Policy Challenges in Modern Health Care

Policy Challenges in Modern Health Care

EDITED BY

D*AVID* M*ECHANIC*

L*YNN* B. R*OGUT*

D*AVID* C. C*OLBY*

J*AMES* R. K*NICKMAN*

Rutgers University Press
New Brunswick, New Jersey, and London

Third paperback printing, 2006

Library of Congress Cataloging-in-Publication Data

Policy challenges in modern health care / [edited by] David Mechanic . . . [et al.].
   p. cm.
   Includes bibliographical references and index.
   ISBN 0–8135–3577–8 (hardcover : alk. paper) — ISBN 0–8135–3578–6 (pbk. : alk. paper)
   1. Medical policy—United States. 2. Health care reform—United States. 3. Health services
accessibility—United States.
   [DNLM: 1. Health Policy—United States. 2. Health Care Reform—United States. 3. Health
Services Accessibility—United States. WA 525 P766 2004] I. Mechanic, David, 1936–
   RA395.A3P588 2004
   362.1'0973—dc22

2004016589

A British Cataloging-in-Publication record is available for this book from the British Library.

The publication program of Rutgers University is supported by the Board of Governors of
Rutgers, The State University of New Jersey.

Manufactured in the United States of America

CONTENTS

v

PREFACE

Our understanding of the distinctions between population health and individual health and their implications for health care and public policies in the United States remains muddled. Population health is considered the province of the public health system, while individual health is the domain of the medical care system. Although these systems both affect health, it is unclear if or how they should interact.

This book is a collection of sixteen essays prepared by awardees of the Investigator Awards in Health Policy Research, a national program of The Robert Wood Johnson Foundation. It contains chapters and public policy recommendations both on the health care system, where the underlying concept is individual health, and on population health, which emphasizes the average health of a group of people bound by common circumstances. It is the first book, to this writer's knowledge, that addresses both those domains, thereby providing an opportunity for further reflection and research. Do the factors that influence population health differ from those that influence individual health? Can we integrate those factors into a single conceptual model of health production? Can policies intended to affect the individual health system have an impact on population health, and the reverse? Is synergy latent, and achievable?

Also juxtaposed in this volume are two seemingly intractable problems that afflict health. First, mechanisms for producing population health—driven by our nation's values, culture, history, and social organization—have yielded low average health in the United States compared with other economically advanced nations. This country also faces wide disparities in health by socioeconomic status, gender, and race/ethnicity. Second, the individually oriented focus of U.S. health care has resulted in a system that is the most expensive in the world and yet is in organizational and functional disarray. Are these two problems related with respect to causes, manifestations, and the public policy solutions proposed by these authors?

The two health production systems interact despite dissimilarities. The distribution of disease in our society places a disproportionate health load on the lower half of the socioeconomic ladder and on other socially disadvantaged segments of the population. Substandard national health status also elevates the need for medical services and increases health care costs. The added cost to the U.S. health care system attributable to substandard health status and large disparities in health could be substantial.

Prominent among causal factors that influence population health are genetic makeup, health behaviors, medical care, cleanliness of the physical environment, the total ecology of all living things, and the characteristics of a society. Causal hypotheses have often been crafted around three concentric rings:

> proximal factors, which include family, friends, neighborhood, work, health behaviors, and local social norms;

> intermediating factors, which include the quality of and participation in governance, the educational system, the regional and local economy, medical and social services, and recreational opportunities; and

> distal factors, which include culture, beliefs, values, racial/ethnic attitudes, standards and resilience of governing institutions, public investment in services, business practices, employment and wage standards, the tax code, physical and social security, and much more.

Integrating these factors, and mindful of the "fundamental" cause concept emphasized by several authors here, the following statement might be valid: systematic variation in social advantage is an important underlying factor in generating wide inequalities in the health of Americans and their poor health relative to other economically advanced countries.

Factors that contribute to dysfunctions in U.S. health and health care might include our individual libertarian culture, belief in unregulated or barely regulated markets, passive acceptance of inequalities, and an inability to resolve issues related to the national heritage, slavery. These historical and cultural factors might have dampened the national will to provide medical care services for all, fired resistance to regulating health care costs, allowed the super-specialization of physicians, and permitted a health care system that commonly discriminates by sex, race, and socioeconomic stature.

Commonality of fundamental causes and policies that join population health and individual health are not the intended subject of this volume. Nevertheless, the recommendations presented here apply to both domains: the political use of moral reasoning, the usefulness of ambiguity in reform policies, the benefits of public-private finance, the search for fundamental causes, and the urgent need for policies to reduce social disadvantage. Other recommendations include the wisdom of applying significant social and legal concepts (from civil rights law, for example) to health law and the need to adopt limits on expenditures that are effective and fair. The authors also express other common themes: the need for multidimensional and multilevel approaches to remedying health disparities, the urgency of underpinning policy proposals with credible research results, and the key role of longitudinal monitoring of health and social programs.

The headwaters are collecting and early momentum is gathering to explore the worth of joining population and individual health into a unified health production concept with overlap of policies. Despite the backlash against tightly managed care in the United States, government and private payers continue to invest in administrative data systems, disease management approaches, and health services research to establish greater links between providing health care and improving health outcomes. Clinical journals are slowly beginning to publish scientific articles on population health. The professional associations of the nation's schools of public health and schools of medicine have been formally meeting for several years in pursuit of common conceptual and operational ground. Finally, this volume is a certain sign that scholars are searching the intellectual spaces beyond their starting disciplines in a quest to enhance the effectiveness of health interventions, to reduce health disparities, and to improve individual and population health outcomes.

Alvin R. Tarlov, MD
Houston, Texas

ACKNOWLEDGMENTS

We are deeply grateful to our many colleagues, including some of the country's most prominent health policy researchers, who made this book possible. The twenty authors who contributed chapters addressed some of the most pressing policy challenges facing our nation and graciously tolerated our editorial prodding.

This volume was supported by The Robert Wood Johnson Foundation through its national program, Investigator Awards in Health Policy Research, that seeks to broaden understanding of health policy challenges and choices. Risa Lavizzo-Mourey, the president and chief executive officer of The Robert Wood Johnson Foundation, and Steve Schroeder, the foundation's past president and CEO, have been especially helpful over the years. Other involved staff members at the foundation include Lori Melichar, Constance Pechura, Robert Hughes, Penny Bolla, Paul Tarini, Joan Barlow, Leoni Infantry, and Deborah Malloy. Alvin Tarlov, who chairs our National Advisory Committee, deserves special acknowledgment. This program has also gained from the participation and commitment of the many other outstanding individuals who have served as members of our National Advisory Committee and from the work of Linda Loranger and Mary Darby of Burness Communications, who have helped the investigators disseminate their research findings.

Thanks are also due to the people who assisted in preparing this book: Marlie Wasserman, Marilyn Campbell, Michele Gisbert, and Nicole Manganaro at Rutgers University Press and Cynthia Church and Elizabeth Cooper at the Investigator Awards National Program Office. Special thanks to Sandra Hackman of Bedford, Massachusetts, who helped to make this book accessible to a broad audience.

Policy Challenges in Modern Health Care

Introduction

⸺⸎⸺

DAVID MECHANIC, LYNN B. ROGUT, DAVID C. COLBY,
AND JAMES R. KNICKMAN

*T*here is widespread consensus that the American health care system underperforms relative to the resources it has available, and that gaps in financing and service delivery pose major barriers to improving health, achieving universal insurance coverage, enhancing quality, controlling costs, and reducing disparities. In addition, while the health care system generously allocates resources to medical services, it devotes far fewer resources to prevention activities and promoting healthier living or lifestyles.

Many of the issues facing the American health system today flow from the enterprise itself, such as advances in technology and science, uncertainty about treatment effectiveness, the explosion of information and its accessibility, and growing demand for services. Other problems reflect American government and policymaking, our distinctive individualistic and activist culture, and our ideological conceptions about health and health care provision. Still others relate to the larger social and economic context, the corporatization and privatization of health care, and difficulties in making medical markets work. Finally, some issues derive from our distinctive history and the history of the medical and other health professions as they compete for autonomy, authority, and public trust.

The U.S. health care system is enormously complex, and its $1.6 trillion annual expenditures—14.9 percent of GNP in 2002—involve many competing interests. The past couple of decades have witnessed much research on health services, although these efforts are minuscule compared to investments in biomedicine. Almost all health services research—and particularly its funding—focuses on immediate and technical challenges that abound in any health care system, especially one as diversified and fragmented as our own. But in our focus on today's most pressing and technical problems, we sometimes lose a broader perspective on how the challenges we face have evolved and on their links with our distinctive history, culture, policymaking processes, and legal and ethical frameworks. Health care now intersects with almost every area of knowledge and all sectors of our economy and social structure. Getting the system right depends as much on economics, politics, behavioral studies, and ethical and philosophical approaches as on the life sciences and the mathematical and material sciences.

This book represents a composite look at some of the striking contemporary

1

challenges we face in health as addressed by some of the nation's leading thinkers from a range of disciplines, backgrounds, and points of view. Thus the volume offers readers a unique opportunity to consider the forces and dilemmas shaping current and future health affairs from the perspectives of individuals active in working to improve health and health policymaking.

We can examine our health system from numerous vantage points. In this volume we seek a broad perspective, one that links our health practices to larger philosophical, cultural, and political issues. This approach gives equal emphasis to promoting health and providing health care services, and focuses on quality and equity as central concerns in health policymaking. As the chapters that follow make evident, these are not isolated issues. They require policymakers to attend carefully to interconnections if decisions on some issues are not to undermine others.

This volume is organized into four sections. The first provides a broad context for understanding how morality, political processes, and economic considerations shape health issues and acceptable policy alternatives. The second section examines population health and the challenges of reducing health and health care disparities, exploring the interconnections among economic and social conditions, the forces promoting and damaging health, the resulting disparities, and how we might reduce them. In this section the discussion ranges from examining broad sociocultural influences to considering how to reduce injury, disease, and death through policies that address smoking, gun safety, and obesity. The authors seek links among these challenges and examine to what degree common approaches are plausible.

The third section moves to the challenge of improving quality, a topic of increasing public and governmental attention following influential reports from the Institute of Medicine of the National Academy of Sciences. These chapters not only describe the opportunities and barriers to change but also reveal how quality issues interconnect with disparities and other aspects of population health. The fourth and final section addresses some of the challenges in ensuring an equitable system of care given the growing gap between expectations and demands and the capacity to meet them.

The Social Context of Health Policymaking

Significant debates about health policy are often highly moralistic and ideological and unrelated to the preponderance of evidence. They inevitably involve questions of personal versus collective responsibility, government versus self-help, individual fault versus social causation, and a broader framing of populations as worthy and unworthy. For example, some debates entail obviously religious perspectives, as with abortion, use of substances, and sexually related diseases. But as James Morone illustrates in his introductory chapter, these same debates encompass broader issues of public responsibility for providing health care, enforcing morality in contrast to reducing social harm (as in providing clean needles to drug users), bringing health care and sex education into schools rather than leaving it to parents, and of social versus individual interventions to combat obesity.

Major policy discussions rarely get very far from notions of good and evil and the worthy and unworthy.

Morone shows how moral ideologies and disputes—and the resulting politics—shape our notions of health and appropriate health policy. Using school-based health clinics and current interest in the epidemic of obesity as examples, he explores the clash between the Puritan ethic and the social gospel and the dangers of demonization.

Theda Skocpol and Patricia Seliger Keenan delve more deeply into political deliberations and the messy politics of health care reform, which inevitably provoke strong partisanship and require ambiguous decisions to allow people with diverse ideologies to come together. Tracing deliberations on important policy questions such as the lack of health insurance and prescription drug coverage, these authors illuminate the extraordinary cross pressures that policymakers confront as they seek to improve health policy. For example, proposals to expand medical benefits or cover the uninsured can easily be derailed by pressures to reduce government spending or to overhaul health care delivery. Yet despite the many political difficulties in hammering out stable agreements, these two authors see some movement among policy elites toward consensus and compromise on some important issues.

Basic to our health care challenges, as Skocpol and Keenan note, is the large and growing population who are uninsured and underinsured. Most insured Americans today face larger out-of-pocket expenditures, as designers of health benefits try to make patients more discriminating and prudent purchasers of health care, as an alternative to the managed care strategies that consumers and health professionals rebel against. The United States is exceptional in its failure to develop universal coverage, but as almost a century of debate shows, reform is difficult to achieve. The growing size and importance of the health sector—and the many interests that have a stake in it—greatly complicate the challenge.

Many observers point to our employer-based system as one significant source of our difficulties with insurance coverage and argue that using employment as the core basis for health coverage is flawed. In contrast, Sherry Glied builds an impressive defense for the advantages of an employer-based system, although she recognizes the need to add other mechanisms for those who are not employed or employed in circumstances where employer coverage is unavailable or not affordable. Employer-based coverage leads to variability in comprehensiveness of coverage and cost, but Glied argues that such insurance offers significant advantages in promoting efficiency, facilitating choice and flexibility, and avoiding the heavy bureaucracy and cumbersome aspects of large governmental systems. In contrast, advocates of a single-payer approach typical of Canada and the U.S. Medicare program point to the relatively low administrative costs compared with the more pluralistic private health care system.

In addition to facing insurance challenges, the health care system is undergoing continuing transformation, as described by James Robinson. With the managed care backlash, insurers have dropped more intrusive controls on doctors and patients and increasingly put responsibility on employers and patients to cover more of the growing costs of health care. Whether a truly competitive marketplace can

be developed, whether patients can make meaningful and thoughtful choices regarding health care alternatives, and whether in the long run they are willing to
accept the cost burdens transferred to them is unclear.

Based on his study of large health care enterprises, Robinson describes
a system of continuing turbulence. The earlier effort to develop integrated health
systems has now lost momentum, and today U.S. medicine is seeing the rise of
single-specialty hospitals and freestanding ambulatory facilities, with specific service chains expanding geographically. Robinson examines new hybrid organizational forms that provide some of the advantages of older organizational forms
but function with greater market flexibility. He views health organizations as highly
adaptive to the vagaries of reimbursement arrangements, particularly under Medicare, as they develop aggressively in areas of medicine where reimbursement is
most favorable. He depicts a system where expectations of continuing growth push
large organizational entities beyond their comparative advantage, which then results in crises and contraction followed by new waves of innovation, expansion,
and disillusion.

Robinson finds shortcomings in the efforts of public authorities to control
the turbulence and growth of unneeded capacity through certificate-of-need legislation and conflict-of-interest regulation, which curb physician referrals to facilities in which they have significant economic interest. In the latter case, for
example, he notes that since physicians both diagnose and provide treatment, the
physician role itself entails self-referral conflict of interest. Thus efforts to limit
such referrals, as in "Stark regulations," may undermine other important goals such
as continuity and coordination of care.

More serious are strategies used by large health plans to segment the market by risk. Such practices make it difficult for health care entities to subsidize
important but unprofitable services and to pool risk across groups. As the system
places more responsibility on consumers and on a pluralistic market, achieving
other important goals such as reducing medical errors, encouraging evidence-based
practice, and addressing population health concerns also becomes more difficult.

Improving Health and Reducing Disparities

The second section of the book deals with promoting population health, reducing disparities, and their interconnections. Although for much of American history social disparities in health and health care were seen as the inevitable result
of people's differing talents and motivations, consensus is growing that disparities
in health according to race, ethnicity, class, and other status attributes are unacceptable. The origin of such disparities is complex and involves not only the biological and social development of individuals and families but also influences that
are intergenerational. Individuals conceived in more deprived social circumstances
face greater risk even in utero, and such risks cumulate over the life course. Much
work now focuses on economic and racial and ethnic disparities in health and health
care. Bruce Link and Jo Phelan address the fundamental causes of health inequali-

ties and raise important questions about the models through which we view the causes of disease.

As they note, the dominant epidemiological model identifies risk factors proximate to the disease outcome and seeks policies and programs to reduce such risks. These authors, however, observe that risk factors change from one period to another, but socioeconomic status—which is associated with such risks at any single point in time—remains strongly related to health outcomes even as risk factors change. Link and Phelan argue that social status is the more fundamental influence because, regardless of the risks, persons with more resources, information, power, and useful networks are better able to marshal these resources to take advantage of what is known about preventing disease and maintaining health. Thus, they argue, we should identify policies that can equalize such coping advantages so that one's socioeconomic status is not such a powerful determinant of health.

Link and Phelan's analysis has some important and perhaps counterintuitive implications for our understanding of social, racial, and ethnic disparities. One might assume that any major health advance, over the long run, would help reduce disparities in health outcomes. But if Link and Phelan are right, any new health opportunity that gives those with money, power, information, and other resources unequal opportunities will widen health disparities, at least initially. Those with resources will be better located to adopt such interventions, whether they are new forms of health screening, preventive opportunities, or innovative treatments. This argues for seeking interventions that are more universal and depend less on the resources of individuals, or at least compensate those most disadvantaged through special targeting efforts. From Link and Phelan's perspective, designing safer vehicles and road systems is more effective in reducing disparities than trying to teach people to drive more safely; fluoridating water is more effective than encouraging better tooth brushing and flossing; and providing healthy foods and opportunities to exercise safely and pleasantly in schools and communities could be more effective than encouraging people to lose weight.

David Hemenway, in his examination of policy on firearms, follows up on the implications of Link and Phelan's analysis by showing how a public health perspective can be a powerful approach to controlling the misuse of guns and reducing injuries and deaths. He reviews the horrendous challenge of the growing availability of guns of enhanced lethality, and shows how policies that address varying aspects of gun production and accessibility—rather than simply gun users—can help control the devastating effects of a gun culture. Here ideological and cultural issues play an especially large role, and advocates for protecting access to guns have energetic support from important sections of the public and much political influence. Thus the public health challenge is particularly difficult. While most Americans favor serious gun control, their commitment is less intense than the commitment of gun advocates to protecting access. When it comes to gun politics and the ability to mobilize voters, the organized gun lobby carries greater weight. Nevertheless, much can be done through technical and regulatory constraints to reduce potential harm while still allowing continued access to guns.

Hemenway provides a menu of policy options, many of which are politically feasible.

Much effort has been devoted to spurring more healthful behavior by encouraging individuals not to smoke or use other substances, to exercise, to eat healthy diets, and the like. Evidence is growing that the factors that relate to poor health outcomes are as embedded in the social and physical environments of people's lives as they are in their behavioral inclinations, and that advancing health depends on social policies that affect the opportunities and constraints of those environments. Population health issues are pervasive, including the nature of the built environment, exposure to environmental risks through traffic, pollution, and crime, lack of access to jobs, ready availability of dangerous substances, and many more. Alternatively, individuals' access to healthy food, opportunities to exercise safely, education and health care, and social integration and support varies widely. Social policies that affect populations and communities' material and environmental resources offer innumerable opportunities to prevent illness and enhance health.

Kenneth Warner—a major contributor to our understanding of the workings of the tobacco industry—analyzes how we have made significant progress in reducing smoking, the single major cause of death. Warner endorses a multi-factor model of smoking prevention and notes the importance of social and tax policies, regulation of cigarette promotion, and cultural constraints on smoking. As he shows, the great advances in combating the forceful efforts of the tobacco industry and inducements to smoke perhaps reflect global social influences and social policies more than efforts to change the hearts and minds of individual smokers. Warner then turns to the next major damaging influence on health: the epidemic of obesity. While noting many differences between the food and tobacco industries, he examines which aspects of the strategies and policies used to combat tobacco can be applied to the growing problem of obesity.

David Williams further develops the disparities issue as it affects racial and ethnic groups. He shows that such health disparities are large and persistent. Like Link and Phelan, he sees them as embedded in larger influences, primarily socio-economic disadvantage, social isolation, and economic marginalization. He notes the multiple pathways through which these larger influences affect health, such as noxious working and living environments, unemployment, exposure to persistent stress, lack of resources to cope and promote healthy living, and constrained access to medical care. Williams makes the essential point that analysts too easily combine people in racial and ethnic groups that are actually heterogeneous and whose members face different life and health challenges. He argues for data that allow us to better unpack such gross and uninformative categories as Hispanic, black, and Asian.

Williams believes that most of our efforts to reduce disparities are unequal to the challenge and that many interventions that would be more effective face social and political barriers. He cites a survey showing that despite all of the media attention to racial disparities in health, more than half of Americans seem not to understand their extent. Thus, like Link and Phelan, he seeks to identify approaches to meaningful policy changes that would win public support and address basic influences.

Sara Rosenbaum and Joel Teitelbaum approach the disparities issue from another angle, asking how the law might become an important instrument to push policy change along. They see law as a powerful instrument in American life and examine how classic civil rights law can be revised and expanded to address discrimination in health and health care, using health financing agencies and associated regulations to convey a strong message. These authors also examine a legal strategy addressing health disparities more directly by eliminating the requirement that individuals demonstrate discrimination, and instead propose rules and standards for reducing disparity. They examine the pros and cons of these alternative legal approaches, alone and in combination. Implementing these ideas, of course, entails many challenges and provides no fast remedy, but disparities will be with us for generations and we need to seek more than a quick fix.

Rosenbaum and Teitelbaum's legal approach to reducing disparities is also innovative in that they suggest approaching remedies through the lens of unequal quality rather than relying on more traditional civil rights strategies of unequal access. This chapter therefore provides a transition to the third section, examining quality in health care and how it can be improved.

The Quality Challenge

In recent years the Institute of Medicine (IOM) has brought to broader public awareness the problems of medical errors and poor quality of health care—problems most experts have known about for decades. The publicity generated by the IOM reports has helped push the quality issue higher on the public agenda, but addressing it in our very complex and decentralized health care system is a massive challenge, and efforts to reduce errors face many barriers. Michael Millenson, a strong voice in the quality improvement movement, describes the numerous quality problems in our health care system and the many efforts being made to address them through new information technology and new approaches to disease management. Although Millenson in other contexts has expressed his frustration at the slowness of change in the conditions that kill and maim so many patients each year, he presents a more optimistic picture here, believing that the many activities needed to improve quality may be moving toward a "tipping point" that will lead to impressive progress. Lucian Leape, an indefatigable advocate and leader in reducing medical errors and adopting a systems approach, and a member of the IOM panel that publicized this issue, describes the many efforts around the country by professional and other groups to push the quality movement forward. He argues the centrality of culture change in this endeavor and recommends a number of approaches for improving patient safety. These include adopting systems approaches to reducing errors in the hospital setting, investing in information technology to computerize medical records and order entry systems, clarifying the labeling of prescription drugs, and increasing federal funding of patient safety research.

Linda Aiken then addresses the role of nursing in providing quality health care, the impending gap between the need for nurses and the supply, the various ways that hospitals and other health organizations are reducing nurse staffing and increasing nurse workloads, and the many challenges these developments pose. Analysts have long known that the quality of nursing is central to preventing errors in hospitals and providing high-quality care. Aiken and her colleagues, as well as others, have demonstrated an association between nurses' workload and the number of deaths in hospitals. These researchers have also shown an association between nurses' education and the number of hospital deaths. Many hospital nurses are highly dissatisfied with their working conditions and lack of autonomy, and many leave nursing because of these dissatisfactions and burnout. Studies have suggested that when nurses have more control over their work, care improves and hospitals function better.

Lisa Iezzoni addresses the quality of care for persons with disabilities and shows how the Medicare program can foster rehabilitation and improve function. While she focuses on the specific question of how existing policy affects persons with difficulty walking because of disease or impairment, millions of Americans who suffer from serious chronic illnesses and disabilities face similar issues. Iezzoni brings to the study of ambulatory problems a passionate personal interest as a scooter-wheelchair-dependent person and an understanding gained from her intensive study of many individuals with limited mobility. She describes some of the catch-22s embodied in public programs that create difficulties for people with chronic illnesses and disabilities, and recommends specific modifications in Medicare that could greatly enhance the lives of many persons who need mobility assistance. Iezzoni, a talented physician who is one of the nation's experts on case-mix adjustment, represents in her personal life the vigorous way one can live as a full participant with appropriate access to the community, transportation, work, medical care, and other supports most people take for granted.

In the final chapter on quality, Rosemary Stevens examines the growing complexity of specialty organizations in American medicine, the disputes among specialties for turf and favorable relative remuneration, and the role of specialty organizations, working individually and together, to set standards for certification and lifelong learning and to introduce new quality initiatives. Stevens describes the complex interconnections between government payment deliberations and specialty concerns and shows how payment decisions can impede high-quality care. Stevens believes, as both an analyst and a participant in specialty deliberations, that specialty associations can play an important role in enhancing quality, and she offers an optimistic view of their recent initiatives and collaboration.

Toward an Equitable System of Health Care

The volume concludes with two chapters on frameworks for fairness in health care policy. First, Richard Frank and Thomas McGuire address longstanding concerns regarding how health insurers separate mental health and substance abuse benefits from most other forms of medical care, and the challenges of integrating mental health and substance abuse care into a more holistic approach. In recent decades we have learned much about the association between mental health and substance abuse and their effects on the course of other medical illnesses, and the enormous disabling consequences of conditions such as major depression, bipolar disease, schizophrenia, and various addictions. These problems cause great distress, interfere with function, lessen productivity, substantially reduce well-being and quality of life, and increase suicide.

Frank and McGuire address several issues related to the challenge of integrating mental health and substance abuse services with other aspects of health care. First, differential insurance coverage for mental health versus other health services results partly from stigmatization, and the fear that coverage will prompt people to use more services at greater cost, a pattern supported by some data. The evidence shows, however, that a managed mental health benefit provided on the same basis as other medical conditions produces only a small additional cost. Still other studies suggest that new kinds of inequality are introduced when behavioral health is managed more strictly than other medical services. Another challenge is the poor medical care persons with mental health morbidities and substance abuse problems receive because of the segmentation of their care. Third are the challenges of designing benefits and financing that lead to efficient and effective services integrated at the point of service. Frank and McGuire explore how to structure an insurance program to produce more equitable and effective results.

In the final chapter Norman Daniels addresses the crucial issue of how we can gain public legitimacy for necessary limits on the provision of health care. Most thoughtful people understand the need for limits in health care as in every other facet of life, but much of the public resists limits when their own health or that of their loved ones is at stake. The backlash against managed care resulted largely from the unwillingness of the public and many health professionals to accept the strategies used by managed care organizations to control the costs of care. Insurance plans have withdrawn from using vigorous utilization management approaches, and as a result health insurance premiums are now rising rapidly, more costs are being transferred to employers and their employees, and more people are becoming uninsured.

Daniels reports on his work with James Sabin on a theory and process they refer to as "accountability for reasonable limits." Daniels argues that decisions on insurance coverage must be transparent and publicly accessible, rest on principles that fair-minded people can accept, allow for challenges and changes when supported by appropriate evidence, and be subject to an oversight process that ensures fidelity to these conditions. Although Norman Daniels is a philosopher and an academic, he and James Sabin, his physician-colleague, have been working with various health insurance plans to test the potential of their ideas and address the practical challenges of implementing them. Daniels offers examples of both progress and difficulties and begins to outline approaches to gaining legitimacy for constraints among patients and professionals. Winning public acceptance for equitable limits is a profound challenge, but failure will eventually result in a many-tiered system of differential care that varies with one's socioeconomic position.

*A*ll of the chapters in this book derive from the Investigator Awards in Health Policy Research, a national program of The Robert Wood Johnson Foundation. Over the past decade, this program has encouraged highly respected and innovative scholars in the social sciences, medicine, and related fields, as well as outstanding scholars early in their careers, to undertake ambitious study of significant health policy issues. Applicants are encouraged to propose projects that apply new perspectives to policy issues and that explore the historical evolution, underlying values, and interplay of social, economic, and political forces that shape emerging structures, processes, and patterns of care. Our belief is that a broader appreciation of forces influencing the health of populations and the organization of health services will result in innovative ideas that will make important contributions to health policy.

There is, of course, no simple, direct path from a research result—however rigorous and innovative—to the making of social policy. Much of the value of health policy research and analysis is in helping frame the perspectives of policymakers, the media, and the educated public, and this is a continuous process. Policymaking is inherently political and depends on much more than perspective and evidence. It requires balancing competing needs and demands, the pressures of various interests both public and private, and public attitudes, values, and beliefs, and thus the perceived legitimacy of policy options.

Many of the program's investigators are influential less because they have succeeded in changing a specific policy decision and more because they help us understand how policymakers and opinion leaders address health policy issues, and because they offer insights on how to improve the process for developing policy. Important changes in the framing of policy questions and the options the public and policymakers see as acceptable often take years, even decades. The major problems in our health care system—managing threats to population health, coverage, financing, quality, and disparities, among others—will remain on our public agenda for years.

Health and medicine are extraordinarily dynamic areas, constituting a seventh of our economy and employing millions of people. Circumstances can change rapidly with the introduction of new knowledge and technologies, evolving economic conditions and financial arrangements, trends in public opinion, and shifts in political power. But the presence of large, important, and powerful interest groups that have a stake in the sector, and the complexity and decentralization of the system, can pose enormous barriers to successfully addressing problems. These characteristics make it especially important that we seek a broader appreciation of how health care functions, and understand that quick technical fixes are unequal to the challenges we face now and in the future.

PART I

The Context of Health and Health Care Policy

CHAPTER 1

Morality, Politics, and Health Policy

———⌾⌾⌾———

JAMES A. MORONE

*A*merican health care policy is different from health policy in other industrial nations. The United States has no national health insurance, of course. However, that difference simply reflects a deeper contrast in the ways we Americans think about politics and health care. European health policy analysts regularly invoke a "solidarity culture"—a staunch belief in sharing resources and concern for what might be called "the people's health" (Morone 2000). European political cultures and institutions often reflect this collective ideal.

What most observers first notice about the American process is the unabashed pursuit of self-interest. In our dynamic (some would say raucous) system, stakeholders and interest groups jockey for advantage on every issue. One wily nineteenth-century politician put it famously after double-crossing a rival: "Politics is not a branch of the Sunday school business" (Morone 1998). This process poses a challenge for health specialists: groups pushing their own interests will stand up and oppose even the most unambiguous scientific findings.

Both scholars and laypeople usually view health policy largely through the lens of interest group politics. Stakeholders and politicians pursue their preferences. They negotiate with one another, cajole neutral parties, and mobilize their own supporters. Constitutional rules bound this process, and an elaborate network of rights protects each individual. The entire political system lurches along, operating its celebrated checks, balancing public programs with private markets, blunting radical changes, and producing incremental adjustments to the status quo. From this perspective, health science constantly wrestles with self-interested politics. Even robust findings are only as good as the policy coalition that assembles around them.

However, interest group politics is only the most obvious story. Two other traditions run through policymaking in the United States. First, Americans also share an intermittent legacy of cooperation—one that grows especially vivid during a crisis. National service programs (such as VISTA and AmeriCorps), town hall meetings (often employed by political campaigns), and attempts to stimulate citizen participation are all familiar efforts to tap the American communal legacy.

Public health advocates, in particular, often try to move beyond competition and appeal to shared interests and values.

Morality offers Americans still another powerful political framework. As foreign observers often point out, the United States remains the industrial world's foremost Puritan nation (Morone 2003a). The Puritan colonists bequeathed America a tendency to turn political differences into moral disputes. The debates that gust up around our social programs often directly concern the moral worth of the beneficiaries: Are they deserving? Such questions put vivid and contested moral images—of virtue and vice, good and evil, us and them—at the heart of American health care politics and policies.

Traditional Models of American Politics

Individualism

Why are Americans so committed to individualism (or what political theorists call classical liberalism)? One of our great national myths offers a popular answer: the first colonists sailed away from old world tyranny and settled a vast "unpopulated" land—the place almost thrust freedom on them. American settlers did not have to push aside kings or nobles to get ahead. Instead, as Tocqueville famously put it, "Americans were born equal instead of becoming so" (Tocqueville 1969, 509; Hartz 1955; Greenstone 1986). Men (and maybe women; the myth gets a bit shaky here) faced extraordinary opportunities. The land and its riches awaited; success simply required a little capital and a lot of work. The irresistible result would be the nation's celebrated individualism, a deep faith in free economic markets (some foreign observers see almost a cult), and a corresponding belief in limited government.

The U.S. Constitution organized this ideology into the nation's political rules. An elaborate system of checks and balances limited national power. But this system also offered political participants many different venues in which to pursue their interests. In the past, political systems had tried to suppress self-interest; the American founders opened the door to it. The answer to the problem of factions, or interests, wrote James Madison in Federalist No. 10 (1787), is injecting an "even greater variety" into the political process. Today political scientists sometimes lament the hyper-pluralism of a system stalemated by competing claims, lobbyists, and lawyers. The practical result is that almost no political arenas stand above the scramble. There are only a very few nonpartisan agencies; there is no prestigious civil service trusted by all sides; and even the judiciary has become another political branch of government (McConnell 1966; Kersh and Morone forthcoming).

The sheer ferocity of this scramble for advantage poses a particular dilemma for health care policy. After all, medical science seeks objective answers to questions about health and health care. It documents, for example, the dangers of smoking, obesity, stress, unsafe sex, and delayed medical care. The surgeon general, the Institute of Medicine, and the Centers for Disease Control and Prevention might issue warnings based on good science. However, any effort to act on those findings simply triggers the politics of self-interest. No cultural mores penalize such a reaction: in politics, economic self-interest is every bit as legitimate as medical science.

The result appears to pose a conflict between medicine and politics. No matter how robust the scientific findings, political interests routinely mobilize and often delay or derail action. The politics of individualism offers health-minded reformers unambiguous advice: use your scientific findings to mobilize your own side. In the political arena, your science is only as strong as your political coalition.

Community

During the 1980s, critics began growing uneasy about unabashed self-interest and untrammeled markets. What happens to the common good when everyone pushes only for number one? Back to early America trooped the social theorists. There they discovered an entirely different American political tradition, one grounded in a robust collective life. In contrast to the legends of rugged individualism, historians documented rich networks of communal assistance. If a barn burned down, townsfolk banded together and helped their neighbor raise another. If iron pots were expensive, families shared them—early American household inventories often list one-half or one-third of a pot or skillet (Morone 2003a, 7).

The communal story sparks enthusiasm across the political spectrum. Here, argue proponents, lies firm ground on which to imagine a renewed civic culture. Americans are not just celebrants of self but partners in a shared public life, not just individualists but communitarians. Conservatives saw an opportunity to restore traditional American values; progressives stressed our obligations to one another, our shared communal fate.

For medical reformers, the legacy of community recalls an often-overlooked public health legacy. After all, American cities have a long history of funding clinics and fighting infectious diseases. A communal heritage—if it can somehow be tapped—opens the prospect of putting self-interest in a larger, civic-minded context (Putnam 2000; Skocpol 2003).

Franklin D. Roosevelt introduced his idea of social security with the classic communal appeal for public health. "The causes of poverty . . . are beyond the control of any individual." So much for the individualistic version of American politics. What was the alternative? Community effort. When a modern civilization faces a disease epidemic, said Roosevelt, "it takes care of the victims after they are stricken." But it also roots out the source of the contagion. Roosevelt proposed an entire social program built on the public health model. He would put aside the "jungle law of economic competition" for "brotherly" cooperation (Roosevelt 1932, 38).

Of course, President Roosevelt introduced his program in response to the Great Depression. The communal alternative has always been the more fragile and intermittent approach, displacing individualism largely during crises and extraordinary circumstances. Moreover, political theorists warn us against romanticizing the American communal tradition. After all, that tradition also animates a painful historical legacy: the urge to reject entire groups based on race, gender, ethnicity, or religion. The Ku Klux Klan, militia groups, and a long, harsh line of nativist organizations also represent communal thinking (Smith 1997).

Still, the communal vision offers a potential rejoinder to the politics of self-interest. Communitarians were critical of the Clinton administration's health reform effort, for example, because officials tried to sell it by promising one group after another that the plan was in their self-interest. The moral of that story, warned White House advisor Paul Starr, is that with "so many people on board . . . our boat may sink from its own weight." The communitarian perspective would have appealed bluntly to the common good—to the notion that we all share values as residents of the same nation (Hacker 1997, 138).

Could such a collective appeal work? Under what circumstances? What conditions stir America's communal legacy? And what about the ugly urge to reject some Americans? We can find answers to these questions in another tradition: American morality politics.

Morality Politics

Americans take religion and morality more seriously than citizens of most other industrial countries. Some 95 percent of all Americans believe in God—a distinct contrast to Sweden (52 percent), France (62 percent), and Britain (76 percent). While other industrial nations grow secular over time, the United States keeps experiencing religious revivals (Morone 2003a, 22). That social fact has deep consequences for U.S. politics. In a nation marked by moral and religious fervor, partisans often import their faith into politics.[1] Moral fervor drove—drives—an extraordinary range of political movements: civil rights, temperance, tobacco, anti-abortion, and many others. Moral judgment seeps into all kinds of political issues in both dramatic and subtle ways.

Moral politics comes with its own founding story. "It seems to me," wrote Alexis de Tocqueville, "that I can see the entire destiny of America contained in the first Puritan who came ashore" (1969, 279). Those first settlers arrived in the New World facing the essential communal question: Who are we? Who were they? The Puritans concocted an extraordinary answer: they were the community of saints. Leadership, in both state and church, went to men who could prove that they were preordained for salvation. The saints could vote, hold office, and enjoy full church membership. (The methodology for proving salvation was complicated, but wealth and health were taken as fairly reliable indicators.) People who were morally uncertain—those who had not demonstrated salvation—were expected to follow the proven saints: they went to church, for example, but did not hold office, vote, or become full church members. And the damned were driven out: witches were hung, Native Americans slaughtered, and heretics sent packing (mainly to Rhode Island, the latrina of New England for all its noxious heresies). In short, moral standing defined leaders, allocated privileges (such as voting), defined communities, and identified the dangerous "other" (Morone 2003a).

The Puritan idea burst out of New England and spread across America (thanks to the purest Puritans, the Baptists). The essential Puritan trope still persists and flourishes: moral virtue continues to define the community, still distinguishes "us" from "them." Moral images specify privilege or punishment, inclusion

or exclusion, deserving poor or dangerous other. These images of potential beneficiaries—often shifting, constantly contested—lie under every U.S. social policy.
"We" get assistance; "they" face social controls.

The traditional individualist model of American politics emphasizes a sharp
line between private realm and public sphere. Constitutional rights bar any public
authority from meddling in people's private lives. "However strange it may seem,"
wrote John Locke in 1689, "the lawgiver hath nothing to do with moral virtues
and vices." In this view, citizens draw on their private desires and values and then
charge into the public, political realm to advance their goals. In the patois of economics, every agent maximizes her own utilities (Locke quoted in Morone 2003a,
6). In contrast, moral politics refuses to honor the private-public distinction. It explicitly enters the private sphere. Individual virtue—character—affects the public
good. Citizens' private behavior, ruled right out of politics in traditional models,
now becomes crucial. Some group's private behavior (real or imagined) seems to
threaten the community.

The Puritans bequeathed the United States two distinct moral visions, two
answers to that political bottom line: Whom should we blame for our troubles? I
call the two answers the Puritan and the social gospel.

Puritans

The Puritan approach focuses on dangerous sinners lurking in our society.
The fears tilt political debates; they sink the communal urge by eroding our sense
of common values and shared fate. The policy problem turns instead to protecting
us from them.

The personal transgressions—the sins—that ostensibly endanger the nation
are most often public health sins. For example, the most sustained moral campaign
in U.S. history targeted substance abuse. Temperance crusaders organized in the
early nineteenth century, won their first statewide prohibition in 1851, managed
national prohibition by 1920, and now inspire a formidable drug war that draws
heavily on Prohibition-era jurisprudence (Morone 2003a).

Sexual threats pose another political perennial. The American Medical Association launched its first great political campaign against abortion—a common
practice in the mid–nineteenth century, when roughly one abortion occurred for
every six live births. Physicians consolidated their own role as social leaders and
healers by turning abortion into a crime. Abortions, they argued, were subverting
the good community by undermining the white, middle-class birth rate while foreign immigrants multiplied and threatened to swamp American blood (Storer 1867;
Morone 2003a).

Similarly, sexually transmitted diseases bred in the urban ghettos and spread
into middle-class families. After all, reported the *American Journal of Public
Health,* "many . . . white . . . boys are going to sow their wild oats" (Allen 1915,
200). In the South, the black syphilis rate became a standard justification for Jim
Crow apartheid. A similar argument reappeared during the first wave of AIDS hys-
teria; frightened Americans dreamed up all sorts of ways to keep homosexuals from
slipping their disease into mainstream culture (Morone 1997).

In each case the same general pattern recurs. Some dangerous personal behavior—drinking, drugs, sexual practices, teen pregnancy, birth control, abortion, the list goes on—threatens the community. The questionable behavior is often associated with some group. Moral politics triggers vibrant stereotypes: Irish drink, Italian immigrants have too many babies, Muslims are terrorists, and black people commit almost every possible sin. Political leaders warn that America faces terrible decline if we don't find a way to rein in the dangerous people and their bad behavior. Standard solutions run to pledges ("just say no" to alcohol, drugs, and sex before marriage), prohibitions, restrictions, regulations, more prisons, and tougher laws.

Of course, all societies impose controls. The political key lies in the emphasis on personal discipline, in the balance between restrictive policies and social welfare benefits. I experienced a vivid illustration of the difference during a debate on the Clinton health reform proposal in 1994.

I was debating a Republican senator who opposed the Clinton plan. We were before a young, liberal audience that was giving the Republican a very chilly hearing. Then, toward the end of the debate, he abruptly turned to face me. The body language said, "Okay, let's quit kidding around." And here's what followed: "Look, professor, you can't expect the hardworking people of suburban Cook County to go into the same health care alliance [a kind of insurance pool] as the crack heads in the city of Chicago." When I turned to face the audience, all set to brush aside this fatuous dichotomy, I saw a room of suddenly sobered liberals. "Yes," they were thinking, "that is a terrible problem." "Hey," I yelped, "those uninsured people in the city of Chicago are college students and hardworking nurses and taxi drivers doing double shifts and single moms holding down two jobs." No dice. In fact, it only got worse. Crack heads and single moms. Our imagined community, struggling together to fix a troubled health care system, had vanished in an instant. Now it was a hardworking us against a drug-abusing, sexually promiscuous them. Forget about extending health care coverage—what "those people" need is moral discipline. The politics of social policy always turns on the mental images we create of the beneficiaries (Morone 2003a).

The Social Gospel
An alternative moral tradition once offered a sharp alternative to blaming individuals. I call it the social gospel (borrowing from a group of reformers at the end of the nineteenth century). Social gospel thinking shifts the focus from individual sinners to an unjust system. The neo-Puritans blame individual misbehavior for society's troubles; the social gospel approach blames society—or socioeconomic pressures—for individual troubles. The causal arrow runs in precisely the opposite direction: the economic system, race prejudice, underprivilege, and social stress put pressure on people. If those people behave badly (by using illegal drugs, for example), it is largely because social and economic forces have pushed them into a tough corner. The social gospel solution appears in countless variations, but they converge on the same familiar points: fix the system and give

every American a fair chance to prosper; don't blame those who fall by the wayside; we all share a common duty to help the disadvantaged.

Thinkers in the late nineteenth and early twentieth century first systematically articulated a version of the social gospel. Reformers like Jane Addams began challenging the dominant Victorian paradigm: poverty caused drunkenness, they said, as much as the other way around. Low salaries and harsh factory conditions—deprivation, not depravity—pushed women into prostitution. This way of thinking came to power with the Roosevelt administration in 1933.[2] Roosevelt constantly articulated the social gospel, and his administration hammered out policies that reflected that approach. The social gospel, like the Puritan perspective, turns on images of health and disease. However, while the neo-Puritans tend to fear contagions, the social gospel seizes on community health as a public policy model.

Roosevelt first introduced the idea of social security while campaigning for president in October 1932. Roosevelt began by declaring that because it was Sunday, he would not be "talking politics" but "preaching a sermon" (Roosevelt 1932, 38). True to his word, the candidate packed his address with religious quotations and allusions. As I noted, he used a public health analogy to draw a picture of the good society, one that protected the weak and the disadvantaged.

Roosevelt brought these generalities down to political earth with sad stories about good people. An 89-year-old neighbor had died while milking a cow, after a blizzard no less; now it was our collective responsibility to help his "83-year-old kid sister," who was languishing in an insane asylum because she had nowhere else to go. Roosevelt was off and running down a roster of needy innocents who needed help: hungry children in public schools, injured workers, sick men and women, crippled children, the unemployed, and many more (Roosevelt 1932, 38). Each example came with the same political spin: poor people are virtuous neighbors who have fallen on hard times. Roosevelt was consciously displacing the past icons of depravity—undisciplined black men and lazy immigrants lounging about the saloons.

That last example, drinking, carried plenty of baggage, for these were the last days of Prohibition. In the New Dealer's hands, excess drinking turned from sin to illness; dry pledges and national prohibition gave way to treatment and education. The fault line between neo-Puritans and social gospel would run right through the next half-century: vice versus illness, crime versus public health, sin versus social responsibility. The social gospel view reached its high tide during the southern civil rights movement and the Johnson administration's Great Society. "Should we double our wealth and conquer the stars," declared Johnson in his most beautiful speech, "and still be unequal to this issue [of racial inequality] then we will have failed as a people and as a nation. For with a country as with a person; what is a man profited, if he shall gain the whole world, and lose his own soul?" (quoted in Morone 2003a, 426).

The Reagan administration eventually buried the whole approach. Reagan scoffed at the idea of collective responsibility. Instead, he turned personal responsibility

—just say no—into a formidable policy mantra. Today the old social gospel idea that drug abuse or crime might stem from underprivilege finds almost no policy traction. Contemporary politics includes plenty of moralizing, but there is scant evidence of the old social gospel idea that we share a collective responsibility to foster social justice for everyone.

Moral Politics in Action

Morality politics are protean and pervasive, springing up in unexpected places and surprising unwary policymakers. Consider two recent cases: school health centers and the politics of obesity.

School-Based Health Clinics

Difficult health problems such as substance abuse, reproductive health, and depression can land teenagers in serious trouble.[3] Given the nature of these problems, perhaps it is not surprising that they are slow to seek care. However, ignoring adolescent health leads to serious problems: one million unintended pregnancies a year, three million sexually transmitted diseases, more than four thousand suicides, and terrible incidents of school violence. The United States has a high adolescent and young adult death rate: 1.5 deaths per thousand young males (in contrast to 0.7 in England, 0.6 in Sweden, and 0.9 in Germany).

One policy response that grew increasingly popular in the 1990s sprang from a simple intuition: put the health care where the kids are. Local hospitals, community health centers, and public health departments opened health centers in schools, especially in poor neighborhoods (Morone, Kilbreth, and Langwell 2001).

Across the country school-based health centers immediately set off a political storm, as they inevitably faced issues such as substance abuse and reproductive health. Cultural and religious conservatives feared that providing treatment (possibly without parental notification) would implicitly condone illegal drug use, underage drinking, and premarital sex. Conservatives countered with calls for stronger discipline, personal responsibility (just say no), and abstinence education. By 1997 the Personal Responsibility and Work Opportunity Reconciliation Act (the welfare reform bill) had introduced abstinence education in schools across the United States (Morone 2003b).

Some liberals confronted the moral issues head on, responding that young people needed counseling on sexuality and chemical dependency. If teens were going to have sex, argued these advocates, they ought to be prepared. Dr. Jocelyn Elders set off a firestorm in her first press conference as director of the Arkansas Department of Health: "We are not going to put them on their lunch trays. But yes, we intend to distribute condoms [through] . . . school based clinics" (Elders 1996, 242).

The battle was on. However, liberals soon discovered that cultural (often Christian) conservatives had formed powerful local organizations across the nation. Those groups focused, in particular, on school boards. In the Northeast conservatives found allies in the Catholic bishops, who were chary of birth control.

In the South and West conservatives acted with the Christian Coalition. In the Pacific states they allied with anti-tax advocates. When the Christian Coalition helped Mike Foster come from far behind and win the governorship of Louisiana, the organization's first demand was an end to the school health centers.

Parental notification posed another difficult issue. When the California legislature passed a bill guaranteeing privacy in school health centers, critics charged the government with undermining parental control. More than ten thousand people rallied against the bill, which conservative talk-show host Dr. Laura turned into a highly publicized cause. Governor Gray Davis responded by vetoing the legislation.

Yet despite ardent opposition, the clinics survived and flourished. Even the school centers in Louisiana weathered the storm and spread. How? Proponents turned moral politics into a classic interest group issue. Where cultural conservatives opposed reproductive health services and sex education, the centers backed off, usually referring their student patients to other providers. But more important, advocates employed that classic political wisdom: build a constituency. As children started receiving treatment, parents, teachers, and health providers rallied around the centers, countering moral complaints with down-to-earth descriptions of kids getting care.

These respectable locals—parents, teachers, and health care providers—told their legislators heartwarming stories about children and the school clinics. Legislators are always primed to deliver concrete benefits to "responsible" community members, and school clinics have proven a prime constituent service. They combine education and health care. They do not bust the budget. They are simple to understand. They offer fine photo opportunities. And they can be doled out one school at a time (Morone, Kilbreth, and Langwell 2001).

In the end the health centers overcame the opposition and expanded, from some 150 in 1990 to more than 1,300 today. But both sides of the story are important. Although advocates defused the moral attack, the criticism powerfully shaped both the health centers and their politics. The health centers reflect the larger politics of public health. Reviewing the response to AIDS, for example, the *American Journal of Public Health* (*AJPH*) reported that Americans engage in far more premarital sex than their British counterparts while condemning promiscuity at much higher rates (Morone 2003a, 481–482). The colonists still adhere to the old Puritan spirit, chortled the *Economist,* reporting on the *AJPH* survey, and they pay the price (Morone 2003a).

American public health policies must steer carefully between sin and censure. When AIDS hit, the more tolerant and abstemious Europeans quickly launched forceful public health campaigns that included leaflets, television advertisements, and needle exchanges. Across the Atlantic, Americans delayed their efforts while squabbling over the exact moral nuance of their message, particularly the degree of emphasis on abstinence. U.S. incidence of AIDS soon measured ten times higher than Britain's (Morone 2003a, 481). Of course, many factors underlie such differences, and, as with the school health centers, Americans eventually sorted out the tension between education and abstinence. But moral conflict again profoundly shaped the health program and its outcomes.

Obesity

In 2001 Surgeon General David Satcher issued a startling report: over 65 percent of Americans were overweight and 30 percent were clinically obese.[4] Obesity, rising at epidemic rates, threatened to overtake tobacco as the chief cause of preventable death. Americans (in fact, residents of almost every nation) suddenly found themselves bombarded by data on obesity's toll—on our lives, our health, and our budgets (Kersh and Morone 2002a).

The issue first provoked derisive commentaries about "big chocolate" and its "menace." The critics drew on the familiar model of America as a nation of individualists who celebrate free markets and vehemently oppose government meddling in private lives (Kersh and Morone 2002b). What could be more personal than the food one eats? The critics were pointing to a genuine dilemma. How might eager public health advocates make a political issue out of such a private matter?

One classic response lies in the moral realm. Nothing moves the political system like a threat from greedy companies who put profits before the public's welfare. Demonizing providers regularly offers reformers a way to cross into the private sphere and control, limit, or prohibit. In the early twentieth century, temperance advocates gained considerable political mileage by charging breweries and saloons with pouring poison into the American workingman. Tobacco offers a more contemporary example. Public health officials spent years trying to publicize the danger, but for political effect nothing matched revelations that the industry had consciously misled the public about the health effects of smoking.

The same kinds of condemnation rapidly entered the obesity debates. Public health scholars explain the startling rise in obesity by pointing to an "unhealthy food environment." For starters, portion sizes have undergone an extraordinary expansion. In his influential book *Food Fight*, Kelly Brownell describes the growth of the all-American burger. In 1957, he reports, the typical hamburger weighed in at one ounce and 210 calories. Today that burger is up to six ounces and 618 calories—and that's before the bacon, cheese, supersized fries (another 610 calories), and double-gulp (sixty-four-ounce) soft drink (Brownell and Horgen 2003, 183). Highly competitive food service entrepreneurs trumpet ever-larger portions: think Whopper, Xtreme gulp, Big Grab, and the Beast. Each innovation ups the ante in serving sizes. Even ostensibly healthy products come loaded with hidden ingredients: sugar (or high-fructose corn syrup) is the first ingredient in Kellogg's Strawberry Nutri-Grain yogurt bars, and the second in Skippy super-chunk peanut butter (Brownell and Horgen 2003; Nestle 2002; Kersh and Morone forthcoming).

Moving from these analyses to charges of corporate villainy required only a small step. As the most ardent critics put it, a cynical industry targets children and reshapes their eating habits. These companies put soda machines in schools and fast food outlets in lunchrooms. The result, argues Eric Schlosser in *Fast Food Nation,* is "a lifetime of weight problems" and "emotional pain." And that is just the beginning. Fast food, he continues, has trashed the countryside, widened the social gap between rich and poor, and turned the meatpacking industry into a labor nightmare (Schlosser 2001, 240). Schlosser's descriptions of the food business are every bit as horrifying as Upton Sinclair's famous expose *The Jungle.*

Schlosser's book became a surprise bestseller, and a steady stream of exposes rapidly followed.

One backlash against fast food muckrakers simply shifts the blame. If some liberals demonize the industry, some conservatives blame overweight individuals. Heavy people lack willpower, they make foolish food choices, they live in unhealthy ways. Like smokers, drug abusers, and heavy drinkers, obese people have made personal choices; they should just say no and push away from the table. The distinct echo from other substance abuse controversies has another unhappy parallel: obesity tends to concentrate in poor and minority communities.

Each picture of blame—the industry versus the individual—carries different policy implications. A focus on the industry suggests requiring better food labels, rethinking school nutrition, restricting advertising, regulating fat content, punishing misleading claims, taxing unhealthy ingredients, and so on. Successfully demonizing big food—directing popular anger at the industry—may cut through the checks and balances of the political system and provoke action.

However, the politics of demonization cuts two ways. Some observers charge that food stamps and school lunches only encourage poor people—who are already fat enough—to overeat (Kaufman 2003). Others have suggested an insurance premium tax on heavy people. Once policymakers begin condemning heavy people, the list of possibilities rapidly grows.

The larger lessons from America's long moral history suggest that demonization is always tempting, since it gets political results, but always dangerous: it fractures communities, limits the range of health policy alternatives, and tends to land hardest on poor and weak populations. In the long run, public health advocates do best when they focus on policies that foster healthy lives and build strong communities.

Past efforts to regulate private behavior, such as alcohol and tobacco use, also take us completely beyond politics and into the cultural realm: Americans dramatically reduced their drinking, their smoking, and even their tolerance for secondhand smoke. When advocates detect a crisis, define a problem, and seek a solution, they are—indirectly, perhaps often unexpectedly—educating the public. The obesity wars are likely to grow, spread, and generate considerable political heat. However, if the history of drinking and smoking serve as a guide, the most important result may lie in the conclusions that citizens draw about their own lifestyles (Kersh and Morone forthcoming).

Epilogue

Moral fears and aspirations profoundly affect American politics. Franklin D. Roosevelt and Martin Luther King made moral arguments as they redefined American social policy. President Ronald Reagan asserted a very different moral framework: neo-Puritan rather than social gospel. The force with which he championed his alternative, and the success he met, may be his most enduring domestic legacy.

When it comes to moral politics, every side seizes on health care. The Puritan approach focuses on threats to public health: drinking, drug abuse, out-ofwedlock births, sexually transmitted diseases, and more. Fears often lead to powerful public action: to restrictions, regulations, and prohibitions.

Proponents of the social gospel alternative reframe the problem away from sin and sinners. They see illness rather than crime, addiction rather than moral weakness. They would treat rather than punish; they look past personal behavior and focus on complex social causes. They constantly echo Franklin Roosevelt's Sunday sermon on social security and call for public health solutions. Puritan drug wars elicit social gospel calls for treatment, education, and harm reduction. More broadly, social gospel pushes for social justice; it promotes collective responsibility toward all members of the community. However, today's call for social gospel programs is only a weak echo of the powerful reforming tradition that dominated American politics in the 1930s and 1960s (Morone 2003a, 407).

Still, down through American history and across a wide political spectrum today, every side uses images of health to articulate its hopes and aspirations, to voice its fears and warnings. The problems we face and the solutions we contrive ultimately revolve around our definitions of health and illness and the pictures we construct of one another. In the end, American morality politics simply reminds us of the importance—the cultural power—of health, health care, and health studies in forging a good society.

Acknowledgments

This chapter is based on my book *Hellfire Nation: The Politics of Sin in American History.* I am grateful to Rogan Kersh and Elizabeth Kilbreth, my collaborators in studying obesity and school health care centers, respectively. Finally, thanks to John DiIulio, Steve Macedo, Gretchen Ritter, Deborah Stone, Rick Vallely, and Sandra Hackman.

Notes

1. People often ask me about the constitutional separation of church and state. In fact, that is precisely what fostered the American religious tumult. By keeping government out of the religious sphere (and refusing to privilege any one sect or faith), the Constitution facilitates robust competition—precisely what makes the American religious culture so fluid and vital.
2. Historians would not categorize Roosevelt with the social gospel thinkers. I have redefined the category around its most salient features and applied it more generally. For details, see Morone 2003a, part IV.
3. This discussion of school centers comes from work I have done with Elizabeth Kilbreth. We are grateful to The Robert Wood Johnson Foundation for funding the research.
4. My discussion of obesity is shaped by the insights of my collaborator, Rogan Kersh.

References

Allen, L. C. 1915. The Negro Health Problem. *American Journal of Public Health* 5: 194–203.

Brownell, K., and K. B. Horgen. 2003. *Food Fight.* New York: Contemporary Books.

Elders, J. 1996. *Joycelyn Elders, M.D.: From Sharecropper's Daughter to Surgeon General of the United States of America.* New York: Avon Books.

Greenstone, D. 1986. Political Culture and American Political Development: Liberty, Union, and the Liberal Bipolarity. *Studies in American Political Development* 1, no. 1: 1–49.

Hacker, J. 1997. *The Road to Nowhere: The Genesis of President Clinton's Plan for Health Security.* Princeton, NJ: Princeton University Press.

Hartz, L. 1955. *The Liberal Tradition in America.* New York: Harcourt, Brace, and World.

Kaufman, Leslie. 2003. Welfare Wars: Are the Poor Suffering from Hunger Anymore? *New York Times,* February 23, WK4.

Kersh, R., and J. A. Morone. 2002a. The Politics of Obesity. *Health Affairs* 20, no. 6 (November/December): 142–153.

———. 2002b. How the Personal Becomes Political: Prohibitions, Public Health, and Obesity. *Studies in American Political Development* 16 (fall): 162–175.

———. Forthcoming. Obesity, Tobacco, and the New Politics of Public Health. *Journal of Health Politics, Policy, and Law.*

Madison, J. 1787. Federalist No. 10. Available at www.constitution.org/fed/federa10.htm.

McConnell, G. 1966. *Private Power and American Democracy.* New York: Knopf.

Morone, J. A. 1997. Enemies of the People: The Moral Dimension to Public Health. *Journal of Health Politics, Policy, and Law* 22, no. 4: 993–1010.

———. 1998. *The Democratic Wish: Popular Participation and the Limits of American Government.* Rev. ed. New Haven, CT: Yale University Press.

———. 2000. Citizens or Shoppers? Solidarity under Siege. *Journal of Health Politics, Policy, and Law* 25 (October): 959–969.

———. 2003a. *Hellfire Nation: The Politics of Sin in American History.* New Haven, CT: Yale University Press.

———. 2003b. American Ways of Welfare. *Perspectives on Politics* 1, no. 1 (March): 137–146.

Morone, J. A., E. Kilbreth, and K. M. Langwell. 2001. Back to School: A Health Care Strategy for Youth. *Health Affairs* 20, no. 1 (January/February): 122–136.

Nestle, M. 2002. *Food Politics: How the Food Industry Influences Nutrition and Health.* Berkeley: University of California Press.

Putnam, R. 2000. *Bowling Alone: The Collapse and Revival of American Community.* New York: Simon and Schuster.

Roosevelt, F. D. 1932. The Philosophy of Social Justice through Social Action. In *The Public Papers and Addresses of Franklin D. Roosevelt.* New York: Random House.

Schlosser, E. 2001. *Fast Food Nation: The Dark Side of the All-American Meal.* New York: Houghton Mifflin.

Skocpol, T. 2003. *Diminished Democracy: From Membership to Management in American Civic Life.* Norman: University of Oklahoma Press.

Smith, R. 1997. *Civic Ideals: Conflicting Ideals of Citizenship in U.S. History.* New Haven, CT: Yale University Press.

Storer, H. R. 1867. *Is It I? A Book for Every Man.* Boston: Lee and Shepherd.

Tocqueville, Alexis de. 1969. *Democracy in America.* New York: Doubleday. (Orig. pub. 1835.)

CHAPTER 2

Cross Pressures

THE CONTEMPORARY POLITICS OF HEALTH REFORM

THEDA SKOCPOL AND PATRICIA SELIGER KEENAN

The past decade has witnessed some amazing twists and turns in U.S. health care politics. Starting in 1993, President Bill Clinton attempted to push through a comprehensive reform that would have guaranteed health insurance to all Americans, extending coverage to low-wage workers who predominated in the ranks of the uninsured. Yet within a year, public opinion turned as interest groups and partisan forces mobilized against the reform proposals, leading Clinton to abandon them (Broder and Johnson 1996; Skocpol 1997). After the 1994 midterm elections, Republicans took control of Congress and redefined health care reform to mean containing costs and restructuring Medicaid and Medicare. But Republican proposals, too, proved unpopular and largely failed (Peterson 1998).

Health reform proposals then concentrated on incremental adjustments until 2003, when Republicans in control of the presidency and both houses of Congress just barely pushed through a major enhancement and restructuring of the Medicare program, which covers 40 million elderly and disabled Americans (on the politics of this episode, see Skocpol 2004). In one of the most extraordinary episodes in U.S. health care politics, Republicans sponsored the addition of a prescription drug benefit to Medicare, a public-sector program they had long questioned, while most Democrats criticized and opposed the legislation even though it mandated expanded benefits.

How are we to understand the contemporary politics of health reform? How do issues rise on the agenda, and what forces determine the shape and fate of legislative proposals? We use insights from political science research on agenda setting and policymaking to examine key episodes and trends, especially the Clinton health reform episode of 1993–1994, the attempted Republican cutbacks of the mid–1990s, and the enactment of Medicare restructuring in 2003. Proposed reforms that make headway, we argue, build on existing public-private arrangements and are more likely to be successfully enacted if they are inherently ambiguous and stress benefits and subsidies rather than cost-constricting regulations or funding cuts. We then draw upon knowledge of past episodes to speculate about the future course of health reform politics.

A Perspective on Reform Episodes

Health reform is inherently multidimensional. Reform can be defined to the public in terms of new benefits, effects on existing benefits, coverage expansions, cost reductions, access to new medical treatments, balance between government role and market-based approaches, effects on small businesses, and so forth. Because of the many dimensions to health reform issues, shifts in definition can create unexpected swings in the direction of policymaking.

The multidimensionality of health care issues—along with the public-private nature of U.S. health care financing and delivery systems—means that major bills are often highly complex. It is not uncommon for major reform proposals to include provisions that simultaneously attempt to expand coverage, contain costs, and address the quality of care—not to mention provisions designed to appeal to policymakers holding diametrically opposed preferences about markets and government. Complexity and ambiguity are necessary to forge compromises in the U.S. political system, which allows many players to exert vetoes as legislation proceeds. Yet when legislation addresses multiple aspects of an issue, it can also become increasingly tricky to reach closure. Choices regarding which element to address first create more avenues for strategic maneuvering, affecting possibilities for success and leading to continuing struggles in the aftermath of both enacted and failed legislation.

Moreover, reform attempts "feed back" into future politics (Hacker 2002; Pierson 2000). However they turn out, reform episodes affect balances of political power, which in turn influence the types of reforms next debated. New interest groups may be activated and new stakes defined. Large-scale health reforms can also alter balances of partisan power. For example, the defeat of the 1993–1994 Clinton plan helped propel Republicans back into control of the House of Representatives for the first time in four decades.

We posit three key phases during episodes of health reform: getting issues onto the agenda, debating policy, and producing outcomes. This analysis enables us to identify when and how key political factors come into play (for further elaborations, see Baumgartner and Jones 1993; Downs 1972; and Kingdon 1995). Early in a reform episode, for example, public opinion typically favors changes, especially those that improve benefits. But once policy debates begin, interest groups and partisan forces can sway public opinion in new directions.

The Public's Influence

Because of persistent trends in the health care system—including increases in the numbers of the uninsured and rising premium and prescription drug costs—the public has favored extending insurance coverage for some time. At any given juncture, specific concerns may vary by subgroup and focus on lack of insurance, costs to those who are covered, or scope of coverage. As they become salient, these public concerns influence the reform possibilities discussed by politicians and help set the legislative agenda.

Coverage and costs were the key public concerns in the early 1990s, when an economic downturn threatened the insurance coverage of many middle-class Americans, even as the rising cost of private insurance greatly concerned employers. The Clinton proposals aimed to address such concerns by linking cost controls and new guarantees for the middle class to coverage extensions for the uninsured. By the mid-1990s, concerns about reducing the federal budget deficit had become salient among much of the U.S. voting public. After capturing control of Congress in 1994, Republicans attempted to link Medicare and Medicaid "reforms" to cutbacks in public spending, which would, they said, help reduce the deficit.

More recently, politicians have focused on another public concern: the adequacy of Medicare in an era when prescription drugs have become central to health care. The needs of low-wage workers without any health insurance coverage are arguably much greater than the needs of elderly Americans for cheaper prescription drugs, as only about a quarter of the elderly lack drug coverage of any kind. Nevertheless, elderly concerns tend to weigh heavily with office-seeking politicians. The elderly are especially attentive to politics, and older voters of all income levels participate in elections at higher levels than their younger counterparts (Campbell 2003). Older voters are a swing constituency vital to both parties, constituting about 25 percent of voters in presidential elections and about 30 percent of voters in off-year congressional contests.

When elderly concerns about paying for prescription drugs grew acute in the 1990s and early 2000s, therefore, office-seeking politicians of both parties paid attention. Indeed, President George W. Bush convinced conservative Republicans, normally opposed to public entitlements, to vote for the Medicare prescription drug benefit in 2003. Republicans believe that denying Democrats an advantage with elderly voters may be the key to retaining governing power in the years ahead.

In short, public concerns spur politicians to keep talking about extending health insurance coverage or other apparently popular goals, especially in election or pre-election years. Nevertheless, as major debates unfold opponents of change can also gain leverage with public opinion. Once proposals begin to move through Congress, considerations apart from simple public hopes play an equal or greater role—especially partisanship, interest group activity, pre-existing institutional arrangements, and budget considerations. As such factors come to the fore, public support for legislative innovations may wane, especially if there are competing proposals for reform or debates switch to a focus on possible cuts in existing benefits.

Such influences certainly sparked shifts in public opinion during the 1993–1994 debates over the Clinton health plan, when the middle class worried that comprehensive reform might threaten existing health insurance (Blendon 1995; Jacobs and Shapiro 2000). During the mid–1990s, Republican proposals for cutbacks in Medicare spending via provider payment reductions also backfired when President Clinton gained popularity after suggesting other means of reducing deficits. Public preferences for benefits thus trumped any general desire for restrained federal spending.

Changes in the focus of debates and accompanying shifts in public opinion were also discernible in the 2003 Medicare reform episode. Even though this legislation passed, public doubts grew as opponents pointed out the gaps in prescription drug coverage and highlighted the ways the new law might undermine broader guaranteed coverage in Medicare. The elderly had high hopes for adding a prescription drug benefit to Medicare (*Washington Post*/Kaiser/Harvard 2002). But by the time the legislation was on the verge of passing, a clear majority of Americans over age fifty opposed it (National Annenberg Election Survey 2003; Skocpol 2003) and doubts remained after the law was enacted (Milbank and Deane 2003). While shifts in public opinion helped to block enactment of major reforms in 1993–1994 and 1995, this time Congress acted before public worries became obvious. Yet public disillusionment may still matter in future skirmishes over issues that the legislation leaves unresolved.

The Role of Parties and Ideology

U.S. parties and legislators approach health reform issues with ideological preferences as well as concerns about elections and public constituencies. In health care, a major source of disagreement concerns the role of government in America's complex and mixed public-private system of health care financing. Liberals want to expand government guarantees and regulations because they believe that competing private insurers, left to their own devices, will tend to exclude sick or costly people. Conservatives, in contrast, believe that market competition maximizes choice and should ultimately lower costs, or at least shift them toward individuals who can make choices and trade-offs.

In recent times, ideological polarization between activists and members of Congress affiliated with the two major parties has grown considerably (Fiorina 2002, 526, figure 4; Poole and Rosenthal 2001). Although the parties are relatively evenly balanced in Congress as well as among the electorate, this polarization means that slight shifts in power can make a big difference in the shape of compromises as well as the chances for legislative success.

Enacted health care reforms tend to reflect complex compromises between public guarantees and private provision. Nevertheless, the party in power sets the framework that governs such compromises. In 1993, President Clinton and congressional Democrats tried to work out a middle-of-the-road system for universal coverage that relied on private insurers and the employer-based insurance system. Still, they aimed for an overarching framework of public guarantees, regulations, and cost containment. In contrast, during the 2003 Medicare reform episode, Republicans tried—and to some degree succeeded—in making the prescription drug benefit conditional on new subsidies for private market forces in Medicare.

Despite these considerations, there are forces that cut against ideological and partisan polarization. Ideology still varies to some degree within each major party, for example, perhaps especially in the Democratic Party, where politicians favoring market competition in public programs coexist with others who would like a unified "single-payer" health insurance system financed entirely through taxation.

Constituency pressures on elected officials also cut across the partisan divide and force them to veer from ideological preferences, especially among Republicans. Regardless of party, for example, legislators from rural areas have distinct goals from those from more populated areas. There may be only one or a few insurance providers in any given rural area; private managed care may remain undeveloped; and rural hospitals struggle to provide comprehensive, convenient services to sparse and often aging populations. Even conservative Republicans may see more limited possibilities for unfettered market competition in such circumstances. Legislators from rural areas thus demand increasing payment rates for rural providers, and the 2003 Medicare legislation could not have passed if it had not included such subsidies.

The Power of Interest Groups

A crowded universe of interest groups also shapes attempts at health care reform, with some groups likely to help set agendas and others more likely to quietly influence the details of legislation.

Since the 1960s, interest groups of many kinds have proliferated in the United States (Berry 1997). Such proliferation has been especially marked in the health care arena—in large part because of increases in federal regulation and spending (Peterson 1993; Skocpol 2003, 146–147, table 4.2; Walker 1991). A rise in the number of public interest groups representing health care consumers creates new capacity for pushing health-related issues onto the public agenda. Nevertheless, professionals run many such public interest groups out of national offices. They may be good at putting problems on the agenda, but they do not usually have the organizational infrastructure or reach to pull millions of citizens into active lobbying on behalf of health care reform (Skocpol 2003). Thus popular issues may appear on the agenda, but lack staying power when ideological divisions occur or opposing interest groups mobilize (cf. Skocpol 1997 for the story of how this happened in the 1993–1994 Clinton health reform episode).

Interest groups representing providers, medical manufacturers, and health insurers have also multiplied. Business groups are highly organized in very specialized ways and they may see huge stakes in even slight adjustments of federal subsidies or regulations. Depending on the issue, the strategies of these groups can range from behind-the-scenes negotiations to increasingly sophisticated public campaigns.

The Clinton health reform episode opened a new chapter in the strategic use of technologies by provider, manufacturer, and insurance groups to reach the general public, key legislators, and grassroots supporters (Broder and Johnson 1996). These groups are often able to affect the details of proposed new legislation as it works its way through congressional committees. Interest-group brokered compromises often increase the complexity and opacity of health care legislation, making it hard for the general public to follow the debate and outcome (Pear and Toner 2003). Pressure from provider and insurance groups may also increase the likelihood that reform proposals will contain expensive subsidies and weak federal regulatory authority, because business interests are looking for profits and room to maneuver in the marketplace.

The Ironies of Budget Politics

Budget constraints have been an almost constant factor in health reform politics since the 1970s. Medical care spending consumes a growing share of federal and state budgets and employer payroll expenses. Congressional rules requiring the "costing out" of reform proposals ensure that their costs play a role in the policy debate. Further complicating matters is the fact that, while budgetary pressures concern policymakers, cost containment is not popular with the public and is often opposed by provider interests as well.

For ideological reasons, politicians disagree about preferred responses to rising costs. Liberals believe in using public clout to control costs, while conservatives favor market competition. Policy experts—including those who share policy goals—may also disagree regarding preferred approaches because of the difficulty of assessing how markets work under imperfect competitive conditions. Ironically, all these cross pressures produce a situation in which politicians pay loud lip service to "cost control," but successful legislation actually provides generous payoffs to beneficiaries and providers—leading to recurrent problems with rising costs.

Efforts to address costs in ways the public can easily perceive have proven politically risky. The Medicare catastrophic legislation of 1988 relied on financing paid by seniors themselves, but seniors soon opposed that step. Their public outcry was most dramatically illustrated by images of a group of angry seniors surrounding Representative Dan Rostenkowski's car, and Congress soon repealed the controversial legislation (Oberlander 2003). The effort to contain costs while expanding coverage was a major factor in the unwieldy design of—and public skepticism about—the Clinton health reform plan (Skocpol 1997).

The public reacted no more favorably in 1995 to Republican legislation that attempted to reduce Medicare payments to health care providers. The widespread shift to managed care in the mid-1990s also provoked public wrath (Blendon et al. 1998). The peculiar gaps in coverage in the Medicare prescription drug legislation were clearly due to the $400 billion ceiling for projected spending, and much of the wariness that seniors are now expressing reflects worries that their drug costs—and perhaps also Medicare premiums—may actually rise.

Public worries about the possible effects of cost controls are magnified by the concerns of business interest groups about limits to federal subsidies or regulatory adjustments that promise to shift rising costs toward private-sector employers, insurers, or providers. Of the three recent efforts at major health care reform—the 1993–1994 Clinton plan; the mid-1990s Republican-sponsored public-sector cuts; and the 2003 Medicare restructuring—the only proposal to actually pass (the 2003 restructuring) was the one that most thoroughly combined weak cost controls on the private sector, benefit increases, and generous subsidies for businesses.

Even though Republicans sponsored and promoted this legislation, it features higher Medicare subsidies for hospitals, physicians, and health maintenance organizations. The final legislation also prohibits federal Medicare authorities from using their regulatory and bargaining powers to lower drug prices. The bill was stripped of provisions that would have the import of cheaper, publicly regulated prescription drugs from Canada. And the final legislation also included subsidies to induce private employers to retain retiree prescription drug benefits. Finally, in adding a modest new drug benefit for all Medicare beneficiaries, the legislation was far from effective "cost control" and guarantees continuing struggles over how to fund Medicare.

Messy Compromises and Future Prospects

Budget constraints promise to loom ever larger in struggles over all aspects of government's role in health care, given recent major tax cuts, a growing federal deficit, the coming retirement of baby boomers, and likely continued increases in health care costs above the overall inflation rate due to ongoing technological change (Newhouse 1992). With strong bipartisan support, lawmakers doubled the National Institutes for Health budget between 1999 and 2003 and enhanced resources for expedited FDA (Food and Drug Administration) review of new drugs, thus fostering the new technology that drives spending growth. These expansions, combined with popular demands for extended health care coverage, are sure to strain the federal budget, giving politicians, including some Democrats, incentives to find "reforms" that reduce costs appearing on public budgets—or at least appear to do so. The recent record, however, is not promising for actually enacting effective budget cuts or cost controls. Though the 1993–1994 Clinton legislation and the mid-1990s Republican reform proposal featured cost controls, both of these efforts fell short of enactment.

Our understanding of past reform debates suggests that if differences do not produce stalemate, compromises necessarily take the form of complex and ambiguous measures that opposing players can interpret as partial victories. From the perspective of expert policy designers, this means that carefully constructed proposals will emerge from the political process—if at all—in substantially altered form. Many provisions of complex compromise bills are designed to satisfy interest groups; while others allow both conservatives and liberals to imagine that they have received "half a loaf" and can return to fight for more or less governmental provision on another day.

Even when efforts are made to forge complex compromises, however, there is no guarantee that proposals will be enacted, or prove stable after initial enactment. Public opinion may turn against complex compromises, as it did in 1993–1994. Or the public may be disillusioned by budget-driven compromises that seek financing from beneficiaries or that limit the scope of benefits, as occurred in extreme form with the repeal of Medicare catastrophic legislation in 1989, and may occur again with the current Medicare prescription drug legislation. Research suggests that cost containment approaches are more politically feasible when they are

less visible to the public and not easily attributable to the actions of readily identifiable politicians (Arnold 1990; Pierson 1994).

Going forward, policymakers face contradictory pressures to expand health
insurance coverage and benefits while, at the same time, limiting increases in federal outlays. Growing ideological polarization also ensures that partisans will want
to head in opposite directions—toward or away from greater government regulation—in each wave of reform. Changes can be stymied by an inability to reach
political compromise over competing approaches and goals, or by lack of commitment to allocate public funds toward expanded benefits desired by the public.

The Medicare prescription drug legislation opens rather than forecloses new
rounds of debate about this vital part of the U.S. health care financing system.
Left unsettled is government's role in regulating pharmaceutical prices and subsidizing health care markets. Reliance on private drug plans to negotiate pharmaceutical prices was key to convincing a Republican-led Congress to pass the
legislation. But if prescription prices continue to rise rapidly, the role of government could easily expand, much as it did in the face of medical price inflation
after Medicare was created in 1965.

The 2003 law reconfigures arrangements and subsidies to private health plans
that serve Medicare beneficiaries and may lead to increased enrollment in HMOs
(health maintenance organizations). Yet it is unclear whether the subsidies will be
enough to attract health plans and Medicare beneficiaries who remain wary following their prior bad experiences with changes in the late 1990s. In earlier rounds
of policymaking for Medicare, many private providers entered the Medicare HMO
market, only to withdraw after government subsidies were trimmed. The new subsidies to private providers are unlikely to produce cost savings to the federal budget. If budget struggles intensify, politicians could once again find it easier to trim
provider subsidies than to trim benefits or raise Medicare premiums. Republicans
may approach such issues with a different mindset than most Democrats, but they,
too, are subject to voter expectations and popular pressures.

Beyond Medicare, expanded coverage for the uninsured remains the great
unsettled question in the mixed U.S. health insurance system. Circumstances in
2004 are in some ways startlingly similar to conditions a decade ago. Private premium increases reached double digits each year from 2001 to 2003, increasing by
13.9 percent in 2003 (Gabel, Claxton, and Holve 2003). Following recent economic
slowdowns, the number of uninsured increased, reaching 43.6 million in 2002
(Mills and Bhandari 2003). A presidential election season induces politicians, especially Democrats, to address issues of coverage and costs with an eye to the concerns of average voters.

But prospects for making headway on coverage for the uninsured are at least
as mixed as in 1993–1994. Public concern regarding health care costs has risen,
but concerns about the economy, war, and terrorism rival health care in public priorities for government action. As with the 1993–1994 reform episode, despite signs
of growing consensus on the need for expanded coverage, proposed policy approaches range widely from those that build on existing programs to those that

make more dramatic departures (Butler 2003; Collins, Davis, and Lambrew 2003; Davis and Schoen 2003; Kahn and Pollack 2001; Meyer and Wicks 2001, 2002).

Thus, even though policy elites have moved closer to consensus, it is unclear whether politicians will seek a financing mechanism for broad-based coverage expansions for the uninsured—especially given the ballooning of projected federal budget deficits (Congressional Budget Office 2003). Democratic primary voters tend to reward candidates whose proposals are more expansive and costly than the general public may be willing to support. The outcome of the 2004 election will affect the prospects for reform, though partisan divisions are sure to persist even if Democrats gain ground. If Democrats and Republicans do not find common ground on measures to aid the uninsured in low-income working families, their plight will remain unresolved. And the political cost of inaction to office seekers may be slight, because lower-income, working-aged Americans do not vote at especially high levels.

In the past, reforms that have moved from conception to enactment have somehow addressed cross pressures—usually by building on existing arrangements and incorporating compromises that give a little to all key players. Looking ahead, coverage expansions—whether in Medicare or to the uninsured—are sure to return to the political agenda because the underlying problems remain salient to the American public. Yet once on the agenda, proposals for expanded benefits tend to become entangled in sweeping visions of how to retool the health care system or reduce federal spending. This makes forging stable compromises difficult. Some reforms may survive the political process in a version that departs substantially from original proposals. But the necessary compromises lead to health policies that will never be perfect from anyone's perspective—whether politician, payer, provider, patient, or policy analyst—inevitably setting the stage for continuing political battles.

Health care reform is certain to remain central to U.S. electoral politics and governance in the years ahead. But it is just as certain to remain unsettled, subject to messy compromises, partisan clashes, and ambiguous decisions.

Acknowledgments

We would like to thank Colleen Barry, Dan Carpenter, Juliette Cubanski, David Cutler, Julie Donohue, Jacob Hacker, Joe Newhouse, Paul Pierson, David Stevenson, and, especially, Bob Blendon for conversations that informed this work, and the editors for helpful suggestions. Any omissions or errors are our own.

References

Arnold, R. D. 1990. *The Logic of Congressional Action*. New Haven: Yale University Press.
Baumgartner, F. R., and B. D. Jones. 1993. *Agendas and Instability in American Politics*. Chicago: University of Chicago Press.
Berry, J. M. 1997. *The Interest Group Society*. 3rd ed. New York: Longman.
Blendon, R. 1995. What Happened to Americans' Support of the Clinton Plan? *Health Affairs* 14: 7–23.

Blendon, R., M. Brodie, J. Benson, et al. 1998. Understanding the Managed Care Backlash. *Health Affairs* 17: 80–94.

Broder, David S., and H. B. Johnson. 1996. *The System: The American Way of Politics at the Breaking Point.* Boston: Little, Brown.

Butler, S. 2003. Laying the Groundwork for Universal Health Care Coverage. Testimony before the Senate Special Committee on Aging, March 13. Washington, DC: Heritage Foundation. Available at *www.heritage.org/Research/HealthCare/test031003.cfm.*

Campbell, A. L. 2003. *How Policies Make Citizens: Senior Political Activism and the American Welfare State.* Princeton, NJ: Princeton University Press.

Collins, S. R., K. Davis, and J. M. Lambrew. 2003. Health Care Reform Returns to the National Agenda: The 2004 Presidential Candidates' Proposals. New York: Commonwealth Fund. Available at *www.cmwf.org/programs/insurance/collins_ reformagenda_671.pdf.*

Congressional Budget Office. 2003. *The Budget and Economic Outlook: An Update.* August. Washington, DC: United States Congress.

Davis, K., and C. Schoen. 2003. Universal Coverage: Creating Consensus. *Health Affairs* (web excl.) W3: 199–211. Available at *www.healthaffairs.org/WebExclusives/ 2203Davis.pdf.*

Downs, A. 1972. Up and Down with Ecology: The Issue-Attention Cycle. *The Public Interest* 28: 38–50.

Fiorina, M. P. 2002. Parties, Participation, and Representation in America: Old Theories Face New Realities. In *Political Science: The State of the Discipline,* ed. I. Katznelson and H. V. Milner, 511–541. New York: W. W. Norton.

Gabel, J., G. Claxton, and E. Holve. 2003. Health Benefits in 2003: Premiums Reach 13-Year High as Employers Adopt New Forms of Cost Sharing. *Health Affairs* 22: 117–126.

Hacker, J. 2002. *The Divided Welfare State: The Battle over Public and Private Social Benefits in the United States.* New York: Cambridge University Press.

Jacobs, L. R., and R. Y. Shapiro. 2000. *Politicians Don't Pander: Political Manipulation and the Loss of Democratic Responsiveness.* Chicago: University of Chicago Press.

Kahn, C. N., and R. F. Pollack. 2001. Building a Consensus for Expanding Coverage. *Health Affairs* 20: 40–48.

Kingdon, J. 1995. *Agendas, Alternatives, and Public Policies.* 2nd ed. Boston: Addison Wesley Longman.

Meyer, J. A., and E. K.Wicks, eds. 2001. *Covering America: Real Remedies for the Uninsured.* Vol. 1. Washington, DC: Economic and Social Research Institute. Available at *www.esresearch.org/RWJ11PDF/full_document.pdf.*

———. 2002. *Covering America: Real Remedies for the Uninsured.* Vol. 2. Washington, DC: Economic and Social Research Institute. Available at *www.esresearch.org/Documents/CovAm2pdfs/CovAm2all.pdf.*

Milbank, D., and C. Deane. 2003. President Signs Medicare Drug Bill; Supporters, Opponents Jockey for 2004 Edge. *Washington Post,* December 9, A1.

Mills, R. J., and S. Bhandari. 2003. Health Insurance Coverage, 2002. Washington, DC: U.S. Census Bureau. Available at *www.census.gov/prod/2003pubs/p60–223.pdf.*

National Annenberg Election Survey. 2003. Public Split on Medicare Bill but Elderly Are Opposed, Survey Shows. November 24. Available at *www.annenbergpublicpolicycenter.org/ naes/press_releases.htm.*

Newhouse, J. 1992. Medical Care Costs: How Much Welfare Loss? *Journal of Economic Perspectives* 6, no. 3: 3–21.

Oberlander, J. 2003. *The Political Life of Medicare.* Chicago: University of Chicago Press.

Pear, R., and R. Toner. 2003. Simple Criticism of Drug Benefit: It's Bewildering. *New York Times,* June 22, A1, A22.

Peterson, M. A. 1993. Political Influence in the 1990s: From Iron Triangles to Policy Networks. *Journal of Health Politics, Policy, and Law* 18: 395–438.

————. 1998. The Politics of Health Care Policy: Overreaching in an Age of Polarization. In *The Social Divide: Political Parties and the Future of Activist Government,* ed. Margaret Weir, 181–229. Washington, DC: Brookings Institution Press.

Pierson, P. 1994. *Dismantling the Welfare State? Reagan, Thatcher, and the Politics of Retrenchment.* New York: Cambridge University Press.

————. 2000. Path Dependence, Increasing Returns, and the Study of Politics. *American Political Science Review* 94: 251–267.

Poole, K. T., and H. Rosenthal. 2001. D-NOMINATE after 10 Years: A Comparative Update to Congress: A Political-Economic History of Roll-Call Voting. *Legislative Studies Quarterly* 26: 5–29.

Skocpol, T. 1997. *Boomerang: Health Care Reform and the Turn against Government.* New York: W. W. Norton.

————. 2003. *Diminished Democracy: From Membership to Management in American Civic Life.* Norman: University of Oklahoma Press.

————. 2004. A Bad Senior Moment. *American Prospect* 15, no. 1: 26–29.

Walker, J. L., Jr. 1991. *Mobilizing Interest Groups in America: Patrons, Professions, and Social Movements.* Ann Arbor: University of Michigan Press.

Washington Post/Kaiser Family Foundation/Harvard University. 2002. *A Generational Look at the Public: Politics and Policy.* August. Washington, DC: Kaiser Family Foundation.

CHAPTER 3

The Employer–Based Health Insurance System

MISTAKE OR CORNERSTONE?

⸻ ∞∞∞ ⸻

SHERRY A. GLIED

*F*or decades, health policy analysts have voiced their disdain for employer-based health insurance. In 1961, Herman and Anne Somers referred to the system as the "'shotgun' marriage of medical care and industrial relations" (Somers and Somers 1961, 227). Critics routinely belittle job-based coverage as an unfortunate historical accident, the by-product of short-lived wartime wage and price controls that moved compensation toward such benefits (Hyman and Hall 2001). Analysts today see the dismantling of this illogical, inefficient institution as an essential step toward the development of universal, equitable health insurance in the United States (Fuchs 1994).

Yet employer-based coverage is a remarkably durable institution. For nearly seventy years most Americans who hold insurance have obtained it through their jobs. Nor is employer-based health insurance peculiarly American, the inadvertent consequence of U.S. policies. Internationally, employer participation in the health insurance system is more the rule than the exception. And far from impeding the development of universal, equitable coverage, the workplace is the foundation of several successful universal insurance systems.

Today American health policymakers have proposed a range of alternatives that either intentionally seek to dismantle employer-based coverage or are likely to undermine it. The orthodox view of job-based coverage implies that policies that lead to its disappearance would be desirable, or at worst benign. The historical and international persistence of this institution, however, suggests the need for a second appraisal of this venerable institution.

The Origins of Employer-Based Coverage

In 2002, 92 percent of all privately insured Americans under sixty-five obtained health coverage through their current or past jobs or through the jobs of family members. The percentage of all Americans under sixty-five who have insurance coverage has fallen from 86 percent in 1987 to 83 percent in 2002, primarily because the cost of health care relative to income has risen (Glied and Stabile 2000). Among those under sixty-five who do hold coverage (private or public), however, the share covered through employment has risen. In 1987, 77 percent of the insured held job-based coverage; today the fraction is 79 percent.[1]

The conventional history of employer-based coverage in the United States begins during and after World War II, when the federal government imposed price and wage controls. Employers seeking to attract workers offered health insurance and other non-wage benefits as substitutes. The inflation-control policy inadvertently contributed to vast growth in insurance coverage—from 1.3 million people in 1940 to 32 million in 1945 (Health Insurance Institute 1970, 17).

Provisions of the tax code further encouraged employer-based coverage (Thomasson 2002). The tax code does not treat employer payments for health coverage as compensation, and thus exempts them from payroll and income taxes (a practice that the Internal Revenue Service formally codified in 1954). This effective subsidy raises overall coverage but has been widely criticized as highly inequitable (favoring the highest-paid employees who are in the highest tax bracket) and often inefficient (favoring those who purchase more costly plans, including plans that encourage excessive utilization) (Glied 1994). Increases in income and payroll taxes since the 1950s have made this tax subsidy ever more valuable, fostering the expansion of employer-based coverage. Employee payments have also been exempt from tax since 1984, if they are channeled through a flexible spending account.

Although this history portrays job-based coverage as an accident, in fact, private health insurance in the United States has always been job based. In the early twentieth century, when income losses owing to ill health were much more important than coverage for medical costs, several large firms, notably Montgomery Ward, began offering disability insurance (and often medical care) to their employees (Faulkner 1940). Today's paid sick days and job-based short-term disability policies are the legacy of these early ventures. Voluntary fraternal organizations also attempted to provide disability insurance (among other benefits) to their members. Membership in the organizations was fluid, and new members attracted by the availability of these benefits tended to be less healthy than anticipated while young, healthy members often defected, ultimately dooming these plans (Witt 2001).

As the costs (and quality) of medical care rose through the 1920s, paying for medical care became a distinct concern. The Committee on the Costs of Medical Care reported that by 1932 about 670,000 workers participated in some form of industrial fixed-payment medical service (Williams 1932). As the depression deepened and paying for care became more difficult, hospitals developed Blue Cross prepayment plans. Hospitals sold these early Blue Cross plans exclusively to job-based groups, including teachers, bank employees, and newspaper workers—before the mid-1930s these plans excluded even dependents (Reed 1947). Plans typically required employer groups to guarantee a fixed level of participation, usually between 40 percent and 75 percent of their employees (Cunningham and

Cunningham 1997). Efforts to sell Blue Cross products to individuals and very small groups during the 1930s led to significant adverse selection (wherein people who anticipate high health costs dominate a risk pool) and nearly bankrupted some regional Blues (Cunningham and Cunningham 1997).

This early history suggests that while price controls and tax policies have been important to the development and persistence of job-based coverage, they were neither necessary nor sufficient. Empirical studies of the effect of tax subsidies on the institutional structure of health insurance strengthen this claim. Although the effect of these tax provisions, at the margin, is to reallocate coverage from the individual market toward the employer-based market, the magnitude of this effect is quite modest. Studies find that this structural effect operates strongly in small firms with fewer than twenty-five or so employees (Stabile 2002; Finkelstein 2002). In the absence of such a subsidy, about half of very small firm employees with job-based coverage would likely lose access to such coverage (their firms would no longer offer it). This implies that offering coverage is subsidy dependent and not fundamentally economically efficient for these small firms. The subsidy appears to have little effect on the choice of job-based rather than individual coverage among employees in larger firms, however. Even without the subsidy, most workers in large firms would continue to obtain health insurance through their jobs.

The importance of job-based coverage in a wide range of institutional contexts around the world attests to the inherent value of organizing health insurance around employment. Well before voluntary employment-based coverage began in the United States, countries with social insurance systems—most notably Germany (also France, Hungary, Czechoslovakia, and several others)—organized the delivery of many mandatory social insurance benefits, including disability and, eventually, medical insurance, through the workplace (Williams 1932). German employers not only contributed to the cost of public social insurance programs (as in the U.S. Medicare program) but also established and managed private insurance plans (or sickness funds) themselves. The German system has become less reliant on management by individual employers over time, but even today, more than a century after the establishment of universal social insurance, many of the largest German employers continue to operate their own health insurance programs (Amelung, Glied, and Topan 2003).

In countries with other forms of universal insurance, publicly financed and organized plans provide major medical coverage. These plans include the National Health Service model in the United Kingdom, the national health insurance model in Canada, and the social insurance system in France. Yet even in many of these situations, employers continue to provide supplemental insurance coverage. Voluntary job-based coverage exists in Belgium, Canada, Denmark, Finland, France, Hungary, Sweden, and the United Kingdom, among others. While such private insurance is much more limited than in the United States (where private job-based insurance pays for about 27 percent of all health care bills), the predominance of job-based coverage in these private markets is striking (Cowan et al. 2002).

In the United Kingdom, for example, job-based coverage accounts for about three-quarters of the market for private health insurance, which covers about 11 percent of residents. The high share of job-based coverage in this small private insurance market is particularly striking because employer payments for health insurance are not tax exempt and all private insurance premiums are subject to an additional tax. In France, supplemental job-based coverage accounts for about two-'thirds of voluntary private health insurance (which pays for about 10 percent of total health expenditures) (OECD 2001). About two-thirds of Canadians are covered by supplemental job-based coverage, which pays the cost of medical services not covered by the national plan, including prescription drugs (Stabile 2002). The average per-employee cost of private coverage in Canada is about 10–15 percent of the per-employee cost of employer-based coverage in the United States.

Finally, job-based coverage is often the only form of health insurance available to middle-income workers in developing countries. Large firms in Brazil, India, and Indonesia (to name a few) routinely provide health insurance to their employees. In other cases, firms provide direct health services in lieu of coverage (Jack 2000; Marzolf 2002; Naylor et al. 1999).

Employment-based coverage, then, is not just an accident of history. Nor is job-based coverage merely a regrettable and inferior way-station, a stage in the maturation of the U.S. health care system on its road to—take your pick—national health insurance or universal, market-based, individual coverage. Rather, job-based coverage is a unique institution that continues to provide the only available basis for a stable private insurance market.

Why Employment-Based Coverage Works

Medium and large firms appear to provide a natural venue for the sale of health insurance. Bigger firms enjoy substantial administrative cost advantages in most of their activities, from purchasing pens and copy paper to offering paid sick leave and disability insurance (Brown et al. 1990). Obvious economies of scale accrue from the ability to make fewer sales calls and process a single payment rather than many. These administrative savings make it advantageous for firms to offer employees a range of benefits and amenities. These advantages are particularly stark in health insurance markets.

The problem of adverse selection plagues markets for all types of insurance, but it is especially difficult in markets where health risks develop over time. Most people would like protection against both the risk that they will experience a negative health event in the coming year (as in all types of insurance) and the risk that they will develop a chronic health condition that will permanently raise their health care costs. In some markets, such as the life insurance market, innovative long-term contracts encourage people to buy coverage when they are young and retain it even if they discover that they are healthier than expected. Developing sustainable long-term health insurance contracts has proven a more intractable problem. Although several economists have described potential models, no going concern has yet adopted them (Cochrane 1995; Pauly et al. 1995). Instead, nongroup health insurance contracts are annual. Thus an event that permanently raises health care costs will permanently raise health insurance premiums—precisely the result people would like to avoid.

Job-based coverage through large firms offers the only existing long-term private health insurance. Such firms can solve both the point-in-time and long-term problem of adverse selection better than voluntary organizations because employees constitute a group formed and sustained for reasons other than the need for health insurance. The group may contain a variety of health risks, but there is little reason to expect people with an exceptional demand for health insurance to dominate. Moreover, people decide to remain at or leave firms mainly (though, noted below, not entirely) for reasons other than their health. Indeed, people whose health deteriorates are more likely to leave their jobs (or retire) than are those who remain healthy.

Voluntary organizations could (and in some instances do—witness the Amish, for example) offer stable health insurance just as effectively as firms do, if the hurdles to joining the organization and maintaining membership and the penalties for exit were as great as those for taking on and leaving a job. Employers provide health insurance mainly because employees value the benefit much more highly than the cost employers incur. The lower loading costs and other inherent advantages of group coverage enable employers to "sell" coverage to their employees at a substantial discount. Firms that do not offer this discounted benefit must pay higher wages to attract similar workers away from competitors that do offer such coverage. Thus the total cost of labor compensation is likely to be lower for firms that can offer both wages and coverage to attract workers than for firms that offer only wages (Famulari and Manser 1989).

This administrative advantage makes employers the essential building blocks of a private health insurance system. Moreover, this employer-based system can operate quite effectively without much regulation.[2] In the nongroup market, regulators aim to moderate rate variation and demand renewable products. By contrast, monitoring the health care costs of potential hires and current employees (and their dependents) at the firm level makes little sense (Bloom and Glied 1991), even without calculating the damage that such a policy would have to the value of the insurance benefit for all employees. Firms have no reason to offer benefits that their employees do not value, so regulation of the content of health insurance can also be minimal. Indeed, under ERISA (the federal law that covers employee benefit plans), medium and large U.S. firms can avoid virtually all substantive regulation of health insurance by self-insuring (Briffault and Glied 2002). While regulation of nongroup markets is full of pitfalls, the employer-based system has operated for about three-quarters of a century as an almost completely unregulated market.

So It Works—So What?

Private health insurance—which, as I have argued, means job-based insurance—operates differently from public insurance. Because it operates in a market, is only lightly regulated, and is highly decentralized, private health insurance can offer much more flexibility than public coverage alone. This flexibility makes private job-based coverage relatively successful in providing insurance to the large subset of Americans who can afford to buy it at current prices, and makes it a useful alternative or supplement to public systems in other countries.

Private employers purchase health insurance in much the same way that they purchase production inputs. In purchasing inputs, employers seek those that will enable them to make, at the lowest-possible cost, products whose characteristics (including price, color, size, and quality) most appeal to consumers. Likewise, in purchasing health insurance, employers wish to obtain, at the lowest-possible cost, the package of compensation (wages, insurance benefits, and pensions) that their employees most prefer. These goals are relatively straightforward—especially compared with the multiple political and policy objectives of public health insurance programs.

The single-minded pursuit of a low-cost product that keeps employees satisfied makes private employers dismiss pleadings from providers (and, to our dismay, makes them equally dismissive of the suggestions of health policy analysts). In markets, purchasers and their dollars rule. This means that private employers can readily purchase products that reduce payments to one provider group in order to expand benefits in another area. In the 1990s, for example, employers added coverage for prescription drugs to employee benefit packages while restricting provider networks and cutting payments to physicians and hospitals (Centers for Medicare and Medicaid Services 2003; Glied 2003). Providers might justifiably complain that they have lost revenue so drug manufacturers can earn more. Employers simply saw the rise in consumer interest in prescription drugs and decided to buy a product that would satisfy their audience. As the Medicare prescription drug debate and similar struggles in Canada suggest, public health insurance programs have much more trouble redividing the pie in this way, even when such a redivision is justified.

When employers blithely select plans that limit choice of provider or fail to cover chiropractors or limit hospital stays, affected providers seek relief from regulators and legislators. Organized provider groups have clout at the legislative level that dissolves once they enter the marketplace.

Employers' disregard for organized providers allows them (or the private insurers with which they contract) to easily adopt and discard benefit, payment, and organizational innovations. Employers have not necessarily been more innovative than governments in the health care market; government researchers developed many of the most significant payment innovations of the past three decades, such as diagnosis-related groups (DRGs) and resource-based relative value scales. However, benefit, payment, and organizational innovations diffuse much differently in the public and private spheres. Governments commission and then legislate new administrative technologies. Private insurers pick and choose among such innovations.

Some private insurers adopted DRGs while others tried capitated payments, for example, but many discarded these methods in favor of others, such as negotiated per diem payments combined with utilization review (InterStudy Reports HMOs Move to per Diem Rates 2001). Employers tried covering alternative medicine in the mid–1990s, but later eliminated these services when added benefits led to overuse and high costs (Edlin 2003). Employers also tried managed-care plans that restricted enrollees' choice of providers, but employees weren't satisfied, so employers added point-of-service options. In the early 1970s, when utilization review was new, both private insurers and Medicare began to implement it. In the 1990s, when it no longer seemed to work, private insurers were quick to dismiss it (Prince 1999).

Private plans may make precipitous decisions regarding which innovations to adopt and reject, but this flexibility can be a valuable antidote to the slow pace of public insurance systems. Dropping a previously covered benefit or changing a payment mechanism takes years of hearings and court rulings under Medicare; it takes a phone call under a private insurance plan.

Employers also gain from their ability to shop for the best prices. Health care is local, so shopping opportunities are often limited, but where national markets exist, as in pharmaceuticals, private markets can be adept at seeking out and exploiting opportunities for savings. The success of private plans in restraining drug costs has led many in Congress to favor the use of such plans in arranging prescription drug benefits for Medicare patients. Of course, government purchasers can also reduce prices, simply by exerting their monopsony clout. The advantage of private competition is that cost reduction efforts are less monolithic. Individual purchasers can negotiate lower prices by offering to purchase in bulk, but across the entire market of purchasers, a variety of similar products can remain viable. Such basic differences between government and market approaches were at the heart of the protracted policy debate about how to structure the Medicare prescription drug benefit (Huskamp et al. 2000).

Finally, private markets permit purchasers to make tradeoffs between the value and cost of new technologies. If people want more of something, or want it faster, and they are willing to pay for it, private markets are likely to arise to sell it to them. This responsiveness has costs. By behaving in this way, private markets translate inequities in income into inequities in the consumption of goods and services. Such responsiveness provides an important signal of consumer demand, however, describing not only what people want but how much it is worth to them.

These benefits—flexibility, responsiveness, shopping—are both the advantages of private insurance and the characteristics that have allowed private job-based health insurance to evolve and survive over time. Job-based coverage has accommodated the pharmaceutical revolution, the development of outpatient surgery, and many other technological changes that have altered the health care delivery system. It has endured the decline of labor unions, the rise of the two-earner household, growing international competition, and other upheavals in the American labor market. Private job-based coverage offers a viable, rapid-response mechanism that complements the ever-changing health care delivery system and labor market. These attributes have made job-based coverage the dominant choice for providing health insurance to average-income working Americans and a source of supplementary benefits in a variety of public health insurance systems.

Yet in both the United States and other nations, the role of private job-based coverage is circumscribed. It operates in contexts where its beneficiaries can pay most of the cost of health care themselves and where the inevitable missteps of private coverage in benefit design, payment mechanisms, and organizational form are bearable. Nowhere does job-based coverage alone provide universal and comprehensive health insurance.

What Job-Based Coverage Cannot Do

Job-based health insurance is a voluntary, market institution. These attributes give the institution its characteristic strengths, but they also limit its use. Despite its strengths, the job-based voluntary private insurance system in the United States leaves over forty million people uninsured.

The most important failing of job-based coverage is in redistribution. Markets and market institutions do not by nature voluntarily redistribute resources.[3] Job-based coverage does seem to foster an unusual degree of redistribution across workers of different incomes within firms (working at a firm with higher-wage colleagues raises the probability that a low-wage worker will have coverage). Structural, regulatory, and tax features all contribute to this cross-subsidization. To avoid adverse selection within the employer pool, many insurers require, as a condition of coverage, that most employees take up insurance. Nondiscrimination rules prohibit insurance arrangements that favor only the most highly paid employees. The substantial subsidies that high-wage workers obtain from the favorable tax treatment of job-based coverage may make them willing to cross-subsidize coverage if that is what it takes to maintain their tax benefit. Yet even with these advantages, the degree of income cross-subsidization under private health insurance is limited.

The job-based health insurance system—like any other private system—never provided health insurance to workers with very low earnings, including disabled workers and those with very few skills. The tax exemption for employer-based health insurance provides very little subsidy for the purchase of health insurance for low-wage workers who already face relatively low marginal tax rates. Given these low subsidy levels, many people in this group do not seek out jobs with health insurance coverage, while others turn down coverage when it is offered. In effect, low-wage workers do not trade off cash for benefits. As the cost of health insurance coverage and the employee share of that cost has risen, a growing number of workers are being priced out of the system and no longer accept job-based coverage when it is offered. Increases in the cost of benefits may lead employers to shift low-wage employees out of the pool of workers eligible for benefits, by contracting out jobs or using temporary workers.

Job-based insurance also generates inequities in the availability of coverage across firms: some firms offer better, more generous coverage than do others. These inequities mirror the many inter-firm disparities throughout the labor market. Small firms pay lower wages than large firms, firms with health insurance benefits tend to also offer pensions and disability coverage, and firms in the apparel industry pay lower wages than those in the transport industry, for example (Brown et al.

1990; Krueger and Summers 1987). Prodigious interventions would be required to smooth such deep-seated variations.

Private health insurance markets may also have difficulty redistributing resources from healthy to sick people. An enduring, and reasonable, concern about job-based health insurance is that employers will discriminate against workers whose health care costs are expected to be higher than average. The substantial value to all workers of coverage that does not drop people when they (or their dependents) become ill, however, suggests that employers may find it economically rational not to discriminate against such workers by firing them or reducing their wages.[4]

Employers might rationally avoid hiring people who are clearly likely to have high health care costs (especially if this information can be inexpensively ascertained). Yet while behaving in this way may make sense, there is little evidence that such discrimination occurs often in practice. Identifying such discrimination may be difficult because employers are unlikely to hire workers whom they anticipate will soon become incapacitated, regardless of whether they do or do not offer health insurance. Still, some evidence shows that private employers do hire people with high future health care costs if they are likely to be able to work. For example, longitudinal studies of people with HIV/AIDS find that about 10 percent who were uninsured moved into private coverage (Smith and Kirking 2001).

Problems of redistribution are the most important reason that people cannot obtain coverage through the job-based system. The connection between employment and health insurance also means that even some people who do earn enough to buy private coverage fit poorly into the system. One group of "misfits" consists of those whose employment situation does not readily lend itself to employment-based coverage. These include new-economy workers with contingent employment contracts, multiple jobs, and part-year employment. This group is relatively small and does not appear to be growing (Hipple 2001). Expanding the misfit group to include people who change jobs often (more than once a year) and those who work for very small businesses that would likely not offer coverage if the tax subsidy did not exist yields a substantially larger group.

A very generous estimate of this expanded group would include all workers in firms of twenty-five or fewer workers (although, in fact, many small, stable firms would continue to find it efficient to offer coverage even without the subsidy). This expanded group accounts for just under half of the active U.S. labor force. Some two-fifths of all Americans under sixty-five live in households that either do not include any workers or include only workers of this misfit type. Even in a system with substantial subsidies for the purchase of insurance, this group would probably not find job-based coverage attractive and would prefer to obtain coverage in a regulated individual market. By contrast, about one-half of all Americans under sixty-five have incomes high enough to afford job-based coverage without a subsidy and are attached to a job that could efficiently offer such coverage.[5]

A system of job-based coverage may find it difficult to accommodate households that deviate from the traditional family. The employer-based system dates from an era when families typically included only one wage earner supporting a spouse and children. Today fewer than 15 percent of households fit this traditional mold. The problems entailed in matching a job-based system to the changing family are apparent in mandatory systems with job-based financing, such as the German health care system (Amelung, Glied, and Topan 2003). The "spousal tax" of job-based coverage can be substantial under these systems because households with two workers subsidize those with only one worker.

The voluntary employer-based health insurance system has, to some extent, adapted to these changes. In particular, by raising the employee share of spousal coverage, private employers have effectively reduced the marriage tax for two-earner households (these households no longer subsidize single-earner households to the same extent). But individually based systems with non-job-based financing (whether private or public) manage such changes in family structure more easily.

Other criticisms of job-based coverage focus on the effects on the labor market of tying health insurance to employment. Many observers have criticized job-based coverage for making U.S. producers less competitive internationally, but this is unlikely in a voluntary system (Reinhardt 1989). Employers have little reason to continue offering coverage unless workers value it enough to pay for it, and if workers pay for coverage through lower wages than they would otherwise receive, health insurance costs cannot affect competitiveness.

More recently, economists have expressed concern that the link between health insurance and the labor market may diminish job mobility—a phenomenon called job lock (Madrian 1994). Job lock can occur if people who anticipate high health care costs are reluctant to leave jobs with health insurance. Job lock implies that current employers treat workers who anticipate high health costs more favorably than nongroup insurers and potential future employers (evidence that job-based coverage offers insurance whose premium does not vary over time). While job lock is very important to individual workers, the best estimates reveal that its impact on the overall U.S. economy is quite small—below 0.1 percent of GDP (gross domestic product) (Gruber and Madrian 2002).[6]

A final set of concerns relates to the effect of job-based coverage on the health care delivery market. Some analysts have argued that employment-based insurance insulates workers from the true cost of health coverage, leading to a more costly health care system than individuals would select on their own. More recently, other critics have argued that in selecting health plans, employers weight cost considerations more heavily than quality measures. In fact, job-based coverage tends to be more generous—in the sense of having greater actuarial value—than coverage that individuals purchase in the nongroup market, but the difference is only on the order of about 10 percent of actuarial value at the median (Gabel et al. 2002).

The greater generosity of employer plans is a predictable result of the open-ended structure of the tax exemption for employer payments, and may not stem from the employment link itself. Studies of plan selection typically find that employers place a lot of weight on price considerations and pay less attention to quality measures (Quality vs. Costs? 2000). In doing so, however, employers mimic the behavior of most workers, who are also typically very sensitive to price and less sensitive to quality (Scanlon et al. 2002). Some workers would undoubtedly prefer higher-quality coverage than their employers select, but most apparently would prefer lower prices. Employers appear to do a fairly good job of mediating between these two virtues. The poor state of information on health care quality—not the role of employers in processing that information—seems paramount in explaining the lack of sensitivity to quality in both public and private health care.

Employer-Sponsored Insurance
in a Reformed Health Care System

The prevailing view of employer-based coverage as a regrettable accident has had important consequences for health policy. By implying that the job-based system is an outgrowth of tax policy rather than a naturally occurring form, this view leads conservative reformers to imagine that a similar, simple tax-based subsidy could trigger development of a large, stable, lightly regulated market offering individual health insurance with stable premiums. This imagined institutional form has never naturally existed anywhere, however. Likewise, by suggesting that employers' role is merely the result of a wartime misstep rather than a flexible vehicle for channeling consumers' demands, this view encourages liberal reformers to believe that a carefully formulated national system can provide a single, equitable level of insurance that covers all the care people desire and will willingly pay for, even as medical care continuously evolves. This structure is also quite uncommon.

A more useful perspective is to see employer-based health insurance as a valuable institution that has unique strengths but is by nature limited in scope. Conservative and liberal reformers are correct that job-based coverage cannot be the sole basis for a universal health insurance system. The most important reason is that the high and rising cost of health care makes it very difficult for lower-income people to purchase insurance coverage, whether in the nongroup market or through employers. The high cost of care implies that expanding the number of people covered by any type of insurance will require substantially raising the level of public redistribution. Even if combined with an appropriate subsidy system, however, employment-based coverage will not be available or appropriate for some people.

What, then, should be the role of job-based coverage in a universal health insurance system? One job-based model considered in the United States is an employer mandate. Hawaii has had such a mandate for nearly twenty years. A mandate, however, would force small, transient firms to provide coverage although it would not be economically efficient for them to do so.

The regulations needed to make a mandate work— including rules about whom employers must cover, how they must treat dual-earner households, and what coverage must include—would erode the flexibility of job-based coverage. The Hawaiian experience also confirms that even with a mandate, a job-based system alone cannot easily produce universal coverage: the state ranked only seventeenth in the nation in 2001 in the proportion of residents with job-based coverage. Building comprehensive universal coverage on an employment base would diminish the strengths of this institution—its flexibility and responsiveness—and accentuate its weaknesses, particularly its poor compatibility with misfit workers and households.

Instead, reform strategies that maintain job-based coverage as a voluntary marketplace would make better use of this institutional form. Conservative and liberal proposals (as well as many other arrangements) for expanding health insurance can adapt such a voluntary market.

Many conservative proposals include refundable tax credits (which may either offset tax obligations or, for people without tax obligations, make direct payments) for the purchase of nongroup coverage. For most of the target population, these proposals offer more generous public subsidies for coverage purchased in the nongroup market than for coverage in the group market. This subsidy design would encourage some uninsured people to purchase coverage, but it would also lead some insured people to shift from employer-based coverage to nongroup coverage, and may induce some employers to stop offering coverage. Shifts in coverage may be appropriate, because some tax credit beneficiaries will be a better fit in the nongroup market. For most others, however, the desirability of shifting out of group coverage will depend on the quality of the new, subsidized nongroup coverage, and this market has never before played a significant role in providing private health insurance.

A better option would be to ensure that the value of subsidies remains the same regardless of where people purchase coverage. One step toward achieving this would be to convert the existing favorable tax treatment of health insurance into a tax credit system (Pauly et al. 1992). Unfortunately, simply offering income-based tax credits might not preserve the long-term risk-pooling benefits of job-based coverage. Healthy beneficiaries would be tempted to leave the employer's health insurance pool and seek inexpensive coverage in the nongroup market. Such defections would likely lead to greater "experience rating" within employer groups and undermine pooling. To preserve pooling, any system must permit (and perhaps even encourage) employers to require employees to participate in their job-based health plan.

Combined with a mandate that individuals purchase coverage (either through work or in the nongroup market) and a publicly regulated or provided fallback option, such as an expanded state employees' purchasing pool or a Medicaid buy-in program, a tax credit system might achieve near universal coverage. Most employers who now offer coverage would probably continue to do so. Job-based coverage would probably be of higher quality than nongroup coverage because of economies of scale, but such a system would be much more equitable than the current one, and likely more equitable than the distribution of virtually any other good or service in the United States.

An alternative model would permit job-based coverage as an alternative or supplement to a universal health insurance program financed by progressive taxation. The tax-financed program would automatically enroll all Americans, but they could choose to opt out of the program. Those who did so might receive a tax credit (set at some fraction of the cost of public coverage) toward the purchase of private insurance.

In this arrangement, job-based coverage would offer a private safety valve for the public system, as in the United Kingdom and Germany. The size of the private job-based market would depend on consumer perceptions of the generosity of public insurance and on the size of the tax credit. Changes in private insurance benefits would reflect consumer demand for new benefits or more generous coverage.

The need to incorporate a voluntary, job-based private market into any public system would complicate its design. A hybrid system would be messy at its edges, where public coverage and private coverage overlapped. The availability of a public insurance system might, for example, lead employers to dump unhealthy workers out of their job-based plans. Regulations could forestall some of this dumping, but some risk selection would likely exist even in a tightly regulated system. Some degree of complexity and inefficiency may be a reasonable price to pay for flexibility.

Permitting private insurance to substitute for public insurance would also inevitably reduce equity relative to an ideal universal system. One option would be to add equity protections to the hybrid system, such as by imposing a redistributive health tax (Glied 1997). Recognizing that retaining parallel systems may be the only practical way to extend coverage in an inequitable society may be more realistic, though. Maintaining job-based coverage will reduce government involvement in the health insurance system and limit explicit redistribution—both features that are likely to make a hybrid system more politically acceptable and easier to implement than a unitary system.

The United States could move toward universal health coverage in several ways. Recognizing and incorporating the strengths of voluntary job-based coverage will likely enrich any of these approaches. Treating employer-based coverage as a historical blunder weakens health policy analysis and proposals. A system that recognizes the near-inevitability of job-based coverage is likelier to prove sturdier, more feasible, and ultimately simpler than one that seeks to design it away.

Acknowledgments

The author thanks Douglas Gould and Bisundev Mahato for research assistance and Dahlia Remler for helpful comments on this chapter.

Notes

1. Author's tabulations of the *Current Population Survey,* Bureau of the Census, Washington, DC, 2003. Note that this fraction declined slightly between 2000 and 2002 after growing steadily through the 1990s. The survey questions changed in 1994, leading to increases in estimates of the proportion of people with employer-based coverage. The proportion has also grown if we use 1994 as the base year, however.
2. By contrast, individual-based private health insurance markets, such as that in the Netherlands, are heavily regulated.

3. A small percentage of firms do adjust health insurance premiums so subsidies are greater for lower-income workers.
4. The situation may be different if fellow employees believe that workers are responsible for their own poor health, as when employers penalize workers who are overweight or smoke, or when employers provide financial incentives for weight reduction and smoking cessation (Aeppel 2003).
5. Author's tabulations of the *Current Population Survey,* Bureau of the Census, Washington, DC, 2002.
6. In part, this is because of federal legislation passed in 1986 (COBRA) and in 1996 (HIPAA). Together these laws mandate that workers who leave their jobs may continue their job-based coverage (by paying 125 percent of its full cost) for up to eighteen months, and that workers who move from one insured job to another are not affected by clauses excluding preexisting conditions.

References

Aeppel, T. 2003. Ill Will: Skyrocketing Health Costs Start to Pit Worker vs. Worker; Employees Gripe That Those with Bad Habits Drive up Insurance Charges for All; Is the Forklift Driver Too Fat? *Wall Street Journal,* June 17.

Amelung, V., S. Glied, and A. Topan. 2003. Health Care and the Labor Market: Learning from the German Experience. *Journal of Health Politics, Policy, and Law* 29, no. 4: 693–714.

Bloom, D., and S. Glied. 1991. Benefits and Costs of HIV Testing. *Science* 252 (June 28): 1798–1804.

Briffault, R., and S. Glied. 2002. Federalism and the Future of Health Care Reform. In *The Privatization of Health Care Reform,* ed. G. Bloche, 49–81. New York: Oxford University Press.

Brown, C., J. Hamilton, et al. 1990. *Employers Large and Small.* Cambridge: Harvard University Press.

Centers for Medicare and Medicaid Services. 2003. *National Health Accounts.* Washington, DC: Department of Health and Human Services. Available at *www.cms.hhs.gov/statistics/nhe/historical/.*

Cochrane, J. H. 1995. Time Consistent Health Insurance. *Journal of Political Economy* 103, no. 3: 445–473.

Cowan, C. A., P. A. McDonnell, K. R. Levitt, and M. A. Zezza. 2002. Burden of Health Care Costs: Businesses, Households, and Governments, 1987–2000. *Health Care Financing Review* 23, no. 3: 131–159.

Cunningham, R., III, and R. M. Cunningham Jr. 1997. *The Blues: A History of the Blue Cross and Blue Shield System.* DeKalb: Northern Illinois University Press.

Edlin, M. 2003. Demand for CAM Grows, but Belongs in a Separate Benefit Category. *Managed Healthcare Executive* 13, no. 6: 38.

Famulari, M., and M. E. Manser. 1989. Employer-Provided Benefits: Employer Cost versus Employee Value. *Monthly Labor Review* 112, no. 12: 24–32.

Faulkner, E. J. 1940. *Accident-and-Health Insurance.* New York: McGraw-Hill.

Finkelstein, A. 2002. The Effect of Tax Subsidies to Employer-Provided Supplementary Health Insurance: Evidence from Canada. *Journal of Public Economics* 84, no. 3: 305–339.

Fuchs, V. R. 1994. The Clinton Plan: A Researcher Examines Reform. *Health Affairs* 13, no. 1: 102–114.

Gabel, J., K. Dhont, et al. 2002. Individual Insurance: How Much Financial Protection Does It Provide? *Health Affairs* (suppl. web exclusives): W172–181. Available at *http://content.healthaffairs.org/webexclusives/index.dtl?year=2002.*

Glied, S. 1994. *Revising the Tax Treatment of Employer-Provided Health Insurance.* Washington, DC: American Enterprise Institute Press.

———. 1997. *Chronic Condition: Why Health Reform Fails.* Cambridge: Harvard University Press.

———. 2003. Health Care Costs: On the Rise Again. *Journal of Economic Perspectives* 17, no. 2: 125–148.

Glied, S., and M. Stabile. 2000. Explaining the Decline in Health Insurance Coverage among Young Men. *Inquiry* 37, no. 3: 295–303.

Gruber, J., and B. C. Madrian. 2002. Health Insurance, Labor Supply, and Job Mobility: A Critical Review of the Literature. Working paper no. w8817. Cambridge, MA: National Bureau of Economic Research.

Health Insurance Institute. 1970. *Source Book of Health Insurance Data.* Washington, DC: Health Insurance Association of America.

Hipple, S. 2001. Contingent Work in the Late 1990s. *Monthly Labor Review* 124, no. 3: 3–27.

Huskamp, H., M. B. Rosenthal, R. G. Frank, and J. P. Newhouse. 2000. The Medicare Prescription Drug Benefit: How Will the Game Be Played? *Health Affairs* 19, no. 2: 8–23.

Hyman, D. A., and M. Hall. 2001. Two Cheers for Employment-Based Health Insurance. *Yale Journal of Health Policy, Law, and Ethics* 2, no. 1: 23–57.

InterStudy Reports HMOs Move to per Diem Rates for Hospitals from Capitation Deals. 2001. *Health Care Strategic Management* 19, no. 6: 9.

Jack, W. 2000. Health Insurance Reform in Four Latin American Countries: Theory and Practice. Working paper. Washington, DC: World Bank.

Krueger, A. B., and L. H. Summers. 1987. Reflections on the Inter-Industry Wage Structure. In *Unemployment and the Structure of Labor Markets,* ed. K. Lang and J. Leonard, 17–47. New York: Basil Blackwell.

Madrian, B. 1994. Employment-Based Health Insurance and Job Mobility: Is There Evidence of Job Lock? *Quarterly Journal of Economics* 109: 27–54.

Marzolf, J. R. 2002. The Indonesia Private Health Sector: Opportunities for Reform: An Analysis of Obstacles and Constraints to Growth. Discussion paper. Washington, DC: World Bank.

Naylor, C. D., P. Jha, et al. 1999. *A Fine Balance: Some Opinions for Private and Public Health Care in Urban India.* Washington, DC: World Bank, Human Network Development.

OECD. 2001. *Private Health Insurance in OECD Countries: Compilation of National Reports.* Paris: Insurance Committee Secretariat.

Pauly, M., P. Danzon, et al. 1992. *Responsible National Health Insurance.* Washington, DC: American Enterprise Institute Press.

Pauly, M., H. Kunreuther, et al. 1995. Guaranteed Renewability in Insurance. *Journal of Risk and Uncertainty* 10, no. 2: 143–156.

Prince, M. 1999. HMO Stirs Debate on Reviews. *Business Insurance* 33, no. 46: 1, 66.

Quality vs. Costs? A Survey of Healthcare Purchasing Habits and Concerns. 2000. *Healthcare Financial Management* 54, no. 7: 68–72.

Reed, L. S. 1947. *Blue Cross and Medical Service Plans.* Washington, DC: U.S. Public Health Service, Federal Security Agency.

Reinhardt, U. 1989. Health Care Spending and American Competitiveness. *Health Affairs* 8, no. 4: 5–21.

Scanlon, D. P., M. Chernew, et al. 2002. The Impact of Health Plan Report Cards on Managed Care Enrollment. *Journal of Health Economics* 21, no. 1: 19–41.

Smith, S. R., and D. M. Kirking. 2001. The Effect of Insurance Coverage Changes on Drug Utilization in HIV Disease. *Journal of Acquired Immune Deficiency Syndromes* 28, no. 2: 40–49.

Somers, H. M., and A. R. Somers. 1961. *Doctors, Patients, and Health Insurance.* Washington, DC: Brookings Institution.

Stabile, M. 2002. The Role of Tax Subsidies in the Market for Health Insurance. *International Tax and Public Finance* 9, no. 1: 33–50.

Thomasson, M. A. 2002. From Sickness to Health: The Twentieth-Century Development of U.S. Health Insurance. *Explorations in Economic History* 39, no. 3: 233–253.

Williams, P. 1932. *The Purchase of Medical Care through Fixed Periodic Payment.* Cambridge, MA: National Bureau of Economic Research.

Witt, J. F. 2001. Toward a New History of American Accident Law: Classical Tort Law and the Cooperative First-Party Insurance Movement. *Harvard Law Review* 114, no. 3: 690–841.

CHAPTER 4

Entrepreneurial Challenges to Integrated Health Care

⸺⤫⸺

JAMES C. ROBINSON

The U.S. health care system is an ongoing experiment in the effort to achieve social goals through market mechanisms—to pursue the public good through private interests. The era of managed care encouraged competition among insurers, capitation contracting between health plans and providers, and the organizational integration of physicians and hospitals to contain costs and foster access to primary care. The ensuing consumer and provider backlash and the failure of many diversified organizations to deliver improvements in quality and efficiency have today substituted a different set of social goals. These include the unwinding of many consolidated organizations, unconstrained access to specialty services, and a commensurate reversion to broad insurance networks and fee-for-service payments. As before, much of the energy for change comes from the private sector. Rather than focus on reducing costs and integrating organizations, however, the entrepreneurial emphasis today is on enhancing revenue and creating niche organizations such as ambulatory surgery centers and single-specialty hospitals.

The record of the private sector during managed care was mixed. That sector marshaled the energy to overcome the organizational fragmentation of the indemnity era but then engaged in overconsolidation. The contemporary drive toward specialization is producing an analogous mix of desirable and undesirable effects. Unbundled services foster managerial and clinical focus, learning-curve efficiencies, and competition within an otherwise consolidated industry. Yet entrepreneurial entrants are targeting only services and patients whose payment rates exceed treatment costs, thereby undermining the implicit subsidies for underpaid services and underinsured patients.

Specialized niche firms also threaten to create a new form of corporate conglomerate by establishing chains of facilities across geographic regions and the nation. Despite talk of focus, the entrepreneurial drive for more revenue is pushing firms into new markets and new products, with the axis of growth shifting from diversification across services within markets (the integrated physician-hospital organization) to diversification across markets within service lines (chains of ambulatory centers and specialty hospitals).

In this environment, integrated delivery systems are shrinking, hobbled by the diseconomies of scope that attend efforts to incorporate services with distinct technologies, professions, customers, and regulatory regimes. Service-specific chains are expanding but face new challenges as they seek to penetrate new geographic markets. Multiservice hospitals—both nonprofit and for profit—are defending themselves by creating subsidiaries and physician joint ventures to achieve the efficiencies attributed to their focused competitors without losing the benefits of diversification. Policy responses—in the form of certificate-of-need regulation and bans on physician referrals to facilities where they have an ownership interest—protect both the public interest (by supporting general hospitals that subsidize care for the needy) and private interests (by sparing general hospitals the rigors of competition).

The remainder of this chapter analyzes the rise of single-specialty hospitals and freestanding ambulatory facilities, emphasizing product and market diversification as alternative strategies for growth. Emphasis is placed on the entrepreneurial, for-profit firms that inject most of the creativity and chaos into the health care delivery system and on responses by nonprofit, full-service institutions. I conclude by highlighting the tendency of every good idea to be pressed too far and every innovative startup to expand beyond the products and markets where it has a distinctive advantage.

Diversification across Services

Depending on one's perspective, the health care ecosystem is either very stable or in a state of continual turbulence. Despite innumerable proclamations of social and corporate transformation, most physicians continue to practice in very small groups, and most hospitals remain full-service, nonprofit institutions. Yet the organizational structure of medicine has seen major experiments in recent decades—some successful and most not. Particularly salient were efforts to integrate professional and institutional services both vertically and horizontally. This entailed creating "integrated delivery systems" (IDS) composed of primary care and specialty physicians, acute and subacute inpatient facilities, ambulatory surgical and diagnostic centers, and other major components of care.

Such integrated entities pursued the administrative and clinical economies of scope that can accrue to organizations that offer mutually supportive products and services (Panzar and Willig 1981; Teece 1980). These efficiencies included cheaper procurement of supplies and information technology; coordination of care from outpatient to inpatient to subacute settings; elimination of excess capacity and duplicate equipment; use of evidence-based guidelines for managing chronic disease; enhanced branding and cross-marketing of services; and financial gains from capitation payments for a full range of services.

The profit opportunity latent in clinical and administrative integration did not escape the notice of those whose mission it is to seek out such opportunities. Investor-owned hospital chains and physician practice management (PPM) firms recognized that most existing delivery systems combined moneymaking with money-losing activities, with losses dissipating any gains. By targeting remunerative services and avoiding services that suffered from below-cost payment, firms could avoid undermining their gains and lay the financial foundation for regional or national expansion.

Investor-owned firms thus adopted a somewhat narrower scope of services than the traditional IDS, focusing on inpatient facilities (hospital chains), physician services (multispecialty PPM firms), or one form of care (specialty PPM firms and rehabilitation or ambulatory surgery chains). These firms expanded by diversifying across markets, thereby obtaining new opportunities while reducing their exposure to the economic and political idiosyncrasies of each region (Lutz, Grossman, and Bigalke 1998; Lutz and Gee 1998; Coddington, Moore, and Clarke 1998; Burns and Robinson 1997; Robinson 1999). The logic of growth then drove many investor-owned firms to diversify across services as they approached the limits of diversification across markets. PPM firms that once focused on primary care added multispecialty clinics, multispecialty PPM firms added independent practice associations and emergency room physician services, hospital chains acquired physician practices, and rehabilitation chains moved into ambulatory services.

The rest is history. The perceived profit opportunity that drew venture capital and entrepreneurial energy into the health care system also attracted the attention of governmental and corporate purchasers, who naturally believed that any surplus should remain with them. The aggressive stance of private purchasers toward health insurance plans in the mid-1990s, compounded by the federal Balanced Budget Act of 1997, cut payments to hospitals and (via the HMOs) to physician organizations.

These moves transformed the profit opportunity from coordinating a full range of services to selectively targeting those that continued to enjoy advantageous payment rates. The squeeze on revenues was accompanied by accelerating costs for multispecialty consolidators, and economic fate was especially harsh for systems that had grown through mergers and acquisitions. Such organizations often found themselves owning overlapping, noncooperative, and overpriced physician and hospital properties, and afflicted with excess capacity, low productivity, and culture clashes.

Many consolidations occurred through bidding wars in which organizations overpaid even for well-performing units, and the practices and facilities most willing to sell were those consolidators should have been least willing to buy. Such acquisitions transformed physician practices from mom-and-pop enterprises—where every dollar saved was a dollar earned—to multispecialty bureaucracies that spread rewards and penalties over the entire system rather than focusing them on responsible parties (Robinson 1999, 2001). Rather than spurring coordination, the amalgamation of primary, specialty, inpatient, outpatient, and ancillary services often led to a financial and cultural war of all against all (Burns and Pauly 2002). Many nonprofit systems and for-profit chains found that the whole of their overbuilt organizations was worth less than the sum of the parts, and they began to divest.

The refocusing of the health care system was nasty, brutish, and short. As usual, Wall Street first sensed the change in industry prospects from high growth to no growth and made an expeditious exit. The collapse of share prices and an inferno of shareholder litigation destroyed PPM firms, which dumped their medical groups onto the market. Many hospital systems also divested the physician practices and ancillary facilities they had acquired, albeit in a more deliberative fashion to retain patient admissions. Investor-owned hospital chains retrenched from national expansion and spun off facilities in markets they could not dominate. Bankruptcy courts opened their arms to embrace the fallen, and one cycle of organizational growth and contraction was complete.

Diversification across Markets

In the aftermath of managed care, a new set of organizational strategies and structures emerged in the health care delivery system. Rather than seek growth and profits by reducing costs under capitation, health care organizations now seek growth and profits by increasing revenues under fee-for-service. Rather than trying to coordinate a continuum of clinical providers and services, entrepreneurial energies now focus on particular specialties, facilities, and procedures where the price-cost margin is most attractive. Primary care physicians and full-service hospitals have been displaced by specialty physicians and single-specialty hospitals, ambulatory surgery centers, and freestanding diagnostic facilities as the heralded components of a new consumer-oriented health care system (Herzlinger 1997; Weaver and Waugh 2002; Triple Tree 2003).

Freestanding Ambulatory Surgery Centers

While much attention has recently focused on single-specialty inpatient facilities, the more important challenge to full-service hospitals is the freestanding ambulatory surgery center. Outpatient procedures as a proportion of total surgeries rose from 20 percent in 1981 to 80 percent in 2003, with almost half of these procedures performed in freestanding facilities or physician offices rather than hospital outpatient departments.

Outpatient surgery has risen partly because changing technologies and incentives have spurred more procedures per capita (Schramm and Gabel 1988; Kozak, McCarthy, and Pokras 1999). The growth in freestanding centers, meanwhile, derives partly from their ability to schedule procedures free from emergency interruptions, enhanced roles for physicians in governance, better architectural designs for operating rooms and supporting facilities, and smaller-scale and more convenient suburban locations. The prospects of these ambulatory surgery companies fluctuate with the financing and regulatory environment. The late 1980s and early 1990s saw an investment surge, as Medicare's payment system reduced the attractiveness of inpatient alternatives, while the late 1990s brought a major contraction owing to pressure from the Balanced Budget Act. Over the past several years the number of freestanding centers has grown dramatically, rising from 2,314 in 1996 to 2,755 in 2000 to 3,400 in 2002 (Cain Brothers 2003; Triple Tree 2003).

Many ambulatory surgery centers are owned by individual physicians or physician partnerships (including specialty group practices), but a growing number are consolidating into national investor-owned chains, including both multiservice hospital chains (such as HCA, Tenet, Universal Health Services, and Triad) and outpatient chains (including AmSurg, United Surgical Partners International). The strong and committed presence of multiservice hospital chains indicates that diversified conglomerates can seize growth opportunities outside their core model. Still, the majority of chain facilities are not affiliated with inpatient hospitals.

HealthSouth, the nation's premiere "focused factory," dwarfs all these ambulatory surgery companies. HealthSouth has fallen on hard times owing to its exceptionally aggressive growth strategy. Formed in 1984 with an emphasis on inpatient rehabilitation, HealthSouth quickly diversified into outpatient rehabilitation and then outpatient diagnostic services, owning 50 outpatient centers by 1990 and 250 by 1994. In 1995 it acquired Surgical Health Corp., the nation's second-largest chain of ambulatory centers, with 37 facilities, plus 12 surgical centers from the nonprofit Sutter Health system in California. The following year HealthSouth acquired Surgical Care Affiliates (67 surgical centers), Health Images (55 diagnostic imaging centers), ASC Network Corp. (29 surgery centers), and National Imaging Affiliates (8 diagnostic imaging centers). In 1998 HealthSouth acquired HCA's ambulatory surgery subsidiary (34 centers) and National Surgery Centers (40 centers).

The firm's acquisitions and growth then stalled, in part because of slowing revenue growth attributable to the Balanced Budget Act and in part because of the inherent difficulties of integrating this many acquisitions so quickly. Throughout the growth period HealthSouth was acclaimed in industry circles as the leading example of what single-service focus and geographic diversification could achieve. However, much of HealthSouth's apparent success was fraudulent, disguised by senior management to its benefit and the detriment of shareholders. Under a wave of government investigations and shareholder lawsuits, all senior managers were replaced (many facing criminal indictments), the firm faced bankruptcy, and creditors insisted that the company divest its surgery centers to cover its financial obligations (Mollenkamp 2003).

Specialty Hospitals

Specialty hospitals resemble ambulatory surgery centers in that they focus on a narrow range of surgical procedures, but the former add inpatient beds and hence can provide more intensive and expensive treatments. The General Accounting Office identified 92 specialty hospitals operating as of February 2003—up from 29 in 1990, with 20 more under development (U.S. GAO 2003a). These facilities included 17 focused on cardiac procedures, 36 on orthopedics, 22 on general surgery, and 17 on gynecology. Three-fourths of the facilities had physician investors or co-owners, and 20 percent were owned completely by physicians. While the ownership stake of any one physician in a specialty hospital is low—usually less than 2 percent—half the facilities with some physician investment reported group ownership stakes of 25 percent or greater (U.S. GAO 2003a). In some markets specialists are merging their practices into larger single-specialty groups precisely to purchase clinical equipment and ambulatory surgical suites (Casalino, Devers, and Brewster 2003). Nonphysician investors in specialty hospitals include nonprofit full-service hospitals, privately held for-profit entities, and one publicly traded corporation. Some one-third of specialty hospitals are independent, one-third are owned by chains, and one-third are owned by general hospitals—the latter usually in the form of joint ventures with local physicians (U.S. GAO 2003b).

The Indianapolis experience illustrates the dynamics of the specialty hospital market, which involves local specialists, outside chains, and incumbent full-service hospitals (Cain Brothers 2003; Katz, Hurley, and Devers 2003; Abelson 2003). In that city a proliferation of heart hospitals began with the threat of a joint venture between local cardiologists and a specialty hospital chain. Two of four multiservice hospital systems then created their own freestanding heart hospitals: St. Vincent Health, in collaboration with the Care Group physician organization, and Community Hospitals Indianapolis, with its staff physicians. Indiana University and Methodist Hospitals then created a cardiac hospital-within-the-hospital, and St. Francis Hospitals moved its heart program to a new facility.

The Center for Studying Health System Change identified ten specialty hospitals in three of the twelve communities it has tracked since 1996 (including Indianapolis). Of these, one was physician owned (medical group), three were owned by local hospitals, two were joint ventures between physicians and local hospitals, and four were joint ventures between physicians and investor-owned chains. The presence of a large single-specialty physician group and the absence of certificate-of-need legislation (under which regulators approve new facilities and equipment) at the state level facilitated the creation of specialty hospitals (Casalino, Devers, and Brewster 2003).

As the sole publicly traded chain of specialty hospitals, MedCath has received the greatest attention, evoking both praise as the harbinger of a new disaggregated health care delivery system and criticism as a financial drain on community hospitals that rely on cardiac surgery profits to subsidize money-losing services such as trauma care. The evolution of MedCath exemplifies the impetus for growth and diversification (Cain Brothers 2003).

Founded in 1988, MedCath went public in 1994 as an operator of mobile cardiac catheterization laboratories; its first heart hospital opened two years later. Caught in the firestorm of investor disillusion with specialty physician practice firms, MedCath went private in 1998 through a management-led leveraged buyout, and then returned to the public capital market with its second initial public offering in 2001. It now co-owns nine facilities with local cardiologists and/or a local hospital, with its stake ranging from 51 percent to 71 percent, and has another three facilities in various stages of development. The newest MedCath facility departs from the smaller, cardiac-only prototype, which averages 58 beds: it contains 112 beds, 12 labor/delivery suites, 16 ICU (intensive care unit) beds, and 36 pure cardiology beds.

The successes enjoyed by the specialized firms reflect astute selection of services and markets as much as efficiency in delivering care. If the business model of a limited range of services were itself the source of competitive advantage, we would observe niche firms in every health care sector. In practice, focused factories concentrate in surgical and diagnostic services where clumsy payment mechanisms by Medicare and private insurers leave money on the table, creating profit for all participants. Traditional hospitals object to the new freestanding entrants precisely for this reason.

Yet the reliance of specialty chains on payment inefficiencies and operating efficiencies leaves them exposed to an eventual wakening of the sleeping giant. There is no reason to assume that Medicare will not slash payments to ambulatory surgery and specialty hospital chains just as it balanced the federal budget on the backs of nursing home and home health chains a few years ago. Implicit but important in the business model of all entrepreneurial health care firms is an exit strategy. Diversification across products and services enables nimble firms to refocus their activities and revenue streams as payment and profit opportunities rise and fall across sectors.

Organizational Hybrids

Rather than the single-service, multi-market chain or the multiservice, single-market hospital dominating the health care delivery system, hybrid organizational forms will likely play a prominent role and share the market with their more focused competitors. In the major non-health sectors of the economy, corporate holding companies with multiple divisions—each responsible for its own products, suppliers, customers, and profit-and-loss accounting—have balanced the virtues of focus and specialization with the virtues of scale and scope. In the language of organizational economics, M-form firms (with multiple semi-autonomous divisions) often dominate U-form firms (those with unitary organizational hierarchies) (Chandler 1962, 1990; Williamson 1985). It is hard to find a single-product firm in any sector, and hard to find a single-market firm among any but the smallest organizations. The M-form firm pursues the advantages of specialization by establishing divisions that mimic the focus of single-product competitors, but it supplements these with the financial, political, and managerial resources of a larger entity.

The M-form organization is already evident in health care. Full-service community hospitals and academic medical centers are experimenting with subsidiaries and physician joint ventures for services most attractive to chain competitors: surgery centers and specialty hospitals. Nonprofit hospitals can create for-profit subsidiaries in which physicians invest, though care must be taken to avoid violating legal and cultural prohibitions on self-referral and fee-splitting.

These subsidiaries take the form of cardiac and orthopedic surgery hospitals, women's health centers, and MRI (magnetic resonance imaging) facilities, among others. They can be located near the mother facility or at other locations that are convenient for physicians and patients. They feature intimate settings for patients and efficient throughput for physicians, who participate as referral sources as well as clinicians. Such facilities can refer more difficult cases to the full-service facility without raising charges of patient dumping. Physicians share governance and net earnings in proportion to their investment and referral volume, rather than equally across the larger hospital's medical staff. Management can be compensated based on the financial performance of the subsidiary in addition to that of the entire organization.

Besides mimicking the potential advantages of single-specialty chains, M-form health care organizations can gain the economies of scale and scope of multi-product firms. The single-specialty subsidiary can be viewed as contributing to the success of the larger organization rather than undermining it—important to physicians, patients, and politicians who worry about the sustainability of institutions that offer unprofitable teaching, safety net, trauma, and primary care services. The M-form is also less likely than the out-of-town chain entrant to evoke the ire of hospital labor unions, philanthropists, and state regulators.

While highlighting the autonomy and accessibility of its subsidiaries, the M-form organization can impose some system-wide requirements, such as that physician-investors also provide care in the mother facility and that some of the subsidiary's profits subsidize money-losing patients and procedures elsewhere. The M-form organization can pursue the "economic credentialing" of its medical staff, denying admitting privileges to physicians who refer their profitable patients to a single-specialty competitor. The M-form firm can tap the larger system's cash flow and borrowing capacity to obtain financial capital, though the value of the diversified firm as an internal capital market varies by its operating margin, debt burden, and credit rating (Standard and Poor's 2003).

The multidivision organization can also plan capacity in a unified manner, responding to rising demand by channeling new beds into specialty facilities rather than expanding the multispecialty hospital. If specialty chains have attracted superior managerial talent through their culture of entrepreneurship, the M-form firm can contract with them to manage their specialty facilities.

The new M-form hospital organizations may be more efficient than the organizations built during the 1980s and 1990s, despite their often diversified, holding-company structures, as they are designed with a clearer emphasis on return on investment. As shown outside the health sector, the least efficient form of diversification is that pursued by large entities in declining industries, where consolidation permits high operating profits, but where possibilities for growth within traditional sectors are limited (Jensen 1986; Jensen and Ruback 1983). Firms with free cash flow (earnings beyond profitable investment opportunities in the industry of origin) are tempted to expand into adjacent products and markets.

Rarely, however, do managers who are well adapted to one set of products, technologies, and customers prove equally successful in new contexts. Much more common are low or negative returns in the new lines of business that must be subsidized by traditional profitable activities. In a competitive economy, these conglomerates will be challenged and ultimately brought down by more focused and efficient competitors, or by hostile takeover (leveraged buyout). In the nonprofit health care sector, competitors in the product market appear in the form of specialty chains, while competitors in the capital market appear through conversions and acquisitions by investor-owned chains (Voelker 2003; Robinson 2000).

During the 1980s and 1990s, the inpatient hospital sector suffered from excess capacity and a lack of internal growth opportunities because of technological changes and capitation payments favoring outpatient care. Many an IDS was built by hospital managers unwilling to fade quietly into the background of the health care industry they once dominated. The acquisition of primary care practices—to say nothing of unproductive mergers with other over-bedded hospitals—were consummated in apparent disregard for financial returns. Now, however, the industry has sweated out excess inpatient capacity, utilization rates are rising, and many hospital organizations need to finance core services (Robinson 2002).

The renovation and expansion of physical facilities, continual updating and replacement of expensive clinical machinery, and long-deferred investment in information systems are making hospitals ever more attuned to the perspectives and priorities of capital markets. The sector has no more free cash flow. Operating surpluses are substantial, at least in consolidated markets with rising hospital admissions, but every dime earned can be invested profitably in the core business. Now hospital systems, both nonprofit and for profit, must justify their capital strategies to investment bankers, equity analysts, bond rating firms, bond insurers, and the other entities that collectively promote the accountability of borrowers to creditors (Gordon, Federbusch, and Nelson 2003). The emerging M-form hospital conglomerate will be subject to line-of-business financial analysis to an extent unknown in previous decades.

The Pyramiding of Regulation

The success of ambulatory surgery chains and specialty hospitals in some markets, coupled with the evident willingness of Wall Street to finance a national expansion, has prompted a virulent response by general multiservice hospitals. The industry has promoted state certificate-of-need (CON) legislation and the extension of federal bans on physician referrals to facilities in which they have an ownership interest. These two types of regulation, singly or in combination, would stifle the challenge from specialized upstarts; almost all specialty facilities are in states without CON legislation, and almost all have physician investors. Proponents of these policies argue that they redress imperfections in the marketplace, while opponents argue that they merely protect incumbents from the rigors of competition.

Certificate of Need

CON statutes date back thirty years to the era when the perceived problems in health care were excess capacity and high-cost technologies in general hospitals, which prompted states to require regulatory approval of new facilities and equipment. CON laws were only partially effective in achieving their goals, as incumbent hospitals lobbied through their desired expansions. Academic critics labeled such influence a form of regulatory "capture," but it appears to have stopped specialized facilities from entering the market (Payton and Powsner 1980). Today incumbent hospitals have an interest in the effectiveness rather than the impotence of regulatory commissions.

The policy argument in favor of CON oversight of specialty facility construction is that general hospitals rely on patients and procedures whose payments exceed costs to subsidize patients and procedures whose payments fall below costs. Specialty facilities that focus their services on the most profitable patients and procedures undermine this cross-subsidy and ultimately may force denials of care in multispecialty general hospitals. More broadly, CON constitutes a form of capacity planning or "upstream rationing," which, in the eyes of its supporters, is needed owing to rampant technological diffusion and cost-unconscious consumer demand. Whereas health planning and regulation fell into disfavor during the two decades of enthusiasm for market-oriented health policy, they now may revive in the wake of the backlash against capitation, vertically integrated delivery systems, and other features of managed care (McDonough 1997).

Critics of CON acknowledge inefficiencies in the mix of health care payment methods in the health care market but despair at the form of entry regulation that CON represents. The standard history of regulation in other industries begins with one market imperfection for which regulatory intervention is the proffered solution. The ensuing regulatory equilibrium is then undermined by changes in technology, consumer demand, and competing products. The declining efficacy of the original regulatory structure generates calls by the regulated industry to limit competition from new sources that heretofore had escaped control (Posner 1971; Banks, Foreman, and Keeler 1999).

Rate regulation of railroads, for example, was justified originally as a response to the potential for exploitive pricing by natural monopolies, and then was used to finance subsidies from highly traveled inter-urban lines to thinly traveled rural lines. The nascent trucking industry targeted inter-urban routes where regulators maintained rates above costs, thereby undermining subsidies to rural routes and leading to an extension of rate regulation to trucks. The regulation of interstate trucking led to high prices, excess capacity, and a range of inefficient practices until it was repealed in the face of intense opposition from the trucking industry and labor (Peltzman 1989; Winston 1993).

The extension of CON to cover specialty hospitals follows a parallel logic, even if the specifics are different. The reliance on administered pricing by Medicare creates categories of profitable and unprofitable procedures, and of profitable and unprofitable patients within each diagnostic category (as hospitals are paid the same rate for patients with illness of different severity levels). The unwillingness of the polity to finance universal health insurance deepens the disparities among profitable (insured) and unprofitable (uninsured) patients. Reliance on general hospitals as the locus of subsidies for unprofitable procedures and patients makes it difficult to subject them to market pressures, as the institutions with the strongest commitment to serving the underserved are most hampered in the effort to attract insured patients. Yet protection of general hospitals from competitive entry by specialty facilities and ambulatory surgery chains also protects them from pressure to improve their performance and hold down their costs.

Over the past decade many hospital markets have become increasingly concentrated through mergers among former competitors, leading to more bargaining power and higher prices (Cuellar and Gertler 2003). The Federal Trade Commission has been unsuccessful in limiting this consolidation. The best hope for competition in local health care markets may come from ambulatory centers and specialty facilities that compete for limited types of services, as new full-service hospitals face high barriers to entry in all but the fastest-growing metropolitan areas.

The pyramiding of regulation is clear. Administered pricing and incomplete insurance coverage create the social need for cross-subsidies, which are threatened by competitive entry. CON limits entry to protect these subsidies but also defends consolidation and monopoly power. Monopoly power in the hospital sector then generates demands for more complete regulation of pricing, presumably through rate setting for all payers. Rate regulation would create new opportunities for cross-subsidies, requiring broader regulation of price and entry for physician services and ancillary providers whose activities might endanger the regulatory equilibrium.

Bans on Referrals to Physician-Owned Facilities

Regulatory prohibitions on physician referrals of Medicare patients to outpatient diagnostic, laboratory, and ancillary facilities in which they have a financial interest date back ten years to reports of excessive and inappropriate referrals (Mitchell 1995; U.S. GAO 1994). Ambulatory surgery facilities and specialty hospitals have been exempt from these so-called Stark regulations—an omission that facilitated their growth. General hospitals support an extension of the self-referral ban to all types of facilities. The 2003 Medicare drug benefit legislation imposed an eighteen-month moratorium on the construction of new specialty hospitals, giving the Medicare Payment Advisory Commission time to study the economic impact of these facilities on general hospitals, and could prompt a permanent extension of self-referral prohibitions to the entire hospital sector. However, these proposed bans pose both conceptual and policy dilemmas, as they undermine the integration between physicians and facilities, thereby throwing out the baby of clinical coordination along with the bathwater of abusive referral practices.

The relationship between a referring physician and a facility in which the physician has an ownership stake is a form of partial vertical integration, intermediate between the extremes of no ownership relationship and full organizational integration (physician as employee of the hospital organization). The ban on physician self-referral would not affect the referral practices of physicians employed in multispecialty medical groups and integrated delivery systems, which expect physicians to refer patients to the facilities of the larger organization.

Indeed, the promotion of vertical integration between physicians and hospitals was premised on the principle that it would facilitate capacity planning, higher utilization rates, attention to a continuum of care, and the ability to measure and reward performance at the system rather than the "silo" level. Stark regulations embody a completely different perspective—one that is skeptical of organizational integration and favors arms-length relationships that do not influence physicians' choices of where to refer patients.

In economic language, the regulations embody a "spot contract" approach to physician and facility relationships. A spot contract is one in which payment and delivery are clearly defined and occur in the same period—as opposed to relational contracts in which price, quantity, and quality are less certain and determined in the future, and depend on long-term mutual dependence among the trading partners (MacNeil 1978). The investment by a physician in an ambulatory surgery facility or specialty hospital provides an incentive for the physician to cooperate with that facility without becoming an employee. Partial integration through investment (targeted by Stark regulations) may not be less desirable than full integration through employment (vertical integration) or arms-length relationships with no ownership incentive (spot contract). Full integration through employment within an IDS potentially creates the same incentive to overutilize a service as investment in a freestanding facility, whereas arms-length spot contracting creates no incentive for coordination between physicians and facilities.

Extension of Stark regulations to ambulatory surgery and specialty hospitals cements one form of organizational relationship—the arms-length spot contract—that has contributed to the fragmentation and inefficiency of the system and is now being superseded by more integrated organizational relationships. The logic of the ban on referrals to services and facilities in which a physician has an ownership interest would prohibit surgical procedures done in a physician's office as well as the ownership of radiological and other clinical equipment by a physician practice. Taken to the extreme, these regulations would prohibit the dual role of the physician as an agent who both diagnoses conditions and recommends treatments, on the one hand, and actually provides (some of) those treatments, on the other. A surgeon who evaluates a patient and recommends a procedure, for example, could be seen as having a conflict of interest if he or she were also a candidate to perform that procedure.

Physicians' opposition to extending self-referral bans stems in part from a longstanding reluctance to become employees of hospitals, which they term the corporate practice of medicine. Bans on physician referrals, state bans on corporate practice of medicine, and CON entry barriers all contribute to the rigidity of the health care system and its difficulty in fostering new organizational forms in response to changes in epidemiology, clinical technology, and patient preferences.

The Health Care Market as Roller-Coaster Ride

Specialty hospital and freestanding ambulatory facilities—combined in multi-market chains, partnered with local physicians, and fueled by venture capital—challenge the organizational status quo in health care. The excessively diversified health care organization presents inviting targets to entrepreneurial entities that target markets, procedures, and patients offering the widest divergence between price and cost. Specialty hospitals and ambulatory facilities potentially reap the administrative and clinical benefits of specialization and replication, doing more of the same thing with the goal of finding ways to do it better and cheaper. The chain structure permits the upstarts to obtain economies of scale in purchasing supplies, hiring managerial talent, and performing back-office functions. More importantly, the chain structure offers the potential for developing benchmarks to monitor, improve, and reward performance across the enterprise. Scale economies and geographic diversification combine with growth opportunities afforded by changes in demography and technology to make the specialty inpatient and outpatient chains the hottest health care sector among capital investors.

But if specialty hospitals and ambulatory facilities offer potential efficiency gains to the U.S. health care system, they also pose new challenges through their tendency to undermine the fragile system of financial subsidies and physician professionalism. The health care system manifests a chaotic mix of payment mechanisms for particular procedures and patients, relying on general hospitals to serve as the locus for the social pooling of health risks. Hospitals earn financial surpluses on services such as cardiac surgery and incur losses on services such as burn care, and hence are imperiled by competitors who provide the former but not the latter. Hospitals tend to earn income from patients covered by commercial insurance and often lose money on patients covered by Medicaid, and hence are imperiled by competitors who focus on the former and avoid the latter. Tensions also arise from the roles of physicians as both referral agents and clinicians, and from the fact that they may earn more money based on their decisions about which patients to refer to which facility than for the care they personally provide.

The health care system manifests numerous inefficiencies that attract entrepreneurial talent and venture capital willing to take high risks for the possibility of reaping high rewards in the largest industry in the largest economy in the world. Once incubated and launched into the delivery system, startups face internal and external expectations for continued growth, which drive them to diversify outside their original niches to new products and new markets. Diversification strategies—whether across products (as in multi-product hospitals) or across markets (as in specialty chains)—inevitably lead startups into domains where their comparative advantages are weak and incumbent competitors are strong. Ignoring warning signs and the lessons of business history, entrepreneurial firms often press forward rather than fall back, apparently pursuing growth as an end in itself. We thus can expect continued cycles of innovation, expansion, and diversification, followed by periods of crisis and contraction, in turn succeeded by new cycles of experimentation, excitement, disillusion, and misery.

Acknowledgments

This research was supported by The Robert Wood Johnson Foundation, through both the Investigator Awards in Health Policy Research and the Health Care Financing and Organization (HCFO) programs.

References

Abelson, R. 2003. Generous Medicare Payments Spur Specialty Hospital Boom. *New York Times*, October 26, 1, 23.

Banks D. A., S. E. Foreman, and T. E. Keeler. 1999. Cross-Subsidization in Hospital Care: Some Lessons from the Law and Economics of Regulation. *Health Matrix: Journal of Law and Medicine* 9, no. 1: 1–35.

Burns L. R., and J. C. Robinson. 1997. Physician Practice Management Companies: Implications for Hospital-Based Integrated Delivery Systems. *Frontiers of Health Services Management* 14, no. 2: 3–35.

Burns L. R., and M. V. Pauly. 2002. Integrated Delivery Networks: A Detour on the Road to Integrated Health Care? *Health Affairs* 21, no. 4: 128–143.

Cain Brothers (investment and merchant banking firm). 2003. If You're Niched, It Might Be Your Fault. *Strategies in Capital Finance* 39 (March): 1–16.

Casalino L. P., K. J. Devers, and L. R. Brewster. 2003. Focused Factories? Physician-Owned Specialty Hospitals. *Health Affairs* 22, no. 6: 56–67.

Chandler, A. D. 1962. *Strategy and Structure*. Cambridge, MA: MIT Press.

———. 1990. *Scale and Scope: The Dynamics of Industrial Capitalism*. Cambridge, MA: Harvard University Press.

Coddington, D. C., K. D. Moore, and R. L. Clarke. 1998. *Capitalizing Medical Groups*. New York: McGraw-Hill.

Cuellar, A. E., and P. J. Gertler. 2003. Trends in Hospital Consolidation: The Formation of Local Systems. *Health Affairs* 22, no. 6: 77–87.

Gordon, B., P. Federbusch, and J. Nelson. 2003. *Moody's Second Quarter 2003 HealthCare Update: Heavy Downgrade Activity Suggests Industry Outlook Moving Towards Negative*. New York: Moody's Investor Service.

Herzlinger, R. 1997. *Market-Driven Health Care*. Reading, MA: Addison-Wesley.

Jensen, M. C. 1986. Agency Costs of Free Cash Flows, Corporate Finance, and Takeovers. *American Economic Review* 76, no. 2: 323–329.

Jensen, M. C., and R. S. Ruback. 1983. The Market for Corporate Control: The Scientific Evidence. *Journal of Financial Economics* 11: 5–50.

Katz, A., R. E. Hurley, K. J. Devers, et al. 2003. *Competition Revs Up the Indianapolis Health Care Market*. Washington, DC: Center for Studying Health System Change.

Kozak, L. J., E. McCarthy, and R. Pokras. 1999. Changing Patterns of Surgical Care in the United States, 1980–1995. *Health Care Financing Review* 21, no. 1: 31–51.

Lutz, S., and E. P. Gee. 1998. *Columbia HCA: Healthcare on Overdrive*. San Francisco: Jossey-Bass.

Lutz, S., W. Grossman, and J. Bigalke. 1998. *Med Inc.: How Consolidation Is Shaping Tomorrow's Healthcare System*. San Francisco: Jossey-Bass.

MacNeil, I. R. 1978. Contracts: Adjustments of Long-Term Economic Relations under Classical, Neo-Classical, and Relational Contract Law. *Northwestern University Law Review* 72: 854–906.

McDonough, J. E. 1997. *Interests, Ideas, and Deregulation*. Ann Arbor: University of Michigan Press.

Mitchell, J. M. 1995. Physician Ownership of Ancillary Services: Indirect Demand Inducement or Quality Assurance? *Journal of Health Economics* 14, no. 3: 263–289.

Mollenkamp, C. 2003. After a Devastating Prognosis, HealthSouth Seeks a Recovery. *Wall Street Journal*, October 21, A1.

Panzar, J. C., and R. D. Willig. 1981. Economies of Scope. *American Economic Review* 71: 268–272.

Payton, S., and R. M. Powsner. 1980. Regulation through the Looking Glass: Hospitals, Blue Cross, and Certificate of Need. *Michigan Law Review* 79, no. 2: 203–278.

Peltzman, S. 1989. The Economic Theory of Regulation after a Decade of Deregulation. Microeconomics paper, 1–41. Washington, DC: Brookings Institution.

Posner, R. A. 1971. Taxation by Regulation. *Bell Journal of Economics and Management Science* 2: 3–21.

Robinson, J. C. 1999. *The Corporate Practice of Medicine.* Berkeley: University of California Press.

———. 2000. Capital Finance and Ownership Conversions in Health Care. *Health Affairs* 19, no. 1: 56–71.

———. 2001. Physician Organization in California: Crisis and Opportunity. *Health Affairs* 20, no. 4: 81–96.

———. 2002. Bond-Market Skepticism and Stock-Market Exuberance in the Hospital Industry. *Health Affairs* 21, no. 1: 104–117.

Schramm, C. J., and J. Gabel. 1988. Prospective Payment: Some Retrospective Observations. *New England Journal of Medicine* 318, no. 25: 1681–1683.

Standard and Poor's. 2003. *Annual Review: 2003 U.S. Not-for-Profit Median Health Care Ratios.* Available at *www.ratingsdirect.com* (accessed September 22, 2003).

Teece, D. J. 1980. Economies of Scope and the Scope of the Enterprise. *Journal of Economic Behavior and Organization* 1: 223–247.

Triple Tree (private investment banking report). 2003. Surgery Centers and Specialty Hospitals: Make Hay While the Sun Shines. *Spotlight Report* 6, no. 2: 1–22.

U.S. General Accounting Office (GAO). 1994. Medicare Referrals to Physician-Owned Imaging Facilities Warrant HCFA's Scrutiny. Washington, DC: GAO HEHS95-2, October 20.

———. 2003a. Specialty Hospitals: Information on National Market Share, Physician Ownership, and Patients Served. Washington, DC: GAO-03-683R, April 18.

———. 2003b. Specialty Hospitals: Geographic Location, Services Provided, and Financial Performance. Washington, DC: GAO-04-167, October 22.

Voelker, R. 2003. Specialty Hospitals Generate Revenue and Controversy. *Journal of the American Medical Association* 289, no. 4: 409–410.

Weaver, N., and T. Waugh. 2002. *Surgery Centers: Industry Report.* Little Rock, AR: Stephens (investment banking firm).

Williamson, O. E. 1985. *The Economic Institutions of Capitalism.* New York: Basic Books.

Winston, C. 1993. Economic Deregulation: Days of Reckoning for Microeconomists. *Journal of Economic Literature* 31: 1263–1289.

PART II

Promoting Population Health and Reducing Disparities

CHAPTER 5

Fundamental Sources of Health Inequalities

———— ∞∞ ————

BRUCE G. LINK AND JO C. PHELAN

$\mathcal{T}$he primacy of social conditions as determinants of health has been observed for centuries. The idea was forcefully articulated by nineteenth-century proponents of "social medicine," who noted strong relationships between health and the dire housing circumstances, poor sanitation, inadequate nutrition, and horrendous work conditions that poor people encountered at that time. This social patterning of ill health led to Virchow's famous declaration that "medicine is a social science" and "politics nothing but medicine on a grand scale" (1848). The idea is also prominent in the work of McKeown, who focused attention on dramatic secular trends toward improved population health (1976). The McKeown thesis, as it has come to be called, states that the enormous improvements in health experienced over the past two centuries owe more to changes in broad economic and social conditions than to specific medical advances.

Nevertheless, this perspective has not always been prominent. In the late twentieth century, the rise and influence of "risk-factor epidemiology" focused attention on individually based biological and behavioral risks for ill health. While this perspective has been enormously successful in providing information that has helped reduce individual risk, and thereby improve population health, its dominance has also helped downplay social conditions as important causes of ill health. Social factors came to be seen not as causes but as clues—starting points in the search for "true" causes that were seen to reside in individual health behaviors and the biological mechanisms that produce pathogenesis. Reflecting this trend, Rothman's influential text on modern epidemiological methods indicated that social class is "causally related to few if any diseases but is a correlate of many causes of disease" (1986, 90).

But risk-factor epidemiology has recently experienced its own crisis, criticized from within for its rote "black box" approach, and for having run out of large risk factors to uncover (Susser and Susser 1996). While numerous factors have contributed to this crisis, two major problems have been the approach's inattention to multiple levels of influence and its inability to understand empirical associations between population characteristics and the health profiles of populations.

For example, both the behavioral and biological risk factors identified by this approach have generally failed to account for or explain gradients in morbidity and mortality associated with socioeconomic status (Lantz et al. 1998; Marmot et al. 1991).

In the context of these problems with risk-factor epidemiology, a revitalization of interest in social and economic factors in health has occurred within social epidemiology and medical sociology. For example, investigators have turned intense attention to macro-level influences on health such as income inequality, social cohesion, and racial segregation and discrimination (Lynch et al. 2000; Kaplan et al. 1996; Kennedy, Kawachi, and Prothrow-Stith 1996; Kawachi et al. 1997; Williams and Collins 2001; Williams, Neighbors, and Jackson 2003). Researchers have also sought to assess multiple levels of social and economic influence, particularly the effects of neighborhood and community-level factors (Diez-Roux et al. 2001; Robert and Li 2001). Finally, analysts have directed intense effort to understanding how these distal causes affect more proximal influences on health to produce pathogenesis, disease, and death (Adler et al. 1994).

Like many of these lines of investigation, the theory of fundamental causes arose in response to the dominant risk-factor approach (House 2002). Instead of social conditions as mere correlates or clues pointing the way to true causes, we claim that social conditions are fundamental causes of health inequalities. We go beyond prior statements regarding the prominence of social factors to indicate why social conditions deserve to be called fundamental and why risk-factor approaches are unsuccessful in accounting for the persistence and pervasiveness of associations between social conditions and health.

Our approach claims that some types of policy interventions will be far more effective in reducing health disparities than others. First, according to the fundamental-cause explanation, social inequality produces health inequality, and thus policies that reduce social and economic inequality will reduce health inequality. Second, policies that benefit people irrespective of individual resources or initiative (for example, fluoridating water versus brushing with fluoride toothpaste) will be more effective in reducing health disparities than policies that require individuals to marshal resources to obtain health benefits. Third, we hold that policies that attend to the social distribution of knowledge about risk and protective factors—and the ability to act on that knowledge—are essential.

Social Conditions as Fundamental Causes

We use socioeconomic status (SES) to exemplify the theory of fundamental causes, although the idea may also pertain to circumstances such as social capital, social stigma, and racism. We begin with the well-established and robust association between mortality and educational attainment, occupational standing, and income (Antonovsky 1967; Sorlie, Backlund, and Keller 1995; Kunst et al. 1998). Biological mechanisms are clearly involved in the SES-disease association. Just as clearly, other mechanisms involving behaviors and environmental exposures must also be present: disease does not flow directly from income, educational, or occupational status into the body. Nevertheless, we cannot understand the effect of SES on mortality by focusing solely on the mechanisms that happen to link the two at any particular time.

To show why, we turn to one of the most striking features of the SES-health association: its persistence across time and place. The association was present in Mulhouse, France, in the early nineteenth century, in Rhode Island in 1865, in Chicago in the 1930s, and occurs in Europe and the United States today (Antonovsky 1967; Sorlie, Backlund, and Keller 1995; Lantz et al. 1998; Kunst et al. 1998). Given the vast differences in life expectancy, risk factors, diseases, and health care systems characterizing these different places and times, the persistence of the SES-mortality association is remarkable. Indeed, it is this persistence that suggests the irreducible nature of SES as a fundamental cause.

Imagine a causal model with SES as the distal factor linked to death by more proximal risk factors. If the proximal risk factors are eliminated, we would expect the SES-mortality association to disappear. However, in several important instances SES disparities in mortality persisted even though major proximal risk factors were eliminated. As a first example consider circumstances in the nineteenth century in which overcrowding, poor sanitation, and widespread infectious diseases such as diphtheria, measles, typhoid fever, tuberculosis, and syphilis appeared to explain higher mortality rates among less-advantaged persons. But the virtual elimination of those conditions and diseases in developed countries in the late twentieth century did not diminish SES inequalities in mortality (Rosen 1979).

As a second example consider that in the twentieth century, countries created national health programs providing free medical care to all with the express purpose of radically altering an important link between SES and health—differential access to care. While such programs addressed important mechanisms and may have kept disparities from growing even larger than they have, SES disparities in mortality nevertheless remained undiminished decades after these programs were implemented (Black et al. 1982). In both examples mechanisms explaining the SES mortality association were dramatically modified. The causal-model approach would predict a substantial reduction in the association between SES and mortality, but that did not happen.

A ready answer to this puzzle is that other mediating risk factors, such as health behaviors and psychosocial stress, have replaced earlier ones. This situation calls to mind Lieberson's description of "basic causes," which have enduring effects on a dependent variable because when the effect of one mechanism declines, others emerge or become more prominent (1985). House and colleagues first suggested that such a process might explain the enduring SES-mortality association (House et al. 1990). Still, although Lieberson's notion of basic causes is critical for understanding the tenacity of the SES-mortality association, it does not tell us what about SES allows it to reproduce its effects even as intervening mechanisms are eliminated.

We have argued that new mechanisms arise because persons higher in socioeconomic status enjoy a wide range of resources—including money, knowledge, prestige, power, and beneficial social connections—that they can utilize to their health advantage (Link and Phelan 1995). Such resources are important in at least two ways. First, they directly shape individual health behaviors by influencing whether people know about, have access to, can afford, and are supported in their efforts to engage in health-enhancing behaviors. Second, resources shape access to broad contexts such as neighborhoods, occupations, and social networks that vary dramatically in associated risk profiles and protective factors. Housing that poor people can afford is more likely to be located near noise, pollution, and other noxious conditions; blue-collar occupations tend to be more dangerous than white-collar occupations; and high-status jobs are more likely to include health care benefits. Thus the processes implied by the fundamental-cause perspective operate at both individual and contextual levels.

As a result, socioeconomic resources shape access to a broad range of circumstances that affect health. Examples include gaining access to the best doctors; knowing about and asking for beneficial health procedures; having friends and family who support healthy lifestyles; quitting smoking; getting flu shots; wearing seat belts; and eating fruits and vegetables. Other examples include exercising regularly; living in neighborhoods where garbage is picked up often, interiors are lead-free, and streets are safe; having children who bring home useful health information from good schools; working in safe occupational circumstances; and taking restful vacations.

This reasoning introduces four essential components of the theory of fundamental causes of morbidity and mortality. First, such causes influence multiple disease outcomes. For example, SES was related to cholera, tuberculosis, and diphtheria in the nineteenth century and is now related to heart disease, stroke, and many types of cancer. Second, such causes operate through multiple risk factors, including but not limited to the items listed above. Third, new intervening mechanisms reproduce the association between fundamental causes and mortality over time. Finally, the "essential feature of fundamental social causes is that they involve access to resources that can be used to avoid risks or to minimize the consequences of disease once it occurs" (Link and Phelan 1995, 87).

Because these resources are general in nature, people can adapt them to changing health-related conditions and use them to protect health no matter what the risks, treatments, and diseases are in a given situation. Thus, for example, socioeconomic resources were equally as useful in avoiding the worst sanitation, housing, and industrial conditions of the nineteenth century as they are in shaping access to health-promoting conditions today. As new discoveries expand our ability to control disease processes, the list of health-enhancing circumstances will only grow. According to our theory, people who command more resources will, on average, hold an advantage in gaining access to and benefiting from this new knowledge.

Evidence for the Fundamental-Cause Theory

An Empirical Test

Phelan and colleagues constructed a test of the theory of fundamental causes by identifying situations where even the richest and most powerful people on earth cannot use resources to escape death. One such situation occurs in the case of potentially fatal diseases that we do not know how to prevent or treat. If the utilization of resources is critical in prolonging life, then in circumstances when resources associated with higher status are useless, high SES should confer little advantage, and the usually robust SES-mortality association should be reduced.

Phelan and colleagues tested this prediction using the National Longitudinal Mortality Study and ratings they developed of the preventability of death from specific causes (1999). The National Longitudinal Mortality Study (Sorlie, Backlund, and Keller 1995; Rogot et al. 1988, 1992) is a large prospective study that uses combined samples of selected Current Population Surveys that are then linked to the National Death Index to determine occurrences and causes of death in a follow-up period of approximately nine years. Reliable ratings (intra-class correlation .85) of the preventability of death were made by two physician-epidemiologists. Causes were categorized into high-preventability and low-preventability groups with common high-preventability causes being cerebrovascular diseases, chronic obstructive pulmonary disease, ischemic heart disease, malignant neoplasm of the trachea, bronchus, and lung, and pneumonia and influenza; and common low-preventability causes being arrhythmias and malignant neoplasms of the pancreas, female breast, and prostate. Gradients according to SES indicators of education and income were then examined separately for high—and low-preventability causes. Consistent with predictions derived from the fundamental-cause theory, Phelan et al. found that the SES-mortality association is much stronger for highly preventable causes of death than for less preventable causes (1999).

Resources versus the Stress of Hierarchical Position

Unlike the fundamental-cause theory, which strongly emphasizes the role of resources, British sociologist Richard Wilkinson argues that the "psychosocial effects of social position" influence the SES gradient more than material conditions such as "bad housing, poor diets, inadequate heating" (1997, 591). Wilkinson believes that the anger, resentment, and envy associated with where one stands in relation to others—along with maladaptive behaviors such as smoking, drinking, and overeating that follow from these emotions—are the most important determinants of SES gradients in health. Support for this view is drawn from ecological studies in industrialized nations, animal studies, and the finely graded nature of status differences in health investigations like the Whitehall study.

Even though SES gradients are apparent within countries, differences in median per capita income between countries are a relatively weak predictor of life expectancy (Wilkinson 1992; Lynch et al. 2000). For Wilkinson, this suggests that relative deprivation is more important than absolute differences in deprivation. Whether conducted in the wild or in captivity, studies of monkeys generally find that a lower position in a dominance hierarchy is associated with worse health, as indicated by measures of atherosclerosis, hyper-secreted cortisol, blood pressure, and immune function (Sapolsky 1990; Shively and Clarkson 1994). Finally, even within the relatively stable employment of the British civil service, and given extensive controls on behavioral and biological risk factors, the Whitehall study found finely graded differences in mortality by occupational level. Because hierarchical position remained a prominent predictor of mortality, and because material deprivation was largely absent in this group of men, the study seems to support the centrality of hierarchy for understanding SES gradients in health.

But the hierarchy-stress explanation cannot account for important changes in the association between SES and specific diseases. According to such an explanation, the stress of low positional location should remain relatively constant across cohorts and therefore produce relatively stable associations between positional location and disease outcomes in different eras. However, evidence concerning two major killers—coronary artery disease and lung cancer—runs counter to this prediction. The link between SES and coronary heart disease shifted dramatically over the last century, changing from a direct to an inverse association (Beaglehole 1990; Marmot, Kogevinas, and Elston 1987). And whereas lung cancer mortality was not related to SES as late as 1931, a large inverse association emerged in the 1950s and 1960s (Logan 1982).

If positional location is the prime determinant of SES gradients in health, one would not expect such dramatic changes; the stress of low position should produce the same inverse gradient across time. On the other hand, from a fundamental-cause perspective, these shifts represent important instances in which SES gradients for specific disease outcomes changed after knowledge about health risk and protective factors emerged. High-SES groups use this new knowledge and its benefits disproportionately, resulting in shifts in the SES-disease/mortality gradient that benefit higher-SES groups.

Intelligence: A Competing Flexible Resource?

Once we have the idea that broadly serviceable resources are required to understand the persistence and the ubiquity of the association between SES and health, we see that a resource other than the social resources identified in the fundamental-cause approach is possible. Intelligence or cognitive ability can also be conceptualized as a broadly serviceable resource that enhances people's abilities to deal with life situations, including situations that have health implications. In seeking to maximize one's chances for a healthy life, one must be able to gain access to information, identify the most salient aspects of one's health situation, and craft an effective approach to addressing it. A case can be made that someone who is more gifted with respect to cognitive ability will fare much better than someone who is not. Moreover, as with other fundamental social causes, people can use intelligence to gain a health advantage no matter the health circumstances of a particular place or time. Because it can be conceptualized in this way, many of the theoretical predictions one might make from a fundamental-social-cause perspective could just as easily be made from a perspective that emphasizes intelligence. Indeed, this is precisely what Linda Gottfredson does in a paper published in the *Journal of Personality and Social Psychology* (2004). By collecting evidence from disparate sources, Gottfredson makes the argument that "general intelligence" may be the fundamental cause of health inequalities. While the evidence she garners is consistent with this possibility, none of it involves direct measures of cognitive ability, SES, and health.

The research issue concerning the role of cognitive ability is relatively straightforward. In our formulation, social and economic resources of knowledge, money, power, prestige, and beneficial social connections are critical, whereas for Gottfredson the psychological resource of intelligence is the source of both the socioeconomic-related resources and health. Critical facts that separate these two interpretations hinge on the importance of cognitive ability for health with SES controlled and the role of SES for health with cognitive ability controlled. To investigate these relationships, Link, Phelan, and Meich located two large public-access data sets—the Wisconsin Longitudinal Study and the Health and Retirement Survey—that provide the requisite measures of SES and IQ and allow us to examine relationships prospectively (2003).

Link and colleagues found no evidence to support the idea that cognitive ability might supplant socioeconomic-related resources of knowledge, money, power, prestige, and social connections in the fundamental-cause framework (Link, Phelan, and Meich 2003). Specifically, in examining mortality and life-threatening illnesses, the investigators found that the effects of education and household income remained significant and were changed only slightly by controls for cognitive ability. In sharp contrast, measures of cognitive ability—though related to health at the bivariate level—declined dramatically, generally to nonsignificant levels, when educational attainment was controlled.

Thus while cognitive ability plays an important role in determining SES resources, it cannot account for the connection between those resources and health. Instead, the findings tell us that within levels of educational attainment, differences in cognitive ability have little consequence for health outcomes. On average, two people with comparable IQ scores, one of whom receives more education, will have different health, but two people with different IQs but the same education will have similar health.

Policy Considerations

The fundamental-social-causes approach leads to very different policies for addressing health disparities than does an individually oriented risk-factor approach. The latter promotes strategies that ask us to locate modifiable risk factors that lie between distal causes (such as SES) and disease, and to intervene in those risk factors to break the link between the distal factors and disease. By addressing intervening factors, the logic goes, we will eliminate health disparities.

But our approach points to the pitfalls of this logic and leads us to recommend policies that take a distinctly population-health perspective in addressing health disparities. Specifically, our approach points to policies that eliminate or reduce the ability to use socioeconomic advantage to gain a health advantage—either by reducing disparities in socioeconomic resources themselves, or by developing interventions that, by their nature, are more equally distributed across SES groups.

We make three general policy recommendations. First, create contextually based health interventions that automatically benefit individuals irrespective of their own resources or behaviors. Second, prioritize interventions that are potentially available and beneficial to people at all socioeconomic levels and target the special needs of resource-poor groups who may face barriers in implementing those interventions. Third, promote policies that increase the SES-related resources available to resource-poor groups.

We assume that social inequalities in health according to SES, race/ethnicity, and other social circumstances are undesirable: that every person, whether rich or poor, black or white, top executive or manual laborer, should have an opportunity to live a healthy life. We hold that something is wrong when social positions of power and privilege determine who lives and who dies, and that efforts to ameliorate such circumstances are desirable. We emphasize this latter point because the goals of improving overall population health and decreasing health disparities may require different kinds of policy initiatives (Marchand, Wikler, and Landesman 1998). Progressive public-health-oriented interventions (such as life-saving screens for colorectal cancer and flu shots) may improve population health without addressing social inequalities in health, and may even contribute to such inequalities if life-enhancing interventions are mal-distributed by SES and other social variables (Mechanic 2002).

Interventions That Benefit Individuals
Regardless of Their Own Resources and Actions

In the United States we tend to emphasize both the ability of individuals to control their personal fate and the importance of doing so (Becker 1993), and thus we carry a strong orientation toward individually based solutions to health problems. But individuals frequently encounter barriers that block their capacity to maximize health. For people at lower socioeconomic levels, lack of money, awareness, understanding, time, social support for health-enhancing behavior, and optimism that adopting certain behaviors will result in a long and satisfying life can be obstacles. When we construct individually based interventions focused on diet, exercise, dental care, illness screening, and the like, we create the possibility that people with greater resources will benefit more from these interventions. This contributes to SES gradients in health. A fundamental-cause approach calls for population-based interventions that influence everyone. When we observe a health problem, we should ask how we can change the context to eliminate the problem or minimize its consequences.

Consider rising asthma rates, particularly in low-income urban areas of developed countries such as the United States (Claudio et al. 1999). Individuals can address known (or strongly suspected) modifiable risk factors and employ medical responses to lessen symptoms and keep asthma from worsening (National Institutes of Health 1997). Medical practitioners can tell individuals that asthma is less severe if homes and apartments are well ventilated and kept spotlessly clean to avoid dust mites, animal dander, and other environmental toxins. Parents can also be informed that cockroach infestation may be problematic for children with asthma and that they should try to eliminate this risk factor from their children's living space. Parents can also be exhorted to get their children away from the television and into the open air. Finally, parents can be told to use preventive medications even when no symptoms are present to reduce the risk of hospitalizations and (rarely) death.

However, while these individually based responses would certainly be helpful to those who implemented them, such a strategy is bound to create SES disparities in the prevalence of severe symptoms of asthma. People with fewer resources are less likely to receive information regarding risk factors and to be able to pursue strategies to counteract them. Resource-poor persons are more likely to live in areas where rodents are common and are unlikely to have household help or equipment for effective cleaning. Roaches are difficult to eliminate from an individual apartment when they infest the entire building, and getting kids away from the television is difficult when open spaces are not available or safe. Finally, uninsured persons are less likely to obtain effective medical interventions to deal with chronic symptoms, and Medicaid reimbursement levels make it hard for doctors to spend enough time to provide parents with needed skills and children with quality care.

Fortunately, pressing individuals to address risk factors is not the only option. Contextually based interventions would seek to encourage city-sponsored rodent and roach reduction efforts that target entire buildings or areas, to provide sponsored activities for children in open areas such as parks, and to locate health screening and medical interventions in schools, where all children can receive them free of charge. Like individually based approaches, contextually based approaches would reduce the overall incidence of asthma symptoms and hospitalizations; but, unlike individual approaches, they would have the added benefit of reducing SES disparities.

Another contextual intervention is to employ air bags rather than seatbelts to reduce road fatalities. Seatbelt use requires each person to secure his or her own belt, and ample evidence shows that people with higher educational attainment are more likely to do so. To the extent that seatbelts are effective, highly educated people benefit more than less-educated people, thereby contributing to a gradient in a health-related outcome. Another contextual intervention concerns the decades-long buildup of lead paint in the homes of many U.S. residents. Will we move from a strategy of warning parents about the dangers of paint chips and paint dust to actually removing the hazard from the environment?

Similar examples include providing vaccinations and health screening in schools, workplaces, and other community settings rather than through private physicians, requiring window guards in all high-rise apartments versus advising parents to watch their children carefully, and adding warning labels to health-hazardous products versus relying on individuals' knowledge of product risks. Other choices include banning smoking in public buildings versus advising people to avoid secondhand smoke, thoroughly inspecting meat instead of advising consumers to wash cutting boards and cook meat thoroughly, and fluoridating water rather than exhorting people to brush often with fluoridated toothpaste. To the extent that interventions influence everyone regardless of the resources they possess or the health behaviors they manifest, we can block the creation of SES gradients: everyone benefits equally. Creative interventions that influence entire contexts rather than individuals could go a long way toward narrowing health disparities.

Monitoring the Dissemination of Health-Enhancing
Information and Interventions

Even if we become far more creative in developing population-based interventions focused on contexts, addressing many health problems will still require individual resources and action. The fundamental-cause idea tells us that resource-rich persons will be far more effective in gaining access to and employing health-enhancing initiatives focused on individuals than people who are resource poor. This means that policy approaches will need to address the consequences of individually targeted information and interventions for health disparities. Two issues are critical.

The first concerns whether we promote initiatives that people with fewer resources may not be able to access. As we seek to create interventions to respond to disease, we need to ask if an intervention is something anyone can potentially adopt, or whether the benefit is available only to people with the requisite resources. The point becomes clear if we take a global view of the medical response to the AIDS epidemic. Research, policy, and investment in the West spawned drugs that have been enormously effective in enhancing the survival and quality of life of people with HIV/AIDS in the United States and Europe. But, because of their cost, these drugs have been unavailable in poor areas of Africa and Asia, creating an enormous resource-related health disparity.

Similar circumstances exist within the United States regarding access to optimal procedures following heart attacks, control of diabetes, rapid response to strokes, and many other interventions. When we create interventions that are expensive and difficult to distribute broadly, we create health disparities. While we might proceed with such interventions because they help some people, and because expensive initiatives sometimes become less expensive with time, we must also weigh the fact that they will create disparities. If our goal is to reduce disparities, we must ask whether we could redirect our intellectual, social, and economic resources to produce a more broadly distributable health benefit.

A second issue in disseminating health-enhancing information and interventions entails understanding why people with fewer resources do not always act on information or adopt health-enhancing ways of life. We call this contextualizing risk and protective factors: that is, understanding what puts people at "risk of risk" and what blocks them from adopting protective strategies (Link and Phelan 1995). The idea is to use such understanding to construct interventions that simultaneously address a risk or protective factor and any barriers to broadly implementing it. For example, interventions that tackle diet and exercise to reduce obesity and encourage a heart-healthy lifestyle would begin with careful attention to all the life circumstances that might create barriers to behavioral change. Examples of such contextual factors include the cost, availability, and convenience of healthful versus unhealthful foods; targeted advertising of convenience and fast foods; access to safe and accessible settings in which to exercise; time for exercise; and support for healthful habits from family, friends, and employers. Absent such efforts, the life circumstances of people with fewer resources will tend to block the adoption of beneficial information, and we will create a health disparity.

A good example of an initiative that has mandated the kind of scrutiny we endorse is the mapping of the human genome. Concerned about the impact of new genetic knowledge, including the possibility that expected benefits might be maldistributed, Congress reserved 5 percent of funding for the Human Genome Project to consider social, ethical, and legal issues (Collins et al. 2003). Whether the initiative will be successful or not remains to be seen; but in general, to the extent that we can anticipate and address factors that produce the unequal distribution of health benefits, the better able we will be to minimize health disparities.

Policies That Distribute Resources to Resource-Poor Populations

The fundamental-cause idea stipulates that people use their knowledge, money, power, prestige, and social connections to gain a health advantage, and thereby reproduce the SES gradient in health over and over again. It follows that if we increase the resources available to resource-poor populations, the relative health of those populations will likely improve. We provide several examples consistent with this prediction.

First, consider an analysis by Peter Arno and James House of the impact of Social Security in the late 1930s. Before Social Security, elders were often extremely resource poor, and death rates were very high. After the advent of Social Security, poverty declined sharply among people sixty-five and older, and death rates also dropped faster than among people under sixty-five. While these data do not prove that Social Security had a causal effect on mortality, they are certainly consistent with that interpretation. If Social Security had an impact on health, it is an indication that providing resources to a group with relatively few resources has health benefits for that group and moves its health profile toward that of groups with more resources.

Another example is the work of Costello and colleagues, who capitalized on a natural experiment where an influx of money from a casino dramatically altered the monetary resources of American Indians living in eleven rural counties in North Carolina (2003). The casino netted each man, woman, and child a monetary stipend that reached six thousand dollars a year in 2001. Costello and colleagues' study of children found substantial improvements in the mental health status (externalizing behaviors) of the children living in these communities from a baseline starting point before the influx of resources to a follow-up point about four years after the monetary stipends began.

A final example is the U.S. Department of Housing and Urban Development's Moving to Opportunity study, which randomly assigned families eligible for housing assistance to one of three groups—those that were given Section 8 vouchers, which help cover housing costs, plus special assistance in moving to low-poverty neighborhoods; Section 8 vouchers alone; or no vouchers at all. Even though only 40 percent of the families receiving assistance actually moved to new housing, the group assigned to Section 8 vouchers plus assistance in relocating to low-poverty areas recorded lower levels of parental anxiety as well as less anxiety and depression among male offspring. Families that actually moved to better neighborhoods showed the greatest improvements (Leventhal and Brooks-Gunn 2003).

Together these studies suggest that providing resources to populations that are resource poor, such as elderly people, American Indians, and people living in areas of concentrated disadvantage, may improve their health profiles. The further up the SES gradient the infusion of resources enables people to move, the more we can expect them to benefit. While the reasons for boosting groups that are relatively resource poor go beyond health benefits, these studies suggest that providing resources to populations at risk of negative health consequences is one important way to reduce health disparities.

Conclusion

Perhaps the strongest policy conclusion we can offer is that standard risk-factor-oriented thinking about social disparities in health will fail to produce policies that can narrow such disparities. We will not be able to eliminate disparities if we focus solely on the individually based risk factors that happen to link SES and health in a given place or time. While the fundamental-cause approach points us away from policy based on a standard risk-factor approach, it points us toward other policies. We endorse three broad types: (1) policies that benefit all people in a context irrespective of their behaviors and resources, (2) policies that minimize resource-related barriers to avoiding risks or implementing beneficial interventions, and (3) policies that distribute resources to resource-poor groups. Pursuing policies like these provides the best opportunity for reducing health disparities in the time ahead.

References

Adler, N., T. Boyce, A. Chesney, et al. 1994. Socioeconomic Status and Health: The Challenge of the Gradient. *American Psychologist* 49: 15–24.

Antonovsky, A. 1967. Social Class, Life Expectancy, and Overall Mortality. *Milbank Memorial Quarterly* 45: 31–73.

Beaglehole, R. 1990. International Trends in Coronary Heart Disease Mortality, Morbidity, and Risk Factors. *Epidemiological Reviews* 12: 1–16.

Becker, M. 1993. A Medical Sociologist Looks at Health Promotion. *Journal of Health and Social Behavior* 34: 1–6.

Black, D., J. Morris, C. Smith, et al. 1982. *Inequalities in Health: The Black Report,* ed. P. Townsend and N. Davidson. Middlesex, UK: Penguin Books Ltd.

Claudio, L., T. Tulton, J. Doucette, et al. 1999. Socioeconomic Factors and Asthma Hospitalization Rates in New York City. *Journal of Asthma* 36: 343–350.

Collins, F., E. Green, A. Guttmacher, et al. (on behalf of the U.S. National Human Genome Research Institute). 2003. A Vision for the Future of Genomics Research. *Nature* 422: 835–847.

Costello, E., S. Compton, G. Keeler, and A. Angold. 2003. Relationships between Poverty and Psychopathology: A Natural Experiment. *Journal of the American Medical Association* 290: 2023–2029.

Diez-Roux, A., S. Merkin, D. Arnett, et al. 2001. Neighborhood of Residence and Incidence of Coronary Heart Disease. *New England Journal of Medicine* 345: 99–106.

Gottfredson, L. 2004. Intelligence: Is It the Epidemiologists' Elusive "Fundamental Cause" of Social Class Inequalities in Health? *Journal of Social and Personality Psychology* 86: 174–199.

House, J. 2002. Understanding Social Factors and Inequalities in Health: 20th-Century Progress and 21st-Century Prospects. *Journal of Health and Social Behavior* 43: 125–142.

House, J., R. Kessler, and A. R. Herzog, et al. 1990. Age, Socioeconomic Status, and Health. *Milbank Memorial Quarterly* 68: 383–411.

Kaplan, G., E. Pamuk, J. Lynch, et al. 1996. Income Inequality and Mortality in the United States. *British Medical Journal* 312: 999–1003.

Kawachi, I., B. Kennedy, K. Lochner, et al. 1997. Social Capital, Income Inequality, and Mortality. *American Journal of Public Health* 87: 1491–1498.

Kennedy, B., I. Kawachi, and D. Prothrow-Stith. 1996. Income Distribution and Mortality: Cross-Sectional Ecological Study of the Robin Hood Index in the United States. *British Medical Journal* 312: 1004–1007.

Kunst, A., G. Feikje, J. Mackenbach, et al. 1998. Occupational Class and Cause-Specific Mortality in Middle-Aged Men in 11 European Countries: Comparison of Population-Based Studies. *British Medical Journal* 316: 1636–1642.

Lantz, P., J. House, J. Lepowski, et al. 1998. Socioeconomic Factors, Health Behaviors, and Mortality: Results from a Nationally Representative Prospective Study of U.S. Adults. *Journal of the American Medical Association* 279: 1703–1708.

Leventhal, T., and J. Brooks-Gunn. 2003. Moving to Opportunity: An Experimental Study in Neighborhood Effects on Health. *American Journal of Public Health* 93: 1576–1582.

Lieberson, S. 1985. *Making It Count: The Improvement of Social Research and Theory*. Berkeley: University of California Press.

Link, B., and J. Phelan. 1995. Social Conditions as Fundamental Causes of Disease. *Journal of Health and Social Behavior* (extra issue): 80–94.

———. 2000. Evaluating the Fundamental Cause Explanation for Social Disparities in Health. In *Handbook of Medical Sociology*, 5th ed., ed. C. Bird, P. Conrad, and A. Freemont. Upper Saddle River, NJ: Prentice Hall.

Link, B., J. Phelan, and R. Meich. 2003. The Resources That Matter: Fundamental Social Causes of Disease and the Challenge of Intelligence. Paper presented at meetings of the American Sociological Association, Atlanta, GA.

Link, B., M. Northridge, J. Phelan, and M. Ganz. 1998. Social Epidemiology and the Fundamental Cause Concept: On the Structuring of Effective Cancer Screens by Socioeconomic Status. *Milbank Memorial Quarterly* 76: 375–402.

Logan, P. 1982. *Cancer Mortality by Occupation and Social Class, 1951–1971*. London: HMSO.

Lynch J., G. Davey Smith, G. Kaplan, et al. 2000. Income Inequality and Mortality: Importance to Health of Individual Income, Psychosocial Environment, or Material Conditions. *British Medical Journal* 320: 1200–1204.

Marchand, S., D. Wikler, and B. Landesman. 1998. Class, Health, and Justice. *Milbank Memorial Quarterly* 76: 449–467.

Marmot, M., and J. Mustard. 1994. Coronary Heart Disease from a Population Perspective. In *Why Are Some People Healthy and Others Not? The Determinants of Health of Populations*, ed. R. Evans, M. Barer, and T. Marmor. New York: Walter de Gruyter.

Marmot, M., G. Davey Smith, S. Stansfeld, et al. 1991. Health Inequalities among British Civil Servants: The Whitehall II Study. *Lancet* 337: 1387–1393.

Marmot, M., G. Rose, M. Shipley, et al. 1978. Employment Grade and Coronary Heart Disease in British Civil Servants. *Journal of Epidemiology and Community Health* 32: 244–249.

Marmot, M., M. Kogevinas, and M. Elston. 1987. Social/Economic Status and Disease. *Annual Review of Public Health* 8: 111–135.

Marmot, M., M. Shipley, and G. Rose. 1984. Inequalities in Death: Specific Explanations of a General Pattern? *Lancet* 1: 1003–1006.

McKeown, T. 1976. *The Role of Medicine: Dream, Mirage, or Nemesis?* London: Nuffield Provincial Hospitals Trust.

Mechanic, D. 2002. Disadvantage, Inequality, and Social Policy: Major Initiatives Intended to Improve Population Health May Also Increase Health Disparities. *Health Affairs* 21: 48–59.

National Institutes of Health. 1997. National Asthma Education and Prevention Program: Clinical Practice Guidelines. Expert panel report no. 2: Guidelines for the Diagnosis and Management of Asthma. *No. 97-4051.*

Phelan J., B. Link, A. Diez-Roux, et al. 1999. "Fundamental Causes" of Social Inequalities in Mortality: A Test of the Theory. Paper presented at meetings of the American Sociological Association, Chicago, IL.

Robert, S., and L. Li. 2001. Age Variation in the Relationship between Community Socioeconomic Status and Adult Health. *Research on Aging* 23: 233–258.

Rogot, E., P. Sorlie, N. Johnson, and C. Schmitt. 1992. *A Mortality Study of 1.3 Million Persons by Demographic, Social, and Economic Factors, 1979–1985: Followup.* No. 92-3297. Bethesda, MD: National Institutes of Health.

Rogot, E., P. Sorlie, N. Johnson, C. Glover, and D. Treasure. 1988. *A Mortality Study of One Million Persons by Demographic, Social, and Economic Factors, 1979–1981: Followup.* No. 88-2896. Bethesda, MD: National Institutes of Health.

Rosen, G. 1979. The Evolution of Social Medicine. In *The Handbook of Medical Sociology*, 3rd ed., ed. H. Freeman, S. Levine, and L. Reeder. Englewood Cliffs, NJ: Prentice Hall.

Rothman, K. 1986. *Modern Epidemiology*. Boston: Little, Brown.

Sapolsky, R. 1990. Stress in the Wild. *Scientific American* 262: 116–123.

Shively, C., and T. Clarkson. 1994. Social Status and Coronary Artery Atherosclerosis in Female Monkeys. *Arteriosclerosis Thrombosis* 14: 721–726.

Sorlie, P., M. Backlund, and J. Keller. 1995. U.S. Mortality by Economic, Demographic, and Social Characteristics: The National Longitudinal Mortality Study. *American Journal of Public Health* 85: 949–956.

Susser, M., and E. Susser. 1996. Choosing a Future for Epidemiology, Part I. *American Journal of Public Health* 86: 668–673.

Virchow, R. 1848. The Public Health Service (in German). *Medizinische Reform* 5: 21–22.

Wilkinson, R. 1992. Income Distribution and Life Expectancy. *British Medical Journal* 304: 165–168.

————. 1997. Socioeconomic Determinants of Health. Health Inequalities: Relative or Absolute Material Standards? *British Medical Journal* 314: 591–595.

Williams, D., and C. Collins. 2001. Racial Residential Segregation: A Fundamental Cause of Racial Disparities in Health. *Public Health Reports* 116: 404–416.

Williams, D., H. Neighbors, and J. Jackson. 2003. Racial/Ethnic Discrimination and Health: Findings from Community Studies. *American Journal of Public Health* 93: 200–208.

CHAPTER 6

A Public Health Approach to Firearms Policy

———— ⟨⟨⟩⟩ ————

DAVID HEMENWAY

*A*n American who dies before the age of forty is more likely to succumb to an injury rather than a disease. The leading cause of injury death in the United States is motor vehicles. The second leading cause of injury death is firearms. In 2001 some 29,500 Americans were killed with firearms in non-war-related events, and about three times that number were wounded seriously enough to be hospitalized. Gun shot injuries are one of the leading causes of both traumatic brain injury and spinal cord injury.

The United States has more firearms in civilian hands than any other high-income nation. About 25 percent of adults in the United States personally own a firearm. Many gun owners have more than one firearm; some 10 percent of adults own over 75 percent of all firearms in the country. The percentage of households with a firearm has declined in the past two decades; about one in three households now contains a firearm.

Among the two dozen or so high-income countries (as classified by the World Bank), the United States is exceptional not only because of the number of firearms in civilian hands but also because so many of our guns are handguns. Our firearm regulations are also relatively permissive. For example, unlike most other industrialized countries, the United States does not have a national firearm licensing or registration system, or laws mandating that all gun owners receive firearm training.

U.S. crime and violence rates—including burglary, robbery, car theft, and assault rates, as assessed in victimization surveys—are comparable to those of other industrialized nations. What is not comparable is our rate of *lethal* violence, and the majority of our homicides are firearm homicides. Studies show that high-income nations that have more guns have more homicides because of higher rates of firearm homicide (Hemenway and Miller 2000; Hepburn and Hemenway 2004).

Studies comparing U.S. regions, states, or cities also find that areas with more firearms have more homicides, primarily because of higher rates of firearm homicide. The association between guns and homicide holds even after controlling for levels of violent crime, unemployment, poverty, urbanization, and alcohol consumption (Miller, Azrael, and Hemenway 2002c). Case-control studies find that a gun in the home is a risk factor for committing a murder and for being murdered (Hepburn and Hemenway 2004). The large majority of perpetrators and victims of lethal violence are male. Few male-on-male homicides appear to be the carefully planned actions of individuals with a single-minded intention to kill. More people are murdered during arguments with someone they know than during the commission of a robbery.

Strong evidence also shows that guns raise the likelihood of suicide in the United States. Nine case-control studies have all found that a gun in the home is a risk factor for completed suicide, and cross-sectional studies find that regions, states, and cities with more guns have more suicides per capita, owing to higher rates of firearm suicide (Miller and Hemenway 1999; Brent 2001; Hemenway 2004). The gun-suicide connection holds even after controlling for poverty, urbanization, divorce, unemployment, education, alcohol consumption, major depression, and suicidal thoughts (Miller, Azrael, and Hemenway 2002d; Hemenway and Miller 2002). A recent study finds that the rate of death from suicide attempts is over 90 percent for firearms, compared with only 2–3 percent for drug overdoses and cutting and piercing, the most common forms of suicide attempts (Miller, Azrael, and Hemenway 2004).

Unintentional firearm injuries are also a problem in the United States. In the 1990s, some fifty people a day were shot unintentionally and about four died. From 1965 to 2000 more Americans were killed in gun accidents than were killed in wars. The majority of Americans who die unintentionally from firearms are under twenty-five years of age. Not surprisingly, in states with more guns, many more youth as well as adults die from firearm accidents (Miller, Azrael, and Hemenway 2001).

TABLE 6.1   *Homicide, Suicide, and Unintentional Firearm Death Rates among 5-to-14-Year-Olds (rates per 100,000, early 1990s)*

	United States	Other countries[a]	Mortality rate ratio
Homicide rates			
Gun homicides	1.22	0.07	17.4
Non-gun homicides	0.53	0.23	2.3
Total	1.75	0.30	5.8
Suicide rates			
Gun suicides	0.49	0.05	9.8
Non-gun suicides	0.35	0.35	1.0
Total	0.84	0.40	2.1
Unintentional firearm death rates	0.46	0.05	9.2

Source: Centers for Disease Control and Prevention 1997, 101–105.

[a]Twenty-five other high-income, populous countries.

TABLE 6.2   *Homicide, Suicide, and Unintentional Firearm Deaths*
among 5-to-14-Year-Olds, 1996–2001

	High-gun states	Low-gun states	Mortality rate ratio (high gun: low gun)
Total population, 5-to-14-year-olds	32.2 million	32.6 million	
Homicides			
Gun homicides	224	82	2.8
Non-gun homicides	152	114	1.4
Total	376	196	2.0
Suicides			
Gun suicides	172	17	10.3
Non-gun suicides	158	107	1.5
Total	330	124	2.7
Unintentional firearm deaths	159	12	13.5

Source: Centers for Disease Control and Prevention, National Center for Injury Prevention and Control, Web-based Injury Statistics Query and Reporting System (WISQARS) (online), 2003. Available at *www.cdc.gov/ncipc/wisqars* (accessed January 15, 2004).

Note: The fifteen states (included in this table) with the highest average levels of household gun ownership (based on the 2001 Behavioral Risk Factor Surveillance System) were Wyoming, Montana, Alaska, South Dakota, Arkansas, West Virginia, Alabama, Idaho, Mississippi, North Dakota, Kentucky, Wisconsin, South Carolina, Utah, and Louisiana. The six states (included in this table) with the lowest average levels of household gun ownership were Hawaii, Massachusetts, Rhode Island, New Jersey, Connecticut, and New York. Data exclude violent deaths caused by the terrorist attacks on September 11, 2001.

Guns are bad for the health of children. Children (aged five to fourteen) in the United States are far more likely than children in other high-income countries to be victims of homicide, suicide, and gun accidents (CDC 1997) (see table 6.1).

Children in states with more guns are also more likely to be murdered, to commit suicide, and to die from unintentional gunshot wounds (Miller, Azrael, and Hemenway 2002a). To illustrate, consider the states at the extremes in terms of gun ownership (see table 6.2). (Because some states with the fewest guns, such as New York and New Jersey, are quite populous, the table compares the fifteen highest-gun states with the six lowest-gun states to obtain equal populations at risk for death.) From 1996 to 2001, children in the high-gun states were far more likely to be victims of homicide, suicide, and gun accidents.

More women are also murdered in high-income countries with more guns, primarily because of higher rates of firearm homicide. Women in the United States are not more likely to commit suicide, but they are far more likely to be homicide victims than women in other industrialized countries. Indeed, over 70 percent of all women murdered in high-income countries are Americans (Hemenway, Shinoda-Tagawa, and Miller 2002).

In states with more guns, women are more likely to be murdered, to commit

TABLE 6.3   *Homicide, Suicide, and Unintentional Firearm Deaths among Women, 1996–2001*

	High-gun states	Low-gun states	Mortality rate ratio (high gun: low gun)
Total population, women	121.4 million	121.1 million	
Homicides			
Gun homicides	2372	709	3.3
Non-gun homicides	2117	2231	1.0
Total	4489	2940	1.5
Suicides			
Gun suicides	2860	461	6.2
Non-gun suicides	2832	2999	0.9
Total	5692	3460	1.6
Unintentional firearm deaths	221	26	8.5

Source: Centers for Disease Control and Prevention, National Center for Injury Prevention and Control, Web-based Injury Statistics Query and Reporting System (WISQARS) (online), 2003. Available at *www.cdc.gov/ncipc/wisqars* (accessed January 15, 2004).

Note: The fifteen states (included in this table) with the highest average levels of household gun ownership (based on the 2001 Behavioral Risk Factor Surveillance System) were Wyoming, Montana, Alaska, South Dakota, Arkansas, West Virginia, Alabama, Idaho, Mississippi, North Dakota, Kentucky, Wisconsin, South Carolina, Utah, and Louisiana. The six states (included in this table) with the lowest average levels of household gun ownership were Hawaii, Massachusetts, Rhode Island, New Jersey, Connecticut, and New York. Data exclude violent deaths caused by the terrorist attacks on September 11, 2001.

suicide, and to be accidentally killed with a firearm. This relationship holds even after accounting for other factors, including urbanization and poverty (Miller, Azrael, and Hemenway 2002b). For example, from 1996 to 2001 women in the fifteen states with the most firearms were over three times as likely to be murdered with a firearm as women in the six states with the fewest firearms. The former were also six times more likely to commit suicide with a firearm, and over eight times more likely to be killed in a firearm accident (see table 6.3).

Male homicide victims are usually shot outside the home, by strangers or acquaintances, while women are more often shot in their own homes, by intimates. Indeed, more than twice as many women are killed with a gun used by their husbands or intimates than are murdered by strangers using guns, knives, or any other means (Kellermann and Mercy 1992). Gun threats in the home against women by intimates appear to be more common than home self-defense uses of guns by women (Azrael and Hemenway 2000). A gun in the home raises the risk to women for homicide, suicide, and gun accidents (Bailey et al. 1997). No study has found that a gun in the home reduces the risk of burglary, robbery, home invasion, spousal abuse, or any crime against women.

Although evidence linking firearm prevalence and violent death is both strong and compelling, firearm issues are among the most contentious in U.S. politics (Hemenway 2004). The gun lobby and other pro-gun advocates continually cite two firearm researchers (and many polemicists) who claim that firearms make us safer, or at least no less safe (Lott 2003; Kleck 1997). Most Internet sites that discuss firearms make repeated claims concerning their benefits for reducing crime and death. Yet the large majority of studies—and all credible studies—show no net benefit from firearms, and usually large social costs.

The gun lobby and pro-gun advocates present a bipolar view of the world: for example, you are either pro-gun or anti-gun. More important, these advocates generally depict people as either violent criminals or decent, law-abiding citizens. According to that worldview, criminals obey no laws and can always obtain firearms whenever they desire. Any firearm law will thus inconvenience only decent, law-abiding citizens, or worse, prevent them from obtaining the firearms they need for protection against violent sociopathic predators. Even with suicide, only two types of people exist: normal people and those who really want to kill themselves and will stop at nothing until they succeed. Firearm laws thus cannot have any effect. Rational firearm policy cannot even reduce accidents, as these are caused by "self-destructive individuals…without guns they would likely find some other way to kill themselves accidentally" (Kopel 1992, 415).

The real world is, of course, much more complex, with many shades of gray. For example, policies that raise the costs of obtaining firearms for criminals, depressed people, and adolescents reduce the likelihood that they will obtain and use them (Hemenway 2004).

The gun lobby claims that an armed citizenry deters crime and that regular citizens are continually protecting themselves with guns and shooting criminals. Yet no credible evidence exists that more guns deter crime. The evidence actually shows the opposite: in all surveys respondents report far more criminal gun uses against them than self-defense uses (Hemenway, Miller, and Azrael 2000; Hemenway 2004).

Some private citizens have undoubtedly benefited by defending themselves with a firearm. Yet most self-defense gun uses reported on private surveys appear to occur during escalating arguments rather than in self-defense against a clear criminal act, and most of these uses appear to be illegal and threaten public safety (Hemenway, Miller, and Azrael 2000). Most gun-owning Americans will never have the opportunity to use their guns against actual robbers or burglars. Untrained in dispute resolution, however, they will have plenty of opportunity to use their guns inappropriately when they are angry, annoyed, tired, drunk, or afraid.

Implicit in the claims of the gun lobby is that people without guns are unarmed and incapable of defending themselves and their property. Yet the large majority of weapon self-defenses occur with weapons other than a firearm. Indeed, homeowners may defend themselves more often with a baseball bat than with a firearm (Hemenway, Miller, and Azrael 2000). Evidence from the National Crime Victimization Surveys indicates that self-defense with any weapon is as likely to prevent an injury as self-defense with a firearm (Kleck and Kates 2001). In any case, the policies suggested by a public health approach to firearms will have little effect on people's ability to protect their homes with a firearm.

The Public Health Approach to Firearms

A public health approach has reduced the burden of infectious disease, tobacco-related illness, and motor vehicle injury, and can also be successful in reducing gun violence. This approach emphasizes prevention, focuses on the community rather than the individual, and encourages collaboration, research, and policies involving many sectors. An important public health insight is that opportunities abound for preventing injuries.

The sharp reduction in motor vehicle injuries over the past fifty years is a public health success story (Hemenway 2001). In the 1950s the traffic safety community focused on the driver. Statistics supposedly showed that driver error caused almost all motor vehicle injuries. Policymakers thus emphasized education and enforcement—training motorists to drive better and fining them when they drove unsafely. Despite these efforts, significant success did not occur until the advent of a more comprehensive approach that did not solely target individual behavior.

For public health experts in the 1950s, the key issue was not which individuals would die in a motor vehicle collision but why over thirty-five thousand fatalities occurred year after year, why some cities and states had higher rates, and why some car makes presented the highest risk. These experts recognized that improving the vehicle and the highway environment would reduce the likelihood of collision more than an exclusive focus on the driver. Over the past forty years cars and roads have become much safer. For example, automobiles now have better braking and a third brake light, roads have better lighting and signage, and interstate highways have been built as limited-access roads with median dividers.

Of prime importance was reducing the likelihood of serious injury once a crash occurred. People are sometimes careless, and they can behave recklessly. But when they do, should they or others die? The goal was to create a system that not only made motorist error less likely, but was also more forgiving when motorists made errors or behaved unlawfully or inappropriately.

The most important traffic safety advances over the past forty years have entailed making motor vehicles safer for human occupants in crashes. For example, we now have collapsible steering columns, airbags, shatterproof windshields, lap and shoulder belts, and non-rupture gas tanks. Roads are also much safer and more forgiving when accidents occur. Many roadside hazards have been eliminated or modified, telephone poles have been removed from the sides of highways, and signs often break away on impact. And improvements in emergency medical services have reduced disabilities caused by crashes. Helicopters now fly the seriously injured to designated trauma centers to receive immediate, high-quality care.

Today's drivers are no better than those of the 1950s—indeed, many believe that road rage has grown along with traffic. Yet motor vehicle fatalities per mile driven have fallen by more than 80 percent. The United States has one of the lowest rates of death per vehicle-mile in the world. The key was reframing the policy question from the fatalistic, "How can we change human nature?" to the realistic, "What are the most cost-effective ways to reduce injury?" (Hemenway 1995). Similarly, while the gun lobby tries to focus exclusively on education and enforcement, injury control practitioners emphasize that directing policy solely to individual users is not cost-effective.

Of course, people should be held accountable for their actions. However, such responsibility pertains not only to gun users but also to gun owners, gun manufacturers, gun distributors, and public officials and other decision makers. The goal of public health is not to find fault. The goal is to prevent mortality and morbidity, and to promote healthy lives.

Only in the mid-1980s did policymakers recognize violence as an important public health issue. In the past twenty years, the public health approach to firearms policy has broadened the discussion from an exclusive criminal justice orientation to one concerned with all firearm injuries, including suicides and unintentional gun deaths. The entry of public health practitioners into the field of firearm injury control has provided new sources of information (including hospital data), new types of statistical analyses (such as odds ratios), new research designs (case-control studies), and many important scientific studies. The public health approach has also attracted new organizations to violence prevention, including the American Academy of Pediatrics. Most important, public health advocates promote science, pragmatism, and optimism in an area long beset by stale polemical debates.

Policy Recommendations

Like the approach to reducing motor vehicle injuries, a public health approach to curtailing problems caused by firearms suggests pursuing a wide variety of policies while maintaining the ability of law-abiding Americans to use guns responsibly. This approach emphasizes the importance of obtaining accurate, detailed, and comparable information each year on the extent and nature of the problem. For each motor vehicle death in the United States, the Fatality Analysis Reporting System collects data on more than one hundred variables, including the make, model, and year of vehicles, speed and speed limit, the location of passengers and whether they were wearing seatbelts, and whether airbags deployed. This information suggests interventions and permits evaluation of which policies are effective and which are not.

A major problem is that detailed national information about firearm injuries does not exist. For example, whether most unintentional firearm injuries occur at home or away from home, or with long guns or handguns, is unknown. Whether adolescents preferentially use certain types of firearms to commit suicide, and whether the percentage of homicides due to inexpensive firearms or assault weapons has been rising or falling, is also unknown.

Many groups have backed the creation of a national violent death reporting system to provide detailed information on all homicides, suicides, and unintentional firearm deaths. The Harvard Injury Control Research Center, working with the Medical College of Wisconsin and others, is coordinating a pilot of this system. Death certificates and reports by medical examiners, police, and crime labs already include this information; it just needs to be assembled consistently. The

Centers for Disease Control and Prevention have funded more than a dozen state health departments to test such a reporting system and are now working to create a comprehensive national system. This is the first step in the public health approach to reducing firearm injuries.

Many other policies directed at gun manufacturers and sellers, firearm owners, and other interested parties could also help reduce firearm injuries.

Manufacturers and Distributors

Although firearms are among the most lethal consumer products, killing tens of thousands of civilians each year, firearm manufacturing is one of the least-regulated industries in the United States. No federal regulatory body has specific authority over firearm manufacturing, which is exempt even from regulation by the Consumer Product Safety Commission. The industry has also escaped any comprehensive examination by Congress. Instead, Congress is considering giving the industry immunity from tort liability for negligence.

A public health approach would create incentives for firearm manufacturers to make products that reduce rather than increase the burden on law enforcement. Rather than producing and promoting firearms that appear primarily designed for criminal use, such as those that do not retain fingerprints, manufacturers could produce guns with unique, tamper-resistant serial numbers. They could also make guns that "fingerprint" each bullet to permit authorities to match bullet and firearm with a high degree of accuracy.

Manufacturers could also improve the safety of their firearms. Unintentional firearm injuries appear to stem partly from a lack of federal safety standards. All firearms could be manufactured so they do not fire when bumped or dropped. Like aspirin bottles, new guns could also readily be made childproof, with minimum trigger pull standards to prevent very young children from shooting them. Since many firearm accidents occur when individuals do not realize a gun is loaded, indicators could alert the user when the gun's chamber contains a bullet, and disconnect devices could prevent a pistol from firing once the user has removed the ammunition magazine, even though a bullet still remains in the firing chamber. The industry could adopt uniform standards for trigger safety mechanisms: the action on some handguns now locks when the manual thumb safety is down, while on others it locks when the thumb safety is up. A lesson from motor vehicles is the key role that can be played by a regulatory agency—with the authority to recall products with hazardous designs and to promote personalized, or smart, guns that only the authorized user can fire.

Gun-making technology is constantly changing. A small but deadly nubugun manufactured in the 1990s looks like a key chain. At the other extreme, recoil compensation mechanisms are making larger-caliber handguns more manageable. Sniper rifles available to civilians can shoot .50-caliber rounds capable of downing helicopters. Caseless ammunition reduces the ability of law enforcement officials to identify a crime weapon by the cartridge left at the scene. Various types of ammunition, such as Glaser safety slugs and flechettes, may create more tissue damage and thus make it more likely that a shooting will result in a death. While Israeli tanks have occasionally fired flechettes—clusters of nail-like projectiles used as anti-personnel weapons—they are controversial because of the danger they pose to civilians. Flechette ammunition can also be used in shotguns and may extend their range and penetrate body armor better than conventional ball shot loads. A regulatory structure could deal quickly and definitively with these and other new technologies that could pose a threat to public safety and health.

The firearm distribution system could also improve. Police stings demonstrate the ease with which felons can obtain firearms directly from licensed dealers. For example, in the Detroit area in 1999, undercover officers acting as prohibited buyers purchased firearms from almost all the dealers they approached. The Bureau of Alcohol, Tobacco, and Firearms, which regulates licensed dealers, could do its job more effectively if given more enforcement authority. For example, ATF agents cannot now pose as felons in sting operations, and serious dealer misconduct is a misdemeanor rather than a felony.

The private sale of firearms is a major loophole in the chain of distribution. Some 40 percent of retail gun sales occur without the involvement of a licensed dealer—at flea markets and gun shows, from car trunks and over the Internet. These sales can occur without background checks, record keeping, or government oversight, making it easy for criminals and terrorists to obtain firearms. Requiring all firearm transfers to pass through licensed dealers, with the required background checks and paper trail, would reduce the enormous flow of firearms to the illegal market.

Investigations of criminal gun use show that adolescents living in states with strict gun-control laws obtain their illegal firearms from states with less restrictive laws. Evidence also shows that a state one-gun-per-month law, which prevents any individual from buying more than one gun each month from any particular dealer, reduces gun running from that state. A national one-gun-per-month law could reduce gun-running across state lines, especially combined with background checks and waiting periods for all sales as well as strong enforcement against scofflaw dealers. Such supply-side restrictions could have an immediate impact on adolescent gun crime; a third of guns used by youth in crime are less than three years old.

Gun Owners

Policies common in other developed countries—registration of handguns, licensing of owners, and background checks for all gun transfers—could reduce the U.S. homicide rate substantially by making it harder for adolescents and criminals to obtain handguns. Such policies would probably have little effect on U.S. rates of assaults, burglary, or robbery, since those crimes usually do not involve guns. Guns are not necessary for most crimes, except perhaps some bank robberies and assassinations. But guns do make crime more lethal.

Illegal-and irresponsible gun-carrying is a major problem in the United States; most gun robberies and gun homicides—particularly of men—occur away from home. Polls show that the majority of Americans do not favor allowing regular citizens to carry firearms. And by more than a ten-to-one margin, Americans do not think regular citizens should be allowed to bring their guns into restaurants, bars, college campuses, hospitals, sports stadiums, or government buildings (Hemenway, Azrael, and Miller 2001). Nonetheless, in the past decade, many states have required police to issue gun-carrying permits to anyone who is not expressly prohibited by statute, even if police have reason to believe that individual may misuse the firearm. Proponents of these policies claim that more gun-carrying by law-abiding citizens will thwart and deter criminals and thus reduce crime. While evidence regarding the effects of these more permissive gun-carrying policies is not conclusive, the best scientific studies suggest that they may increase rather than reduce crime overall (Ayres and Donohue 2003). It is not clear why allowing individuals whom the police want to prohibit from carrying guns to do so should boost public safety.

Parents, Physicians, and Teachers

Although firearm safety experts urge owners to store guns appropriately, many leave their guns loaded even when they are not intended for protection. Many individuals, such as concerned parents, could become more assertive in this arena. Asking about guns and gun storage in the homes that children visit could become as commonplace as ensuring that a child's seatbelt is securely fastened. Women could also become better informed about their own homes. Many women appear to believe—incorrectly—that there are no guns in the house or, if there are, that they are unloaded and locked up (Azrael, Miller, and Hemenway 2000).

Clergy, teachers, labor leaders, and physicians could also take active steps to help reduce our gun problem. For example, psychologists and psychiatrists often treat depressed and manic adolescents, yet many do not even discuss firearms or firearm storage with their parents, even though most adolescents who commit suicide do so with firearms.

The Power of the Gun Lobby

The policies discussed in this chapter should not face Second Amendment barriers. Although the gun lobby claims an individual right to gun ownership, most U.S. courts have found no such right in the U.S. Constitution. For example, the Supreme Court let stand a decision upholding an ordinance in Morton Grove, Illinois, that banned the possession of handguns within its borders. A policy statement of the American Civil Liberties Union, proud defender of the Bill of Rights, states, "The ACLU agrees with the Supreme Court's long-standing interpretation of the Second Amendment that the individual's right to bear arms applies only to the preservation or efficiency of a well-regulated militia....There is no constitutional impediment to the regulation of firearms" (quoted in Hemenway 2004, 159). While many state constitutions provide special protections for gun ownership, the federal constitution provides little more protection for firearms than it does for the ownership of cars, chain saws, or swimming pools, none of which the public health community has a desire to ban.

Polls consistently show that the overwhelming majority of the U.S. public wants reasonable firearm policies. They want tamper-resistant serial numbers for guns, childproof firearms, magazine safeties, background checks for gun sales between private individuals, personalized guns, registration of hand guns, and licensing of gun owners. A solid majority even favors prohibiting citizens from carrying guns. These results are not a passing fancy spurred by school shootings or terrorist bombings, nor are they rigged results that reflect unclear wording of survey questions. Every independent poll, year after year, shows the same results (Smith 2001). The vast majority of the population—and even a majority of gun owners and NRA (National Rifle Association) members—want more government action to make guns safer and keep them out of the wrong hands.

If such policy measures could make a difference and the large majority of Americans desire them, why haven't they been enacted? One reason is the power of special interests in U.S. politics; in this instance, that of the gun lobby. Interestingly, compared with industries such as alcohol and cigarettes, firearm manufacturing and distribution are quite small and employ relatively few people. The power of the gun lobby reflects not so much corporate money as the ability to mobilize grassroots support. Gun leaders do this partly by fomenting fear and anger among gun owners, portraying any minor gun policy initiative as a veiled attempt to confiscate everyone's guns. To prevent this catastrophe, people rally with funds and commitment, preventing the enactment of many reasonable gun laws.

The gun lobby is filled with individuals who are knowledgeable and passionate about guns, and they share a common interest. While the lobby represents only a small minority of gun owners, it still totals some three million members. This lobby can readily mobilize groups of ten or more individuals to attend even the most local political events. By contrast, gun-control groups have smaller memberships, and many members have little knowledge of firearms; their common interest is often only that they or their loved ones were victims of firearm violence. Only a political commitment keeps them together. The rest of the American public—the large majority—hopes that reasonable gun policies are enacted but does not actively work to ensure that result.

Creating a Regulatory Firearm Agency

The public health approach to reducing gun violence emphasizes the need for prevention as well as punishment, recognizes that alterations in the product and the environment are more likely to be effective than attempts to change individual behavior, and urges the pursuit of multiple strategies to tackle the problem. The public health community understands the importance of involving the entire community and sees roles for many groups, including educational institutions, religious organizations, medical associations, and the media.

The concern of public health advocates regarding firearms is similar to its concern about stairs, swimming pools, and motor vehicles: the manufacture and use of such products can affect community safety and well-being. The goal of the public health community is to prevent violence and injury, not to ban swimming pools, motor vehicles, or guns.

Since guns move easily across state boundaries, federal rather than state and local policies will often be the most effective. A useful step might be to endow an agency with the power to regulate firearms as consumer products. The National Highway Traffic Safety Administration (NHTSA) mandates that automobiles have seatbelts and shoulder belts, collapsible steering columns, and shatterproof windshields; a firearm agency could similarly require that firearms are childproof, that pistols have magazine safeties, and that serial numbers are tamper resistant. Just as NHTSA bans unsafe products such as three-wheeled all-terrain vehicles, a firearm agency might ban regular civilian use of caseless ammunition and .50-caliber bullets. Certainly a federal firearm regulatory agency should have the power to require companies to recall defectively designed products. An effective agency would respond rapidly to changes in technology and the marketplace.

An effective agency would also have the ability to promote new technologies that could help make society safer. For example, personalized, or smart, guns that only authorized users can fire could limit criminal use of stolen guns and reduce the chance of unintentional injury to children and adolescents. Improvements in less-lethal firearms—such as tranquilizer and beanbag guns and electric stunphasers—could help prevent deaths and serious injuries in police, civilian, and even criminal shootings. All adults, including gun owners, should be responsible for their behavior. Motorists in the United States must obtain a driver's license and register their automobiles. Other industrialized nations commonly license gun owners and register all handguns. Their experience suggests that these measures may help reduce firearm violence.

Not only gun owners and users but also gun dealers and manufacturers have responsibilities. Some gun dealers do not act in a socially responsible way, and government regulators need to bring the dealers under greater scrutiny. To help ensure that inappropriate people cannot easily obtain firearms, every gun transfer should occur through a licensed dealer, after a background check.

The public health approach does not focus on finding fault; it emphasizes prevention. The threat of punishment can deter criminals, and incarceration can help prevent them from harming other members of society; criminal justice (like tort law) is part of the prevention package—but only one part. Instead of looking exclusively at the pathologies of hundreds of thousands of perpetrators and victims of firearm violence and injuries, public health advocates try to understand why these events occur year after year, and to determine how best to break the cycle.

The first step is to obtain detailed, consistent data each year on the extent of the problem. Like NHTSA's national data system, a national violent death reporting system could provide detailed information on the circumstances surrounding all fatal shootings, information that is crucial for evaluating regulations. Such data should be readily available to all, along with funds for scientific research.

Accurate data and good science are usually critical for ensuring success in public health; reliable information helps change social norms. For example, before science showed the dangers to public health, spitting on the subway was acceptable and smoking was sophisticated. It is time to change the norm that accepts gun violence as a routine part of American life. Fortunately, more and more Americans are seeing firearm violence as a uniquely U.S. problem—and one that a public health approach can tackle.

Acknowledgments

The Robert Wood Johnson Foundation, the Joyce Foundation, the Packard Foundation, and the Open Society Institute helped fund this research.

References

Ayres, I., and J. J. Donohue III. 2003. Shooting Down the "More Guns Less Crime" Hypothesis. *Stanford Law Review* 55: 1193–1312, 1371–1386.

Azrael, D., and D. Hemenway. 2000. "In the Safety of Your Own Home": Results from a National Survey on Gun Use at Home. *Social Science and Medicine* 50: 258–291.

Azrael, D., M. Miller, and D. Hemenway. 2000. Are Household Firearms Stored Safely? It Depends on Whom You Ask. *Pediatrics* 106: e31.

Bailey, J. E., A. L. Kellermann, G. W. Somes, et al. 1997. Risk Factors for Violent Death of Women in the Home. *Archives of Internal Medicine* 157: 777–782.

Brent, D. A. 2001. Firearms and Suicide. *Annals of the New York Academy of Sciences* 932: 225–239.

Centers for Disease Control and Prevention (CDC). 1997. Rates of Homicide, Suicide, and Firearm-Related Death among Children: 26 Industrialized Countries. *Morbidity and Mortality Weekly Report* 46 (February 7): 101–105.

Hemenway, D. 1995. Guns, Public Health, and Public Safety. In *Guns and the Constitution: The Myth of Second Amendment Protection for Firearms in America*, ed. D. A. Henigan, E. B. Nicholson, and D. Hemenway. Northampton, MA: Aletheia Press.

———. 2001. The Public Health Approach to Motor Vehicles, Tobacco, and Alcohol, with Applications to Firearms Policy. *Journal of Public Health Policy* 22: 381–402.

———. 2004. *Private Guns, Public Health*. Ann Arbor: University of Michigan Press.

Hemenway, D., and M. Miller. 2000. Firearm Availability and Homicide Rates across 26 High-Income Countries. *Journal of Trauma* 49: 985–988.

———. 2002. The Association of Rates of Household Handgun Ownership, Lifetime Major Depression, and Serious Suicidal Thoughts with Rates of Suicide across U.S. Census Regions. *Injury Prevention* 8: 313–316.

Hemenway, D., B. P. Kennedy, I. Kawachi, and R. D. Putnam. 2001. Firearm Prevalence and Social Capital. *Annals of Epidemiology* 11: 484–490.

Hemenway, D., D. Azrael, and M. Miller. 2001. National Attitudes concerning Gun-Carrying in the United States. *Injury Prevention* 7: 282–285.

Hemenway, D., M. Miller, and D. Azrael. 2000. Gun Use in the United States: Results from Two National Surveys. *Injury Prevention* 49: 985–988.

Hemenway, D., T. Shinoda-Tagawa, and M. Miller. 2002. Firearm Availability and Female Homicide Victimization across 25 Populous High-Income Countries. *Journal of the American Medical Women's Association* 57: 1–5.

Hepburn, L., and D. Hemenway. 2004. Firearm Availability and Homicide: A Review of the Literature. *Aggression and Violent Behavior* 9: 417–440.

Kellermann, A. L., and J. A. Mercy. 1992. Men, Women, and Murder: Gender-Specific Differences in Rates of Fatal Violence and Victimization. *Journal of Trauma* 33: 1–5.

Kleck, G. 1997. *Targeting Guns: Firearms and Their Control*. Hawthorne, NY: Aldine de Gruyter.

Kleck, G., and D. B. Kates. 2001. *Armed: New Perspectives on Gun Control*. New York: Prometheus Books.

Kopel, D. B. 1992. *The Samurai, the Mountie, and the Cowboy: Should America Adopt the Gun Controls of Other Democracies?* Buffalo, NY: Prometheus Books.

Lott, J. R., Jr. 2003. *The Bias against Guns*. Washington, DC: Regnery Press.

Ludwig, J., and P. J. Cook, eds. 2003. *Evaluating Gun Policy*. Washington, DC: Brookings Institution.

Miller, M., and D. Hemenway. 1999. The Relationship between Firearms and Suicide: A Review of the Literature. *Aggression and Violent Behavior* 4: 59–75.

Miller, M., D. Azrael, and D. Hemenway. 2001. Firearm Availability and Unintentional Firearm Deaths. *Accident Analysis and Prevention* 33: 477–484.

———. 2002a. Firearm Availability and Unintentional Firearm Deaths, Suicides, and Homicides among 5- to 14-Year-Olds. *Journal of Trauma* 52: 267–275.

———. 2002b. Firearm Availability and Unintentional Firearm Deaths, Suicide, and Homicide among Women. *Journal of Urban Health* 79: 26–38.

———. 2002c. Household Firearm Ownership Levels and Homicide across U.S. States and Regions, 1988–1997. *American Journal of Public Health* 92: 1988–1993.

———. 2002d. Household Firearm Ownership Levels and Suicide across U.S. Regions and States, 1988–1997. *Epidemiology* 13: 517–524.

———. 2004. The Epidemiology of Case-Fatality Rates for Suicide in the Northeast. *Annals of Emergency Medicine* 43: 723–730.

Smith, T. W. 2001. *National Gun Policy Survey of the National Opinion Research Center: Research Findings*. Chicago: National Opinion Research Center.

CHAPTER 7

Tobacco Policy in the United States

LESSONS FOR THE OBESITY EPIDEMIC

※

KENNETH E. WARNER

On June 16, 2004, cigarette smoking killed some twelve hundred Americans. That shocking death toll warranted no headlines. Neither did the same outcome—some twelve hundred more deaths—the following day, nor the day after. Indeed, it is the rare headline that informs the public that smoking accounts for nearly one of every five deaths in the United States, one in three during middle age. Smoking is simply too commonplace, too mundane. Yet it is far and away the nation's—and increasingly the world's—leading killer. In this chapter I examine the burden smoking has imposed on society and what we have learned in attempting to deal with that burden. I then consider lessons drawn from this experience for addressing the most rapidly growing behavioral cause of chronic disease: the epidemic of obesity, the only behavior that threatens to overtake smoking as a cause of death.

The Toll of Smoking

Cigarette smoking currently kills over four hundred thousand Americans annually. The vast majority are long-time smokers—smoking kills about half of lifelong smokers—but thousands are nonsmokers, victims of exposure to smoke from other people's cigarettes (U.S. Department of Health and Human Services 1989; Samet 2001; Glantz and Parmley 1995).

The lethal danger lies in the chemical stew that is cigarette smoke and the frequency with which it is inhaled. Cigarette smoke consists of more than four thousand chemical compounds, including arsenic, hydrogen cyanide, formaldehyde, benzene, naphthalene, vinyl chloride, lead, polonium-210, cadmium, ammonia, carbon monoxide, and, of course, nicotine. More than forty of the chemical compounds in smoke are known carcinogens. Taking about ten puffs per cigarette, a pack-a-day smoker inhales this potpourri of chemicals 200 times daily, or 73,000 times per year. Over a lifetime of fifty years of smoking, a pack-a-day smoker inhales 3.65 million times, having consumed more than a third of a million cigarettes. There may be no greater testimony to the strength of the human organism than the fact that roughly half of lifelong smokers survive this remarkable chemical assault.

The vast majority of smokers begin smoking as children, when they have no conception of their own mortality and every expectation that they will not continue to smoke as adults. For at least half, this expectation will not be realized, for they quickly become addicted. As smokers grow into adulthood and fail to quit, cognitive dissonance kicks in, allowing them to believe that the dangers of smoking are exaggerated and that, in any case, the dangers are not relevant to them personally. Smokers—especially heavy smokers—systematically underestimate the risks they are incurring (Weinstein 2001).

On surveys, over 70 percent of smokers report that they would like to quit, yet only about 2.5 percent succeed in doing so each year, and these are disproportionately the most educated. Because both quitting and initiation rates reflect educational status, smoking has progressively become concentrated in lower socioeconomic groups that may have less motivation and fewer resources with which to quit. Thus, while only 9 percent of survey respondents with a postgraduate degree smoke today, 29 percent of people lacking a high school degree are smokers (Warner and Burns 2003).

Given the adverse publicity about smoking and social disapproval, remaining smokers may constitute "hard-core" individuals unable or unwilling to quit. The issue is controversial—quit rates have not declined—but evidence is accumulating that future efforts to reduce smoking may require new and more effective methods (Warner and Burns 2003).

The Antismoking Campaign

The modern assault on smoking began in earnest following publication of epidemiological studies linking smoking to lung cancer in the early 1950s, with major health organizations leading efforts to involve the government in a public stance against smoking (U.S. Department of Health and Human Services 1989). Publicity surrounding the publication of the first surgeon general's report on smoking and health in January 1964 was so intense that per capita cigarette sales plummeted 15 percent by March of that year (U.S. Public Health Service 1964). By year's end the decline measured 5 percent after sales recovered, but the drop was significant when measured against the nearly annual increases that had occurred since the beginning of the century. The year 1963, it turned out, marked the pinnacle of cigarette consumption in this country.

One indicator of the success of the antismoking campaign is the fact that adult per capita consumption (total cigarettes divided by the population over seventeen years of age) declined from forty-two hundred in 1963 to two thousand in 2001. The U.S. antismoking campaign divides into three phases, the first occurring predominantly through the early 1970s.

The Campaign's First Phase: Public Education and Exhortations to Quit

The naïve expectation of public health campaigners was that, newly informed about the dangers of smoking, smokers would see the error of their ways and quit.

Educated kids would not start. This proved both more difficult and less successful than expected. Through the 1960s, cigarette advertising dominated the airwaves and filled magazine pages. In striking contrast, the public health community, with meager resources, had to rely on news coverage, donated space for antismoking messages, and pleas to school boards to incorporate antismoking education into health curricula.

Two policy developments gave the antismoking message newfound prominence. Shortly after the release of the 1964 surgeon general's report (itself a prime example of public information), and prompted by the Federal Trade Commission, Congress mandated that "one side" of cigarette packs include a health warning label beginning in 1966. Although research later questioned the effectiveness of these warnings, coverage of the debate and the novelty of the warnings themselves undoubtedly had some early impact (U.S. Department of Health and Human Services 1989).

Around the same time, the Federal Communications Commission ruled that its Fairness Doctrine should apply to broadcast advertising of cigarettes. Developed to ensure a diversity of views on political issues, the Fairness Doctrine required broadcasters to donate airtime to the "other side" of controversial issues to produce "balance." The commission concluded that smoking was then a controversial issue and that the heavy presence of cigarette ads demanded a countervailing force. As a result, broadcasters were required to donate airtime to antismoking messages.

The Fairness Doctrine affected broadcasters from mid-1967 through the end of 1970. At their peak, antismoking messages received approximately one minute of airtime for every three minutes of cigarette advertising. Research showed that the novel Fairness Doctrine ads depressed cigarette consumption far more than cigarette ads increased it. Adult per capita cigarette consumption declined during all four years that the antismoking ads aired—the first time in history that per capita consumption had fallen more than two years in a row. And two-year declines had occurred only twice before: during the Great Depression and following the first epidemiological research linking smoking to lung cancer (Warner 1979).

Supported, quietly, by the cigarette industry—which fully appreciated the devastating effect of the Fairness Doctrine ads on sales—Congress banned cigarette ads from radio and TV effective January 2, 1971. This removed the need for broadcasters to donate time to the antismoking message, and the volume of antismoking ads plummeted. Per capita consumption rose for the next three years—the first, and last, multiple-year increase since publication of the surgeon general's 1964 report.

The public health community responded in part by adopting a more aggressive—but still publicity-based—approach to reducing smoking, one inaugurated in the Fairness Doctrine ads. From informing smokers about the dangers of smoking in the 1960s, the strategy shifted in the early 1970s toward exhorting smokers to quit, in part by attempting to embarrass or shame them into doing so. Antismoking "marketers" portrayed smoking as antisocial and stupid; they made a mockery of smoking and often smokers. Such marketers also appealed to smokers' concern for their loved ones by disseminating images of young children, often with tears in their eyes, begging their parents to quit.

The first decade of the antismoking campaign yielded mixed results. Per capita cigarette consumption had leveled off, and research indicated that per capita consumption would have continued to rise without the campaign, reaching 20–30 percent higher by 1975 (Warner 1977). Yet these aggregate figures masked developments that created cause for concern. One of the most striking effects of the campaign was its differential impact on smokers depending on their education. In the mid-1960s, smoking prevalence varied little by educational attainment. Shortly thereafter a gap emerged, with prevalence declining steadily among the nation's most educated population but changing little among the least educated. This gap widened over the years (Warner and Burns 2003).

The message was clear, if not then widely appreciated: education and exhortation were working for the educated populace; the strategy was failing for the less educated. Overall, the campaign had succeeded in stabilizing smoking but not in achieving the major declines its leaders had expected. Some smokers were responding to the antismoking message but many were not. Given the steady rise of smoking among women during the decade preceding the antismoking campaign, mortality was rising (U.S. Department of Health and Human Services 1989). All was not well.

The Campaign's Second Phase: The Nonsmokers' Rights Movement

In a 1972 report, Surgeon General Jesse Steinfeld observed that cigarette smoke might damage nonsmokers' health (U.S. Department of Health, Education, and Welfare 1972). This was the first official mention of the possibility, and one of the few cases where a surgeon general's report "scooped the field." Significant scientific evidence that environmental tobacco smoke (ETS) harmed the health of nonsmokers did not emerge until a decade later (U.S. Department of Health and Human Services 1989). Since then, a wealth of studies has shown that cigarette smoke causes lung cancer in heavily exposed but otherwise healthy nonsmoking adults, also likely causes a large number of heart disease deaths, and damages the respiratory function and health of children (Glantz and Parmley 1995). Based on the scientific evidence, in 1992 the Environmental Protection Agency declared ETS a Class A carcinogen (U.S. Environmental Protection Agency 1992). If the association with heart disease proves causal, as appears likely, environmental tobacco smoke may induce forty thousand to fifty thousand deaths per year, placing involuntary or passive smoking just behind active smoking, obesity, and alcohol as the leading behavior-related causes of death in our society.

While the scientific evidence on ETS dates from the early 1980s, public concern—first with the "fairness" of nonsmokers being exposed to ETS and then with its health effects—emerged much earlier. In 1973 Arizona adopted the first modern state law restricting smoking in public places for public health reasons. Two years later Minnesota adopted the first comprehensive clean indoor air law. Other states rapidly followed suit, with laws growing more restrictive over time. Today forty-five states have some restrictions on the books. The latest trend is toward banning smoking completely in restaurants and bars, mandatory, as of this writing, in five states and dozens of cities and counties.

The nonsmokers' rights movement is the most sustained and in many ways most transforming phase of the antismoking campaign. Now spanning three decades, this phase converted smoking from a socially acceptable behavior to one pursued by social pariahs. Clean indoor air laws and associated private policies (smoking prohibitions in businesses, no-smoking policies in private homes) have both followed and contributed to the evolution of a nonsmoking ethos. Clearly, the majority support required to pass a law derives in some fundamental way from the will and support of the public. But the growing presence of such laws itself transforms public attitudes toward smoking.

The proportion of the citizenry stating that they prohibit smoking in their own homes has risen dramatically, following the adoption of public policies on clean indoor air. These private policies serve as a major indicator of the social attitude toward smoking, especially since their growth has considerably exceeded the rate of decline in smoking prevalence (Soliman, Pollack, and Warner 2004). More visible, and equally compelling, is the rash of state laws and city and county ordinances prohibiting smoking in all restaurants and bars.

Prohibitions on indoor smoking, intended to protect the health and rights of nonsmokers, have succeeded (Hopkins et al. 2001). An additional impact—one not publicly anticipated by those urging their adoption—is a rise in the rate of smoking cessation. Studies principally comparing workplaces with and without smoking prohibitions consistently find higher rates of cessation among employees in firms prohibiting smoking (Fichtenberg and Glantz 2002). That impact ranks clean indoor air laws and policies as among the most effective tobacco-control policy measures available.

The Campaign's Third Phase: Comprehensive State Tobacco-Control Programs

In 1988, California activists successfully passed an initiative raising the state's cigarette excise tax by twenty-five cents per pack, with some $100 million of the new revenues dedicated annually to tobacco control. Thus was born the first comprehensive state-based tobacco-control program. Through an aggressive antismoking media campaign, support and passage of strong local clean indoor air ordinances, support of telephone stop-smoking hotlines, and other initiatives, the California program led to declines in per capita consumption well above those in the rest of the nation. Declining smoking-related mortality rates were also associated with the program (Farrelly, Pechacek, and Chaloupka 2003; Glantz and Balbach 2000).

In 1992, Massachusetts successfully followed with a similar ballot initiative raising the state's cigarette excise tax by a quarter per pack, with a portion of the revenues used to create the Massachusetts Tobacco Control Program. Like the California experience, the Massachusetts program is credited with producing significant declines in smoking among both children and adults. Several other states have now developed comprehensive programs of their own, including Arizona, Oregon, Maine, and Alaska. National initiatives launched by the National Cancer Institute, American Cancer Society, and The Robert Wood Johnson Foundation have provided funding to most states to begin tobacco-control programs (Farrelly, Pechacek, and Chaloupka 2003).

The Centers for Disease Control and Prevention (CDC) concluded that comprehensive state-based programs are an effective and cost-effective means of controlling tobacco use and of achieving significant public health gains. CDC developed a guide to comprehensive state programs, identifying nine components and estimating state-specific funding needs (Centers for Disease Control and Prevention 1999). The Institute of Medicine has also endorsed comprehensive programs as a cost-effective investment in public health (National Cancer Policy Board 2000), and a recent econometric analysis reveals a clear association between states' tobacco-control investments and ensuing declines in smoking (Farrelly, Pechacek, and Chaloupka 2003).

For a brief historical moment, the air was filled not with smoke but with optimism that soon all states would mount credible, comprehensive tobacco-control programs. In 1998, the state attorneys general announced a settlement of their Medicaid lawsuits against the tobacco industry (the Master Settlement Agreement, or MSA), which included an unprecedented payout of $206 billion to forty-six states over a twenty-five-year period. Four other states had settled individually with the industry prior to MSA; the total payout from both efforts came to $246 billion. The attorneys general most heavily involved in the MSA negotiations envisioned that all states would dedicate a significant proportion of the settlement funds to an aggressive assault on youth smoking.

Such was not to be. Although a few states used settlement funding for tobacco control, only a handful ever achieved CDC's minimum funding level for a comprehensive program. Instead, states devoted the vast majority of the money to other purposes, ranging from education to road repair. More recently, many states have drawn on their future MSA payments to help cover large budget deficits. Massachusetts has cut its model program by 90 percent. California's program, which often struggled with a legislature intent on redirecting excise tax revenues, has found the problem intensifying as the state grapples with the nation's largest state deficit. The national funding initiatives are drying up.

It is far too early to declare the demise of the era of comprehensive state tobacco-control programs; in a rebounding economy the tobacco-control community's numbers, sophistication, and influence could revitalize these efforts. But it is also clear that the promise of the California and Massachusetts experiments cannot come to full realization nationwide under these circumstances. From the heady days of the mid- to late-1990s, the antismoking campaign has entered an uncertain, uncomfortable, and mostly discouraging period, with abundant resources having disappeared as precipitously as they appeared on the scene just a few years ago.

The Tobacco Lawsuits

The state lawsuits, and the resulting MSA, constituted one highly visible component of lawsuits that have dotted the tobacco-control landscape for years. The lawsuits themselves divide into three distinct "waves" (Rabin 2001). The most recent wave—which includes the state suits and a variety of class-action lawsuits—has clearly changed the face of tobacco control in the United States and abroad.

The suits have exerted a profound impact on multiple aspects of smoking and health. Electronic publication of lawsuit-generated internal documents has created a treasure trove of facts and incriminating statements. The MSA has raised cigarette prices, restricted marketing, and created a national countermarketing campaign. Other suits have occasionally even threatened the manufacturers with the prospect of financial ruin.

These impacts notwithstanding, with the exception of the MSA, much of the lawsuits' potential to affect smoking still lies in the future. Verdicts favoring plaintiffs will have to survive a lengthy appeals process to impose a truly substantial financial burden on cigarette manufacturers, one that would force prices up dramatically or even cause the manufacturers to seek protection from bankruptcy. It remains to be seen whether, collectively, the lawsuits will fundamentally alter the landscape of tobacco use in the future or merely constitute a fascinating (and temporally important) chapter in tobacco control history.

Other Dimensions of the Antismoking Campaign

Preeminent among other facets of the campaign has been cigarette taxation. Raising cigarette prices, primarily through taxation, is one of the most effective policy tools to reduce smoking, and a popular one (Chaloupka et al. 2000). Raising the tax rate allows legislators to do good while doing well: while decreasing the health burdens of smoking, a tax increase also boosts government revenues.

Congress has raised the federal cigarette tax infrequently and only modestly, a reflection of the influence of tobacco states. An increase in the federal tax also reduces state revenues: the tax induces quitting, while a state's take per pack has not changed. Absent some quid pro quo, states thus oppose increases in the federal cigarette tax.

In contrast, tax increases have been frequent in many states and have resulted in high per-pack taxes in some; as of July 1, 2003, New Jersey tops the list, with a tax of $2.05 per pack. Thirteen other states (and the District of Columbia) have tax rates of $1.00 or more per pack. (New York City imposes a $1.50 tax per pack in addition to the state's $1.50 tax.) Historically, state tax increases have come (and gone) in waves. From 1964 through 1972, numerous states increased their taxes, causing the real price of cigarettes to rise substantially. Over the next decade, concerns that tax-induced interstate price differences were fostering cigarette smuggling from low- to high-priced states led to a period of few increases; real prices actually fell. Taxes and prices cycled back up and then down again. In very recent years prices have risen substantially, the result of MSA-induced price increases (used to fund the state payments required of the industry) and a new spate of state tax increases responding to burgeoning state deficits. Cigarette consumption has always varied inversely with real price.

Antismoking efforts also include restrictions on cigarette sales to or purchases by youth, restrictions on advertising, modification of warning labels, and so on. An effective tool, inaugurated during the Fairness Doctrine period in the late 1960s, is the use of media countermarketing. Several states have made media campaigns a centerpiece of their efforts. The MSA included a provision that led to a national media campaign known as "Truth." Evidence from these experiences supports the proposition that well-designed, well-funded, and sustained counteradvertising campaigns can have a significant impact on smoking among both youth and adults (Farrelly, Niederdeppe, and Yarsevich 2003).

The Anti-antismoking Campaign: The Role of the Tobacco Industry

No discussion of the antismoking campaign would be complete without recognition of the obstructionist role of the tobacco industry. The industry has worked hard and often successfully to deceive the public about the dangers of smoking, silence critics, and buy the silence of potential critics such as the media. The industry has also used financial largesse to enlist organizational allies to develop the charade of grassroots opposition to tobacco-control measures, and again relied on deep pockets to develop close-knit relationships with legislators who block public health measures designed to reduce smoking (Advocacy Institute 1998).

The campaign of deception dates from a 1954 industry ad entitled "A Frank Statement to Cigarette Smokers" (Tobacco Industry Research Committee 1954). The ad assured the American public that the companies "accept an interest in people's health as a basic responsibility, paramount to every other consideration in our business. . . . We always have and always will cooperate closely with those whose task it is to safeguard the public health." Internal industry documents reveal that the "frank statement" represented the first step in a public relations campaign to deny the dangers of smoking and challenge the public health establishment at every turn.

As recently as 1994, the CEOs of all the nation's major cigarette companies testified before Congress that they did not believe that smoking was addictive and did not know that it caused fatal disease. Their own scientists and lawyers had known both facts for decades and had been consistently telling them so.

Today the cigarette companies are trying to present a "new face" to the public. They acknowledge the dangers and addictiveness of smoking and claim, much as they did in 1954, that they want to cooperate with public health authorities to keep kids off cigarettes and help smokers who wish to quit to do so. The tobacco-control community is justifiably skeptical.

Evaluating the Antismoking Campaign and Its Future

The numerous, disparate, and uncoordinated efforts to combat smoking—public sector and private, institutional and individual—that constitute America's national antismoking campaign have produced a remarkable record of public health success. As a result of the campaign, smoking prevalence has fallen by nearly half. Extrapolating from earlier research, one can conclude that, had the antismoking campaign never occurred, well over 100 million U.S. adults would have smoked in 2003—in contrast with fewer than half that number who actually did smoke. In 2001 Americans consumed two thousand cigarettes per adult. Had the campaign never materialized, the figure would be in the vicinity of six thousand cigarettes. Literally millions of Americans have each enjoyed an average of fifteen to twenty additional years of life as a result of their decisions not to smoke or to quit in response to the campaign. No other public health movement in the past half-century has produced comparable health benefits.

At the same time, 45 million Americans continue to smoke, despite a highly unsupportive social environment. Beyond the resulting deaths, additional millions live with smoking-induced emphysema, heart disease, and cancer. The continuing presence of smoking serves as a stark reminder of the tenacity of nicotine addiction, both for individuals and historically. In the late sixteenth century, Turkish Sultan Murad IV decreed tobacco smoking punishable by death. This rather austere to-bacco-control policy (the first to prove that smoking was, in fact, hazardous to health) did not stop smoking in Turkey. It is perhaps not surprising, therefore, that our own smoker-unfriendly environment is not sufficient to clear the air.

Indeed, a few tobacco-control leaders are now contemplating a next phase for the antismoking campaign: an era of harm reduction. Harm reduction entails offering inveterate smokers—those who cannot or will not quit—the option of switching from cigarette smoking to a hopefully less hazardous form of ingesting nicotine. The notion of harm reduction is highly controversial (Martin, Warner, and Lantz 2004). But its serious consideration reflects the continuing burden of smoking, the fact that notwithstanding the enormity of its accomplishments, the antismoking campaign remains a long way from victory.

Lessons for Public Health

Tobacco-control successes would multiply if proponents could apply lessons from the experience elsewhere in public health. All too often, the public health "community" functions as a series of isolated silos, each enclosing advocates and professionals dedicated to a single issue, such as unprotected sex, lack of exercise, or tobacco. Those who do make occasional forays outside their silos often produce useful insights.

Tobacco and alcohol abuse—seemingly a natural set of subjects for cross-fertilization—have benefited from such interdigitation on occasion, but far less often than one might expect. And those interactions that have occurred have been only partially productive. Advocates in the alcohol field relied heavily on the to-bacco-control experience in securing congressional legislation mandating alcohol warning labels. The tobacco experience indicated, however, that small labels placed in obscure locations were not likely to be effective. Yet the alcohol label is itself small, wordy, and more obscure than any cigarette label. Did advocates of alcohol labels ignore the evidence, or did they believe, as one concluded, that it was not the labels per se that mattered, but rather the "noise" in Congress and the media surrounding debate over legislation?

On the other side of the exchange, tobacco-control advocates drew on the alcohol-control community's experience to push for state laws prohibiting minors from buying cigarettes. Such laws are now universal throughout the country. But their effectiveness relies on enforcement, something the experience with alcohol should have taught. Only recently has the tobacco-control community begun to address the enforcement issue aggressively, but with mixed success. As the alcohol example demonstrated long ago, even reasonably well-enforced minimum-age-of-purchase laws cannot stop minors from acquiring a product (Wakefield and Giovino 2003).

Reflecting the many decades of experience with the antismoking campaign, tobacco control likely has more to offer other domains of public health than they have to offer it. Many lessons are direct and self-evident, and many have been applied. Taxation as a successful deterrent to teen smoking has had applications in alcohol taxation, for example. A congressional hearing several years ago focused on taxation of cigarettes and bullets, the latter seen as a (small) deterrent to gun violence. Most recently, the novel and successful experience with state and class-action tobacco lawsuits generated a similarly reasoned legal assault on guns. Today the intellectual leaders of the tobacco lawsuit strategy provide direct guidance to lawyers and nutrition experts exploring the use of lawsuits against the food industry to address America's burgeoning obesity epidemic.

That epidemic has all the signs of becoming America's next tobacco crisis. Thus it seems particularly appropriate to explore how the tobacco-control experience might inform the public health assault on the country's newest epidemic.

Lessons from the Antismoking Campaign for Controlling Obesity

Today's obesity epidemic bears a striking resemblance to the tobacco epidemic at mid-century in many ways. Driven by both biology and behavior, the product of an environment that seduces and induces abuse (consider junk food and fast-food advertising directed at children), the rising tide of excess weight has created the second-greatest source of preventable, premature mortality in our society. With smoking on the decline and obesity rising rapidly, the latter may soon overtake the former as a cause of death (Centers for Disease Control and Prevention 2003).

Biologically, humans are hard-wired to seek out high-calorie, fatty foods. Whenever our early ancestors captured animal prey, they stuffed themselves to survive the long periods when they would go without. In an era of plentiful, inexpensive, and easily accessible food, much of it laden with fat, we continue to crave the tastes that permitted our ancestors to survive and now threaten our health. Eating occurs in a "toxic environment" that fosters the now-counterproductive behavior of bingeing on fatty, high-calorie foods (Brownell and Horgen 2003).

Economic and social factors create a real challenge for most people to avoid overeating. Food manufacturers find it especially profitable to advertise sugary cereals and fast-food meals to children. Budget-challenged school systems contract for corporate food sponsorships and vending in exchange for new resources. Low prices make unhealthy manufactured foods far more affordable than fresh produce. The economics of food preparation lead to gigantic portions in restaurants. In their convenience and low cost, attractive and ubiquitous fast-food restaurants easily compete with work-stressed parents intending to prepare meals at home. The information-age work environment has greatly diminished physical activity, which burned off calories. Suburban sprawl makes walking and biking endangered modes of transportation. What's more, like smoking today, obesity disproportionately afflicts the most disenfranchised members of society. The poor care more about food prices, have less access to fresh produce, and find dangerous streets and lack of fitness facilities deterrents to regular exercise.

As an epidemic, obesity has become a national concern only recently. The response has a familiar ring to students of the early phases of the antismoking campaign. Efforts are inaugurated to educate the public about healthy eating habits and the need for regular physical exercise. Calls for parental responsibility dominate responses to children's lust for fast food. Discussions about limiting food advertising on children's TV shows reappear. Leading food manufacturers and purveyors are urged to produce and promote healthy food. The government seeks to collaborate with the industry in finding solutions. Advocates call for more informative labeling of manufactured food products and new labeling of restaurant meals.

Like the first phase of the antismoking campaign, the obesity-prevention information and exhortation effort will win converts. Some people—primarily drawn from the most highly educated segment of society—will take (and indeed have taken) public health messages to heart and will modify their behavior accordingly. In the face of nearly overwhelming social forces, however, the odds of a substantial turnaround are low. As long as it persists in its current form, the "toxic environment" will poison efforts to make "individual responsibility" an important answer to the problem. Consider the challenge confronting well-intentioned parents who wish to guide their children toward a healthy diet. What those children hear from their parents contradicts what they see on TV and billboards, what they are offered in school, and what their friends consume.

A principal implication is that education, exhortation, and the theme of individual responsibility cannot do it all, as they could not with tobacco. In particular, they are likely to have the least impact on those most burdened—people mired in poverty. More assertive public policy interventions will be needed, many possibly of a regulatory nature. The public health community will have to confront the toxic environment directly, in a manner that risks creating an adversarial relationship with the food industry. This will be a source of discomfort for many people on both sides. Furthermore, as the tobacco-control experience recommends, public health forces will need to develop multipronged and comprehensive strategies, and remain for the long haul (Mercer et al. 2003). Indeed, in a public health battle against a behavior-related health problem, be it obesity, smoking, illicit drugs, teen pregnancy, or gun violence, "victories" are tallied by the reduction in damage wrought, not by the final conquest of the risk factor in question.

The similarities between the early assault on tobacco and the contemporary attack on obesity raise an intriguing question: Must a full-fledged public health campaign begin with the least combative and coercive intervention—information— before launching into an adversarial mode? To persuade disinterested but necessary parties that more assertive methods are essential, proponents may need to try this most "reasonable" of all approaches first. However, the obesity campaign seems to be mixing more assertive, even combative, elements of a public health campaign with multiparty "discussion" of the problem. For example, prominent activists and scientists have called for and, in some instances, achieved "snack taxes." Their interest in using an excise tax to simultaneously deter unhealthy eating and raise funds to combat it derives directly from the successes of cigarette taxation. Calls for bans on food advertising aimed at children also resemble tobacco-control strategies, as do efforts to remove soft drink sponsorship from schools.

An excise tax on "bad foods" deserves explicit attention, especially if it can be combined with a food subsidy program for the poor that facilitates purchase of "good foods" such as fresh produce. The tax-and-subsidy combination is attractive for both practical and political reasons. Practically, the tax would raise revenues to support a food subsidy program that, in budget-strapped times, likely could not be sold without a new revenue source. The tax would also likely discourage junk-food eating more among the price-sensitive poor than among the rich. Meanwhile, subsidizing the purchase of fresh produce for the poor would allow substitution of now less expensive fruits and vegetables for now more expensive snack foods. The availability of "fresh produce food stamps" could dramatically boost the number of retail outlets selling fresh produce in the nation's inner cities. The paucity of retail availability of fresh produce constitutes a significant barrier to healthy diets among poor people. Selling a snack tax may be far easier if revenues are designated to help the poor, especially poor children, secure healthier diets. One survey after another has found that Americans are especially supportive of cigarette taxes if revenues are earmarked for programs designed to prevent youth smoking.

Targeting population subgroups with interventions believed to be more effective for them is likely to emerge as an important feature of the national attack on obesity. In the early antismoking movement, campaigners failed to distinguish between high- and low-education smokers, for example, and between African American and white smokers. Over time we learned which interventions had the most impact on which subgroups. Early media campaigns worked best with educated white smokers. Later media campaigns targeted different socioeconomic and ethnic groups. California's campaign, for example, included messages developed specifically for Hispanics, Koreans, and African Americans.

Success with antismoking countermarketing recommends using the media to sell healthy eating behaviors. A large, sustained, professionally developed media campaign could provide at least a modicum of competition for pervasive enticements to consume soft drinks, cookies, candy bars, potato chips, and fast-food meals. The tobacco-control experience emphasizes that a campaign that is poorly funded, of short duration, and prepared by well-meaning amateurs is unlikely to have much impact. Reliance on donated airtime will not work. Scores of worthy causes compete for scarce public-service announcement spots. Substantial financing would have to be secured to mount an effective campaign, probably on the order of $100 million or more annually. Snack taxes could contribute here, too—a modest national tax could generate billions of dollars—as might voluntary "goodwill" contributions from food manufacturers, many of whom would have a direct financial interest in moving America's dietary habits in a salutary direction.

The fact that some food producers might participate in such an endeavor suggests a potentially fundamental difference between the tobacco and obesity cases. Smoking-prevention campaigns often portray tobacco companies as exploiting the young. Through media portrayals, as well as news conferences and congressional hearings, the tobacco-control community strives to reveal companies' disinterest in the futures of their young victims. Many food manufacturers are inextricably linked to Big Tobacco—Kraft owns Nabisco, and Philip Morris (recently renamed Altria) owns Kraft, for example—and it is easy to see them as driven by similar greed and disdain for the customer.

The situations are not entirely the same, however. Food manufacturers produce low-fat versions of their traditional products and, increasingly, trans-fat-free snacks. Soft drink producers have introduced diet versions of their mainstay products. Fast-food purveyors have reduced their use of unhealthy oils and added salads to their menus. One can ask whether these alternatives have made much of a difference in the U.S. diet, as Americans' weights have burgeoned, but food manufacturers' behavior appears less reprehensible on the surface than that of the tobacco companies. Cigarette manufacturers, in contrast, sell only unhealthy products (although their emerging emphasis on harm reduction products bears some resemblance to snack food producers' introduction of low-fat snacks) (Martin, Warner, and Lantz 2004). Evil tobacco companies thus make for a far more appealing public policy target than mixed-message food manufacturers.

More generally, the obesity issue presents a far more complicated picture than does tobacco control. Cigarettes offer smokers few benefits other than satisfying nicotine cravings; the product is clearly not needed to sustain life. And as addictive as nicotine is, smokers can cease cigarette consumption entirely. Half of all Americans who have ever smoked have done so. Especially today, given smoke-free workplaces and public buildings, and with cigarette billboards now removed from the landscape, former smokers can reside in an environment relatively free of cues to smoke.

In obvious contrast, food is essential. Obese people must eat, and the cues to eat are ubiquitous. At the personal level, this helps explain why the battle of the bulge is so much more difficult than quitting smoking: the agent is ever-present, literally "in your face." At the public level, the necessity and positive values of food mean that policy cannot create a "food-free" environment. The clean indoor air law that has transformed Americans' attitudes toward smoking and boosted quitting in environments (notably workplaces) that prohibit smoking has no equivalent in the world of obesity. This means that very few dieters manage to sustain significant weight loss, far less than the fraction of former smokers who remain abstinent.

Some lessons from the clean indoor air movement do apply to the obesity epidemic, however. While one cannot envision (nor desire) a food-free environment, one can easily imagine a junk-food-free environment. This is the goal of people working to remove the pervasive influence of junk food in schools, some of it sponsored by the manufacturers, much of it in response to student demand. Research has shown that replacing soft drinks with fruit juices and bottled water in vending machines improves students' diets (Brownell and Horgen 2003). Replacing pizza, burgers, and fries with salads and healthy sandwiches in cafeterias could also alter students' diets. Clearly, achieving such changes will be extraordinarily difficult; but think back twenty-five years. Who would have believed it possible that major cities, entire states, would ban smoking in all restaurants and bars?

Much of this discussion focuses on community and other social interventions; much, either implicitly or explicitly, emphasizes prevention rather than attempts to treat obesity. However, the case for treating obesity may be compelling, and lessons from tobacco may be relevant here as well. Broader social interventions probably use scarce resources more cost-effectively than individualized clinical treatment of smoking addiction. Still, clinical treatment for smoking cessation is "the gold standard of health care cost-effectiveness" (Eddy 1992). Only a minority of treated smokers succeeds in quitting, but the low cost of treatment, combined with the high health benefits of success, create an attractive cost-effectiveness outcome. Especially given that individualized treatment may be necessary for certain smokers to quit—namely, those who do not respond to social interventions—health groups should urge providers and insurance companies to cover cessation counseling and treatment. That many providers do not offer such treatment reflects a constellation of problems surrounding the delivery of behavioral counseling in the health care setting (Warner 1997).

Likely, the most important message from the antismoking campaign is that tackling the obesity problem requires a sustained, thoughtful, well-resourced, multidimensioned effort. Such an effort must begin with education and exhortation: with creative use of the media to get the word out. It must include concerted attempts to convince major economic interests—including food producers and fast-food purveyors—to engage in enlightened self-interest by supporting constructive initiatives (a healthy-eating campaign) and dissociating themselves from destructive ones (product placement in schools). It should engage the broader community in encouraging physical activity (such as by creating convenient walking and bike paths). An obesity-control movement must be prepared to fight the prolonged and painful battles to achieve meaningful public policy.

Improved food labeling is one such battle that has been fought with considerable success. Junk food excise taxes constitute another, where forays have achieved mixed success at best, with a limited number of small taxes having been adopted to date, several of which have been eliminated subsequently. Anti-obesity campaigners must remain vigilant for external developments that may profoundly affect their work and figure out how to maximize the benefits from them. The tobacco lawsuits are a case in point, one that lawyers viewing obesity as a new target of opportunity have already borrowed. Finally, underpinning both policy and treatment interventions must be a sound base of research. Its contribution to tobacco control has been vital (Warner 2004).

The remarkable achievements of the antismoking campaign notwithstanding, the public health community is a long way from declaring victory over tobacco. The lesson is clear: obesity-control campaigners must set realistic goals, derive satisfaction from partial victories, and commit for the long run.

References

Advocacy Institute. 1998. *Smoke and Mirrors: How the Tobacco Industry Buys and Lies Its Way to Power and Profits*. Washington, DC: Advocacy Institute.

Brownell, K. D., and K. B. Horgen. 2003. *Food Fight: The Inside Story of the Food Industry, America's Obesity Crisis, and What We Can Do About It*. Chicago, IL: Contemporary Books.

Centers for Disease Control and Prevention. 1999. *Best Practices for Comprehensive Tobacco Control Programs*. Atlanta, GA: National Center for Chronic Disease Prevention and Health Promotion, Office on Smoking and Health. Available at *www.cdc.gov/tobacco/research_data/stat_nat_data/bpcitation.htm* (accessed September 22, 2003).

———. 2003. *U.S. Obesity Trends, 1985–2001*. Atlanta, GA: National Center for Chronic Disease Prevention and Health Promotion, Division of Nutrition and Physical Activity. Available at *www.cdc.gov/nccdphp/dnpa/obesity/trend/maps/* (accessed September 22, 2003).

Chaloupka, F. J., T-W. Hu, K. E. Warner, et al. 2000. The Taxation of Tobacco Products. In *Tobacco Control in Developing Countries*, ed. P. Jha and F. J. Chaloupka. New York, NY: Oxford University Press.

Eddy, D. M. 1992. David Eddy Ranks the Tests. *Harvard Health Letter* July suppl.: 10–11.

Farrelly, M. C., J. Niederdeppe, and J. Yarsevich. 2003. Youth Tobacco Prevention Mass Media Campaigns: Past, Present, and Future Directions. *Tobacco Control* 12 (suppl. 1): i35–i47.

Farrelly, M. C., T. F. Pechacek, and F. J. Chaloupka. 2003. The Impact of Tobacco Control Program Expenditures on Aggregate Cigarette Sales, 1981–2000. *Journal of Health Economics* 22: 843–859.

Fichtenberg, C. M., and S. A. Glantz. 2002. Effect of Smoke-Free Workplaces on Smoking Behaviour: Systematic Review. *British Medical Journal* 325: 188–194.

Glantz, S. A., and W. W. Parmley. 1995. Passive Smoking and Heart Disease: Mechanisms and Risk. *Journal of the American Medical Assocation* 273: 1047–1053.

Glantz, S. A., and E. D. Balbach. 2000. *The Tobacco War: Inside the California Battle*. Berkeley: University of California Press.

Hopkins, D. P., P. A. Briss, C. J. Ricard, et al. 2001. Reviews of Evidence Regarding Interventions to Reduce Tobacco Use and Exposure to Environmental Tobacco Smoke. *American Journal of Preventive Medicine* 20 (suppl. 2): 16–66.

Martin, E. G., K. E. Warner, and P. M. Lantz. 2004. Tobacco Harm Reduction: What Do the Experts Think? *Tobacco Control* 13, no. 2: 123–128.

Mercer, S. L., L. W. Green, A. C. Rosenthal, et al. 2003. Possible Lessons from the Tobacco Experience for Obesity Control. *American Journal of Clinical Nutrition* 77 (suppl): 1073S–1082S.

National Cancer Policy Board. 2000. *State Programs Can Reduce Tobacco Use*. Institute of Medicine/National Research Council. Washington, DC: National Academies Press.

Rabin, R. L. 2001. The Third Wave of Tobacco Tort Litigation. In *Regulating Tobacco*, ed. R. L. Rabin and S. D. Sugarman. New York: Oxford University Press.

Samet, J. M. 2001. The Risks of Active and Passive Smoking. In *Smoking: Risk, Perception, and Policy*, ed. P. Slovic. Thousand Oaks, CA: Sage.

Soliman, S., H. A. Pollack, and K. E. Warner. 2004. Decrease in the Prevalence of Environmental Tobacco Smoke Exposure in the Home during the 1990s in Families with Children. *American Journal of Public Health* 94: 314–320.

Tobacco Industry Research Committee. 1954. A Frank Statement to Cigarette Smokers (ad in over four hundred U.S. newspapers). Available at *http://tobaccodocuments.org/ctr/ CTRMN043095–3096.html* (accessed September 22, 2003).

U.S. Department of Health and Human Services. 1989. *Reducing the Health Consequences of Smoking: 25 Years of Progress. A Report of the Surgeon General*. Public Health Service, Centers for Disease Control, Center for Chronic Disease Prevention and Health Promotion, Office on Smoking and Health. DHHS publication no. (CDC) 89–8411. Washington, DC: U.S. Government Printing Office.

U.S. Department of Health, Education, and Welfare. 1972. *The Health Consequences of Smoking. A Report of the Surgeon General: 1972*. Health Services and Mental Health Administration, Public Health Service. DHEW publication no. (HSM) 72–7516. Washington, DC: U.S. Government Printing Office.

U.S. Environmental Protection Agency. 1992. *Respiratory Health Effects of Passive Smoking: Lung Cancer and Other Disorders*. EPA/600/6-90/006F. Washington, DC: Office of Air and Radiation, Office of Research and Development.

U.S. Public Health Service. 1964. *Smoking and Health: Report of the Advisory Committee to the Surgeon General of the Public Health Service*. U.S. Department of Health, Education, and Welfare, Center for Disease Control. PHS publication no. 1103. Washington, DC: U.S. Government Printing Office.

Wakefield, M., and G. Giovino. 2003. Teen Penalties for Tobacco Possession, Use, and Purchase: Issues and Evidence. *Tobacco Control* 12 (suppl. 1): i6–i13.

Warner, K. E. 1977. The Effects of the Anti-Smoking Campaign on Cigarette Consumption. *American Journal of Public Health* 67: 645–650.

———. 1979. Clearing the Airwaves: The Cigarette Ad Ban Revisited. *Policy Analysis* 5: 435–450.

———. 1997. Cost-Effectiveness of Smoking Cessation Therapies: Interpretation of the Evidence and Implications for Coverage. *PharmacoEconomics* 11: 538–549.

———. 2004. Tobacco Policy Research: Insights and Contributions to Public Health Policy. In *To Improve Health and Health Care*, vol. 8, ed. S. L. Isaacs and J. R. Knickman. New York: Jossey-Bass.

Warner, K. E., and D. M. Burns. 2003. Hardening and the Hard-Core Smoker: Concepts, Evidence, and Implications. *Nicotine and Tobacco Research* 5: 37–48.

Warner, K. E., and H. A. Murt. 1983. Premature Deaths Avoided by the Antismoking Campaign. *American Journal of Public Health* 73: 672–677.

Weinstein, N. D. 2001. Smokers' Recognition of Their Vulnerability to Harm. In *Smoking: Risk, Perception, and Policy*, ed. P. Slovic. Thousand Oaks, CA: Sage.

CHAPTER 8

Patterns and Causes
of Disparities in Health

————— ∞∞ —————

DAVID R. WILLIAMS

The health of the U.S. population has improved markedly over time. Average life expectancy at birth increased by 30 years in the last century, from 47 in 1900 to 77 in 2000 (National Center for Health Statistics 2003). Yet different social groups in the United States continue to experience dramatically varying levels of health. For example, the life expectancy of Asian American women in Bergen County, New Jersey, is 97.7 years, while that of American Indian men in a cluster of counties in South Dakota is 56.6 years (Murray et al. 1998). This 41-year difference in life expectancy indicates that some social groups have health experiences reminiscent of the nineteenth century while others enjoy twenty-first-century health status. Sentiment is growing in many quarters that such large disparities in health are unacceptable.

This chapter provides an overview of social disparities in health in the United States. It begins by outlining the complex social forces that combine to produce variations in health. It then considers the patterns of racial/ethnic differences in health and shows how these must be understood in the context of the heterogeneity of those groups, and the even larger disparities by socioeconomic status (SES) and gender. The chapter concludes by focusing on the opportunities and challenges for reducing social disparities in health in the United States.

Determinants of Health

Analysts estimate that behavioral patterns account for 40 percent of U.S. deaths, with social circumstances and environmental exposures accounting for 20 percent, genetics 30 percent, and inadequacies in medical care 10 percent (McGinnis, Williams-Russo, and Knickman 2002). Differential exposure to a broad range of social and behavioral factors can importantly affect the distribution of disease, disability, and death. Race, SES, and gender are social categories that are linked to varying exposures to health-enhancing or health-damaging factors in multiple social contexts, including family, neighborhood, and work environments.

The types of stressors to which individuals are exposed, the availability of resources to cope with stress, and the patterned nature of responses to environmental challenges are shaped by the larger social and economic contexts of people's lives. Although the specific pathways and social processes that determine exposure may differ, the extent to which racial, gender, and SES groups are differentially exposed to common social influences and risks is striking. A brief overview of environmental factors that can increase the risk of health problems follows.

Unemployment and Working Conditions

Participation in meaningful work is important to psychological as well as economic well-being. Men, low-SES individuals, and disadvantaged racial/ethnic groups are differentially exposed to economic marginalization and separation from the labor force. For example, compared with women, men are much more likely to be incarcerated, homeless, or residents of substance abuse treatment facilities (Williams 2003). Because of historic and continuing individual and institutional discrimination, lower levels of preparation for the labor market, and the mass movement of jobs from areas with concentrated minority and low-income populations, racial minorities and low-SES persons have markedly higher levels of unemployment and job instability than their more socially advantaged peers (Williams and Collins 2001).

The health of lower-SES groups, racial minorities, and men is also affected by their disproportionate exposure to occupational stress and poor working conditions. Low-SES individuals and members of disadvantaged racial/ethnic groups are more likely to be employed in occupational settings and job categories characterized by high levels of psychosocial stress, physical demands, and exposure to toxic substances (Williams and Collins 1995). Similarly, men are more likely than women to work in dangerous occupations and industries, and to have higher rates of occupational-related diseases and deaths. For example, men account for 90 percent of job fatalities in the United States (Courtenay 2000).

Stress, Resources, and Health Practices

Exposure to stress is a risk factor for health problems, but coping responses can ameliorate at least some of these negative effects. Compared with their more economically favored counterparts, disadvantaged minorities and low-SES individuals have higher levels of stress and fewer resources to cope with it. With the exception of employment-related stress, men are not more exposed to stress than women, but women employ more effective coping strategies. They are more likely than men to express their distress via their emotions and to seek and receive interpersonal support, especially from other women (Taylor et al. 2000). Men's cultural scripts urging them to avoid displaying emotional vulnerability lead them to cope with stress through externalizing responses such as substance use and antisocial behavior. Thus, while severe emotional distress among women often gives rise to anxiety and mood disorders, it often manifests in men in alcohol and drug abuse (Rosenfield 1999). In turn, substance use and abuse are important contributors to accidents, family problems, criminal behavior, health care costs, and premature mortality (Williams 2003).

Stress is importantly linked to alcohol and drug use. Higher levels of stress are associated with the initiation and continuation of substance use, as well as with relapse (Brady and Sonore 1999). Alcohol and drug abuse are strongly patterned by SES, with the rates being two to three times higher for the lowest compared with the highest SES category (Kessler et al. 1994). African Americans (or blacks) and other minorities do not consistently have elevated rates of substance use compared with whites, but their use tends to begin at later ages, and heavy use continues for a longer time (McLoyd and Lozoff 2001). Moreover, a given level of substance use and cigarette smoking has stronger negative effects on the health of blacks than on that of whites (Sterling and Weinkam 1989; Williams 2003).

The discussion of substance use highlights the more general role of personal health practices (such as eating, drinking, and exercise) as determinants of health. These behaviors are all socially patterned and play a role in accounting for SES, gender, and racial/ethnic differences in health. Beliefs about masculinity and manhood often lead men to be more likely than women to engage in a broad range of high-risk behaviors and to shun health-promoting activities (Courtenay 2000). SES and racial/ethnic status shape exposure to many different psychosocial and environmental risks for health (Williams and Collins 1995). For example, low-SES persons have higher levels of high-risk behaviors (such as smoking, physical inactivity, and poor nutrition), acute and chronic stress, and hostility and depression, and lower levels of social support and perceptions of control (House and Williams 2000).

Differential Access to Medical Care

Although medical care plays an important role in health, its contribution is much weaker than typically assumed. Clinical medicine has played a small role in improving population health over the last two centuries, yet better nutrition and sanitation and higher living standards have been more important. Moreover, improved access to medical care spurred by national health programs has exerted only limited effect, if any, on socioeconomic inequalities in health. At the same time, timely and appropriate preventive medical services, as well as effective therapies to manage acute and chronic illnesses, can improve health, enhance the length and quality of life, and reduce disparities in health (Politzer et al. 2001).

Socially disadvantaged racial groups and persons of low SES have lower levels of insurance coverage than their socially and economically favored counterparts, and thus are less likely to have access to care (NCHS 2003). However, removing the economic barriers alone would still leave care substantially underutilized (Weinick and Zuvekas 2000). Besides access differences, social groups differ greatly in their utilization of care. For example, although men and women in the United States tend to have similar levels of health insurance coverage, men utilize preventive medical services less often than women (NCHS 2003). The differences for men are linked to male tendencies to project strength and to suppress vulnerability and need (Courtenay 2000). Analysts have identified multiple barriers at both the institutional and the individual level that can lead to lower utilization of care. These include organizational characteristics of the health care system that make it easier for socioeconomically favored individuals to extract maximal benefits, language and cultural barriers, and historic incidents and prior experiences in medical and other social institutions that prompt greater distrust of health care providers and institutions (Smedley, Stith, and Nelson 2003).

Differences in the way health care providers and institutions respond to social groups also leads to variations in the quality of care they receive. Compared with whites, minority men and women receive less-intensive and poorer quality of care (Smedley, Stith, and Nelson 2003). The sources of these differences are many, but systematic—though often unconscious—discrimination based on negative racial stereotypes is likely an important cause. Similar processes operate for persons of low SES (van Ryn and Burke 2000). In male-dominated health care contexts, providers do not view men in general more negatively than women. Nonetheless, health care providers spend less time with men than women in medical encounters, and offer men fewer services, fewer recommendations to make behavioral changes, less health information, and less medical advice (Courtenay 2000). Health care providers appear to project larger cultural norms regarding the absence of vulnerability and need among men onto their male patients and withhold care and advice that they perceive as unnecessary.

Social Disparities in Health

The patterning of health status mirrors the variation in social and behavioral risk factors among people of different race/ethnicity, SES, and gender. Many different pathways may lead to disparities. Socioeconomic deprivation and exposure to poor living and working conditions are central determinants of poor health for socially disadvantaged racial/ethnic and low-SES groups. In contrast, men are advantaged in social, economic, and political power relative to women. At the same time, deeply held cultural views about maleness have shaped men's beliefs and the practices of social institutions in ways that increase health risks for men.

Racial/Ethnic Disparities in Health

Table 8.1 presents the magnitude of racial differences in mortality for the U.S. working-age population. Two patterns are evident in the data. First, blacks and American Indians (or Native Americans) have mortality rates that are higher than those of whites. These differences are especially marked between the ages of twenty-five and fifty-four; the patterns for the three groups converge in later years. The residential separation of blacks and American Indians has been distinctive in U.S. history and is a key determinant of racial differences in SES and health status for African Americans and the 60 percent of American Indians who live on or near reservations (Williams and Collins 2001).

For example, a study of young African Americans showed that eradicating residential segregation would eliminate differences between blacks and whites in earnings, high school graduation, and unemployment rates, as well as two-thirds of the racial difference in single motherhood (Cutler, Glaeser, and Vigdor 1997). A recent modest decline in black-white residential segregation has not reduced the concentration of urban poverty, the residential isolation of most African Americans, and the number of census tracts where African Americans are a high per-

TABLE 8.1   *Age-Specific Death Rates for Working-Age Adults (per 100,000 population) for Whites and Minority/White Ratios, 2000*

Age	White (W) rate	Black/W ratio	Am Ind[a]/W ratio	API[b]/W ratio	Hispanic/W ratio
15–24	75.6	1.6	1.6	0.6	1.1
25–34	96.2	2.0	1.6	0.5	1.1
35–44	180.3	2.0	1.7	0.5	0.9
45–54	391.8	2.1	1.3	0.5	0.9
55–64	948.9	1.7	1.2	0.6	0.8
65–74	2,375.1	1.4	1.0	0.6	0.7

Source: U.S. Department of Health and Human Services, 2003.
[a]Am Ind is for American Indian.
[b]API is for Asian and Pacific Islanders.

centage of the population (Williams and Collins 2001). The continuing residential social isolation and economic marginalization of many blacks and Native Americans suggest that their socioeconomic and health challenges will continue.

The table also reveals a second pattern: equivalent or lower rates of mortality among Hispanics (or Latinos) and Asian and Pacific Islanders (API) compared with whites. At every age, API mortality rates are markedly lower than rates for whites. Hispanic mortality rates are slightly higher than those of whites for the two younger age groups (fifteen through thirty-four), but are lower than those of whites between ages thirty-five and seventy-four. The large number of immigrants within the Asian and the Hispanic populations importantly affects the health status of these groups. Immigrants of all major racial/ethnic groups in the United States have lower rates of adult and infant mortality than their native-born counterparts (Singh and Yu 1996; Hummer et al. 1999). However, because Latinos and Asians differ in their SES levels upon arriving in the United States, and in their trajectories for socioeconomic mobility, they are likely to have diverging patterns of health.

The health literature has paid inadequate attention to the SES characteristics of various immigrant groups. Table 8.2 presents the rate of college graduation and white-collar (managerial and professional) employment for major immigrant groups and the native-born population. Several Asian immigrant groups have higher levels of education and occupational status than native-born Asians and other native-born Americans, including whites. Thus, although the health advantage of Asian immigrants declines somewhat as they assimilate into American culture, their continued relatively high SES profile suggests that Asians are likely to continue to lead the other groups on many health indicators (Frisbie, Cho, and Hummer 2001; Cho and Hummer 2000).

Table 8.2 also highlights considerable variation within the Asian group (similar to the heterogeneity within all major racial/ethnic populations). Cambodian, Laotian, and, to a lesser extent, Vietnamese immigrants have lower levels of edu-

TABLE 8.2   *Socioeconomic Status of Immigrants and Native-Born Persons, 1990*

Group	College grad[a] (%)	White collar job[b] (%)
NATIVE BORN		
All U.S. born	20.3	27
Asian (U.S. born)	35.9	34
White (non-Hisp.)	22.0	29
Black (non-Hisp.)	11.4	18
Pacific Islanders	10.8	18
Am. Indian	9.3	18
Puerto Rican	9.5	17
Mexican (U.S. born)	8.6	16
IMMIGRANTS		
All foreign born	20.4	22
Asian		
India	64.9	48
Taiwan	62.2	47
Philippines	43.0	28
Japan	35.0	39
Korea	34.4	25
China	30.9	29
Vietnam	15.9	17
Cambodia	5.5	9
Laos	5.1	7
Hispanic		
Mexico	3.5	6
Dominican Repub.	7.5	11
El Salvador	4.6	6
Cuba	15.6	23
Nicaragua	14.6	11
Black		
Africa	47.1	37
Jamaica	14.9	22
Haiti	11.8	14

Source: Rumbaut 1996.
[a]College Grad indicates college graduation or more for persons aged twenty-five years or older.
[b]White collar job indicates professionals, executives, and managers.

cation and managerial employment than U.S.-born persons. Laotians, Hmong, and Cambodians also have higher rates of poverty and lower levels of family income than blacks and American Indians (Williams 2001). Thus, combining all Asians into one category, or focusing only on subgroups with a long history of settlement in the United States, masks Asian subgroups with higher levels of risks. Where disaggregated health data are available, Laotians, Hmong, Cambodians, and

Vietnamese have poorer health than other Asian groups and the white population (Cho and Hummer 2000; Frisbie, Cho, and Hummer 2001). The combination of APIs into a single group has been similarly problematic because Pacific Islanders have elevated levels of morbidity and mortality compared with the overall U.S. population (Frisbie, Cho, and Hummer 2001; Zane, Takeuchi, and Young 1994). The Office of Management and Budget's recent revision of racial/ethnic categories to include a separate category for Native Hawaiians and other Pacific Islanders will permit better tracking of the health of this group.

The socioeconomic profile of Latino immigrants differs markedly from that of Asians. The rate of college graduation is low for immigrants from Mexico, the Dominican Republic, and El Salvador. Immigrants from Cuba and Nicaragua have higher levels of education but still lag behind the native-born U.S. population on both education and occupational status. In light of this low SES profile, the surprisingly good mortality profile of Latinos has been termed the "Hispanic paradox."

Several factors put the Hispanic health profile into perspective. First, Hispanic immigrants, like other immigrants, are selected on health. Second, the health advantage of Hispanic immigrants declines with length of stay in the United States and acculturation to American society. Adult and infant mortality, psychiatric disorders, psychological distress, substance use, low birth weight, poor health practices, and other indicators of morbidity all rise as Hispanic immigrants adopt the behaviors of their host society (Finch et al. 2002; Vega and Amaro 1994). Third, the trajectory of Hispanic health is likely to differ markedly from that of Asians because of the limited socioeconomic mobility of Latinos. The low SES profile of Hispanic immigrants, the low SES levels of native-born Latinos, and their lack of educational and occupational opportunities are likely to combine to increase the effects of low SES on Hispanic health. These influences also mean that the health of Latino immigrants is likely to decline more rapidly than that of Asians, and to be worse than the U.S. average in the future (Camarillo and Bonilla 2001). Unlike Asian immigrants, who report lower levels of morbidity than their native-born counterparts, Latino immigrants rate themselves lower than native-born Hispanics on indicators of morbidity such as self-rated health (Frisbie, Cho, and Hummer 2001; Finch et al. 2002).

Table 8.2 also shows that black immigrants from Africa have rates of college graduation more than twice those of the overall U.S.-born population and four times those of native-born blacks. Most black immigrants in the United States come from the Caribbean. Jamaican immigrants have SES levels that are slightly higher than those of native-born blacks but lower than those of all U.S.-born persons. The SES levels of Haitian immigrants are similar to those of native-born blacks. Like other immigrants, black immigrants have lower mortality rates than native-born blacks, but their morbidity levels vary by specific group and health outcome (Williams 2001). At least some black immigrants experience serious challenges to socioeconomic mobility. Thus, monitoring the SES and health of black immigrants and their children can help identify how SES, acculturation, and exposure to racism relate and combine to affect health and health trajectories.

TABLE 8.3   *Life Expectancy at Age 25: Race, Income, and Gender Differences*

Family income (1980 dollars)	Males			Females			Gender diffs[a]	
	White	Black	**Race diffs**	White	Black	**Race diffs**	**White**	**Black**
All	50.1	45.7	**4.4**	56.7	52.4	**4.3**	**6.6**	**6.7**
<$10,000	45.0	41.6	**3.4**	54.5	50.3	**4.2**	**9.5**	**8.7**
$10,000–24,999	50.2	47.4	**2.8**	56.9	53.7	**3.2**	**6.7**	**6.3**
$25,000+	52.9	50.2	**2.7**	57.8	55.3	**2.5**	**4.9**	**5.1**
Income diffs.	**7.9**	**8.6**		**3.3**	**5.0**			

Source: Lin et al. 2003.
[a]Diffs = Differences.

Race, SES, and Gender Disparities

The simultaneous consideration of race/ethnicity, SES, and gender in table 8.3 provides important insight into the nature of social disparities in health. There are large racial differences in life expectancy. White men and women have a life expectancy at age twenty-five that exceeds that of their black counterparts by 4.4 and 4.3 years, respectively. Consistent with other research, the racial differences in life expectancy become smaller when comparing blacks and whites at similar levels of income. At the same time, striking racial differences in life expectancy persist at every level of income. At the lowest income level, white males and females live 3.4 and 4.2 years longer, respectively, than their black peers. Even at the highest income level in the table, white men and women at age twenty-five outlive their black counterparts by 2.7 and 2.5 years, respectively. The persistence of racial differences in health after SES is controlled could reflect the noncomparability of SES indicators across race, the residual effects of early life adversity, or the contribution of risk factors linked to racism (Williams and Collins 1995).

Research has documented substantial differences in health by SES, with the largest effects at the lowest SES levels. As SES levels rise, health improves in a stepwise progression—the association is evident even at middle and high levels of SES. Table 8.3 shows that high-income white and black men at age twenty-five live at least 8 years longer than their low-income counterparts. These differences by income are almost twice as large as the black-white difference. Income differences in life expectancy are smaller for women than for men, with the lowest-income white and black females having a life expectancy that is shorter by 3.3 years and 4.3 years, respectively, than their highest-income peers. Income levels fluctuate considerably with stages of the life cycle, with about 40 percent of the U.S. population experiencing large income gains and losses during their working years (McDonough et al. 2000). Both income losses and the persistence of low income predict elevated mortality risk (McDonough et al. 1997).

Large gender differences can be found in a broad range of health status indicators (Williams 2003; Courtenay 2000). Table 8.3 shows that black and white women have a life expectancy at age twenty-five that is 6.7 and 6.6 years longer, respectively, than that of their male counterparts. The gender differences are largest for the lowest-income groups. Low-income white women outlive their male counterparts by 9.5 years, and the comparable number for blacks is 8.7 years. At the highest income level, both black and white women have a 5-year advantage in life expectancy over their male counterparts. Moreover, the effect of multiple social categories is additive. Race, income, and gender all make independent contributions to disparities in health. As table 8.3 shows, white women with the highest level of income have the highest life expectancy at age twenty-five (58 years), while low-income black males have the lowest (42 years). The difference in life expectancy between these two groups at age twenty-five is more than 16 years. This is almost four times as large as the overall black-white difference in life expectancy, more than twice as large as the gender difference for both races, and almost twice the size of the largest income differences in life expectancy.

The observed differences in life expectancy are sizeable and have important implications for individuals, families, and society. A gain in life expectancy of a month from a preventive intervention targeted at populations of average risk and a gain of a year from an intervention targeted at a high-risk population are considered significant improvements (Wright and Weinstein 1998). To place such gains in context, demographers estimate that if a magic bullet eliminated cancer or heart disease overnight, the gain in life expectancy for the U.S. population would be only two or three years. Disparities in health also have considerable economic costs. Economists have estimated the median value of an additional year of life at $70,000 (Viscusi 1993). Poorer health status also affects participation in the workforce and in income support programs. A recent study found that differences in illness levels between blacks and Native Americans, on the one hand, and whites, on the other, accounted for a large part of racial differences in employment rates and in participation in public assistance programs and Social Security, especially among forty-five- to sixty-four-year-olds (Bound et al. 2003).

An important characteristic of social disparities in health is their persistence despite overall improvements in the health of populations. For example, although the health of all Americans improved markedly during the twentieth century, social disparities in health remained large or even widened. Infant mortality rates by race illustrate this trend (NCHS 2003). In 1950, the infant mortality rate was twenty-seven per one thousand live births for whites and forty-four for blacks. By 1999, the infant death rate for whites (six per one thousand) was more than four times lower than the 1950 level, and that of blacks (fifteen per one thousand) was almost three times lower. And the absolute racial difference in the rates had been cut in half (from seventeen to nine).

Nonetheless, a large disparity persisted in 1999, and the relative difference had widened because the decline in infant mortality was more rapid for whites than for blacks. The odds that a black infant would die before his or her first birthday compared with his/her white counterpart had risen from 1.6 in 1950 to 2.5 in 1999. Other data also reveal that socioeconomic inequalities in health have persisted or widened in the United States and elsewhere (Williams and Collins 1995).

For example, despite major changes in the causes of death between 1911 and 1981 in England and Wales, the elevated mortality risks for individuals in lower social classes remained large compared with those of professional and managerial classes (Marmot 1986). Moreover, increases in the quantity and effectiveness of medical care during this period, and more equitable access owing to the introduction of the British National Health Service in 1948, appear to have had no effect on reducing SES inequalities in health.

Reducing Disparities in Health

Healthy People 2010 is the third iteration of national health goals first launched by the United States in 1979. This initiative seeks to increase the years of healthy life and eliminate racial/ethnic disparities in health in six target areas by the year 2010 (U.S. DHHS 2000). To accomplish this, the initiative identifies 467 specific objectives in twenty-six priority areas. While expansive in scope, the large number of objectives is overwhelming, lacks focus, and reflects inconsistencies across priority areas (Davis 1998, 2000). I use this initiative as the backdrop for assessing the challenges and opportunities for reducing social disparities in health.

In theory, there are four potential approaches to eliminating disparities in health status, and success may well require initiatives in each area (Mackenbach and Stronks 2002). These include reducing SES disadvantage in the population, reducing the effects of health on SES disadvantage, changing the intervening factors that mediate the effects of SES on health, and reducing deficiencies in medical care. Healthy People 2010 initiatives primarily address the latter two strategies.

Reducing SES Disadvantage in the Population

Healthy People 2010 has devoted little attention to addressing the underlying contexts in which ill health and disparities in health emerge. Given that specific health risks are embedded in larger social and political contexts, effective intervention must take into account the historical and cultural factors that shape the experiences and living conditions of various social groups. Intervention can alter features of these environments to maximize health-enhancing activities and buffer negative exposures. Potential policies to reduce SES inequalities include enhancing educational achievement among low-SES children and improving employment opportunities, neighborhood and housing quality, and transportation services. Other possible strategies include new tax and income support policies to assist the most vulnerable, and reducing long-term poverty through initiatives that enable the chronically unemployed to find work.

Few policies designed to improve SES conditions have been rigorously examined for their health effects, but there is some limited evidence that such strategies would work. For example, the Moving to Opportunity Program, which provided assistance to randomly selected families in high-poverty neighborhoods to move to less-poor neighborhoods, showed that the mental health of both parents and sons had improved three years later (Leventhal and Brooks-Gunn 2003).

A recent natural experiment similarly assessed the impact of an income supplement on the psychopathology of American Indian children (Costello et al. 2003). The study found that higher family income (because of the opening of a casino) was associated with declining rates of deviant and aggressive behavior. Moreover, although a definitive causal connection cannot be established, a narrowing of the racial income gap from 1968 to 1978 was associated with a larger decline in overall mortality for African American men and women aged thirty-five to seventy-four than for similarly aged whites, on both a percentage and an absolute basis (Cooper et al. 1981). Similarly, as the income of blacks fell relative to that of whites between 1980 and 1991, the life expectancy of blacks dropped, absolutely and relative to that of whites (Williams and Collins 1995). Experiments with a negative income tax during the 1970s found that supplemental income to mothers was associated with higher birth weight for their children without any health intervention (Kehrer and Wolin 1979).

A U.S. task force recently identified over two hundred community-based interventions that could be used to improve social environments and health (Anderson et al. 2003). The task force identified six key factors in the social environment that are determinants of health. These include (1) neighborhood living conditions; (2) opportunities for learning and capacity development; (3) community development and employment opportunities; (4) prevailing norms, customs, and processes; (5) social cohesion, civic engagement, and collective efficacy; and (6) health promotion, disease and injury prevention, and health care opportunities. Within each domain, a wide range of specific strategies were identified. At the same time, the task force acknowledged that there was ample evidence documenting the effectiveness of only two interventions: early childhood development programs for low-income children and rental assistance programs for low-SES families (Anderson et al. 2003).

A report commissioned by the British government—usually referred to as the Acheson report—also concluded that reducing health inequalities requires intervening in the social determinants of health (Department of Health 1998). While acknowledging differences between the United States and the United Kingdom, U.S. observers saw merit in the Acheson report and called for a similar high-level U.S. commission that would be comprehensive in its solutions to social disparities in health (Newman 2001; Tarlov 2000). Proponents argue that such a body would not only broaden American understanding of the determinants of health, but also prompt us to consider the health implications of tax, education, employment, and housing policies.

Reducing the Effects of Health on SES Disadvantage

Reducing disparities in health also requires attending to reverse causation (i.e., the notion that sickness leads people to become economically disadvantaged) by reducing the effects of health on SES disadvantage. Such efforts could include maintaining benefit levels for the long-term disabled, modifying work conditions to boost work participation levels of the chronically ill and disabled, and designing health interventions that would remove barriers to paid employment for persons who now receive government benefits (Mackenbach and Stronks 2002). Such policies would not address primary prevention but can improve the quality of life and economic productivity of those who are already ill.

Changing the Intervening Factors

A third approach to reducing disparities in health would alter the intervening factors that mediate the effects of SES on health. Healthy People 2010, which calls for many health promotion programs aimed at improving the health practices of individuals, emphasizes this approach. However, a greater focus on environmental measures, such as providing free fruit in elementary schools, raising tobacco taxes to reduce consumption, and reengineering work to reduce occupational stress, would strengthen the likelihood that Healthy People 2010 initiatives will succeed.

In general, the results of large-scale health interventions targeted at individuals have been disappointing. For example, the Multiple Risk Factor Intervention Trial (MRFIT)—an ambitious and intensive U.S.-based experiment—did not significantly reduce cardiovascular risk factors in the targeted group of high-risk men compared with men in the control group (MRFIT Research Group 1982). At the same time, several small-scale interventions with quasi-experimental designs have reduced SES influences on health indicators. For example, in the Netherlands, school health promotion programs eliminated SES variations in tooth brushing and reduced smoking initiation among low-income students (Mackenbach and Stronks 2002). Similarly, changes in working conditions among manual laborers reduced physical workload and absences from work due to illness.

While some interventions targeted at communities find no effects, others have found significant effects on health behaviors for at least some population groups (Emmons 2000). For example, although a community-level intervention to reduce cigarette smoking in eleven matched pairs of communities did not yield significantly lower quit rates for heavy smokers, quit rates increased significantly among both less-educated smokers and light-to-moderate smokers (Emmons 2000). Economic analysis indicates that if the results of community trials were applied to the population level, they would be as cost-effective as accepted medical interventions (Emmons 2000).

Changes in cigarette smoking over time show that successful interventions require a coordinated and comprehensive approach (Warner 2000). Reductions in cigarette smoking require the active involvement of professionals and volunteers from a broad range of organizations, including government, health professional groups, community agencies, and business. The use of multiple channels—including media, workplaces, schools, churches, medical and health societies—and multiple interventions is also essential. The latter include efforts to inform the public about the dangers of cigarette smoking (smoking cessation programs, warning labels on cigarette packs), economic inducements to avoid tobacco (excise taxes, differential life insurance rates), and laws and regulations restricting tobacco use (clean indoor air laws, restricting smoking in public places, and restricting sales to minors). Even with all these interventions, progress is only partial.

At the same time, since behavioral risk factors appear to account for only about 10–20 percent of SES differences in morbidity and mortality, interventions addressing health behaviors alone are unlikely to eliminate disparities (House and Williams 2000). Experience over the last one hundred years suggests that interventions on intermediary risk factors will have limited success in reducing social inequalities in health as long as more fundamental social inequalities remain intact (House and Williams 2000).

Improving Medical Care

Healthy People 2010 appropriately calls for improving access and quality of care for vulnerable populations. The initiative also notes the critical need to ensure that health services are responsive to patients who do not speak English or who are from other cultures. A recent review of published studies using an experimental or quasi-experimental design concluded that patients who received culturally competent care had significant improvement on multiple health outcomes, compared with those who did not (Kehoe, D'Eramo Melkus, and Newlin 2003). However, the range of outcomes these studies examined was limited, the definition and use of culturally relevant and competent care was variable, and the long-term efficacy of the interventions is unclear.

Some forms of training that emphasize mastering specific information about particular social groups may actually enhance negative stereotypes and lead to unconscious discrimination. Such unconscious bias is likely an important contributor to a pervasive pattern of racial and ethnic differences in the quality and intensity of U.S. medical care (Smedley, Stith, and Nelson 2003). More process-oriented approaches to understanding and responding to the unique needs of every patient are essential. In fact, key aspects of culturally appropriate care appear to include devoting adequate time and attention to the patient, providing individual or group support, or both, and improving quality of care (Kehoe, D'Eramo Melkus, and Newlin 2003).

Improving access to care for vulnerable populations requires addressing the shortage of primary care physicians in disadvantaged areas. Reducing the underrepresentation of minorities in the health professions is also likely to improve quality of care for minority populations. For example, only 2.9 percent of U.S. doctors in 1999 were black, but black and Hispanic physicians are more likely than others to care for the uninsured and those covered by Medicaid, and to practice in underserved urban and rural areas (*Lancet* editorial 1999; Komaromy et al. 1996). A recent study of patients in sixteen urban primary care practices found that race-concordant visits averaged two minutes longer than race-discordant encounters among both black and white patients (Cooper et al. 2003). Patients in race-concordant visits also reported higher levels of satisfaction and judged physicians' participatory decision-making style more positively. Moreover, independent ratings of audiotapes of the encounters indicated that race-concordant visits had a more positive emotional context (as indicated by voice tone) and a slower pace, as reflected in slower speech by both the physician and the patient.

Targeting the Most Vulnerable

Healthy People 2010 seeks to improve overall health while reducing disparities in health. In practice, accomplishing both these aims at once is difficult. Many
policies likely to have the greatest impact on population health can lead to growing disparities (Mechanic 2002). Given that the same social factors undergird various disparities in health, a comprehensive approach that improves health and
reduces health inequalities is possible. However, such an approach will have to
increase prosperity and improve services for all while trying to improve the health
of the most vulnerable *faster* than that of the rest of the population (Mackenbach
and Stronks 2002).

Ensuring Long-Term and Realistic Goals

The Healthy People 2010 target of eliminating racial disparities by 2010 is
unrealistic. For example, the target for cigarette smoking is virtually unattainable,
given the past twenty-five years of experience with smoking cessation (Mendez
and Warner 2000). More generally, the U.S. experience with tobacco reduction efforts over the last forty years shows that behavioral changes to improve health require a long-term commitment that continually builds on incremental success
(Warner 2000). The earlier Healthy People 2000 initiative met only 15 percent of
its objectives and made progress on an additional 44 percent (Marwick 2000), suggesting that goals should be appropriately modest based on prior experience. More
realistic expectations are evident in other programs to reduce disparities. The European region of the World Health Organization aims to reduce SES disparities
by 25 percent in all member states by 2020 (Davis 2000). The Netherlands seeks to
reduce the gap in healthy life expectancy between high- and low-SES groups from
twelve to nine years by the year 2020 (Mackenbach and Stronks 2002).

The Need for National and Regional Cooperation

The goals for Healthy People 2010 were developed through a national con-
sultative process involving over 350 national organizations, 270 state agencies, public health experts, and public representatives (Davis 2000). However, the report
produced by this effort does not, for the most part, indicate which agencies and
organizations are accountable for achieving most of the initiative's objectives (Davis
2000). Nor does it clearly articulate the responsibility of the federal government
even in areas such as the use of motorcycle helmets, where federal policy has had
a large impact (Davis 1998).

Governments can do much to improve health and health care, and strong
federal leadership is indispensable to improving health in the United States (Lurie
2002). However, given the multiple factors underlying disparities in health, a coordinated effort by multiple departments and agencies is essential. Yet Healthy
People 2010 is an initiative of the Department of Health and Human Services. Taking seriously the broad social determinants of health would require enlisting multiple sectors of society, as well as mounting crosscutting efforts by federal agencies
to maximize government spending to improve health and reduce health inequalities.

Reducing inequalities in health requires national leadership that provides direction and financial resources, government action at the regional and local level, and active support and commitment from community organizations and individuals. This combination of a national vision and resources with local action allows for flexibility in planning at the local level. One of the most successful community interventions on record adopted this approach and dramatically reduced residents' rate of coronary heart disease. Importantly, this intervention in North Karelia, Finland, began when the community perceived that it had a problem (the world's highest death rate from heart disease), requested help from public health experts, and worked with multiple sectors not only to increase information and education but also to produce environmental changes (Puska et al. 1985).

The Need for Evaluation

Healthy People 2010 has drawn criticism because competing interests and compromise shaped its final recommendations (Davis 1998). For example, the initiative's targets and strategies often reflect prevailing political ideology rather than current research (such as the failure to suggest a tax on cigarettes). Nevertheless, significant gaps remain in the knowledge base regarding what interventions work, and the need for rigorous scientific evaluation of the health and social results of various interventions is urgent. Few of the many interventions implemented internationally have been subject to rigorous scientific evaluation, and most efforts that have been evaluated have been modest (Mackenbach and Stronks 2002; Stronks 2002). In addition, many major social interventions have not been evaluated for their health consequences. Moreover, since well-intentioned and plausible interventions may have unintended effects, both the positive *and* negative effects of interventions and their cost-benefit ratios must be assessed (Petticrew 2003).

Drawing on examples from smoking cessation efforts, Warner notes the need for constant reevaluation because of the changing nature of the problem (2000). A community-based intervention in Baltimore similarly highlights the need to sustain initially beneficial effects (Levine et al. 2003). In that city a hypertension control program using nurse-supervised community health workers reduced blood pressure over a four-year period and doubled the percentage of hypertensive patients who adequately controlled their blood pressure. However, although the declines in blood pressure were marked during the first twenty-seven months, both the systolic (plus seven) and diastolic (plus four) measures rose between month twenty-seven and the end of the program (month forty). This finding highlights the importance of long-term evaluation of interventions to assess how long any initial beneficial effects can be sustained, and if and when reinforcement or "booster shots" may be necessary.

Overcoming the Barriers

Evidence clearly shows that social disparities in health are large, pervasive across health status measures, persistent over time, and costly to society. Moreover, interventions aimed at improving health that are not coupled with those that seek to reduce social disadvantage are unlikely to substantially reduce disparities.

Healthy People 2010, a federal initiative to eliminate racial/ethnic disparities in health, is narrow in scope and unlikely to be effective given its neglect of broad social determinants.

At least two major barriers may hamper efforts to address these social disparities. First, most Americans are unaware of the problem. A national survey in 1999 by the Kaiser Foundation found that more than half of all whites, Latinos, and African Americans were unaware that blacks had shorter life expectancy and higher infant mortality rates than whites (Lillie-Blanton et al. 2000). This finding is striking, given that racial differences have been central in the reporting of U.S. health data for many decades. And in all likelihood public awareness of disparities linked to race is greater than awareness of disparities related to gender and SES. A society that is largely unaware of a problem is unlikely to be highly motivated to address it.

The second and arguably more important issue is one of political feasibility and political will to do what is necessary to address health disparities. Some observers argue that the American tendency to focus on individual success and opportunity undermines the sense of collective good needed to make a strong national commitment to equity (Leeder 2003). At a minimum, the question of political feasibility means that policymakers must identify real and perceived barriers to implementing programs to address social disparities in health. In particular, decision makers need to determine how to frame such initiatives to ensure that they resonate with American ideals and are perceived as attractive. American norms of equality of opportunity and the dignity of the individual, as well as today's emphasis on improving health care quality, could build public support to improve the health of all. While we await more information on the effectiveness of interventions, we could greatly enhance the health of many U.S. residents if we made applying all the knowledge that we already have a national priority.

Acknowledgments

Work on this chapter was supported in part by grants from The Robert Wood Johnson Foundation Investigator Awards in Health Policy Research program and the National Institute of Mental Health, and by the John D. and Catherine T. MacArthur Foundation Research Network on Socioeconomic Status and Health. I am grateful to Car Nosel, Han Nah Kim, and Trisha Matelski for research assistance and preparation of the manuscript.

References

Anderson, L. M., S. C. Scrimshaw, M. T. Fullilove, et al. 2003. The Community Guide's Model for Linking the Social Environment to Health. *American Journal of Preventive Medicine* 24 (3S): 12–20.

Bound, J., T. Waidmann, M. Schoenbaum, et al. 2003. The Labor Market Consequences of Race Differences in Health. *Milbank Memorial Quarterly* 81, no. 3: 441–473.

Brady, K. T., and S. C. Sonore. 1999. The Role of Stress in Alcohol Use, Alcoholism Treatment, and Relapse. *Alcohol Research and Health* 23: 263–271.

Camarillo, A. M., and F. Bonilla. 2001. Hispanic in a Multicultural Society: A New American Dilemma? In *America Becoming: Racial Trends and Their Consequences,* ed. N. J. Smelser, W. J. Wilson, and F. Mitchell. Vol. 1. Washington, DC: National Academies Press.

Cho, Y., and R. A. Hummer. 2000. Disability Status Differentials across Fifteen Asian and Pacific Islander Groups and the Effect of Nativity and Duration of Residence in the U.S. *Social Biology* 48, no. 3–4: 171–195.

Cooper, L. A., D. L. Roter, R. L. Johnson, et al. 2003. Patient-Centered Communication, Ratings of Care, and Concordance of Patient and Physician Race. *Annals of Internal Medicine* 139, no. 11: 907–916.

Cooper, R. S., M. Steinhauer, A. Schatzkin, et al. 1981. Improved Mortality among U.S. Blacks, 1968–1978: The Role of Antiracist Struggle. *International Journal of Health Services* 11: 511–522.

Costello, E. J., S. N. Compton, G. Keeler, et al. 2003. Relationships between Poverty and Psychopathology: A Natural Experiment. *Journal of the American Medical Association* 290, no. 15: 2023–2029.

Courtenay, W. H. 2000. Constructions of Masculinity and Their Influence on Men's Well-Being: A Theory of Gender and Health. *Social Science and Medicine* 50: 1385–1401.

Cutler, D. M., E. L. Glaeser, and J. L. Vigdor. 1997. Are Ghettos Good or Bad? *Quarterly Journal of Economics* 112: 827–872.

Davis, R. M. 1998. Healthy People 2010: National Health Objectives for the United States. *British Medical Journal* 317: 1513–1517.

———. 2000. Healthy People 2010: Objectives for the United States—Impressive, but Unwieldy. *British Medical Journal* 320: 818–819.

Department of Health. 1998. *Independent Inquiry into Inequalities in Health Report.* London: The Stationery Office.

Emmons, K. M. 2000. Behavioral and Social Science Contributions to the Health of Adults in the United States. In *Promoting Health: Intervention Strategies from Social and Behavioral Research*, ed. B. D. Smedley and S. L. Syme. Washington, DC: National Academies Press.

Finch, B. K., R. A. Hummer, M. Reindl, et al. 2002. Validity of Self-Rated Health among Latino(a)s. *American Journal of Epidemiology* 155, no. 8: 755–759.

Frisbie, W. P., Y. Cho, and R. A. Hummer. 2001. Immigration and the Health of Asian and Pacific Islander Adults in the United States. *American Journal of Epidemiology* 153, no. 4: 372–380.

House, J. S., and D. R. Williams. 2000. Understanding and Reducing Socioeconomic and Racial/Ethnic Disparities in Health. In *Promoting Health: Intervention Strategies from Social and Behavioral Research*, ed. B. D. Smedley and S. L. Syme. Washington, DC: National Academies Press.

Hummer, R. A., R. G. Rogers, C. B. Nam, et al. 1999. Race/Ethnicity, Nativity, and U.S. Adult Mortality. *Social Science Quarterly* 80: 136–153.

Kehoe, K. A., G. D'Eramo Melkus, and K. Newlin. 2003. Culture within the Context of Care: An Integrative Review. *Ethnicity and Disease* 13: 344–353.

Kehrer, B. H., and C. M. Wolin. 1979. Impact of Income Maintenance on Low Birth Weight: Evidence from the Gary Experiment. *Journal of Human Resources* 14: 434–462.

Kessler, R. C., K. A. McGonagle, S. Zhao, et al. 1994. Lifetime and 12-Month Prevalence of DSM-III-R Psychiatric Disorders in the United States. *Archives of General Psychiatry* 51: 8–19.

Komaromy, M., K. Grumbach, M. Drake, et al. 1996. The Role of Black and Hispanic Physicians in Providing Health Care for Underserved Populations. *Black and Hispanic Physicians and Underserved Populations* 334, no. 20: 1305–1310.

Lancet editorial. 1999. Affirmative Action. *The Lancet* 353, no. 9146: 1.

Leeder, S. R. 2003. Achieving Equity in the Australian Healthcare System. *Medical Journal of Australia* 179: 475–478.

Leventhal, T., and J. Brooks-Gunn. 2003. Moving to Opportunity: An Experimental Study of Neighborhood Effects on Mental Health. *American Journal of Public Health* 93, no. 9: 1576–1582.

Levine, D. M., L. R. Bone, M. N. Hill, et al. 2003. The Effectiveness of a Community/Academic Health Center Partnership in Decreasing the Level of Blood Pressure in an Urban African-American Population. *Ethnicity and Disease* 13: 354–361.

Lillie-Blanton, M., M. Brodie, D. Rowland, D. Altman, and M. McIntosh. 2000. Race, Ethnicity, and the Health Care System: Public Perceptions and Experiences. *Medical Care Research and Review* 57: 218–235.

Lin, C. C., E. Rogot, N. J. Johnson, et al. 2003. A Further Study of Life Expectancy by Socioeconomic Factors in the National Longitudinal Mortalilty Study. *Ethnicity and Disease* 13: 240–247.

Lurie, N. 2002. What the Federal Government Can Do about the Nonmedical Determinants of Health. *Health Affairs* 21, no. 2: 94–106.

Mackenbach, J. P., and K. Stronks. 2002. A Strategy for Tackling Health Inequalities in the Netherlands. *British Journal of Medicine* 325: 1029–1032.

Marmot, M. G. 1986. Social Inequalities in Mortality: The Social Environment. In *Class and Health: Research and Longitudinal Data*, ed. R. D. Wilkinson. London: Tavistock.

Marwick, C. 2000. Healthy People 2010 Initiative Launched. *Journal of the American Medical Association* 283, no. 8: 989–990.

McDonough, P., G. J. Duncan, D. R. Williams, et al. 1997. Income Dynamics and Adult Mortality in the U.S., 1972–1989. *American Journal of Public Health* 87, no. 9: 1476–1483.

————. 2000. The Impact of Income Dynamics on Mortality in the United States. In *The Mortality Crisis in Transitional Economies*, ed. G. A. Cornia and R. Paniccia. New York: Oxford University Press.

McGinnis, J. M., P. Williams-Russo, and J. R. Knickman. 2002. The Case for More Active Policy Attention to Health Promotion. *Health Affairs* 21, no. 2: 78–93.

McLoyd, V. C., and B. Lozoff. 2001. Racial and Ethnic Trends in Children's and Adolescents' Behavior and Development. In *America Becoming: Racial Trends and Their Consequences,* vol. 1, ed. N. J. Smelser, W. J. Wilson, and F. Mitchell. Washington, DC: National Academies Press.

Mechanic, D. 2002. Disadvantage, Inequality, and Social Policy. *Health Affairs* 21, no. 2: 48–59.

Mendez, D., and K. E. Warner. 2000. Smoking Prevalence in 2010: Why the Healthy People Goal Is Unattainable. *American Journal of Public Health* 90, no. 3: 401–403.

Multiple Risk Factor Intervention Trial (MRFIT) Research Group. 1982. The Multiple Risk Factor Intervention Trial: Risk Factor Changes and Mortality Results. *Journal of the American Medical Association* 248: 1465–1477.

Murray, C. J., C. M. Michaud, M. T. McKenna, and J. S. Marks. 1998. *U.S. Patterns of Mortality by County and Race, 1965–1994.* Cambridge, MA: Harvard University Press.

National Center for Health Statistics (NCHS). 2003. *Health: United States, 2003.* Hyattsville, MD: National Center for Health Statistics. DHHS publication no. 2003-1232, September.

Newman, K. S. 2001. After Acheson: Lessons for American Policy on Inequality and Health. In *Income, Socioeconomic Status, and Health: Exploring the Relationships*, ed. J. Auerbach and B. K. Krimgold. Report no. 299. Washington, DC: National Policy Association.

Petticrew, M. 2003. Presumed Innocent: Why We Need Systematic Reviews of Social Policies. *American Journal of Preventive Medicine* 24 (3S): 2–3.

Politzer, R., J. Yoon, L. Shi, et al. 2001. Inequality in America: The Contribution of Health Centers in Reducing and Eliminating Disparities in Access to Care. *Medical Care Research and Review* 58, no. 2: 234–248.

Puska P., A. Nissinen, J. Tuomilehto, et al. 1985. The Community-Based Strategy to Prevent Coronary Heart Disease: Conclusions from the Ten Years of the North Karelia Project. *Annual Review of Public Health* 6: 147–193.

Rosenfield, S. 1999. Gender and Mental Health: Do Women Have More Psychopathology, Men More, or Both the Same (and Why)? In *A Handbook for the Study of Mental Health: Social Contexts, Theories, and Systems*, ed. A. Horowitz and T. Scheid. Cambridge, UK: Cambridge University Press.

Rumbaut, R. G. 1996. Origins and Destinies: Immigration, Race, and Ethnicity in Contemporary America. In *Origins and Destinies: Immigration, Race, and Ethnicity in America*, ed. S. Pedraza and R. G. Rumbaut. Belmont, CA: Wadsworth.

Singh, G. K., and S. M. Yu. 1996. Adverse Pregnancy Outcomes: Differences between U.S.- and Foreign-Born Women in Major U.S. Racial and Ethnic Groups. *American Journal of Public Health* 86: 837–843.

Smedley, B. D., A. Y. Stith, and A. R. Nelson, eds. 2003. *Unequal Treatment: Confronting Racial and Ethnic Disparities in Health Care*. Washington, DC: National Academies Press, Institute of Medicine.

Sterling, T. D., and J. Weinkam. 1989. Comparison of Smoking-Related Risk Factors among Black and White Males. *American Journal of Industrial Medicine* 15: 319–333.

Stronks, K. 2002. Generating Evidence on Interventions to Reduce Inequalities in Health: The Dutch Case. *Scandanavian Journal of Public Health* 30 (suppl. 59): 20–25.

Tarlov, A. R. 2000. Public Policy Frameworks for Improving Population Health. In *The Society and Population Health Reader: A State and Community Perspective*, ed. A. R. Tarlov and R. F. St. Peter. New York: New Press.

Taylor, S. E., L. C. Klein, B. P. Lewis, et al. 2000. Biobehavioral Responses to Stress in Females: Tend-and-Befriend, Not Fight-or-Flight. *Psychological Review* 107: 411–429.

U.S. Department of Health and Human Services (DHHS). 2000. *Healthy People 2010*. 2nd ed. Washington, DC: U.S. Government Printing Office.

———. 2003. Centers for Disease Control and Prevention, National Center for Health Statistics. *Mortality Tables*. Available at *www.cdc.gov/nchs/datawh/statab/unpubd/mortabs.htm*.

van Ryn, M., and J. Burke. 2000. The Effect of Patient Race and Socio-Economic Status on Physicians' Perceptions of Patients. *Social Science and Medicine* 50, no. 6: 813–828.

Vega, W. A., and H. Amaro. 1994. Latino Outlook: Good Health, Uncertain Prognosis. *Annual Review of Public Health* 15: 39–67.

Viscusi, W. K. 1993. The Value of Risks to Life and Health. *Journal of Economic Literature* 31: 1912–1946.

Warner, K. E. 2000. The Need for, and Value of, a Multi-Level Approach to Disease Prevention: The Case of Tobacco Control. In *Promoting Health: Intervention Strategies from Social and Behavioral Research*, ed. B. D. Smedley and S. L. Syme. Washington, DC: National Academies Press.

Weinick, R. M., and S. H. Zuvekas. 2000. Racial and Ethnic Differences in Access to and Use of Health Care Services, 1977 to 1996. *Medical Care Research Review* 57 (suppl. 1): 36–54.

Williams, D. R. 2001. Racial Variations in Adult Health Status: Patterns, Paradoxes, and Prospects. In *America Becoming: Racial Trends and Their Consequences,* vol. 2, ed. N. Smelser, W. J. Wilson, and F. Mitchell. Washington, DC: National Academies Press.

———. 2003. The Health of Men: Structured Inequalities and Opportunities. *American Journal of Public Health* 93, no. 5: 724–731.

Williams, D. R., and C. Collins. 1995. U.S. Socioeconomic and Racial Differences in Health. *Annual Review of Sociology* 21: 349–386.

———. 2001. Racial Residential Segregation: A Fundamental Cause of Racial Disparities in Health. *Public Health Reports* 116: 404–415.

Wright, J. C., and M. C. Weinstein. 1998. Gains in Life Expectancy from Medical Interventions: Standardizing Data on Outcomes. *New England Journal of Medicine* 339, no. 6: 380–386.

Zane, N.W.S., D. T. Takeuchi, and K.N.S. Young. 1994. *Confronting Critical Health Issues of Asian and Pacific Islander Americans*. Thousand Oaks, CA: Sage.

CHAPTER 9

Addressing Racial Inequality in Health Care

SARA ROSENBAUM AND JOEL TEITELBAUM

Focusing on the role of race in health policy is not easy. Any such analysis raises a host of complex issues that lie at the policy intersection of health care and civil rights. More fundamentally perhaps, such an exploration cannot proceed without confronting two matters that many might prefer to avoid. The first is the historical dominance of racially biased attitudes, beliefs, and customs in medicine no less than in other areas of life, such as education, employment, housing, transportation, public accommodations, and even marriage and family formation. The second, which follows on from the first, is the need for the medical system itself to be an equal player in a broad national undertaking, which includes active policy interventions when necessary, to find ways to erase discrimination's vestiges.

Some may believe that race is too profound a societal issue to lend itself to a public policy response. Research on health and health care unfortunately tends to bolster this perception by failing to push beyond statistical analysis of racial disparities to explore their underlying causes.[1] Even more troubling are the disparity studies that conclude by speculating on the possible roles of patient attitudes and preferences without giving equal weight to the possible roles of systemic factors. There are far too few studies, such as that conducted by Schulman and colleagues (1999), which attempt to probe the role in health disparities that may be played by physician perception and clinical judgment. Furthermore, it is not uncommon to find that such evidence is either met with denial or whitewashed when it is presented (Geiger 2004).

In their watershed chronicle of race and health care, *An American Health Dilemma,* W. Michael Byrd and Linda A. Clayton present an almost overwhelming picture of a problem that lies at the juncture of culture and policy (2002). In the authors' view, the attitudes, preferences, and beliefs that must change are not those of individual patients but those of the health care system itself. This study depicts a threefold dilemma: a social expectation that minority Americans will experience substandard health status; a highly privatized health system that accords broad discretion to entrepreneurs and marginalizes poor and minority members;

and a widespread refusal to acknowledge the problem of racial segregation and exclusion in health care. This exhaustive exploration underscores that were the nation to minimize the role of law and policy in changing health care culture, it would commit an error as serious as ignoring policy tools in other social settings.

Using the law to move a nation to address race is inherent to democratic government. Law can be understood as the formal language by which society shapes, institutionalizes, and preserves its mores (Friedman 2002); and thus, the notion that racial matters should be addressed in laws that govern the health care system is hardly radical. Indeed, official racial segregation sanctions once dominated the law, not merely in the southern states, but also as part of the federal Hospital Survey and Construction Act of 1946 (Hill Burton), which authorized the construction of segregated facilities (Smith 1999). Just fifty years have passed since *Brown v. Board of Education*, and it has only been forty years since *Simkins v. Moses Cone Hospital*, in which the federal courts declared segregated health facilities unconstitutional.[2] Furthermore, scores of communities managed to preserve health care's racial divide even after this decision, through the use of laws and policies governing hospitals' medical staffing privileges (Smith 1999; Byrd and Clayton 2002; Bobinski 2003; Trubek and Das 2003; IOM 2003; U.S. Commission on Civil Rights 1999).

Not only do the specific remedial tools that public policy can bring to bear on social problems argue for a vibrant role for law in race and health care. The very use of the legal process itself signals the nation's willingness to use a public, democratic forum—its most formal, transparent, and visible means of social ordering—to address race. Robert Caro's description, in *Master of the Senate* (2002), of the debate over the 1957 Civil Rights Act illuminates the role of lawmaking in challenging racial beliefs. As Caro notes, the true import of this debate for national civil rights policy lay far less in the law that ultimately emerged (true reform would not arrive until the Civil Rights Act of 1964) than in the act of public debate itself. The issue of race in health care is simply too important to leave to the less visible world of shifting social attitudes.

Despite the distance yet to travel, the paucity of data measuring racial progress, and lingering barriers to care, efforts to address race in health care reveal the profound impact of laws. These include legislation desegregating U.S. hospitals and creating public financing programs, which exerted an enormous impact on systemic barriers to care (Smith 1999). Legislation also established community health centers in medically underserved, disproportionately minority communities (Davis and Schoen 1977; IOM 2003; U.S. Commission on Civil Rights 1999; Byrd and Clayton 2002; GAO 2003; Shone et al. 2003).

Addressing race and health care requires understanding the interaction between civil rights law and the vast body of law that collectively defines and influences the financing and provision of health care (Rosenbaum and Teitelbaum 2003). One law in particular—Title VI of the 1964 Civil Rights Act—has tended to dominate legal analysis of race and health care. Title VI prohibits discrimination in federally assisted programs and services and defines virtually all sources of public health care financing as a form of federal assistance. Furthermore, Title VI reaches not only intentional discrimination (known as disparate treatment) but also seemingly neutral conduct that nonetheless—as shown by statistical evidence—has an adverse impact on racial and ethnic minority groups (Perez 2003). This latter form of conduct has long been termed "disparate impact" and has obvious parallels to more recent discussion of health disparities.

This classic legal construct, which grounds the problem of disparities in the law of civil rights, may now be giving way to shared ownership with the law of health care quality. Shifting the legal paradigm from civil rights to health quality may make the conversation easier and remedies more attainable. Certainly, the task of proving a legal wrong cannot be any more challenging under a quality paradigm than as a civil rights violation. Proving the latter is extraordinarily difficult given the lack of a universal and compulsory system for collecting data on patient care by race, the most crucial evidence in a disparate treatment claim.

Even assuming statistics do exist, litigating a case of discrimination requires a plaintiff to be able to prove not only injury but also at least proximate causation, a very high bar. The result is that only those acts that have the most visible and overt potential impact on minority populations, such as hospital closures or relocations, or the segregation of patient floors or wings by race, have tended to be litigated (Rosenbaum, Markus, and Darnell 2000). Furthermore, many of the most troubling examples of racial disparities may be replete with confounding factors where the law is concerned. Proving a civil rights claim requires isolating these potential confounders to show that the injury was indeed racial rather than economic or tied to health status. In this regard, of course, an added complication is the extent to which physicians' choice of diagnosis and treatment approaches in specific types of cases affects the outcome of care (IOM 2003). Basing treatments on individuals' financial status or ability to "benefit" from treatment may be troubling but nonetheless may not violate Title VI, whose scope is confined to racially identifiable injury. Health care discrimination cases brought under Title VI thus remain relatively few and far between (Rosenbaum, Markus, and Darnell 2000; Watson 1990).

Federal oversight of civil rights compliance—groundbreaking in the early years of the Civil Rights Act—has also become virtually nonexistent (U.S. Commission on Civil Rights 1999). The near-total absence of federal enforcement has become an even more critical problem in the wake of the 2001 Supreme Court decision in *Alexander v. Sandoval*.[3] That decision virtually eliminated individuals' ability to bring suits aimed at halting practices with discriminatory effects at least against private recipients of federal funds, such as hospitals, nursing homes, and managed care organizations (Rosenbaum and Teitelbaum 2003).

The modern consumerism movement might have given new strength to challenges to perceived discrimination in health care. But modern health care consumerism has its roots in the law of markets, not in the law of civil rights; and, as a result, the legal framework of open markets applies (Havighurst 2002). Market advocates emphasize information, choice, and transparency rather than the establishment of legal rights of patients and substantive operational duties on the part of providers (Halvorson and Isham 2003). While the concept of transparency might propel such advances in industry practices as the greater availability of racially relevant information on quality and utilization, the disproportionately weak purchasing power of many racial and ethnic minority groups, related to their higher poverty, health risks, and lack of insurance, makes this result unlikely.

Health policy debates that focus on race are thus fraught with legal complications and raise issues that the nation—especially the medical care system—would prefer to avoid. Furthermore, the relatively limited power of minority consumers as a group may serve to undermine rather than advance their position in an age of consumerism. Still, despite these challenges, the discussion of race and health care has not only persisted but broadened to include health care quality along with civil rights. Indeed, the continued dominance of race as a public policy matter in both legislatures and the courts has, if anything, reinforced the search for the means to advance the issue of race in health policy.[4]

What Does the Evidence Show?

Considerable research into racial disparities in health supports several basic conclusions. First, while patient preference and what is referred to as "lifestyle" may play some role, socioeconomic factors appear to be powerful drivers of racial disparities in health. This is particularly true for measures of mortality and morbidity from preventable causes as well as complications of illness (IOM 2003; Bobinski 2003; U.S. DHHS 2000). Second, even when patient characteristics are controlled, differences in use and outcomes are evident, a finding that suggests the role of the medical care system itself in contributing to racial disparities (Geiger 2004). Barriers seem to arise after individuals have already entered the medical care system, when practice style rather than individual behavior tends to dominate the course of events (IOM 2003).

Third, racial disparities in access to health care and outcomes appear pervasive, affecting numerous health conditions and health care settings, even when investigators control for insurance status and income. Were race a predictor of health care and outcomes only in isolated circumstances, the inference might be weaker, but the pattern surmounts the bounds of mere coincidence (IOM 2003; Kaiser Family Foundation 2003; Collins, Hall, and Neuhaus 1999; Geiger 2004).

Fourth, for a number of reasons, the nation's approach to health insurance significantly discriminates against racial and ethnic minorities. In a voluntary, employment-based health care system, economically disadvantaged individuals (who are more likely to be members of racial and ethnic minority groups) are more likely to be either uninsured or publicly insured (Kaiser Family Foundation 2003; Hall, Collins, and Glied 1999). These racial disparities permeating the health insurance system persist even into old age. Among Medicare beneficiaries aged sixty-five and older, non-Latino white beneficiaries are significantly more likely to possess supplemental employer-sponsored or other private coverage, while their minority counterparts are six to seven times more reliant on Medicaid to supplement Medicare (Kaiser Family Foundation 2003).

Fifth, large racial gaps appear in patients' access to health care, even when personal characteristics are held constant. Minority patients, particularly those of Latino descent, are more likely to lack a usual source of health care and less likely to use any medical services. Regardless of whether the measure is primary care or specialty care, minority populations also show a consistent pattern of lower levels of utilization, and disparities persist even when researchers control for income (Kaiser Family Foundation 2003).

Finally, and perhaps most compelling from a policy standpoint, even when minority patients have entered the health system, they are less likely to receive the level of care accorded nonminority patients for the same conditions regardless of insurance status (Bobinski 2003; IOM 2003). Medicare managed-care enrollees, for example, receive differential levels of treatment based on race for comparable cardiovascular conditions such as acute myocardial infarction (Schneider, Zaslavsky, and Epstein 2002). Latino and African American patients with public insurance do not receive coronary artery bypass surgery at rates comparable to their white, publicly insured counterparts. African American patients are also less likely to receive treatment for early-stage lung cancer and, not surprisingly, post lower five-year survival rates. Minority nursing home residents with cancer are more likely to experience untreated daily pain (Kaiser Family Foundation 2003).

Studies reveal important racial disparities in managing chronic illness as well. Medicaid-insured African American and Latino children use less primary care, depend more extensively on emergency departments, experience higher rates of hospitalization, and die at significantly higher rates than their white counterparts (IOM 2003; Kaiser Family Foundation 2003). Together, these results reveal a broad and consistent relationship between the race of patients and the use and outcome of care, regardless of whether treatment entails primary care or specialized services. The health care financing system intensifies these results because it works least well for economically disadvantaged racial and ethnic minority groups.

The cumulative evidence flowing from this immense body of research supports several major policy inferences. The most controversial is the inference that the medical care system itself acts in ways that are discriminatory in result, if not in design. This inference is controversial because its ultimate evidentiary source is real clinicians and institutions interacting with real patients. It suggests that the very act of medical decision making can increase the potential for racially identifiable outcomes even where none are intended (Bloche 2001).

This link between the conduct of individual physicians and institutions and patterns of patient care is hardly a new one. In a compelling study conducted nearly forty years ago, two Yale researchers, physician Raymond Duff and sociologist August Hollingshead, chronicled the relationship between patients and clinicians at Yale New Haven Hospital. They observed a correlation between patients' economic and racial characteristics and the extent to which the hospital and its medical staff—as a result of both individual conduct and institutional protocols—acted as their "committed sponsors." Patients who experienced what Hollingshead and Duff brilliantly termed "committed sponsorship" from their physicians showed better survival rates and health outcomes; those who did not fared poorly, as measured by mortality, morbidity, and overall health quality (Duff and Hollingshead

1968). This seminal work points to the fundamental connection between the relationship between physicians and patients, on one hand, and good results in a complex health system, on the other. This finding should hardly surprise anyone who knows the system, yet it has only recently reemerged as a focus of policy attention.

The potential of the U.S. health care enterprise to produce racially identifiable results extends beyond the individual conduct of clinicians and institutions, however. Equally important to both minority patients and minority communities are the broad discretion accorded the health care industry—at both the practitioner and corporate entity level—to select both product and geographic markets and the general lack of governmental standards or oversight of aggressive market conduct (Rosenbaum 2003). It is true that the government has made modest investments in programs to compensate for market failure in the area of primary care, such as community health centers and other community-based and publicly supported services. But these providers (whose services are consistently recognized for their high quality) hardly can overcome the effects of an immense and inaccessible system of specialized and extended health services.

Discretion over the design of health care markets can have important racial implications. With the demise of health planning in most states and communities, providers' decisions regarding location and services—such as whether to stay in the city or move to the suburbs and whether to offer outpatient and diabetes management programs—become matters of business strategy rather than community need. U.S. civil rights law has been particularly unhelpful regarding the basic business of health care: virtually every case challenging health care closures and relocations on civil rights grounds has lost. One review of cases from 1965 to 1998 suggests that Title VI claims tend to succeed only when evidence shows discrimination within a particular market or institution, rather than refusal by a health care provider to either enter or remain in a market (Rosenbaum, Markus, and Darnell 2000). Similarly, although refusal by hospitals and nursing homes to accept Medicaid patients has been shown to have a disproportionate adverse impact on minority patients in violation of Title VI, this evidence has virtually never been used by courts or legislatures to compel provider participation in Medicaid.

Managed care had the potential to open new markets to publicly insured minority patients by imposing on network providers a contractual duty of care toward plan members. However, this is not how managed care has in fact played out. Residential segregation in many communities has limited care networks to the physicians and safety net providers already serving affected neighborhoods. Moreover, those physicians who are members of networks have resisted the "all-products" clauses that insurers attempted to write into their provider agreements, insisting on maintaining the right to select their patients (Rosenbaum et al. 1997).

Medicaid managed care is especially important for minority populations, given the tendency toward a racially identifiable distribution of health plan members by payer type. Medicaid has played a fundamental role in reducing disparities, and its value for persons with chronic illness and disabilities compared with more limited conventional insurance can hardly be overstated (Rosenbaum 2002; Weil 2003). But Medicaid managed care today is dominated by specialty companies typically affiliated with safety net providers who already treat beneficiaries. As impressive as the health care safety net has been in terms of clinical quality and overall commitment to community-wide outcomes, individual clinics continue to report serious problems ensuring access to specialty care for their publicly insured patients (Gusmano, Fairbrother, and Park 2002). Although the growing dominance of managed care organizations in public insurance for lower-income patients may appear to have improved access by integrating service delivery and financing, the extent of improvements remains an open question characterized by a conflicting body of evidence (Rosenblatt, Law, and Rosenbaum 1997).

The Law and Policy Implications of Race and Health Care

Maintaining a focus on the intersection between racial disparities and legal interventions remains an important policy priority. Legislation introduced in both the House and the Senate in 2003 attests to the persistence of racial inequality in health care as a target of legal intervention. This legislation would address racial disparities through an array of venues, from more active enforcement by civil rights agencies to additional programs and services aimed at improving minority access to health care.[5]

A good part of the problem of using civil rights laws aimed at the protection of racial and ethnic minority groups to address racial disparities in health and health care is the confounding effects of socioeconomic and health insurance status. In this regard, legislation reforming insurance coverage would by definition amount to a legal intervention aimed at reducing racial disparities. For example, a uniform, universal health insurance scheme that did not distinguish by employment, family income, or place of residence in either coverage or financing might be expected to reduce barriers to health care and improve the supply and distribution of health resources in poorer communities. Past efforts to expand Medicare and Medicaid coverage certainly are dramatic testaments to the power of major insurance reform in fostering racial equality (Davis and Schoen 1977; Kaiser Family Foundation 2003).

But favorable racial results are a possible byproduct of insurance reform rather than a specific remedy aimed squarely at reducing documented disparities. Furthermore, the evidence shows that financing improvements alone might well mitigate the role of race in health care only modestly, since, even controlling for income and coverage, researchers find that disparities persist (IOM 2003).

These studies suggest the importance of addressing racial disparities in health and health care directly, rather than hoping for progress as a felicitous byproduct of insurance reform. From a public policy standpoint, reducing disparities requires a formal and enforceable scheme that promotes accountability toward discrete subgroups of patients as well as the overall population. Such a scheme would act as a lever for advancing reforms that otherwise might languish, and whose importance easily can be obscured by the aggregated results of generalized improvement activities.

The power of law to compel change in custom and practice is fundamental to the premise of law itself, and evidence of this power is visible in civil rights laws such as Title VI of the 1964 Civil Rights Act, financing programs such as Medicare and Medicaid, and laws aimed at improving health care quality (Smith 1999; Rosenblatt, Law, and Rosenbaum 1997). Perhaps the most famous articulation of the role of law in altering outmoded or inappropriate custom arises in the context of legal accountability for one's conduct, in the landmark case of *The T. J. Hooper*. In that 1932 case, Judge Learned Hand emphasized that reasonable conduct—determined by objective evaluation of relevant evidence rather than by industry custom—was the proper legal standard for ensuring public accountability.[6]

Two important legal traditions could anchor a formal scheme of public accountability for reducing health disparities: the law of civil rights and the law of health care quality. The point at which these two legal traditions converge in the flow of federal Medicare and Medicaid funds deserves careful attention because of the power of financing to shape the structure and process of medical care.

Innovations in Civil Rights Law

Individual enforcement has always been a central tool of civil rights law because of the lack of agency oversight, but in this regard the *Alexander v. Sandoval* decision represents an unprecedented diminution of individuals' ability to counter industry practices that have discriminatory effects (Rosenbaum and Teitelbaum 2003). In a post-*Sandoval* world, even if individuals claiming disparate impact surmount barriers such as the lack of data, cost of litigation, and difficulty in meeting the legal burden of proof, this decision amounts to a total bar to individual enforcement of Title VI's de facto discrimination ban, at least regarding private entities.

But *Sandoval* addressed only the question of whether individuals could enforce the discriminatory impact rule. It did not grapple with whether Title VI's effects test is enforceable by federal agencies. This crucial fact raises once again the notion of breathing new life into direct federal enforcement of providers' legal obligations under federal civil rights law. A policy statement released by Justice Department officials in the wake of the *Sandoval* decision reiterated the power of agency enforceability. Moreover, recent administration actions regarding access to care by persons with limited English proficiency suggest a renewed willingness to use civil rights law to reduce health disparities (Rosenbaum and Teitelbaum 2003).

Civil rights laws that link eligibility for federal grants and contracts to nondiscrimination standards could be effectuated by conditioning Medicare and Medicaid payments on evidence of provider adherence to specific conduct aimed at promoting access and quality of care for minority patients. The standards could then be enforced through the reporting of patient care data by race. In essence, this is the approach taken by the Office for Civil Rights in its formulation of standards of conduct for programs and entities serving non-English speaking persons. This approach could be extended to other aspects of health care operations as well, including service arrangements, the design and implementation of residency and health professions training programs, and other practices linked to access to care.

Such a regulatory approach effectively mirrors the early days of Title VI, when federal officials conditioned eligibility for Medicare and Medicaid payments on a showing of nondiscrimination (Smith 1999). For this approach to work, officials would have to develop specific performance standards in areas that research links to reducing disparity. For example, agencies might condition federal payments on modifications in facility staffing, training programs, clinical affiliations, practice techniques, and diversity training. To be legally viable as a Title VI-propelled standard, the conduct in question must be reasonably related to disparate racial outcomes and need not be linked to evidence of intentional discrimination. A second civil rights-based approach—closely linked to the first but cast as an incentive—would be to establish legal "safe harbors." The federal guidance regarding the obligations of health care providers toward persons with limited English proficiency (LEP) contains the seeds of this approach. This guidance, originated by the Clinton administration in 2000 and revised by the Bush administration in 2003, details broad standards that federally assisted providers must satisfy to comply with Title VI. (Ironically, perhaps, the *Sandoval* decision also involved barriers to such federally assisted services.) Although the Bush administration exempted physicians in private practice whose only source of federal assistance is Medicare, these guidelines nonetheless retain considerable breadth. In effect, the LEP guidance creates legal safe harbors against civil liability for "disparate impact" under Title VI.

This approach is loosely modeled on strategies for enforcing antitrust and fraud and abuse statutes that could be used to address other goals for reducing health disparities as well. Recent research links improvements in health care quality to reductions in racial disparities (Sehgal 2003). Thus, tying training programs and quality improvement activities to data on access and outcomes by race might ensure compliance by health care institutions with federal civil rights standards.

In short, developing health-care-related Title VI standards for racial and ethnic minority patients similar to the LEP standard should be feasible. Such standards could establish goals aimed at eliminating health care disparities and allow providers to show compliance with those goals by collecting, analyzing, and publishing data. This approach borrows heavily from the methods developed for measuring improvements in health care quality now widely accepted by providers and purchasers alike.

Developing such policies would be complex, but no less so than creating any performance measurement system that is valid, reliable, and reasonably calculated to measure the desired conduct, adjusted to control for individual cases. Given systems for collecting information by racial and ethnic origin, providers can adapt systems for measuring quality to those measuring progress in reducing racial disparities. This approach would acknowledge the basic link between civil rights law and efforts to remedy racial disparities through health care financing.

The Law of Health Care Quality

For decades, civil rights law has "owned" the concept of racial disparities; indeed, the concept of disparity in treatment originated in civil rights theory and practice. Racial disparities as a distinct concept in health quality, in contrast, first loomed large in the late 1990s as part of a deliberate effort by the Clinton administration to broaden the legal and policy approach to race in health care. This new paradigm has gained sufficient momentum so that the Bush administration has continued to emphasize racial disparities as a separate and independent measure of health quality, albeit by softening the language about the effects (or extent) of disparities in its reports to Congress (Geiger 2004).

In reconceptualizing racial disparities as an independent measure of health quality, federal officials have succeeded in accomplishing what two generations of civil rights legal advocacy could not: framing evidence of racial disparities as related not only to legal discrimination but to poor quality. This reframing has not only expanded public understanding of the problem, but also served to minimize the need to distinguish between economic and racial factors, a necessary step in using civil rights law as legal leverage over the health care system. Disparities in health care have become an all-important component of the growing effort to identify formal interventions aimed at promoting health care quality. Research suggests a focus on three distinct areas: health care management and practice (staff privilege rules, clinical program affiliations, training programs, and participation in public insurance programs), the process of care (staff training and education and clinical practice style), and clinical outcomes and consumer experiences. Of particular importance, in our view, is broadening the avenues into and through care and the nature of health professionals who achieve formal status and influence. In view of the link between the physician-patient relationship and health quality, public programs could link institutional eligibility for training funds to race-conscious admissions policies, as permitted by the Supreme Court in 2003. Also important could be incorporating cultural training into education curricula, as it appears to influence the quality of clinical care (Betancourt 2003).

As with a civil rights approach, enforcing the law of quality could entail both regulations and incentives. Enforcement of a quality-based model could occur through not only federal payers (Medicare, Medicaid, and the Children's Health Insurance Program) but also state payers (and regulatory and licensure agencies) and even public and private employers. The latter could include private employer-sponsored health plans and public employee plans for both civilian and military workers, such as the Federal Employees Health Benefits Program, which can achieve similar results through contractual specifications.

A health quality agenda for reducing racial disparities requires widespread acceptance of the need to collect and publish much more extensive data on patients' race, payer, and income. The health care system has ferociously resisted collecting such data in a civil rights context, so these efforts do not exist outside of a few Medicare reporting systems. Indeed, one of the best-known pieces of civil rights litigation stemmed from the secretary of Health and Human Services' unsuccessful effort to mandate a collection system (Rosenbaum, Markus, and Darnell 2000).

The world of health quality has no equivalent to *Sandoval.* No court has ruled that individuals cannot sue over quality of care and medical negligence, and basic common law principles could form the foundation for medical tort claims under state law (Rosenblatt, Law, and Rosenbaum 1997). Extending confidentiality to information collected for studying racial disparities could address this legal exposure, just as the law protects information stemming from medical peer review (Marchev 2003).

Achieving consensus on the use of law and policy to encourage efforts to reduce racial disparities would be difficult, but the discomfort caused by this debate only underscores its importance. Ideally U.S. mores, preferences, attitudes, and beliefs would be free of racial overtones. But despite decades of progress, race remains very much alive in the American consciousness and national experience. Thus race in all its complexity must continue to play a central role in the U.S. health policy debate, no matter how painful the discussion or complex the policy response. In our view, belief in simpler solutions such as better insurance coverage and more patient choice overlooks more than two centuries of history as well as a litany of studies showing that race really matters. The sooner the nation actively adopts the goal of reducing disparities in health care policy and practice, the stronger the health care system will be.

Notes

1. A comprehensive treatment of race and health policy would focus not only on medical care but also on the inequalities in health determinants that underlie disparities in health (Bobinski 2003).
2. *Brown v. Board of Education,* 347 U.S. 483 (1954); *Simkins v. Moses H. Cone Memorial Hospital,* 323 F.2d 959 (4th Cir. 1963).
3. *Alexander v. Sandoval,* 532 U.S. 275 (2001).
4. *Grutter v. Bollinger,* 123 S. Ct. 2325 (2003).
5. Healthcare Equality and Accountability Act, S. 1833; H.R. 3459 (108th Cong., 1st sess., 2003).
6. *The T. J. Hooper,* 60 F. 2d 737, 2d Cir. (1932).

References

American Medical Association. 2002. *Letter to Department of Health and Human Services re: HHS Regulatory Reform Initiative and Various Relief Issues.* March 5. Available at *www.ama-assn.org/ama/pub/article/5922–5984.html* (accessed August 22, 2003).

———. 2003. *Letter to Brenda Aguilar.* April 21. Available at *www.ama-assn.org/ama/pub/article/6073–5812.html* (accessed August 22, 2003).

———. 2003. *Comments on the Proposed Rule to Modify Certain Standards in the Rule Entitled "Standards for Privacy of Individually Identifiable Health Information."* Available at *www.ama-assn.org/ama/pub/article/6073–5812.html* (accessed August 22, 2003).

Albert, T. 2003. Doctors Say Medical Assistance Should Face Lawsuit in Girl's Death. *American Medical News,* August 18. Available at *www.ama-assn.org* (accessed August 22, 2003).

Betancourt, J. 2003. Cross Cultural Medical Education: Conceptual Approaches and Frameworks for Evaluation. *Academic Medicine* 78: 560–569.

Bloche, M. G. 2001. Race and Discretion in American Medicine. *Yale Journal of Health Policy, Law, and Ethics* 1: 95–130.

Bobinski, M. A. 2003. Health Disparities and the Law: Wrongs in Search of a Right. *American Journal of Law and Medicine* 29, no. 2–3: 363–381.

Burris, S. 2003. Envisioning Health Disparities. *American Journal of Law and Medicine* 29, no. 2–3: 151–159.

Byrd, W. M., and L. A. Clayton 2002. *An American Health Dilemma: Race, Medicine, and Health Care in the United States, 1900–2000.* New York: Routledge.

Caro, R. 2002. *Master of the Senate.* New York: Knopf.

Collins, K. C., A. Hall, and C. Neuhaus. 1999. *U.S. Minority Health: A Chartbook.* New York: Commonwealth Fund. Available at *www.cmwf.org/programs/minority/collins_minority_chartbook_321.pdf* (accessed January 3, 2004).

Davis, K., and C. Schoen. 1977. *Health and the War on Poverty.* Washington, DC: Brookings.

Duff, R., and A. B. Hollingshead. 1968. *Sickness and Society.* New York: Harper & Row.

Friedman, L. M. 2002. *Law in America: A Short History.* New York: Modern Library.

Gatzman v. Salamatin. 2003. Muskogee County, OK. Pet. CJ-03-1024. Filed June 30.

Geiger, H. J. 2004. Why Is HHS Obscuring a Health Care Gap? *Washington Post*, January 27, A-17.

General Accounting Office (GAO). 2003. *Health Care: Approaches to Address Racial and Ethnic Disparities.* GAO-03-862R. Washington, DC: General Accounting Office.

Gornick, M. 2001. Understanding Disparities in the Use of Medicare Services. *Yale Journal of Health Policy, Law, and Ethics* 1: 133–171.

Gostin, L. O. 2002. *Public Health Law and Ethics: A Reader.* Los Angeles: University of California Press; and New York: Milbank Memorial Fund.

Gusmano, M., G. Fairbrother, and H. Park. 2002. Exploring the Limits of the Safety Net: Community Health Centers and Care for the Uninsured. *Health Affairs* 21, no. 6: 188–194.

Hall, A., K. S. Collins, and S. Glied. 1999. *Employer-Sponsored Health Insurance: Implications for Minority Workers.* New York: Commonwealth Fund. Available at *www.cmwf.org/programs/minority/hall_minorityinsur_314.asp* (accessed January 3, 2004).

Halvorson, G. C., and G. J. Isham. 2003. *Epidemic of Care.* San Francisco: Jossey-Bass.

Havighurst, C. G. 2002. Is the Health Revolution Finished? How the Health Care Revolution Fell Short. *Law and Contemporary Health Problems* 65: 55–99.

Institute of Medicine (IOM). 2003. *Unequal Treatment: Confronting Racial and Ethnic Disparities in Health Care.* Washington, DC: National Academies Press.

Johnson, H., and D. Broder. 1997. *The System.* New York: Random House.

Kaiser Family Foundation. 2003. *Key Facts: Race, Ethnicity, and Medical Care.* Washington, DC. Available at *www.kff.org/sections.cgi?section=minority&disp=10* (accessed August 22, 2003).

Link, B., and J. Phelan. 1995. Social Conditions as Fundamental Causes of Disease. *Journal of Health and Social Behavior* 87: 80–94.

Marchev, M. 2003. *Medical Malpractice and Medical Error Disclosure: Balancing Facts and Fears.* Portland, ME: National Academy for State Health Policy.

Mayberry, R. M., F. Mili, and E. Ofili. 2000. Racial and Ethnic Differences in Access to Medical Care. *Medical Care Research and Review* 57 (suppl.): 108–146.

Perez, T. 2003. The Civil Rights Dimensions of Racial and Ethnic Disparities in Health Care. *Unequal Treatment: Confronting Racial and Ethnic Disparities in Health Care.* Washington, DC: National Academies Press.

Rosenbaum, S. 2002. Health Policy: Medicaid. *New England Journal of Medicine* 343 (February 21): 635–640.

————. 2003. The Impact of U.S. Law on Medicine as a Profession. *Journal of the American Medical Association* 289: 546–557.

Rosenbaum, S., A. R. Markus, and J. Darnell. 2000. U.S. Civil Rights Policy and Access to Health Care by Minority Americans: Implications for a Changing Health Care System. *Medical Care Research and Review* 57 (suppl.): 236–260.

Rosenbaum, S., and J. Teitelbaum. 2003. Civil Rights Enforcement in the Modern Healthcare System: Reinvigorating the Role of the Federal Government in the Aftermath of *Alexander v. Sandoval*. *Yale Journal of Health Law and Policy* 5: 1–71.

Rosenbaum, S., and P. Shin. 2003. *Health Centers as Safety Net Providers: An Overview and Assessment of Medicaid's Role*. Washington, DC: Kaiser Family Foundation. Available at *www.kff.org/content/2003/4113/4113.pdf* (accessed August 22, 2003).

Rosenbaum, S., C. Sonosky, P. Shin, L. Repasch, and M. Zakheim. 1999. *Negotiating the New Health System: A Nationwide Study of Medicaid Managed Care Contracts*. Washington, DC: George Washington University Medical Center.

Rosenbaum, S., R. Serrano, M. Magar, and G. Stern. 1997. Civil Rights in a Changing Health Care System. *Health Affairs* 16: 90–105.

Rosenblatt, R. A., S. Law, and S. Rosenbaum. 1997. *Law and the American Health Care System*. New York: Foundation Press.

Schneider, E. C., A. M. Zaslavsky, and A. Epstein. 2002. Racial Disparities in the Quality of Health Care for Enrollees in Medicare Managed Care. *Journal of the American Medical Association* 287: 1288–1294.

Schulman, K. A., J. Berlin, W. Harliss, et al. 1999. The Effect of Race and Sex on Physicians' Recommendations for Cardiac Catheterization. *New England Journal of Medicine* 340: 618–626.

Sehgal, A. 2003. Impact of Quality Improvement Efforts on Race and Sex Disparities in Hemodialysis. *Journal of the American Medical Association* 289: 996–1000.

Shone, L., A. Dick, C. Brach, et al. 2003. Race and Ethnicity in SCHIP in Four States: Are There Baseline Disparities, and What Do They Mean for SCHIP? *Pediatrics* 112, no. 6, pt. 2: e521.

Smith, D. B. 1999. *Health Care Divided*. Ann Arbor: University of Michigan.

Teitelbaum, J., and S. Rosenbaum. 2003. Medical Care as a Public Accommodation: Moving the Discussion to Race. *American Journal of Law and Medicine* 29, no. 2–3: 381–395.

Trubeck, L. G., and M. Das. 2003. Achieving Equality: Healthcare Governance in Transition. *American Journal of Law and Medicine* 29, no. 2–3: 395–422.

U.S. Commission on Civil Rights. 1999. *The Health Care Challenge: Acknowledging Disparity, Confronting Discrimination, and Ensuring Equality*. Vol. 2, *The Role of Federal Civil Rights Enforcement Efforts*. No. 005-902-00063-1. Washington, DC: USCCR.

U.S. Department of Health and Human Services (DHHS). 2000. *Healthy People 2010*. Available at *www.health.gov/healthypeople* (accessed August 22, 2003).

————. 2003. *Guidance to Federal Financial Assistance Recipients Regarding Title VI Prohibition against National Origin Discrimination Affecting Limited English Proficient Persons*. Office for Civil Rights. 68 Fed. Reg. 47311–47323. August 8.

Watson, S. D. 1990. Reinvigorating Title VI: Defending Health Care Discrimination: It Shouldn't Be So Easy. *Fordham Law Review* 58: 939–1002.

Weil, A. 2003. There's Something about Medicaid. *Health Affairs* 22, no. 1: 13–30.

PART III

*Improving Quality
of Care*

CHAPTER 10

Still Demanding Medical Excellence

———— ∞ ————

MICHAEL L. MILLENSON

Years before the Institute of Medicine began issuing health system quality alerts with nearly the same frequency as Microsoft warnings of rifts in software security, I painstakingly gathered much the same evidence the IOM used to such highly publicized effect.

I was a veteran journalist transformed by the magic wand of a Robert Wood Johnson Foundation Investigator Award into a health policy researcher. As I read and reread the articles, studies, and reports piled on every surface in my small academic office, I was appalled: years of research on important ways to make medical care safer and more effective had produced scarcely any effect on doctors and hospitals. I was also anxious. The trail of clues pointing to needless deaths and injuries seemed to me to be Poe's purloined letter—damning evidence hidden in plain sight. Naturally, I wondered why more seasoned researchers had not already sounded the alarm. Was I failing to detect some mitigating circumstance?

No matter how conservative I tried to be with the actual numbers, the grim bottom line remained. As I would eventually write in a book entitled *Demanding Medical Excellence: Doctors and Accountability in the Information Age,* "From ulcers to urinary tract infections, tonsils to organ transplants, back pain to breast cancer, asthma to arteriosclerosis, the evidence is irrefutable. Tens of thousands of patients have died or been injured year after year because readily available information was not used—and is not being used today—to guide their care. If one counts the lives lost to preventable medical mistakes, the toll reaches the hundreds of thousands" (Millenson 1997, 353).

Since I began my investigator work in early 1994, and since the words above appeared in late 1997, the movement to measure and manage the quality of medical care has gained significant clinical and political traction. Bits and pieces of the quality improvement (QI) ethos—and in some cases much more than bits and pieces—have become institutionally embedded in medical practice. What has not yet happened, however, is the kind of transformation that would signal a clinical, ethical, and economical clean break with the past. It is as if, in reaction to the thundering condemnation of medical education contained in the 1910 Flexner report, a few schools had overhauled their curriculum while the rest had simply added a couple of biology courses and created an assistant dean for scientific affairs.

I believe the situation regarding medical excellence has changed so slowly because effective quality measurement and management does, in fact, demand true transformation. The IOM's ringing assertion that "systems of care"—which include organizational processes as well as information technology—can prove more important than training for individuals represents a radical departure (IOM 2001). Operationalizing the blueprint for change spelled out by the IOM requires a wholesale reexamination of deeply ingrained practices and beliefs.

As science historian Thomas Kuhn famously pointed out, the traumatic process of adopting a new paradigm does not occur until the defenders of the old ways "can no longer evade anomalies that subvert the existing tradition" (1970, 6). In a similar vein, quality pioneer W. Edwards Deming concluded that systematic quality improvement carries such a large burden of individual and organizational upheaval that it is embraced only when it offers the sole path "out of the crisis" (Deming 1986). Yet while health care pundits regularly and solemnly invoke the notion of "crisis," day-to-day reality belies this broad-brush characterization. In fact, the myriad payers, providers, insurers, and patients who comprise this $1.6 trillion chunk of the U.S. economy remain quite comfortable with traditional approaches, both economically and culturally.

All of which reinforces the insight of Boston surgeon Ernest Amory Codman some ninety years ago. Contemplating the failure of his proposal to improve medical "efficiency" (his phrase for more reliable, high-quality care) by publicizing the outcomes of individual surgeons and hospitals, Codman wrote, "For whose *interest* is it to have the hospital efficient? Strangely enough, the answer is: No one. . . . There is a difference between interest and duty. You do your duty if the work comes to you, but you do not go out of your way to get the work unless it is for your interest" (1934, xviii).

Are the "interest" and "duty" to promote "efficiency" finally converging? I believe they are—not because I am convinced that widespread transformation is already under way, but because irreversible groundwork is now being laid for that transformation. Call it cautious optimism, but optimism nonetheless.

Diffusing Innovations

In his classic work *Diffusion of Innovations,* Everett Rogers wrote that five characteristics hold the key to an innovation's adoption. These include its relative advantage over what already exists; its compatibility with existing values and behaviors; its lack of complexity; its ability to undergo experiment ("trialability"); and its ability to produce results everyone can see ("observability") (Rogers 2003).

The first of Rogers's rules—that an innovation produces "relative advantage"—is roughly equivalent to Codman's rueful realization that those asked to change must believe it is in their interest to do so. The advantage must not only be real; it must be *perceived* as real. Surmounting this barrier can prove surprisingly difficult. Here outside pressure has played a key role in health care QI, as contrasting tales of the patient safety movement and the effort to reduce inappropriate variation in medical practice reveal.

There was no patient safety movement in 1994 when I began my Investigator Award work; today, there is a strong one. No stunning new research emerged during the interim. In 1994 it was well documented that medical errors were common; that doctors and hospitals were in denial about their frequency; that system changes, not "punishing the perpetrators," was needed to eliminate them; and that those changes, particularly when computerized, could be extraordinarily effective.

The 1991 Harvard Medical Practice Study, with its groundbreaking documentation of both the extent and impact of medical mistakes, had exerted virtually no impact on provider behavior. In December 1994 a frustrated Lucian Leape, one of the study's authors, wrote in the *Journal of the American Medical Association (JAMA)* that the profession largely continued to ignore the preventability of medical mistakes, whose death toll equaled that of a crash of two 747s every three days (Leape 1994).

After Leape's accusations (and his airline crash analogy) drew media attention, "hate mail began pouring in" to *JAMA* from AMA members outraged that the journal had printed the piece. Recalled then-editor George Lundberg, "I was accused of being on the side of the lawyers, a damned turncoat and traitor to the cause" (Lundberg 2000). Small wonder that when the *Boston Globe* in early 1995 broke the story of the painful death by chemotherapy drug overdose of its young medical columnist, Betsy Lehman, the American Medical Association's official reaction was that "isolated and sometimes egregious mistakes" happen (McAfee 1995).

Changing Perceptions

So how did perceptions of the relative advantage of comprehensive patient safety reform finally change? To begin with, Lehman's death at a nationally renowned cancer hospital convinced the intellectual leaders of American medicine to directly confront the inadequacy of the "people, not systems" approach. The "best and the brightest" had manifestly failed to protect someone much like themselves—an articulate and informed patient who complained about the drug's effect but was ignored, someone who many medical leaders knew personally.

Lehman's death represented a turning point for the news media as well. Investigations into medical mistakes became a staple of the health care beat, which, in turn, maintained public and political pressure (Millenson 2002). In Boston, physician and hospital organizations formed a coalition to prevent errors, and in Chicago the American Medical Association reversed course and established a National Patient Safety Foundation, which specifically rejected the idea that errors were "uncommon" and endorsed "systematic" efforts to prevent errors.

The 1999 IOM report *To Err Is Human* took the patient safety movement to the next level. The very first effort by the IOM's Committee on the Quality of Health Care in America concluded that forty-four thousand to ninety-eight thousand Americans died in hospitals every year because of preventable medical errors.

Moreover, the report noted pointedly, "Silence surrounds this issue. For the most part, consumers believe they are protected" (IOM 2000, 3).

The research was not new, but the IOM report placed it in a radically different context. First, its statistics were in a simple form designed for maximum public impact: more deaths occurred yearly from medical errors than from breast cancer or AIDS, plus the ever-popular crashing 747 comparison. Moreover, researchers affiliated with the nation's scientific elite had authored this indictment of American medicine for failing to act. Finally, the report linked abstract concepts to concrete consequences. The very first paragraph of *To Err Is Human* named three individual victims, all of whom (including Lehman) had been identified through local newspaper investigations. National television coverage of the IOM report turned those names into faces and families whose fate struck an instant chord with the American people.

A few weeks after *To Err Is Human* was released one poll found that an astonishing 51 percent of the public was aware of its conclusions (Kaiser Family Foundation 1999). Within a year, the U.S. General Accounting Office had produced a report on adverse drug events; members of Congress had introduced legislation requiring reporting of medical errors; and millions of dollars to fight medical mistakes had been channeled to the Agency for Healthcare Research and Quality. State legislators, usually deferential to hospitals and doctors, introduced a brace of error-prevention measures and passed some of them. Separately, a coalition of Fortune 500 employers known as the Leapfrog Group launched an initiative pushing hospitals to install computerized systems for physicians' orders to prevent medication errors. All these moves helped change the perception among providers of the relative advantage of change.

Crucially, pressure for safety improvement has continued, manifested by national and local media attention and a variety of initiatives by legislators, accreditors, and payers at both national and local levels. In one potent symbol, Massachusetts announced in January 2004 the creation of the Betsy Lehman Center for Patient Safety and Medical Error Prevention. Its mission is to promote patient safety through work with governmental agencies, providers, and patients.

Putting Innovation into Practice

The IOM report, the AMA's reversal of its stance on errors, and continuing public pressure also helped galvanize a broad spectrum of professional organizations to address safety, thereby signaling compatibility "with existing values and behaviors"—Rogers's second requirement. One example is the aggressive effort to limit "wrong site" surgery, led by the American Academy of Orthopaedic Surgeons.

Professional support has also proven critical to Rogers's third requirement: "trialability"—specific actions individuals can take to test an innovation. For example, the Boston-based Institute for Healthcare Improvement, a respected independent nonprofit founded by pediatrician and researcher Donald Berwick, has set up "best practice" collaboratives to help organizations handle the nitty-gritty details of instituting the IOM's safety recommendations. Meanwhile the Pittsburgh

Regional Healthcare Initiative is involving the entire provider and payer community in its goal of implementing "zero tolerance" for preventable medication errors and hospital-caused infections. Many provider organizations have launched similar, if less ambitious, efforts.

All these initiatives not only make error-reduction "trialable," but also reduce the complexity of innovation, Rogers's fourth requirement. State-of-the-art safety improvement no longer requires a research infrastructure. Premier, Inc., an alliance of over two hundred hospitals and health care systems, offers a quality prize and says the best safety efforts are now coming from "frontline" hospitals rather than academic research centers. Fairview Hospital of Great Barrington, Massachusetts, with only twenty-four beds, implemented such sweeping safety improvements that it became a national finalist for the American Hospital Association's 2002 Quest for Quality Prize. Meanwhile, efforts to reduce complexity continue. In early 2003, the federal Agency for Healthcare Research and Quality launched a Web-based patient safety and quality improvement forum that features interactive learning modules, online discussion, and expert analysis of medical errors reported anonymously (see *www.webmm.ahrq.gov/*).

Change over the past decade regarding the last item on Rogers's list—observable results—has been striking. Stories of successful efforts to reduce errors have gone from invisible to ubiquitous in professional journals (including articles on impressive successes in reducing errors by the Veterans Health Administration and Boston's Brigham and Women's Hospital), the trade press, conference proceedings, and monthly listservs.

Creating a "Social Epidemic"

Both collectively and synergistically, these safety improvement efforts have begun creating what Malcolm Gladwell calls, in *The Tipping Point* (2000), a "social epidemic." What an intervention needs to shift common practice, Gladwell writes, is not "an avalanche of new or additional information" but rather specific information that allows individuals to understand how the intervention fits "into their lives" (2000, 98). A staple of professional meetings on patient safety, for example, includes a slide with a scribbled prescription that seems to indicate one drug or dosage but actually prescribes something quite different. The same pointed message has also seeped into the public realm, as evidenced by a 2003 *Dilbert* cartoon where Dilbert asks his physician, "What if your bad handwriting causes the pharmacy to give me a harmful medication?" The doctor responds blithely, "That's a little thing I call marketing."

Still, while U.S. medical practice may have reached the tipping point on patient safety, the new paradigm is by no means universal. Safety efforts also remain inpatient focused; outpatient errors, not addressed in the 1999 IOM report, are only beginning to receive sustained attention. Finally, the speed of change sometimes suggests that what has been tipped over is a jar of molasses. In one not atypical example of lionizing the Lilliputian, the Ohio Department of Health related proudly how it was working with provider groups to stop the use of five dangerous abbreviations in prescriptions. The department characterized this effort, which began in early 2003, as a response to the IOM report of 1999. The department said it is "hoping" to eliminate these dangerous and "very easy" to eliminate abbreviations by 2005. Not surprisingly, a 2002 survey by Blendon and colleagues found that practicing physicians do not share the same "sense of urgency expressed by many national organizations" regarding preventing errors (Blendon et al. 2002).

Unvarying Variation

Moreover, the patient safety story is the good news. At the other end of the spectrum is the battle against inappropriate variation in medical practice. In the early 1970s, John Wennberg published his first papers demonstrating high variation in surgical procedures performed on similar types of patients in different areas of the country and within individual states and counties (see Wennberg and Gittelsohn 1973). The road to publication was bumpy, and Dr. Wennberg faced significant resistance from editors at major journals before his papers were ultimately accepted. For his trouble, he was cursed by fellow doctors and lost his academic job.

In the early 1980s, as health care costs soared, Wennberg's research received prominent attention professionally and through Senate hearings and media coverage. Yet efforts to address practice variation did not take hold. In the early 1990s Wennberg's data on variation reemerged into the spotlight with efforts to reform the national health care system; but, once more, no sustained change in practice ensued. A decade later, in 2003, reports of variation in practice seemingly unjustified by better patient outcomes started appearing yet again in publications as diverse as *Self* and *Business Week*.

Viewed within a framework of diffusing innovation, the Wennbergian wheelspinning is not surprising. While the patient safety movement raises sensitive issues, its basic goals are clearly consonant with the bedrock professional value of "first, do no harm." For physicians, protecting patient safety is also financially neutral or positive, as it can help them avoid malpractice suits. Studies of variations in clinical practice, by contrast, can threaten physician income; the purchasers and policymakers who flocked to Wennberg's work were attracted by the possibility of reducing the "high" outliers (surgeons who were likely to operate for a certain problem) to the lower norm, not by the intellectual challenge of discovering whether a higher rate of surgery or a lower rate was really better. In addition, doctors often view studies examining medical variation as clashing with "existing values and behaviors." As medical sociologist Eliot Freidson has observed, "The model of the clinician . . . encourage[s] individual deviation from codified knowledge on the basis of personal, first-hand observation of concrete cases. This deviation is called 'judgment' or even 'wisdom'" (1970, 347). Within that context, variation in medical practice is often seen as a legitimate response to patients' individuality.

Moreover, while patients themselves intuitively understand and are disturbed by "mistakes," variation is a far more elusive concept. Patients may believe that more care represents better care, or that the judgment of their doctors differs from that of their peers because the former are smarter.

Finally, even clinicians who want to reduce inappropriate variation have had no reliable and "non-complex" means of doing so. As Harvard Medical School's Barbara McNeil noted in her 2001 "Shattuck Lecture," efforts to reduce uncertainty and rationalize care have suffered from both a lack of definitive data and delays in translating the information that does exist into usable clinical form.

Breaking the Deadlock

One might ask whether quality measurement and management in the early twenty-first century has dwindled to an effort to implement advice offered by Puritan preacher and physician Cotton Mather at the end of the seventeenth century: "Let this advice for the *sick* be principally attended to: *Don't kill 'em.*" I believe the answer is no—which is where my cautious optimism comes in. For many years attempts to address variation in professional practice and, more broadly, improve outcomes have bogged down in "town-gown" arguments. Practicing physicians have worried that academics unfamiliar with real-world ambiguity were second-guessing their clinical reasoning, while researchers were equally suspicious that in-the-trenches docs respond more to peer pressure and self-interest than to science. Over the past few years, however, several factors have emerged to break this deadlock.

First is the quantity and quality of research linking quality defects to measurable financial and health outcomes. The IOM issued a call to arms in 1998 and then 2001 against the overuse, underuse, and misuse of care (Chassin, Galvin, and National Roundtable 1998). Patient safety efforts have focused on the human and financial costs of misuse; now overuse and underuse are coming in for a similarly focused examination that fits the facts into a specific social context. In the overuse category, for instance, two breakthrough articles by Elliott Fisher and colleagues in *Annals of Internal Medicine* examined how variations in Medicare spending affected measures of access, satisfaction, utilization, and outcomes (2003a and 2003b). The authors concluded that Medicare enrollees in higher-spending regions receive an extraordinary 60 percent more care "but do not have better health outcomes or satisfaction with care" (Fisher et al. 2003a, 286). Invited political, clinical, and economic commentaries highlighted the importance of the research given growing provider and social concern about health care affordability.

At the other end of the spectrum, a national review by Elizabeth McGlynn and colleagues in the *New England Journal of Medicine* found that physicians provide the preventive, acute, and chronic care called for by medical literature just 55 percent of the time. This failure poses "serious threats to the health of the American public," the authors concluded. They linked specific procedures (such as replacement of broken hips and treatment of stomach ulcers) to specific failure rates (a compliance rate of less than a third with evidence-based recommendations) (McGlynn et al. 2003). Other reports have provided a steady stream of data on defects in care for specific conditions and series of conditions at individual institutions.

The Advent of Evidence-Based Medicine

A second important factor in breaking the town-gown deadlock is the way data on quality defects are being translated into actionable information. Recall that a "tipping point" requires that individuals understand how an intervention fits "into their lives." The evidence-based medicine (EBM) movement, with its focus on applied knowledge, is starting to provide that type of information. Moreover, it is doing so within a context compatible with existing clinical values. If studies of variations in medical practice seemed, to physicians, to invite statistics-based second-guessing, and "continuous quality improvement" could not shake the feel of the factory floor, EBM is dressed in the comfortable Flexnerian robes of scientific practice. Although some clinicians still fret about "cookbook medicine," EBM has entered the medical mainstream. A Medline search of journal abstracts for 1993 found just six uses of the term "evidence-based medicine," all but one of which were basic explanations of the concept. A similar 2003 Medline search found 2,315 citations, beginning with the clearly nonbasic "guidelines for the treatment of oligodendroglioma." More important in terms of putting theory into practice, EBM has benefited from a decade of technological advances that have made QI innovations extraordinarily "trialable" and "observable."

Computers allow clinicians, hospitals, and health plans to track adherence to well-established processes (for example, annual eye exams for diabetics) and even some outcomes. A host of organizations offer collaboratives, courses, and other educational interventions designed to help providers make specific changes that will improve these measures. At an even more sophisticated level, a handful of vendors have begun using neural network "artificial intelligence" techniques to integrate data from pharmacies and laboratories with data on health care utilization and diagnosis. The goal is to compare outpatient treatment of individual patients to the "best-care" standards, and to intervene to improve that care through "alerts" to the treating physician when clinically appropriate. In hospitals, informatics vendors are starting to provide similar actionable information to clinicians in real time. In both cases, the technology will only become more reliable, more usable, and less expensive. Finally, the growing movement toward networked medical records—spurred in part by government pressure—promises to make clinical analysis both cheaper and far more reliable.

To be sure, important analytical barriers remain, particularly concerning data at the individual clinician level (Landon et al. 2003). But the adoption of computer-enabled decision aids is sweeping through society; the move toward more timely and actionable EBM-based information in health care is unstoppable.

Pressure from Outside the System

A third important factor is breaking the town-gown gridlock. Reliable data and actionable data are not enough; there must be a compelling reason to use the information. Here health care transformation has long stalled in a quagmire of ego, financial self-interest, ignorance, and inertia—with substantial contributions from all parties. Frank Davidoff has written of a physician who stated he simply could not accept the findings of a new study on diabetes treatment because it meant admitting to patients that he had been wrong. Concluded Davidoff, "The experience of shame helps to explain why improvement—which ought to be a 'no-brainer'— is generally such a slow and difficult process" (2002).

One way to persuade providers to use QI information is through peer pressure, a strategy that has produced modest success. The more effective method, as the literature on innovation diffusion makes clear, is to combine internal with external pressure. Economist Kenneth Arrow wrote in a seminal 1963 essay, "The social obligation for best practice is part of the commodity the physician sells, even though it is a part that is not subject to thorough inspection by the buyer" (965). In the Information Age, the second part of that sentence is fast losing its validity.

For instance, the Internet has given patients easy access to "translated" versions of the same general evidence-based guidelines as their physicians. Patients with some conditions, such as cancer and heart disease, can now go to a Web site sponsored by a trusted patient advocacy group, answer a detailed clinical questionnaire, and receive a customized printout of the best medical evidence of care for individuals with similar conditions. This is truly the "abstract" (EBM) made concrete ("my care"), and it brings the issue of variation directly to the patient (see *www.nexcura.com*).

Once the for-profit affiliate of Wennberg's Foundation for Informed Medical Decision Making peddled to doctors' offices decision-making videodisc equipment, which sold poorly and was used infrequently. Now that affiliate has grown to a $100 million business by coaching health plan members and corporate employees on "best practice" in helping patients talk with their doctors as decision-making equals. Other vendors now sell data that reveal procedure-specific outcomes by hospital.

Patients not motivated to act on their own may find their employer or health plan providing not-so-subtle pressure to become "empowered." Disease management vendors now contact tens of millions of Americans on behalf of health plans as well as employers who are convinced that higher-quality care means lower cost—particularly if efforts focus on patients who are the most likely to pile up substantial expenditures. Clinical prediction rules and algorithms that were largely the playthings of theoreticians in 1994 are mass-produced in 2004 as desktop PC rules for nurses and software for doctors' Palm Pilots. Codman's "end-result idea"—which called for measuring and disclosing outcomes—is, in a sense, being reincarnated as computer code.

Kissing the Frog

The economic incentive for using information on quality improvement—the "interest" versus "duty" equation of Codman's time—has also begun to change. The first pay-for-performance pilot programs are now being gingerly rolled out by both large private purchasers and, importantly, Medicare. I believe these programs will inevitably expand, particularly in the wake of the Medicare Prescription Drug, Improvement, and Modernization Act of 2003, which links public reporting by hospitals of ten quality indicators to a modest increase in reimbursement. Similarly, the Federal Trade Commission in early 2004 was considering new rules that would ease prohibitions on presumed anti-competitive physician and hospital collaborations if they included QI elements such as comprehensive safety improvements and measurement and reporting of outcomes.

On a parallel track, the "consumer-driven health care" movement—whose origins lie in the fervent desire of private payers to share the burden of rising medical costs with employees—is starting to understand that it cannot succeed unless it provides information to individuals on the quality of care as well as its cost. In 2003, an estimated 1.5 million Americans enrolled in these types of plans, which typically involve health spending accounts and customized network or benefit selection (Gabel, Lo Sasso, and Rice 2002).

Certainly, the economic fruits of "best care" must be shared. Too often, providers who have pioneered evidence-based practices that keep patients healthy have been economically penalized. Similarly, "consumer-driven" care must evolve from mantra to meaningful action; patients who suspect that "evidence-based medicine" is invoked only to eliminate overused services but not to support underused ones will respond by seeking the protection of regulators, legislators, and the courts.

Transformation is instantaneous only in fairy tales; alas, waving a magic wand or passionately kissing a frog accomplishes little in the real world. The Flexner report at the beginning of the twentieth century provoked a "crisis" in medical education that could be solved only by "subvert[ing] the existing tradition," to use the terminology of Deming and Kuhn. At the beginning of the twenty-first century, I believe that an accumulation of social, economic, and clinical pressures is slowly but surely bringing the same transformation to everyday medical practice.

Fortunately, evidence-based medicine resonates with providers and the public in a way that the cerebral "practice variation" and cold-blooded "managed care" never did. After all, if there is anything Americans crave more than "more," it is "best." At the same time, transparency of information and a balancing of autonomy and accountability are secular trends, a "social epidemic," if you will, to which medicine is not immune. Teachers now debate "outcomes-based" report cards, while law enforcement officials explore the merits of "evidence-based policing."

Nonetheless, the pace with which QI innovations will be implemented still depends upon the persistence and sense of urgency of patients, of providers who are patient champions, and of those with the power to intervene on patients' behalf. The price of inaction is painfully high by any yardstick—economic, clinical, and moral. At the beginning of the twenty-first century, as at the start of the last one, we must still demand medical excellence. Fortunately, signs are growing that we are.

References

Arrow, K. 1963. Uncertainty and the Welfare Economics of Medical Care. *American Economic Review* 53: 941–973.

Blendon, R. J., C. M. DesRoches, M. Brodie, et al. 2002. Views of Practicing Physicians and the Public on Medical Errors. *New England Journal of Medicine* 347: 1933–1940.

Chassin, M. R., R. W. Galvin, and the National Roundtable on Health Care Quality. 1998. The Urgent Need to Improve Health Care Quality: Institute of Medicine National Roundtable on Health Care Quality. *Journal of the American Medical Association* 280: 1000–1005.

Codman, E. A. 1934. *The Shoulder*. Boston: Thomas Todd.

Davidoff, F. 2002. Shame: The Elephant in the Room. *Quality and Safety in Health Care* 11: 2–3.

Deming, W. E. 1986. *Out of the Crisis*. Cambridge, MA: MIT Press.

Fisher, E. S., D. E. Wennberg, T. A. Stukel, et al. 2003a. The Implications of Regional Variations in Medicare Spending. Part 1: The Content, Quality, and Accessibility of Care. *Annals of Internal Medicine* 138: 273–287.

———. 2003b. The Implications of Regional Variations in Medicare Spending. Part 2: Health Outcomes and Satisfaction with Care. *Annals of Internal Medicine* 138: 288–298.

Freidson, E. 1970. *Profession of Medicine: A Study of the Sociology of Applied Knowledge*. New York: Dodd, Mead.

Gabel, J., A. T. Lo Sasso, and T. Rice. 2002. Consumer-Driven Health Plans: Are They More Than Talk Now? *Health Affairs* July–Dec., Suppl. Web Exclusives: W395–407. Full text available at *http://content.healthaffairs.org/cgi/reprint/hlthaff.w2.395v1*.

Gladwell, M. 2000. *The Tipping Point*. New York: Little, Brown.

Institute of Medicine (IOM). 2000. *To Err Is Human: Building a Safer Health System*. Washington, DC: National Academies Press.

———. 2001. *Crossing the Quality Chasm: A New Health System for the 21st Century*. Washington, DC: National Academies Press.

Kaiser Family Foundation/Harvard Health News Index. 1999. Available at *www.kff.org/content/2000/1565/HNI%20Nov-Dec1999.pdf* (accessed January 18, 2004).

Kuhn, T. S. 1970. *The Structure of Scientific Revolutions*. 2d ed. Chicago: University of Chicago Press.

Landon, B. E., S. L. Normand, D. Blumenthal, and J. Daley. 2003. Physician Clinical Performance Assessment: Prospects and Barriers. *Journal of the American Medical Association* 290: 1183–1189.

Leape, L. L. 1994. Error in Medicine. *Journal of the American Medical Association* 272: 1851–1857.

Lundberg, G. D., with J. Stacey. 2000. *Severed Trust: Why American Medicine Hasn't Been Fixed*. New York: Basic Books.

McAfee, R. E. 1995. Malpractice System Needs Reform, letter in Voices of the People, *Chicago Tribune,* May 12, sec. 1, 27.

McGlynn, E. A., S. M. Asch, J. Adams, et al. 2003. The Quality of Health Care Delivered to Adults in the United States. *New England Journal of Medicine* 348: 2635–2645.

McNeil, B. J. 2001. Shattuck Lecture: Hidden Barriers to Improvement in the Quality of Care. *New England Journal of Medicine* 345: 1612–1620.

Millenson, M. L. 1997. *Demanding Medical Excellence: Doctors and Accountability in the Information Age*. Chicago: University of Chicago Press.

———. 2002. Breaking Bad News: Effective Public Accountability in Health Care Demands Effective Communication to the Public. *Quality and Safety in Health Care* 11: 206–207.

Rogers, E. M. 1995. Lessons for Guidelines from the Diffusion of Innovations. *Joint Commission Journal on Quality Improvement* 21: 324–328.

———. 2003. *Diffusion of Innovations*. 5th ed. New York: The Free Press.

Wennberg, J., and A. Gittelsohn. 1973. Small Area Variations in Health Care Delivery. *Science* 182: 1102–1108.

CHAPTER 11

Preventing Medical Errors

———⊸∞⊶———

LUCIAN L. LEAPE

Most people first became aware of the problem of medical errors in late 1999, when the National Academy of Sciences' Institute of Medicine (IOM) released *To Err Is Human,* which announced that up to ninety-eight thousand people die each year from medical errors (IOM 2000). Although the shocking mortality figures came from studies published up to eight years previously (Leape et al. 1991; Brennan et al. 1991; Thomas et al. 2000), they were new to most readers and came now from an impeccable source. Congress promptly scheduled hearings, and shortly thereafter the president called on all federal health agencies to implement the IOM recommendations (Quality Interagency Coordination Task Force 2000).

The IOM brought to public attention a slow-growing safety movement that began in 1995 with the coincidence of disaster and opportunity. The disaster was a series of highly publicized serious medical errors, most notoriously, the death of Betsy Lehman, a health reporter for the *Boston Globe,* from a massive overdose of chemotherapy at the respected Dana Farber Cancer Institute. That such a tragic error could happen at such a prestigious medical institution shook both public and professional confidence. The opportunity was the discovery by health care leaders of the potential for preventing errors by using industrial human factors approaches, particularly the recognition that the cause of most human errors is neither carelessness nor incompetence, but defects in the systems in which people work (Leape 1994). For example, system characteristics such as look-alike labels and sound-alike names, conditions of work (long hours and heavy work loads), and managerial style (diffused responsibility and lack of teamwork) make it more likely that an individual will make a mistake. Errors can be reduced by redesigning the systems.

The implications of this concept for medicine are profound because it runs counter to classical medical training that focuses on faultless individual performance, reinforced by shaming and blaming. However, the systems approach is based on a wealth of studies in cognitive psychology and human factors engineering, as well as substantial experience in industries such as aviation, which have found that achieving safety requires much more than training individuals to be careful (Reason 1990, 1997; Helmreich 2000).

Also in 1995 studies began to appear indicating the feasibility of applying the systems analysis approach in health care (Bates et al.1995; Leape et al. 1995). Several leaders turned this opportunity into action. At the American Medical Association (AMA), legal counsel Martin Hatlie, long frustrated with attempts at tort reform, quickly recognized the potential of these new insights. He and James Todd, executive vice president, persuaded the AMA Board of Regents that it would be more productive to focus on reducing errors and that they could take the lead by establishing a foundation of stakeholders to promote patient safety. At the same time, Dennis O'Leary, president of the Joint Commission on Accreditation of Healthcare Organizations (JCAHO), recognized the need for that organization to change its approaches to safety. Within the year, the AMA and the JCAHO joined the American Association for the Advancement of Science and the Annenberg Foundation in organizing the first multidisciplinary conference on medical errors. At this meeting, which was held in 1996, the AMA announced the formation of the National Patient Safety Foundation, with Hatlie as its executive director, and O'Leary announced that the JCAHO was making its reporting system nonpunitive.

During the mid-1990s, a small number of hospitals began to take actions to better protect patients from medical errors. The Dana Farber Cancer Institute, badly shaken by the Lehman tragedy, underwent a major reorganization. New leaders, particularly James Conway, chief operating officer, undertook a major transformation of institutional culture to drive out blaming and to redesign systems. At the Veterans Health Administration, Kenneth Kizer, then under secretary for health, decided to make safety a system priority. Both Conway and Kizer spoke of their experiences and plans at the Annenberg Conference.

Yet continued research on medical errors, the application of systems theory to making changes in hospital systems, and experiments by some hospitals to improve care systems did not create much of a groundswell for greater focus on patient safety. Indeed, patient safety was not a major concern of most hospitals, doctors, or the general public until the IOM report made this "insider" information public (Leape et al. 2000). Release of the report triggered a media blitz and captured the attention of President Clinton and members of Congress. Overnight, public and professional awareness of the seriousness of the medical error problem spread from hundreds to millions.

Since the IOM Report

In the previous chapter, Michael Millenson describes the acceleration of activity in patient safety since the IOM report, which he presents as an encouraging example of the diffusion of innovation. While one might dispute that rosy scenario, a fair assessment would conclude that a remarkable amount of progress has been made in a relatively short period of time. Almost everyone is now aware that we have a serious problem—the public, Congress, government bureaucrats, payers, hospital managers, hospital boards, professional societies, and frontline workers.

TABLE 11.1   *NQF-Endorsed Set of Safe Practices*

1. Create a healthcare culture of safety.
2. For designated high-risk, elective surgical procedures or other specified care, patients should be clearly informed of the likely reduced risk of an adverse outcome at treatment facilities that have demonstrated superior outcomes and should be referred to such facilities in accordance with the patient's stated preference.
3. Specify an explicit protocol to be used to ensure an adequate level of nursing based on the institution's usual patient mix and the experience and training of its nursing staff.
4. All patients in general intensive care units (both adult and pediatric) should be managed by physicians having specific training and certification in critical care medicine ("critical care certified").
5. Pharmacists should actively participate in the medication-use process, including, at a minimum, being available for consultation with prescribers on medication ordering, interpretation and review of medication orders, preparation of medications, dispensing of medications, and administration and monitoring of medications.
6. Verbal orders should be recorded whenever possible and immediately read back to the prescriber—i.e., a health care provider receiving a verbal order should read or repeat back the information that the prescriber conveys in order to verify the accuracy of what was heard.
7. Use only standardized abbreviations and dose designations.
8. Patient care summaries or other similar records should not be prepared from memory.
9. Ensure that care information, especially changes in orders and new diagnostic information, is transmitted in a timely and clearly understandable form to all of the patient's current health care providers who need that information to provide care.
10. Ask each patient or legal surrogate to recount what he or she has been told during the informed consent discussion.
11. Ensure that written documentation of the patient's preference for life-sustaining treatments is prominently displayed in his or her chart.
12. Implement a computerized prescriber order-entry system.
13. Implement a standardized protocol to prevent the mislabeling of radiographs.
14. Implement standardized protocols to prevent the occurrence of wrong-site procedures or wrong-patient procedures.
15. Evaluate each patient undergoing elective surgery for risk of an acute ischemic cardiac event during surgery, and provide prophylactic treatment of high-risk patients with beta blockers.
16. Evaluate each patient upon admission, and regularly thereafter, for the risk of developing pressure ulcers. This evaluation should be repeated at regular intervals during care. Clinically appropriate preventive methods should be implemented consequent to the evaluation.

(continued)

As envisioned by the IOM, the Agency for Healthcare Research and Quality (AHRQ) has become a national focus for safety, funding safety research, convening policy groups to set agendas, disseminating safety information, and supporting the development of standards for reporting and safe practices. Under the forceful direction of Kenneth Kizer, the National Quality Forum (NQF), a public-private partnership of purchasers, providers, payers, accrediting organizations, government agencies, and consumer groups, has convened expert panels to work on improving patient safety in the hospital setting. These panels produced a standardized list of serious reportable events for states to use in their mandatory re-

TABLE 11.1 *NQF-Endorsed Set of Safe Practices (continued)*

17. Evaluate each patient upon admission, and regularly thereafter, for the risk of developing deep vein thrombosis (DVT)/venous thromboembolism (VTE). Utilize clinically appropriate methods to prevent DVT/VTE.
18. Utilize dedicated anti-thrombotic (anti-coagulation) services that facilitate coordinated care management.
19. Upon admission, and regularly thereafter, evaluate each patient for the risk of aspiration.
20. Adhere to effective methods of preventing central venous catheter-associated blood stream infections.
21. Evaluate each pre-operative patient in light of his or her planned surgical procedure for the risk of surgical site infection, and implement appropriate antibiotic prophylaxis and other preventive measures based on that evaluation.
22. Utilize validated protocols to evaluate patients who are at risk for contrast media-induced renal failure, and utilize a clinically appropriate method for reducing risk of renal injury based on the patient's kidney function evaluation.
23. Evaluate each patient upon admission, and regularly thereafter, for risk of malnutrition. Employ clinically appropriate strategies to prevent malnutrition.
24. Whenever a pneumatic tourniquet is used, evaluate the patient for the risk of an ischemic and/or thrombotic complication, and utilize appropriate prophylactic measures.
25. Decontaminate hands with either a hygienic hand rub or by washing with a disinfectant soap prior to and after direct contact with the patient or objects immediately around the patient.
26. Vaccinate health care workers against influenza to protect both them and patients from influenza.
27. Keep workspaces where medications are prepared clean, orderly, well lit, and free of clutter, distraction, and noise.
28. Standardize the methods for labeling, packaging, and storing medications.
29. Identify all "high alert" drugs (e.g., intravenous adrenergic agonists and antagonists, chemotherapy agents, anticoagulants and anti-thrombotics, concentrated parenteral electrolytes, general anesthetics, neuromuscular blockers, insulin and oral hypoglycemics, narcotics and opiates).
30. Dispense medications in unit-dose or, when appropriate, unit-of-use form whenever possible.

Source: National Quality Forum 2003. See the full report for applicable care settings for each practice, detailed specifications, background, and references.

porting systems and identified thirty proven safe practices that JCAHO and others can require hospitals to implement (see table 11.1) (National Quality Forum 2002, 2003).

JCAHO has toughened its stance on safety. Accreditation surveys are no longer scheduled months in advance: JCAHO auditors now arrive without warning to conduct audits of health care facilities. In 2002, the accrediting organization required that hospitals implement eleven specific safe practices, with promise of more to follow. These include methods to ensure proper identification of surgical patient identity and operative site, standardization of abbreviations, and removal of hazardous chemicals from nursing units. The National Patient Safety Foundation (NPSF) has also been a strong advocate, funding safety research and convening many regional and national conferences to inform, motivate, and instruct safety leaders.

A number of other organizations are focusing on patient safety. Professional organizations, such as the American College of Physicians, have begun to make patient safety a priority in their meetings and journals. The American Hospital Association (AHA) disseminated to all member hospitals a set of recommended medication safety practices, tools for systems analysis of medication systems, and survey instruments and safety leadership recommendations for hospital executives. The Accreditation Council for Graduate Medical Education (ACGME) recently established limits on the number of hours residents can work. With the American Board of Medical Specialties (ABMS), it is leading specialty societies to develop standards and measures of competency, including safe practices and systems analysis.

Safety coalitions have developed in fifteen states (Rosenthal et al. 2001). In response to programs initiated by these groups, many hospitals have made changes in their medications systems (Massachusetts Coalition for the Prevention of Medical Errors 2001; Shapiro 2000; Delaware Valley Healthcare Council 2001). In addition to peer pressure, coalitions provide technical support, public visibility, and positive publicity for participating hospitals.

Purchasers brought their power to quality and safety in 2000, when the Leapfrog Group, the health care purchasing coalition of the Business Roundtable, announced that it would only pay for care in institutions that met certain standards. These included the use of computerized physician order entry and the presence of an intensivist to monitor the care provided in intensive care units. The Leapfrog Group established volume minimums for certain complex operations and other procedures and pays for these procedures only when performed in hospitals that meet the volume standards (Milstein et al. 2000). Other payers have recently endorsed similar measures.

Since the IOM report, safety activities in hospitals have increased. Virtually every hospital now has launched some sort of a safety program, and many are trying to create a nonpunitive environment that encourages workers to report errors and to identify systems failures. Several large health care systems, including HCA (formerly known as Hospital Corporation of America), Premier, VHA (formerly known as Voluntary Hospitals of America), and Allina, have recommended various safe practices (mostly in the medication realm) to their member hospitals (VHA 2000). However, the outstanding leader is the Veterans Health Administration, which has implemented nonpunitive reporting, use of computerized order entry systems, bar coding, team training, and other initiatives.

Patients have also become significantly more involved in their own care in response to the explosion of information available about illnesses, treatments, and patient experiences as well as entreaties by consumer advocacy groups (Ponte et al. 2003). A variety of national and regional organizations, such as NPSF and the AHA, state and regional coalitions, and AHRQ have published safety tips for consumers and have encouraged hospitals to establish full disclosure programs and partner with patients.

A few hospitals have implemented an impressive number of new practices. Luther-Midelfort Hospital in Eau Claire, Wisconsin, for example, has implemented more than twenty new practices and policies, such as nonpunitive error reporting, leadership training, protocols for managing hazardous drugs such as insulin and anticoagulants, and methods to ensure that prescribed medications match those taken prior to hospitalization (Rozich and Resar 2001; Pronovost et al. 2002; Randolf and Pronovost 2002).

Yet despite fairly widespread activity since the IOM report, actual implementation of changes to prevent accidental injury of hospitalized patients has been incredibly slow. Instead, what we see in most hospitals can be most charitably labeled marginal: the implementation of a few changes in the medication system or the announcement of a new policy for surgical site identification, but often not much more. Most health care institutions have not made safety a priority nor devoted significant resources to preventing errors. Even public tragedies often result in "damage control" and cover-up, rather than reassessment of policies and practices and major changes.

Overall, there is no evidence that the rate of accidental injury is falling. In its first annual report, AHRQ analyzed changes in its patient safety indicators as measured by ICD-9 discharge codes in a random sample of hospitalized patients. There was no significant change from 1994 to 2000 (AHRQ 2003).

Why Has Progress Been So Slow?

Given the magnitude of the problem—a million preventable injuries each year and one hundred thousand preventable deaths—and extensive knowledge about how to reduce them, one might reasonably have expected a huge national effort—a "moon shot" type of governmental commitment. Instead, the only major action for patient safety taken by Congress in four years was to appropriate, starting in 2001, approximately $50 million annually to AHRQ for research on patient safety. While this order-of-magnitude increase in research support is welcome, it pales in comparison to funding for research in any of the conditions (heart disease, AIDS, arthritis, etc.) addressed by individual National Institutes of Health.

Why hasn't patient safety become a national priority, commanding the resources, leadership, talent, and effort that it seems so obviously to require? One reason for political inertia is that there is not sufficient public pressure to overcome the powerful forces to maintain the status quo. The initial public furor that sparked presidential and congressional responses at the time of the IOM report has subsided, and with it any sense of political urgency. Media accounts of individual outrageous cases of preventable deaths or injuries still appear as before, but, as before, seldom lead to systemic changes.

Loss of public concern is dramatically evident in an opinion poll taken in 2002. Despite widespread dissemination in late 1999 of the IOM's alarming figure of ninety-eight thousand preventable deaths annually, three years later more than 60 percent of the public believed that the number of preventable deaths was five thousand or less. Yet 10 percent also reported a family experience with a preventable death (Blendon et al. 2002). Adjusting for the time span of recall and possible double counting, this yields a national estimate of approximately five hundred thousand preventable deaths annually—five times the shocking IOM estimate!

(Presumably the low estimates of risk came from the other 90 percent of those who were polled.)

A second reason that safety has not become a burning political issue is that its advocates have not succeeded in making the case that specific policy changes will result in significantly safer care. A case in point is reporting of adverse events and errors. Congress has tried unsuccessfully each year since the IOM report to pass legislation protecting from legal discovery information about medical errors and adverse events when they are reported to a central agency (such as AHRQ or JCAHO). However, there is little evidence that enhanced reporting would improve safety, or how it would do so in the absence of intensive (and expensive) investigation of underlying causes. No cost-benefit analysis has been done.

Another example is the lack of federal support and funding for information technology, particularly the standardized electronic medical record (EMR). No one questions the value of an EMR. It would vastly improve communication between all parties, including doctors and patients, and it would greatly facilitate measurement of all aspects of quality. It would permit aggregation of national data to quickly detect complications of a new drug, for example. However, advocates have only recently succeeded, via the IOM, in convincing government officials of the need to address issues related to the standardization of information and formats and the compatibility of existing technology so that commercial EMR systems will be able to communicate with one another.

Third, in the current political climate, there is a great reluctance to expand government's regulatory powers. Given the immensity of the problem of medical errors and accidents, one might think a first step would be to create a federal agency with the power, scope, and funding of the Federal Aviation Agency. Not so. Such a proposal would be strongly opposed by the pharmaceutical and device industries, the AMA, and the hospital industry. In fact, even the relatively small support for AHRQ, a non-regulatory agency which has done a superb job of providing advice to policymakers and funding research, is shaky.

Culture Change Is Needed

Progress would be slow even if safety were a national priority, because making health care safe is much more complicated than launching a moon shot. What is needed is not just new techniques or rules. Nor is the challenge just to adopt an innovation, such as a new hybrid strain of peas, or even one as complex as the automobile or implementing national health insurance. It is to change the medical culture (Weeks and Bagian 2000; Hatlie and Wagner 1999). Culture change of this magnitude is not an innovation; it requires a host of innovations at multiple levels—personal, professional, organizational, and societal.

An oft-cited model for a culture of safety is high reliability organizations (HROs), companies in highly hazardous industries such as commercial aviation, nuclear power, aluminum production, and aircraft carrier operations, that have succeeded in becoming highly safe. The distinguishing characteristic of HROs is their culture of mindfulness, accountability, and commitment to safety (Roberts, Stout, and Halpern 1994; Grabowski and Roberts 1997). Safety is not just an organizational priority, it is *the* priority, articulated at the highest level and translated into shared values and beliefs throughout the organization. Safety is an explicit goal, supported by a host of policies and practices that are carefully, even compulsively, followed.

HROs value organizational learning. They do not just respond to accidents, but constantly and proactively search for hazards. They have created open cultures characterized by easy and frequent communication both between workers and across organizational levels. Most work occurs in multidisciplinary teams, yet every individual has a sense of personal responsibility to practice safely, to identify hazards, and to take action to reduce them. Because errors are recognized as indicators of systems failures, the response to individuals who make mistakes is nonpunitive. At the same time, misconduct or reckless behavior is not tolerated. There is no ambiguity about who is responsible for implementing safe practices, who monitors compliance, and who is responsible for taking action when performance fails. Safety is not a program; it is a way of life (Weick, Sutcliffe, and Obstfeld 1999).

By contrast, most modern health care organizations are very dysfunctional. They are more inclined to cover up problems than to solve them, to be concerned about reputation over substance, and to adopt a blaming, fix-the-problem-and-don't-let-it-happen-again approach when things go wrong. The peculiar administrative arrangements in hospitals whereby the dominant professionals, physicians, consider themselves independent contractors makes establishing accountability and organizational coherence difficult.

The Hospital Safety Agenda

The safety agenda for hospitals is huge. To begin to approach the high levels of safety seen in HROs, hospitals must implement a broad array of new policies and practices (see table 11.2). These include prohibiting punishment for errors, while still holding personnel accountable for poor performance or misconduct; demonstrating respect for workers through humane hours and work loads; and demonstrating respect for patients by requiring full, honest, and prompt disclosure of errors.

All health care organizations need to give higher priority to implementing known safe practices, such as checking patient identity prior to starting procedures or administering medication, and proper hand disinfection. The NQF list of thirty proven safe practices is a good place to start (see table 11.1). These practices also need to be enforced. For example, a hospital that is serious about safety would revoke the privileges of a physician who refuses to disinfect his hands between patients. All these, and more, are part of a culture of safety.

Barriers to Culture Change

There are many barriers to achieving a safe culture in health care. One of the most challenging is the specialization and isolation of workers, many of whom

TABLE 11.2   *The Hospital Safety Agenda*

Create a nonpunitive learning environment where practitioners feel free to report and talk about their mistakes without fear of punishment while also feeling personally responsible to identify and remedy unsafe conditions that they encounter in their work.

Respond promptly to reports of accidental injuries to patients using a systems approach to find and remedy underlying failures.

Proactively seek out hazards ("accidents waiting to happen") and correct faulty systems. Create safety by design.

Break down hierarchical barriers and prohibit demeaning behavior in order to develop strong multidisciplinary teams in which the contributions of all members to patient care are valued.

Establish clear lines of accountability for implementing, monitoring, and enforcing compliance with safe practices.

Implement all known safe practices (such as computerized order entry, various medication safety practices, surgical site verification, etc.). These include, at a minimum, those recommended by the National Quality Forum, American Hospital Association, and the Joint Commission on Accreditation of Health Care Organizations.

Implement a full-disclosure policy whereby patients are promptly and compassionately informed of errors in their care and are provided with appropriate support.

Provide humane and reasonable working conditions, including appropriate staffing ratios for nurses, reasonable work loads for physicians, and strictly enforced limits on working hours for both nurses and physicians.

Take responsibility for physicians with behavioral or competency problems by developing programs to promptly identify them and deal with them by providing remediation, retraining, or, if necessary, restriction of practice.

---

are locked into outdated paradigms of individual performance and expertise and organized in so-called "silos." Physicians in one specialty, for example, often have little understanding of the practice of those in another, or even when to call on them. Clinic nurses lack expertise to work in the intensive care unit, and vice versa.

Modern health care is also extraordinarily complex. The variety of devices, operations, types of imaging, and expertise required are mind-boggling. Physicians must choose from among more than nine thousand prescription drugs, for example. The diversity of the workforce reflects the myriad specialized skills that are required to make it work.

Another barrier is the lack of meaningful accountability in most institutions. Because no single person is responsible for major systems such as medication, no one has the authority to make needed changes. Most physicians don't feel that they work for anyone, least of all the hospital administrator. They feel entitled to flaunt rules that they don't agree with—such as disinfecting hands between patients. Financial incentives in this fragmented system are often antithetical to changing systems to improve quality. For example, a program that reduces complications in diabetic patients so that fewer require hospitalization reduces the income of both hospitals and physicians.

Ironically, physicians are often a barrier to progress. Although the leaders of the safety movement are mostly physicians, the vast majority of doctors have been remarkably passive—many don't choose to believe there is a serious problem. In a blaming culture, it is shameful to admit that patients are injured by our mistakes (Davidoff 2002; Hilfiker 1984). But, in fairness, it is also true that most physicians don't see mistakes very often in their own practices, however numerous they are in the aggregate. The IOM figure of ninety-eight thousand preventable deaths per year, for example, averages out to only one every six years per physician. Since typically fewer than half of errors are recognized by the person making them, an average physician might perceive himself as responsible for at most one preventable death every ten to twelve years—hardly a cause for alarm in a profession where death is a common occurrence. They don't perceive a need to change.

Doctors also tend to be skeptical about the concept of systems causes of errors. It runs against everything they were taught and have believed: that if you are well prepared and careful, you will not make mistakes. The systems approach smacks of irresponsibility for those who do not understand it (Casarett and Helms 1999). It also implies—correctly—some loss of autonomy as individual preference defers to required safe practice.

Often, hospital chief executive officers also don't perceive a need to change because they receive few reports of errors. In the typical hospital blaming culture, most errors are not reported, and even fewer make their way to the front office. Thus, the CEO really doesn't see a problem. In the absence of pressure from either their physicians or the public, there is little incentive for major change. Pressure from regulators or the JCAHO can be responded to by implementing the prescribed practices rather than revamping systems.

Culture Change from the Bottom Up

Conventional wisdom and historical evidence indicate that a culture change of the magnitude needed in health care requires both a major crisis and strong leadership. But individuals dying from medical errors one by one, however many there may be in a year, are not perceived as a crisis; and, so far, a national leader has not emerged. When customs and practices are strongly entrenched as they are in medicine, change is even harder to accomplish.

Yet the culture is changing. We are witnessing culture change in the absence of national leadership or perceived crisis. It is change from the bottom up: piecemeal, spotty, and slow, but enduring and spreading. It is driven by a relatively small number of individuals who believe passionately in what they are trying to do, a belief that gets reinforced with each success.

The "transforming concept," that errors are caused not by bad people, but by bad systems, has struck a profound chord in many health professionals, not just physicians, but also nurses and pharmacists who are at the "sharp end," making errors that hurt patients. In our blaming culture, many—perhaps most—nurses live in constant fear of making a serious mistake and are burdened with guilt when they do. Systems theory, almost like a new religion, offers a way out, lifting the burden of guilt while offering a path to prevention. Not surprisingly, many nurses embraced it enthusiastically. They are changing the systems, bit by bit, unit by unit—not just implementing new medication practices, but also experimenting with working better in teams, fuller disclosure to patients, adjustment of work loads and hours, and building a variety of other aspects of a safe culture. They are doing it because it is the right thing to do.

The recognition of the intrinsic validity of this transforming concept has also motivated leaders of government and accrediting and professional organizations, as described earlier. While it was the IOM report that galvanized many to action, they have been sustained by a vision of what needs to be done. No grand plan, no national program, no national leadership exists, yet these leaders are moving ahead in hundreds of ways because it is the right thing to do.

Will It Do the Job?

A central policy question is how to facilitate this progress in the absence of a major commitment by the federal government. Clearly, one course is to continue pressing for incremental change. The IOM report, *Fostering Rapid Advances in Health Care: Learning from System Demonstrations,* would be a good place to start (IOM 2002). The report calls for the federal government to support bold regional demonstration projects in five critical areas, two of which, information and communications technology and malpractice liability, are critical to patient safety. These recommendations should be accepted and funded.

But much more than demonstration projects are needed. The government has finally moved on setting standards for computerized patient records and has committed to making a model patient record available in 2004. However, the costs of purchasing and implementing these computer systems are substantial. Without government subsidies, hospitals and practitioners are unlikely to adopt them. Major federal funding, on the order of $20–40 billion over five years, should be actively sought for the rapid implementation of computerized medical records and order entry systems in every hospital, office, and patient care facility in the nation. Politically, such an appropriation could be achieved if all major health organizations (the AMA, AHA, professional societies, and JCAHO) were to focus on that single goal.

AHRQ's research initiative on patient safety should be further expanded with a target of doubling expenditures every five years. This effort builds both the knowledge base and the expertise needed for hospitals to improve patient safety. Within AHRQ, the Center for Quality Improvement and Patient Safety's role as sponsor of safe practice development and validation is crucial to progress and should be fully funded. The agency should also receive adequate funding to meet its mandate to monitor progress in safety by annually collecting and analyzing hospital data on safety indicators.

The Food and Drug Administration (FDA) must also play a more active role in reducing medication errors. Insufficient attention to packaging, labeling, naming, and standardizing medications has made it too easy for patients to make mistakes when taking prescription drugs. Errors could be reduced if the FDA required manufacturers to provide all drugs in unit of use and to modify labels so that the names of drugs are clearly displayed in large print.

Policymakers, politicians, and all who are concerned about safe health care should support the continuing efforts of health-related organizations to advance safe practices and policies. ACGME and ABMS need to complete their project to define performance standards and indicators and promote implementation of these measures within hospitals to monitor and improve physician performance. The moment of truth is at hand for ACGME: Will it enforce restrictions on residents' hours that went into effect in July 2003? If so, it can move onto other tough issues, including methods and standards for training residents to respond to adverse events, carry out systems analysis, and respond to patients with honesty and sensitivity.

Specialty societies, such as the American College of Physicians and the American College of Surgeons, should be encouraged to expand their efforts in safety at all levels by:

- Scheduling presentations and courses in such safety issues as systems analysis, teamwork, leadership, and disclosure at their annual and regional meetings;
- Showcasing safety studies at research forums;
- Featuring safety topics in their journals; and
- Establishing expert panels to identify, validate, and disseminate safe practices unique to each specialty.

All payers should adopt the model advanced by the Leapfrog Group, and the model should be broadened each year to include additional safe practices. Payers, in turn, should expand the use of indicators, such as those pioneered by the National Committee for Quality Assurance and NQF, and publish annual report cards of each hospital's compliance with safe practices and policies, as determined by independent audits. Health plans should play the primary role in the dissemination of tools and instruction for implementation of safe policies and practices.

Of all organizations, the JCAHO has the most potential to motivate hospitals to change their cultures and make safety a true priority. With the recent shift to unannounced inspections, the commission has the opportunity to demonstrate to hospitals and to the public that it is serious about safety. It must do so. It would not be unreasonable for the JCAHO to expect every hospital to implement all of the NQF safe practices within two or three years, and to begin to levy sanctions against those that are laggards. It is also time for the JCAHO to issue meaningful public reports of all hospital evaluations. Safety is too important to be kept a secret.

How much more consumers can do is unclear. While patient advocacy groups have had an impact on safety organizations such as NPSF and the Institute for Healthcare Improvement (an organization in Boston that is working with stakeholders on quality improvement initiatives), their impact on public policy and funding is less apparent. Certainly, keeping public pressure on for safer health care is important, however.

Medical Errors are Symptoms of a Dysfunctional Health System

Although pressure from all stakeholders will continue the push to adopt safer practices, if we are to achieve the culture change necessary to raise safety to a level comparable to that in high reliability industries, it will be necessary to address fundamental deficiencies in the organization and delivery of health care to Americans. As the IOM report pointed out, the challenges of patient safety are but one aspect of the much larger problems of access, financing, and coordination of care that confront the American health care system (IOM 2001). The IOM called for a complete overhaul of the health care system.

The Physicians' Working Group for Single-Payer National Health Insurance provided additional pressure by proposing a universal health care system, supported by taxes that would effectively expand Medicare to all Americans (Woolhandler et al. 2003). An essential feature of their proposal is that basic health care should be non-commercial and not-for-profit. While that seems unlikely to happen, some realignment of financial incentives will be necessary to achieve safe health care. Payment systems must be devised that reward, not punish, safe practices. For example, serious errors in the management of patients taking anticoagulants (blood-thinning drugs) such as warfarin are much less common when the process is managed by a nurse-run clinic. Yet some payers will not provide reimbursement unless the service is provided by a physician.

Finally, to create a culture of safety we must deal with the problems posed by the tort system. More than any factor, the threat of malpractice suits inhibits physician participation in safety programs and poisons their relationships with patients. To solve this problem, we must address the issues that the tort system is supposed to address: compensation and negligence. No-fault compensation offers a promising alternative for compensating injured patients and has been implemented in Sweden and New Zealand. The IOM recently called for federal funding of state demonstration projects to test the feasibility of that approach here in the United States (IOM 2002).

However, it seems unlikely that state legislatures will adopt no-fault compensation plans without substantial improvement in the methods for dealing with the other objective of tort law—deterring negligence. Prevention of negligent acts must occur within the hospital or physician practice, for that is where the precursors of negligence—incompetence, disruptive behavior, substance abuse, and mental and physical illness—first manifest themselves. Hospitals need to develop more effective programs for doctors with problems, to identify unsafe behavior before it results in patient injury, and to retrain and rehabilitate as many physicians as possible. To do this, they need support and direction from state licensing boards, health departments, and the JCAHO.

Making the changes necessary for safe health care requires a major change in our thinking: not just about what we do, but about what we are. Achieving safe health care requires much more than changing some practices, developing some new systems, and putting some new rules in place. It requires that all health professionals fundamentally reassess their concepts of professional autonomy (Can physicians learn to share authority in teams?), responsibility (for *all* patients and systems, not just our individual work), and how to improve, how to move from perfecting individuals to perfecting systems.

No other industry has succeeded in achieving a high level of safety without heavy regulation. But health care is very different from other industries: medical professionals have a strong sense of duty and responsibility to patients. It is possible that voluntary effort at the front line and pressure from many stakeholders will be sufficient to change hospital cultures. We should all hope so.

References

Agency for Healthcare Research and Quality (AHRQ). 2003. *National Health Care Quality Report*. AHRQ publication no. 04-RG003. Washington, DC: DHHS.

Bates, D. W., D. J. Cullen, N. Laird, et al. 1995. Incidence of Adverse Drug Events and Potential Adverse Drug Events. *Journal of the American Medical Association* 274: 29–34.

Blendon, R. J., C. M. DesRoches, M. Brodie, et al. 2002. Views of Practicing Physicians and the Public on Medical Errors. *New England Journal of Medicine* 347: 1933–1940.

Brennan, T. A., L. L. Leape, N. Laird, et al. 1991. Incidence of Adverse Events and Negligence in Hospitalized Patients: Results from the Harvard Medical Practice Study I. *New England Journal of Medicine* 324, no. 6: 370–376.

Casarett, D., and C. Helms. 1999. Systems Errors versus Physicians' Errors: Finding the Balance in Medical Education. *Academic Medicine* 74: 19–22.

Davidoff, F. 2002. Shame: The Elephant in the Drawing Room. *Quality and Safety in Health Care* 11: 2–3.

Delaware Valley Healthcare Council. 2001. Regional Medication Safety Program for Hospitals. Philadelphia. Available at *www.dvhc.org/rr/medsafeprogram.htm*.

Grabowski, M., and K. Roberts. 1997. Risk Mitigation in Large-Scale Systems: Lessons from High Reliability Organizations. *California Management Review* 39: 152–162.

Hatlie M., and S. Wagner. 1999. The National Patient Safety Foundation: Creating a Culture of Safety. *Surgical Services Management* 5: 35–37.

Helmreich, R. L. 2000. On Error Management: Lessons from Aviation. *British Medical Journal* 320: 781–785.

Hilfiker, D. 1984. Facing Our Mistakes. *New England Journal of Medicine* 310: 118–122.

Institute of Medicine (IOM). 2000. *To Err Is Human: Building a Safer Health System*. Washington, DC: National Academies Press.

———. 2001. *Crossing the Quality Chasm*. Washington, DC: National Academies Press.

———. 2002. *Fostering Rapid Advances in Health Care: Learning from System Demonstrations*. Washington, DC: National Academies Press.

Leape, L. L. 1994. Error in Medicine. *Journal of the American Medical Association* 272, no. 23: 1851–1857.

Leape, L. L., A. I. Kabcenell, T. K. Gandhi, P. Carver, T. W. Nolan, and D. M. Berwick. 2000. Reducing Adverse Drug Events: Lessons from a Breakthrough Series Collaborative. *Joint Commission Journal on Quality Improvement* 26, no. 6: 321–331.

Leape, L. L., D. W. Bates, D. J. Cullen, et al. 1995. Systems Analysis of Adverse Drug Events. *Journal of the American Medical Association* 274, no. 1: 35–43.

Leape, L. L., T. A. Brennan, N. M. Laird, et al. 1991. The Nature of Adverse Events in Hospitalized Patients: Results from the Harvard Medical Practice Study II. *New England Journal of Medicine* 324, no. 6: 377–384.

Massachusetts Coalition for the Prevention of Medical Errors. 2001. *MHA Best Practice Recommendations to Reduce Medication Errors.* Available at *www.mhalink.org/mcpme/mha_best_practice_recommendation.htm* (accessed June 24, 2002).

Milstein, A., R. S. Galvin, S. F. Delbanco, P. Salber, and C. R. Buck Jr. 2000. Improving the Safety of Health Care: The Leapfrog Initiative. *Effective Clinical Practice* 3: 313–316.

National Quality Forum. 2002. *Serious Reportable Events in Patient Safety: A National Quality Forum Consensus Report.* Washington, DC: National Quality Forum.

———. 2003. *Safe Practices for Better Health Care: A Consensus Report.* Washington, DC: National Quality Forum.

Ponte, P. R., G. Conlin, J. B. Conway, et al. 2003. Making Patient-Centered Care Come Alive: Achieving Full Integration of the Patient's Perspective. *Journal of Nursing Administration* 33: 82–90.

Pronovost, P. J., M. Jenckes, M. To, et al. 2002. Reducing Failed Extubations in the Intensive Care Unit. *Joint Commission Journal on Quality Improvement* 28: 595–604.

Quality Interagency Coordination Task Force. 2000. *Doing What Counts for Patient Safety: Federal Actions to Reduce Medical Errors and Their Impact.* Washington, DC: Agency for Healthcare Research and Quality.

Randolph, A. G., and P. Pronovost. 2002. Reorganizing the Delivery of Intensive Care Could Improve Efficiency and Save Lives. *Journal of Evaluation in Clinical Practice* 8: 1–8.

Reason, J. 1990. *Human Error.* Cambridge, UK: Cambridge University Press.

———. 1997. *Managing the Risks of Organizational Accidents.* Hants, UK: Aldershot; Brookfield, VT: Ashgate.

Roberts, K., S. Stout, J. Halpern. 1994. Decision Dynamics in Two High-Reliability Military Organizations. *Management Science* 40: 614–624.

Rosenthal, J., M. Booth, L. Flower, and T. Riley. 2001. *Current State Programs Addressing Medical Errors: An Analysis of Mandatory Reporting and Other Initiatives.* Portland, ME: National Academy for State Health Policy.

Rozich, J., and R. Resar. 2001. Medication Safety: One Organization's Approach to the Challenge. *Journal of Clinical Outcomes Management* 8: 27–34.

Shapiro, J. P. 2000. Industry Preaches Safety in Pittsburgh. *U.S. News and World Report*, July 17.

Thomas, E. J., D. M. Studdert, H. R. Burstin, et al. 2000. Incidence and Types of Adverse Events and Negligent Care in Utah and Colorado. *Medical Care* 38, no. 3: 261–271.

VHA. 2000. *The Patient Safety Organizational Assessment.* Washington, DC.

Weeks, W. B., and J. P. Bagian. 2000. Developing a Culture of Safety in the Veterans Health Administration. *Effective Clinical Practice* 3: 270–276.

Weick, K. E., K. M. Sutcliffe, and D. Obstfeld. 1999. Organizing for High Reliability. *Research in Organizational Behavior* 21: 81–123.

Woolhandler, S., D. U. Himmelstein, M. Angell, and Q. D. Young. 2003. Proposal of the Physicians' Working Group for Single-Payer National Health Insurance. *Journal of the American Medical Association* 290, no. 6: 798–805.

CHAPTER 12

Improving Quality through Nursing

———⊸⊶⊸———

LINDA H. AIKEN

Both the public and physicians rank nurse understaffing of hospitals as one of the most serious threats to patient safety (Blendon et al. 2002). Two-thirds of hospital bedside nurses concur that there are not enough nurses in their hospitals to provide high-quality care, and close to half score in the high-burnout range on standardized tests. Almost one in four intends to leave his or her job in the hospital within a year (Aiken et al. 2001). Federal estimates suggest that the shortfall of nurses could approach 275,000 by 2010 and 800,000 by 2020 (U.S. DHHS 2002). Until very recently, policymakers and health care leaders have not associated hospital nurse understaffing and burnout with medical errors and adverse patient outcomes, as evidenced by the few references to nursing in the Institute of Medicine's first two major quality reports (Institute of Medicine 2000, 2001). This chapter explicates the link between nursing and quality and discusses the implications for the nation's quality improvement agenda.

The Role of Nurses in Promoting Quality of Care

Nursing is the care of the sick (and those who may become sick) and the maintenance of the environment in which care occurs (Diers 2004). Nurses are responsible for fulfilling those aspects of the medical regimen delegated to them by physicians, such as administering medication, but they are legally and professionally responsible for their own actions when fulfilling delegated tasks. In the case of administering medications, nurses are responsible for ascertaining that the dose is correct for the age of the patient and that the route of administration is proper. Nurses have a professional and legal scope of practice that is complementary to that of physicians and includes assessing and intervening within their areas of expertise, such as skin and wound care, managing pain and providing comfort, and teaching patients and their families how to manage their care after hospital discharge, among myriad other responsibilities. Nurses are also responsible for maintaining a safe and patient-centered care environment. Thus, nurses routinely step in when non-nursing support services are not available or are inadequate to maintain a clean environment. They ensure that patients receive adequate nourishment, enforce infection control practices, and prevent hazards such as improper disposal of needles and sharps that could transmit blood-borne pathogens to unsuspecting staff and visitors.

Two of nurses' most important functions associated with patient safety, quality of care, and patient outcomes are providing surveillance for early detection of adverse events, complications, and medical errors and mobilizing institutional resources for timely intervention and rescue. A number of factors influence the effectiveness of nurse surveillance, including patient-to-registered-nurse ratios, the education of registered nurses at the bedside, and the numbers of licensed practical nurses and aides relative to registered nurses (often referred to as the skill mix of nursing personnel). Once a nurse detects potentially hazardous clinical signs, the work environment and institutional culture can promote or impede timely and successful resolution of the problem.

Nurses' relationships with physicians are particularly important in ensuring that patients receive the help they need. Since U.S. physicians typically combine office-based medical practice with caring for hospitalized patients, nurses are often physicians' eyes and ears at the hospital bedside. This arrangement works best in organizations that employ enough well-qualified staff, where nurses and physicians have a high degree of mutual respect and trust, and where top administrators facilitate patient-centered services throughout the institution (Aiken, Clarke, and Sloane 2002). Increasingly, nurses, particularly nurse practitioners, have assumed the same important roles in primary care and ambulatory settings.

Patients have high regard for nurses. For many years Gallop polls have reported that nurses top the list of occupations that the public most trusts and respects; indeed, nurses rank considerably higher than physicians, pharmacists, health care executives, and all others who work in health care. Nurses interact with the public in a variety of roles across the life span from birth to death, providing support in labor, consultations on breastfeeding and infant care, well-child care in medical offices and schools, occupational health in the workplace, care for the chronically ill and elderly, and care for the dying and support for their families. Patients and families often seek out nurses to translate information imparted by physicians, perhaps because there is less social distance between nurses and their patients than between doctors and patients. Nurses have been the key advocates for some of the innovations that have made modern health care more humane and patient-centered, such as demedicalizing normal births, liberalizing visiting hours and family participation in hospital care, and providing alternatives to invasive medical interventions at the end of life, such as hospice care. The high regard in which the public holds nurses is a source of personal gratification for them and the basis, along with their close interface with physicians, for their influence and authority in health care.

The Adequacy of Nurse Staffing

The adequacy of nurse staffing in hospitals and other health care settings is a matter of considerable debate, largely because of concerns about costs. Registered nurses constitute the largest group of health professionals in hospitals and account for a significant share of their operating expenses. Using a conservative total compensation estimate of $60,000 a year for a registered nurse, hospitals that add 50 nurses a year would have to pay out a total of $3 million. At present the nation's hospitals employ some 1.2 million nurses. It is generally easier for hospitals to base nurse staffing levels on budgetary resources than to use objective case-mix standards which would require additional financial resources.

An underappreciated aspect of the debate over the adequacy of nurse staffing concerns the impact of understaffing on annual nurse turnover rates, which are estimated to average about 13 percent nationally and over 20 percent at some hospitals. Aiken and associates examined the hypothesis that a minimum level of staffing is required to retain nurses and minimize turnover (Aiken et al. 2002). They found that each patient added to the workload of a hospital bedside nurse was associated with a 23 percent increase in burnout and a 15 percent rise in job dissatisfaction—both precursors to voluntary job resignation. Forty percent of nurses who were dissatisfied and burnt out intended to leave their jobs, compared with only 10 percent who were satisfied and not burnt out.

Assessing Nurse Staffing Adequacy

Two different perspectives dominate perceptions of hospital nurse shortages. One focuses on vacant budgeted positions and the influence of vacancies on costs and revenues. The other—often held by clinical nurses and physicians—evaluates the extent to which existing staff can provide needed services, taking into account the illness burden and intensity of care their patients require. Measuring shortages by vacancy rates has led to the widely held belief that nurse shortages are cyclical and self-correcting in response to changing market conditions (Aiken and Mullinix 1987; Buerhaus et al. 2002). The expectation that nurse shortages will not last long has tempered efforts to address nurses' dissatisfaction and claims that inadequate investment in nursing is undermining quality of care. However, the factors associated with predictions of greater national need for nurses are not cyclical. They include population aging, prevalence of chronic illness, rising per capita use of health services, and greater use of nurse-intensive technologies. These factors have prompted federal workforce planners to forecast a growing gap between nurse supply and demand (U.S. DHHS 2002).

Hospitals have experienced substantial increases in the intensity of services and case-mix complexity and shorter lengths of stay since the advent of prospective payment in 1980. This new payment system reimbursed hospitals based on patient diagnosis rather than length of stay. Since hospitals received the same amount regardless of whether patients with hip replacements remained in the hospital for three days or two weeks, prospective payment drove many hospitals to shorten patient stays. As large numbers of patients were discharged before they fully recuperated from surgery or illnesses, the condition of patients remaining in hospitals became more serious, requiring more intensive services and care.

Before the 1980s, hospitals commonly admitted preoperative patients several days before surgery for tests and evaluation. Nurses used that preoperative time to develop a trusting relationship, prepare patients and their families for what to expect following surgery, and assess the patient's usual physical and mental state, to be able to evaluate abnormalities and detect complications postoperatively. Today few patients are admitted to the hospital before the day of their scheduled surgery, and nurses see most patients for the first time when they are leaving the recovery room still groggy from anesthesia. They do not know the extent to which a patient can see, hear, or communicate under normal circumstances, or the patient's normal color, breathing patterns, and blood pressure. Patients may have more than one surgical site, multiple monitors, an artificial respirator, and an intravenous line administering powerful drugs that can result in death if the infusion rate is not correct. On average, nurses care for five to six postoperative patients at a time. Every day about a third of nurses' patients arrive directly from the operating room or have been admitted in an acute medical crisis; a third are in the early stages of recovery or stabilization, with many requirements for nursing time; and a third are being discharged, often with complicated home care requirements.

Hospitals have not added enough new registered nurse positions to offset the substantial rise in case-mix complexity. Between 1981 and 1993, the total percentage change in full-time-equivalent nursing personnel—adjusted for patient days and case-mix complexity—declined by more than 7 percent nationally and by over 20 percent in some states, including Massachusetts, New York, and California (Aiken, Sochalski, and Anderson 1996). Pennsylvania hospitals experienced a 21 percent increase in patient acuity between 1991 and 1996, and no change in the number of employed licensed nurses (RNs and LPNs). The result was a 14 percent decrease in the ratio of licensed nurses to case-mix-adjusted patient days of care (Unruh 2002).

Because increases in case-mix complexity and faster admission/discharge cycles have placed a burden on nurses that hospitals have not adequately recognized, about 85 percent of nurses work longer on a daily basis than their scheduled hours. Recent research has documented a substantial increase in the rate of errors associated with nurses working more than twelve consecutive hours, and close to half of hospital staff nurses commonly work longer than twelve hours (Rogers 2004). Presently no policies govern safe working hours for nurses, in contrast to other occupations in which vigilance is a matter of life and death. Lack of understanding by institutional managers and public policymakers of how shortened stays and greater case-mix complexity have adversely affected the work of nurses and the safety of patients—and failure to add enough nurse positions to ensure high-quality care—lie at the heart of the nurse shortage and perceptions that hospitals are unsafe.

Nurse Staffing and Patient Outcomes

Many research studies have now linked nurse staffing and patient outcomes. One of the first such contemporary studies was the national halothane study, which documented a twelve-fold variation in surgical mortality from this form of anesthesia across the nation. The study found nurse staffing among the significant determinants of mortality (Moses and Mosteller 1968). Public availability of Medicare data for U.S. hospitals also generated a series of studies on the factors underlying variations in mortality; these studies focused primarily on non-nursing correlates such as for-profit versus nonprofit hospital ownership (Shortell and Hughes 1988; Hartz, Krakauer, and Kuhn 1989; Silber et al. 2000). Each study reported in passing that nurse staffing was significantly related to mortality, but no one took much notice of these collective findings until nurse investigators began designing studies to examine the effects of nurse staffing on patient outcomes.

In 1996 the Institute of Medicine published the results of its study on the adequacy of hospital nurse staffing, acknowledging the evidence from health services research suggesting a link between nurse staffing and patient outcomes, but concluding that insufficient evidence existed for recommending safe staffing levels (Institute of Medicine 1996). The IOM's call for funding more research spawned new studies reinforcing the link between nurse staffing and patient outcomes.

In a study of outcomes following common surgical procedures for over 230,000 patients in 168 hospitals, Aiken and colleagues documented a strong association between staff nurse workloads and surgical mortality and failure to rescue patients who had developed complications (Aiken et al. 2002). Hospital staffing ranged from about 4 to 8 patients per nurse; 50 percent of hospitals had a patient-to-nurse ratio of 5 to 1 or lower. After adjusting for over 130 patient and hospital factors, the results suggested that each additional patient in a nurse's workload raised the odds of mortality by 7 percent. Thus the risk of death and failure to rescue patients with complications was nearly 30 percent higher in hospitals where nurses' average workload was 8 patients than in hospitals where nurses cared for 4 patients. The effect was linear, so reducing nurses' workloads from 8 to 7 patients produced the same 7 percent decline in mortality risk as cutting the workload from 5 patients to 4. (The sample included too few hospitals to reliably estimate the effect beyond 8 patients per nurse.)

There is a growing literature of well-designed studies demonstrating a variety of better patient outcomes associated with more favorable staffing of registered nurses (Kovner and Gergen 1998; Blegen, Goode, and Reed 1998; Cho et al. 2003). For example, Needleman and associates documented a significant relationship between nurse staffing and urinary tract infections, pneumonia, shock, hemorrhage in the upper gastrointestinal tract, and length of stay in medical patients, as well as failure to rescue in surgical patients (2002). Person and associates showed that the odds of dying from first-time acute myocardial infarction were significantly lower in hospitals with more favorable nurse-to-patient ratios (2004). Studies have also linked better nurse staffing to lower rates of medication errors and reduced needle-stick injuries to nurses (Blegen, Goode, and Reed 1998; Clarke, Sloane, and Aiken 2002).

Nursing Skill Mix and Patient Outcomes

Nursing skill mix varies substantially, with some hospitals employing predominantly registered nurses (RNs) and others a mix of RNs, licensed practical nurses (LPNs), and aides. The organization of nurses' work and the deployment of non-RNs have changed over time. In the 1960s division of labor within hospital nursing commonly occurred in a team structure, where RNs provided assessments, medications, and treatments to all patients while directing LPNs and aides who attended to personal hygiene, ambulation, and other routine patient care. As the number of registered nurses employed by hospitals grew, RNs saw the value of maintaining a closer relationship with patients than team nursing allowed and the opportunity to shed the unwanted responsibility for supervising LPNs and aides. Nurses advocated returning the care of all patients to RNs under a model referred to as primary nursing, and hospital managers supported the transition from team to primary nursing. The result was a substantial decline in the employment of LPNs in hospitals nationally and a skill mix in which RNs represented the majority of nursing personnel.

During the hospital restructuring movement to contain costs in the 1990s, many hospitals once again substituted LPNs and aides for RNs (Brannon 1996; Norrish and Rundall 2001). However, research findings consistently support the conclusion that the most important factor in improving patient outcomes is the number of registered nurses. Aiken and associates found no relationship between patient-to-LPN ratios or patient-to-aide ratios and variation in mortality, but they did find a substantial effect of patient-to-RN ratios on surgical mortality and failure to rescue (Aiken et al. 2002). Jarman and associates found the higher the proportion of the least-trained auxiliary nursing personnel in English hospitals, the higher the mortality (1999). The weight of evidence suggests that lesser-trained nursing personnel are not substitutes for RNs in ensuring quality of care and patient safety.

Nurses' Education and Patient Outcomes

Registered nurses in the United States receive their basic education in one of three types of programs, all of which qualify graduates to take the registered nurse licensing examination. These programs include three-year hospital-sponsored diploma programs, two-year associate degree programs in community colleges, and four-year baccalaureate nursing programs in colleges and universities. Freidson described nursing as an incompletely closed profession because of its inability to establish minimum education requirements for entry (1970).

In 2001 hospital diploma programs—which had educated almost all nurses in the 1960s—graduated just 3 percent of new nurses. Associate degree programs replaced diploma programs, accounting for over 60 percent of new entrants to nursing in 2001, while about 36 percent of new nurses were baccalaureate graduates (National Council of State Boards of Nursing 2001). Close to 45 percent of nurses nationally had a baccalaureate or higher degree in 2000, and almost one in four obtained the degree following basic education in a diploma or associate degree program (Spratley et al. 2001). Many other countries, including Canada, Australia, New Zealand, Ireland, Iceland, and Cuba, have eliminated multiple educational pathways into nursing by establishing the baccalaureate as the entry-level degree for new nurses. The United Kingdom has moved nursing education within higher education but has not yet completed the full transition to a baccalaureate degree.

Research is surprisingly scanty on variations in nurses' education across institutions and health care settings and on the impact of nurses' educational levels on clinical practice and patient outcomes. A few studies have suggested that baccalaureate-prepared nurses are more likely to demonstrate professional behaviors important to patient safety, such as problem solving, performance of complex functions, and effective interdisciplinary communication (Hickam et al. 2003; Blegen, Vaughn, and Goode 2001). Nurse executives in teaching hospitals prefer baccalaureate-prepared nurses and aim to have at least 70 percent of their staff nurses trained at the baccalaureate level, while community hospital nurse executives reportedly prefer that 50 percent of nurses have BSNs (Goode et al. 2001). With only about 43 percent of hospital staff nurses holding a baccalaureate degree, not enough are available to meet these targets.

Aiken and colleagues observed that the proportion of hospital staff nurses holding a baccalaureate degree ranged from none to 77 percent across Pennsylvania hospitals, and they designed a study to find out if variation of that magnitude was associated with differences in patient outcomes (2003). The answer was yes. The researchers found that hospitals with a larger proportion of baccalaureate-prepared nurses had significantly lower surgical mortality rates, after adjusting for patient and hospital characteristics (such as size, teaching status, and technology) as well as patient-to-nurse staffing ratios, nurse experience, and whether the patient's surgeon was board certified. Every 10 percent increase in the proportion of nurses holding a baccalaureate degree was associated with a 5 percent decrease in both the likelihood that patients would die within thirty days of admission and the odds of failure to rescue patients with complications.

Moreover, the effects of nurse staffing and education were found to be additive. The best outcomes occurred in hospitals where nurses took care of four or fewer patients each and 60 percent of staff nurses were educated at the baccalaureate level or higher. The worst outcomes occurred in hospitals where nurses cared for eight or more patients each and only 20 percent had baccalaureate degrees. The effect on mortality of a 20 percent rise in the percentage of baccalaureate-prepared nurses was roughly equivalent to adding enough nurses to reduce the mean workload by two patients. Thus, hospitals might be able to stem the growing need for more nurses per one hundred inpatient days by moving to a more highly educated RN workforce.

Nursing faces special challenges in raising educational requirements commensurate with trends in other health professions because of modern hospitals' dependence on large numbers of nurses. Hospital employers seem to prefer training nurses quickly and inexpensively and inculcating interchangeable skills and modest career expectations. However, this scenario clashes with the aspirations of many people attracted to nursing with hopes of upward mobility and opportunities for personally gratifying careers and reasonably remunerated work. The number of applicants to nursing schools who already have college degrees is growing rapidly, and universities have responded with programs as short as one year for college graduates who wish to earn a BSN.

Nurse Practice Environments

Flood and Scott describe hospitals as having dual bureaucratic and professional structures that represent opposing approaches to managing complex tasks (1987). Conventional bureaucracies subdivide work among many participants and control their activities through externally imposed rules and hierarchies. Organizations with professional structures support the efforts of self-regulating individuals who exercise considerable discretion in carrying out their work (Freidson 1970). Hospital nurses are agents of a bureaucracy but hold professional values and seek peer relationships and professional modes of organizing their work. Etzioni described professional-bureaucratic conflict as a major concern for complex health care organizations such as hospitals, suggesting that "the authority of knowledge and the authority of administrative hierarchy are basically incompatible" (1969, viii). Indeed, research on hospital nurse burnout is consistent with this view, showing that organizational conflict far outweighs the psychological and physical stress associated with caring for ill and dying patients (Aiken and Sloane 1997).

Studies have devoted relatively little attention to the impact of organizational context and culture on patient outcomes, focusing instead on the effects of staffing. One of the first studies of nursing to integrate a sociological perspective with outcomes such as mortality examined the performance of magnet hospitals (Aiken, Smith, and Lake 1994). Such hospitals were originally designated in the early 1980s based on their success in attracting and retaining nurses when other local hospitals were experiencing nurse shortages (McClure and Hinshaw 2002). Compared with other institutions, magnet hospitals had higher nurse satisfaction, and their nurses reported more autonomy, greater control over resources required for high-quality care, and better relations with physicians.

As a first step in exploring the effects of organizational features common to magnet hospitals, Aiken and colleagues matched the 39 original magnet hospitals with 195 control hospitals selected from all non-magnet U.S. hospitals. Using a multivariate matched sampling procedure—propensity scoring—that controlled for twelve hospital characteristics including size, teaching status, technology, and proportion of board-certified physicians, the investigators found that magnet hospitals had a 4.5 percent lower Medicare mortality rate than matched hospitals (Aiken, Smith, and Lake 1994). Nurse staffing alone did not explain this outcome: organizational cultures that devolved greater autonomy and control to nurses and promoted good relations between nurses and physicians were also associated with better patient outcomes.

Aiken and colleagues further explored the relationship between nurse practice environments and patient and nurse outcomes in a subsequent study making use of a natural experiment in the organization of care associated with the AIDS epidemic. A multiple-site study was designed that included forty units in twenty hospitals. Ten of these hospitals had dedicated AIDS units and were matched with comparable hospitals without such units. The study included two magnet hospitals without AIDS units for comparison. The investigators found that risk-adjusted AIDS mortality within thirty days of admission was substantially lower and patient satisfaction was significantly higher in dedicated AIDS units and magnet hospitals than in conventionally organized general medical units (Aiken et al. 1999). More favorable nurse staffing and practice environments were among the important explanations for these better patient and nurse outcomes.

Aiken and colleagues have since studied nurse practice environments in a large representative group of hospitals to determine the extent to which features are associated with nurse retention and patient outcomes. That study—which included over seven hundred hospitals in five countries—found that nurses in hospitals in the United States, Canada, the United Kingdom, Germany, and New Zealand face common challenges regarding nurse understaffing and high levels of burnout and job dissatisfaction. Nurses in all these countries also associate deficiencies in quality of care with inadequate staffing and poor nurse work environments (Aiken et al. 2001; Aiken, Clarke, and Sloane 2002). Germany is the only country with substantially lower nurse burnout, which may reflect its significantly longer average length of stay.

Remarkably, given the many differences in culture and nurses' education across countries, at least some hospitals in every country have organizational features similar to those of U.S. magnet hospitals. Nurse and patient outcomes are better in magnet-like hospitals, which devolve greater autonomy and control to nurses and provide a more supportive environment for professional practice. For example, the frequency of patient falls with injuries, medication errors, and hospital-acquired infections is lower in hospitals across the five countries where nurse staffing is more favorable, the administration supports high-quality nursing, nurses have career development opportunities, and physicians and nurses have good relations.

Nursing and Quality Improvement

There is one area of potential discordance between the research evidence documenting better outcomes when hospitals devolve more authority to nurses and ongoing efforts to protect patients from medical errors. Much of the evolving thinking about how to reduce medical errors suggests developing systems that standardize medical decision-making and minimize professional discretion. Do the aims of patient safety systems conflict with evidence that organizations that devolve more authority and autonomy to nurses have better outcomes?

Nurses have long been responsible for many of the safeguards in hospital care, such as counting sponges and instruments in the operating room to ensure that they are not left inside patients, storing dangerous drugs in locked cabinets, having two nurses check the compatibility of blood before transfusion, and notifying physicians when a medication order seems out of the ordinary before administering it. Nurses have been the de facto safety system in hospitals for over a hundred years. Indeed, recent studies confirm that nurses find most of the medication errors that are detected in hospitals. However, nurses understand the vulnerabilities of the people-dependent safety provisions on which hospitals rely. Indeed, a common fear of nurses—and one that contributes to their high levels of burnout—is that with their increasingly heavy workloads they will fail to detect an error committed by someone else or commit an error themselves that will hurt a patient. Hence, more effective safety systems that minimize the opportunity for human error would improve the work environment and mental health for nurses more than for any other hospital workers.

However, minimizing errors is only one strategy for improving quality of care in hospitals. Good nurse-patient relationships are at the heart of safe and effective hospital care. A myriad of situations still require expert clinical judgment, including recognizing early signs that a patient may not be doing well and mobilizing a timely institutional response, and determining when and under what circumstances a patient can be safely discharged. Moreover, in addition to caring for patients, nurses are responsible for maintaining the environment in which care takes place, which requires authority as well as status within an organization. Nurses must have some control over the resources required for meeting patients' needs, such as safe nurse staffing levels, timely responses from physicians, accessible supplies and equipment, and support departments, such as housekeeping, pharmacy, central supply, and blood bank, that run efficiently and effectively around the clock.

The international hospital outcomes study aimed to show that nurse autonomy was consistent with—rather than antithetical to—effective interdisciplinary team functioning. Researchers documented that hospitals in which nurses had greater autonomy and more control over resources were more, not less, likely to have well-developed and effective interdisciplinary teams (Rafferty, Ball, and Aiken 2001). Research by Aiken and associates suggests that hospitals that promote the full exercise of the professional nurse role and devolve authority to nurses in their areas of expertise also create effective interdisciplinary care cultures, patient-centered environments, and better patient outcomes. Such institutions will probably be at the forefront of establishing new and better systems to reduce human error because their professional culture values clinical excellence informed by evidence-based practice.

Both new systems that reduce human error and an organizational context that enables the best performance from each health professional are essential in ensuring safe and effective care for hospitalized patients. The IOM reports on quality, which initially gave little attention to nursing, have now focused explicitly on the need to transform the nurse work environment to keep patients safe. This suggests a merging of two previously separate areas of concern—nurse shortages and patient safety—into a more unified approach to quality that is likely to yield important new initiatives to ameliorate both problems.

References

Aiken, L. H., and C. F. Mullinix. 1987. The Nurse Shortage: Myth or Reality? *New England Journal of Medicine* 317: 641–646.

Aiken, L. H., and D. M. Sloane. 1997. Effects on Organizational Innovation in AIDS Care on Burnout among Hospital Nurses. *Work and Occupations* 24: 455–479.

Aiken, L. H., D. M. Sloane, E. T. Lake, et al. 1999. Organization and Outcomes of Inpatient AIDS Care. *Medical Care* 37: 760–772.

Aiken, L. H., H. L. Smith, and E. T. Lake. 1994. Lower Medicare Mortality among a Set of Hospitals Known for Good Nursing Care. *Medical Care* 32: 771–787.

Aiken, L. H., J. Sochalski, and G. Anderson. 1996. Downsizing the Hospital Workforce. *Health Affairs* 15: 88–92.

Aiken, L. H., S. P. Clarke, and D. M. Sloane. 2002. Hospital Staffing, Organizational Support, and Quality of Care: Cross-National Findings. *International Journal for Quality in Health Care* 14: 5–13.

Aiken, L. H., S. P. Clarke, D. M. Sloane, et al. 2001. Nurses' Reports of Hospital Quality of Care and Working Conditions in Five Countries. *Health Affairs* 20: 43–53.

Aiken, L. H., S. P. Clarke, D. M. Sloane, et al. 2002. Hospital Nurse Staffing and Patient Mortality, Nurse Burnout, and Job Dissatisfaction. *Journal of the American Medical Association* 288: 1987–1993.

Aiken, L. H., S. P. Clarke, R. B. Cheung, et al. 2003. Education Levels of Hospital Nurses and Patient Mortality. *Journal of the American Medical Association* 290: 1617–1623.

Blegen, M. A., C. J. Goode, and L. Reed. 1998. Nurse Staffing and Patient Outcomes. *Nursing Research* 47: 43–50.

Blegen, M. A., T. Vaughn, and C. J. Goode. 2001. Nurse Experience and Education: Effect on Quality of Care. *Journal of Nursing Administration* 31: 33–39.

Blendon, R. J., C. M. DesRoches, M. Brodie, et al. 2002. Views of Practicing Physicians and the Public on Medical Errors. *New England Journal of Medicine* 347: 1933–1940.

Brannon, R. L. 1996. Restructuring Hospital Nursing: Reversing the Trend toward a Professional Work Force. *International Journal of Health Services* 26: 643–654.

Buerhaus, P. I., J. Needleman, S. Mattke, et al. 2002. Strengthening Hospital Nursing. *Health Affairs* 21: 123–132.

Cho, S. H., S. Ketefian, V. H. Barkauskas, et al. 2003. The Effects of Nurse Staffing on Adverse Events, Morbidity, Mortality, and Medical Costs. *Nursing Research* 52: 71–79.

Clarke, S. P., D. M. Sloane, and L. H. Aiken. 2002. Effects of Hospital Staffing and Organizational Climate on Needlestick Injuries to Nurses. *American Journal of Public Health* 92: 1115–1119.

Diers, D. 2004. *Speaking of Nursing...Narratives of Practice, Research, Policy, and the Profession*. Sudbury, MA: Jones and Bartlett.

Etzioni, A. 1969. *The Semi-Professionals and Their Organizations: Teachers, Nurses, and Social Workers*. New York: Free Press.

Flood, A. B., and W. R. Scott, eds. 1987. *Hospital Structure and Performance*. Baltimore, MD: Johns Hopkins University Press.

Freidson, E. 1970. *Professional Dominance: The Social Structure of Medical Care*. New York: Atherton.

Goode, C. J., S. Pinkerton, M. P. McCausland, et al. 2001. Documenting Chief Nursing Officers' Preference for BSN-Prepared Nurses. *Journal of Nursing Administration* 31: 55–59.

Hartz, A. J., H. Krakauer, and E. M. Kuhn. 1989. Hospital Characteristics and Mortality Rates. *New England Journal of Medicine* 321: 1720–1725.

Hickam, D. H., S. Severance, A. Feldstein, et al. 2003. *The Effect of Health Care Working Conditions on Patient Safety*. Rockville, MD: Agency for Healthcare Research and Quality, Department of Health and Human Services.

Institute of Medicine. 1996. *Nursing Staff in Hospitals and Nursing Homes: Is It Adequate?* Washington, DC: National Academies Press.

————. 2000. *To Err Is Human: Building a Safer Health System*. Washington, DC: National Academies Press.

————. 2001. *Crossing the Quality Chasm*. Washington, DC: National Academies Press.

————. 2004. *Keeping Patients Safe: Transforming the Work Environment of Nurses*. Washington, DC: National Academies Press.

Jarman, B., S. Gault, B. Alves, et al. 1999. Explaining Differences in English Hospital Death Rates Using Routinely Collected Data. *British Medical Journal* 318: 1515–1520.

Kovner, C., and P. J. Gergen. 1998. Nurse Staffing Levels and Adverse Events Following Surgery in U.S. Hospitals. *Image: Journal of Nursing Scholarship* 30: 315–321.

McClure, M. L., and A. S. Hinshaw. 2002. *Magnet Hospitals Revisited*. Washington, DC: American Nurses Association.

Moses, L. E., and F. Mosteller. 1968. Institutional Differences in Postoperative Death Rates. *Journal of the American Medical Association* 203: 492–494.

National Council of State Boards of Nursing. 2001. *Annual Report 2001*. Available at *www.ncsbn.org/public/about/res/AnnRpt_FY01.pdf* (accessed May 2, 2003).

Needleman, J., P. Buerhaus, S. Mattke, et al. 2002. Nurse-Staffing Levels and the Quality of Care in Hospitals. *New England Journal of Medicine* 346: 1715–1722.

Norrish, B. R., and T. G. Rundall. 2001. Hospital Restructuring and the Work of Registered Nurses. *Milbank Memorial Quarterly* 79: 55–79.

Person, S. D., J. J. Allison, C. I. Kiefe, et al. 2004. Nurse Staffing and Mortality for Medicare Patients with Acute Myocardial Infarction. *Medical Care* 42: 4–12.

Rafferty, A. M., J. Ball, and L. H. Aiken. 2001. Are Teamwork and Professional Autonomy Compatible, and Do They Result in Improved Hospital Care? *Quality in Health Care* 10 (suppl. 2): ii32–ii37.

Rogers, A. 2004. Work Hour Regulation in Safety-Sensitive Industries. In *Keeping Patients Safe: Transforming the Work Environment of Nurses*, ed. A. Page. Institute of Medicine, Committee on the Work Environment for Nurses and Patient Safety. Washington, DC: National Academies Press.

Shortell, S. M., and E.F.X. Hughes. 1988. The Effects of Regulation, Competition, and Ownership on Mortality Rates among Hospital Inpatients. *New England Journal of Medicine* 318: 1100.

Silber, J. H., S. K. Kennedy, O. Even-Shoshan, et al. 2000. Anesthesiologist Direction and Patient Outcomes. *Anesthesiology* 93: 152–163.

Spratley, E., A. Johnson, J. Sochalski, et al. 2001. *The Registered Nurse Population, March 2000: Findings from the National Sample Survey of Registered Nurses*. Access no. HR-0900603. Rockville, MD: U.S. Department of Health and Human Services.

U.S. Department of Health and Human Services (DHHS). 2002. *Projected Supply, Demand, and Shortages of Registered Nurses, 2000–2020*. Rockville, MD: National Center for Health Workforce Analysis, Health Resources and Services Administration.

Unruh, L. 2002. Nursing Staff Reductions in Pennsylvania Hospitals: Exploring the Discrepancy between Perceptions and Data. *Medical Care Research and Review* 59: 197–214.

Vahey, D. C., L. H. Aiken, D. M. Sloane, et al. 2004. Nurse Burnout and Patient Satisfaction. *Medical Care* 42: 1157–1166.

CHAPTER 13

Improving Medicare for Beneficiaries with Disabilities

—❧—

LISA I. IEZZONI

A few lines caught my eye near the end of a lengthy *New York Times* article on June 11, 2003. The article recounted the growing likelihood that Congress would add prescription drug benefits to Medicare and itemized the trade-offs required to trim projected expenses (Pear 2003a, A21). After describing various components of proposed Senate legislation, the article concluded, "To help offset the costs, Medicare would freeze payments for home medical equipment, like wheelchairs and oxygen, for seven years."

Of course, the legislation signed by George W. Bush in December 2003 bore little resemblance to this June proposal. In particular, Congress did not overturn Medicare's central tenet: coverage of only those services that are "reasonable and necessary for the diagnosis or treatment of illness or injury or to improve the functioning of a malformed body member" (42 C.F.R. Sec. 402.3), services that fit snugly within the standard medical armamentarium. Although policymakers have strayed occasionally, such as adding coverage for selected screening tests and palliative care, Medicare's guiding mandate remains inviolate.

Given this context, the acceptability of freezing Medicare payments for wheelchairs and home-based oxygen comes as little surprise—although limiting oxygen payments carries a mischievous symbolism (certainly, oxygen should meet Medicare's reasonable and necessary standard). This proposal exemplifies a more basic and vexing reality that extends well beyond Medicare: The American health care system fails to meet the daily health and function-related needs of many people with chronic, disabling medical conditions. Although technologies and therapies exist to maintain, restore, or maximize function, they often fall outside health insurance coverage boundaries. Such gaps in coverage prevent people from obtaining services and equipment that are costly to purchase out-of-pocket, needlessly compromising lives.

This observation draws upon long historical roots. Achieving passage of the Medicare program required years of political maneuvering, compromises, and reduced expectations. The Medicare program did cover more non-acute care, including limited stays in skilled nursing homes and home-based rehabilitation, than any other governmental, nonprofit, or commercial insurer at the time (Fox 1993). Nonetheless, in the end, "Left out were provisions that addressed the particular problems of the chronically sick elderly: medical conditions that would not dramatically improve and the need to maintain independent function rather than triumph over discrete illness and injury" (Marmor 2000, 153). Forty years later, little has changed.

Although these problems wend throughout the health care delivery system, I concentrate on Medicare policies for several reasons. Medicare is huge. In 2002, Medicare insured roughly 40.6 million persons, including 6.0 million individuals under age 65 with disabilities (Centers for Medicare and Medicaid Services [CMS] 2003b). Of an estimated $236.5 billion expenditures in 2001, Medicare spent $31.9 billion on beneficiaries with disabilities (CMS 2002). Furthermore, unlike Medicaid programs and private health plans, Medicare's rules extend nationwide, although specific implementation decisions can vary across regions. Over the years, Medicare policies have frequently infiltrated the rest of the health care system. Therefore, Medicare offers an excellent starting point to examine health care policies for persons with disabilities.

Demographic Trends Breed Urgency

Countless persons with disabilities daily slip through the fault lines crisscrossing the health care delivery system. Why is this issue so pressing now? Numbers offer a clear answer.

Almost one-fifth of U.S. residents—19.3 percent of people age 5 years and older, or 49.7 million—report disabilities (U.S. Census Bureau 2003b). As table

TABLE 13.1   *Estimates of Disability from the 2000 U.S. Census (population in millions)*

Disability[a]	Age 16 to 64 years						Age 65 years and older					
	Total	(%)	Males	(%)	Females	(%)	Total	(%)	Males	(%)	Females	(%)
Population	178.9	(100.0)	87.6	(100.0)	91.1	(100.0)	33.3	(100.0)	13.9	(100.0)	19.4	(100.0)
With any disability	33.1	(18.6)	17.1	(19.6)	16.0	(17.6)	14.0	(41.9)	5.6	(40.4)	8.3	(43.0)
Sensory	4.1	(2.3)	2.4	(2.7)	1.7	(1.9)	4.7	(14.2)	2.2	(15.6)	2.6	(13.2)
Physical	11.2	(6.2)	5.3	(6.0)	5.9	(6.4)	9.5	(28.6)	3.6	(25.8)	6.0	(30.7)
Mental	6.8	(3.8)	3.4	(3.9)	3.3	(3.7)	3.6	(10.8)	1.4	(9.9)	2.2	(11.4)
Self-care	3.1	(1.8)	1.5	(1.7)	1.7	(1.9)	3.2	(9.5)	1.0	(7.5)	2.1	(11.0)
Ability to leave the home	11.4	(6.4)	5.7	(6.4)	5.8	(6.4)	6.8	(20.4)	2.3	(16.8)	4.5	(23.0)
Employment	21.3	(11.9)	11.4	(13.0)	9.9	(10.9)	—		—		—	

Source: adapted from the U.S. Census Bureau 2003b.

[a]Items 16 and 17 on the 2000 long-form census questionnaire addressed disability. The questions and the definition of disability are described elsewhere (U.S. Census Bureau 2003a).

13.1 shows, persons age 65 and older report any disability at higher rates than younger people—41.9 percent compared with 18.6. At younger ages, males generally have higher rates of disability than females, while the reverse occurs over age 64 years. Physical disabilities are more common than sensory or mental health disabilities. Racial and ethnic minority populations have higher disability rates than do whites (see table 13.2).

Even more compelling numbers come from looking ahead. By 2030, the number of people age 65 years and older will rise to 69.4 million (20 percent of the population) from 34.7 million (12.6 percent) in 2000 (Day 1996). Persons age 85 years and older will become the most rapidly growing segment of the population, rising from 4.3 million (1.6 percent) in 2000 to 18.2 million (4.6 percent) in 2050.

This growth reflects lengthening life expectancies, even in recent decades. The average male born in the United States in 1970 could anticipate living to roughly 67 years of age compared with over 74 years for those born 30 years later (Arias 2002). Life expectancy for females rose from 75 years in 1970 to almost 80 years in 2000. Declining death rates from heart disease substantially prolonged longevity, expanding the numbers living with chronic, nonfatal, but disabling conditions. Persons with significant physical disabilities are also living longer, largely because of fundamental medical breakthroughs like advances in antibiotics. According to the National Spinal Cord Injury Statistical Center (2001), persons who become paraplegic at age 40 and survive 1 year following injury can expect to live another 29 years, compared with 38 years for persons without spinal cord injury.

Aging does not invariably produce disability, at least not until near death. Centenarians often remain reasonably healthy until shortly before dying. Recent reports suggest that rates of serious functional deficits are declining among older

TABLE 13.2   *Disability by Race and Ethnicity Groups, 2000 U.S. Census*

	Age	
Racial/ethnic groups[a]	16 to 64 years (%)	65+ years (%)
Total	18.6	41.9
White alone	16.8	40.6
Black or African American alone	26.4	52.8
Asian alone	16.9	40.8
American Indian or Alaskan Native alone	27.0	57.6
Native Hawaiian, other Pacific Islander alone	21.0	48.5
Some other race alone	23.5	50.4
Two or more races	25.1	51.8
Hispanic or Latino (of any race)	24.0	48.5

Source: adapted from the U.S. Census Bureau 2003c.

[a]For the first time, during the 2000 census respondents could indicate membership in more than one race or ethnicity group.

individuals, although evidence about the most severe disabilities is contradictory (Freedman, Martin, and Schoeni 2002). Multiple factors likely underlie improvements in functional abilities among older persons, including new medical therapies and healthier lifestyle. Nevertheless, "disability is not something that happens only to a minority of humanity, it is a common (indeed natural) feature of the human condition. . . . Over the lifespan, [disability is] a universal phenomena" (Üstün et al. 2003, 82).

With the aging population, the absolute number of Americans with functional limitations will rise by over 300 percent by 2049 if the age-specific prevalence of major chronic conditions remains unchanged (Boult et al. 1996). Arthritis, the leading cause of disability among adults, affected 70 million adults in 2001, including 60 percent of people age 65 and older (Centers for Disease Control and Prevention 2003). If current rates remain unchanged, the number of persons over age 65 with arthritis will double by 2030, causing more physical impairments than ischemic heart disease, cancer, and dementia combined. Obesity among adult Americans is also rising, growing from 12 percent in 1991 to 20.9 percent—or 44.3 million persons—in 2001 (Mokdad et al. 2003). Apart from causing disability itself, obesity contributes to other debilitating conditions, including diabetes, arthritis, high blood pressure, and asthma. Many more persons will therefore have multiple coexisting, chronic, disabling conditions in coming years.

Medicare covers more than just people age 65 and older. Rising numbers of disabled workers receive Medicare through qualifying for Social Security disability insurance (SSDI). The average annual rate of growth in Medicare enrollment between 1973, when SSDI recipients could first get Medicare, and 1999 was 4.3 percent for disabled beneficiaries compared with 1.7 percent for aged enrollees (CMS 2003a). In 2002, 5.5 million disabled workers received benefits from the Social Security Administration (SSA). Today's SSDI recipients look different than those of prior years (IOM 2002b). In 1960, when persons younger than 50 years of age could first receive SSDI benefits, the average disabled worker was 57.2 years old; by 2002, the average age fell to 51.0 years. In 1957, when SSDI benefits first became available, only 20 percent of disabled workers were women, compared with 45 percent in 2002. Disabled women workers receive lower monthly payments than men: $709 compared with $936 in December 2002 (SSA 2003). Thus, on average, those receiving SSDI today will likely stay on the rolls longer and have less disposable income than former beneficiaries.

One final demographic issue involves social, economic, and health disadvantages experienced by many persons with physical, sensory, and psychiatric disabilities. Compared with others, persons with disabilities have less education and higher rates of poverty, unemployment, tobacco use, obesity, and fair or poor health. They are also more likely to live alone and report feeling frequently depressed, anxious, fearful, or under stress. Even with insurance, persons with disabilities could still risk poor health outcomes because of complex underlying medical conditions that need to be treated by diverse clinical specialists, poor coordination of care, inadequate communication or discordant expectations between physicians and patients, physically inaccessible care sites, insufficient health literacy, and financial barriers. Medicare beneficiaries with disabilities spend $1,532 out-of-pocket annually for health care services; this amount rises to $2,175 for persons with two or more limitations of activities of daily living (Foote and Hogan 2001).

Targets for Policy Changes

As the Disability Policy Panel of the National Academy of Social Insurance acknowledged, "Despite its gaps in covered services, Medicare is an essential source of health care coverage for Social Security disability beneficiaries" as well as chronically debilitated older adults (Mashaw and Reno 1996, 144). Indeed, Medicare meets many high-cost service needs of enrollees with disabilities, such as inpatient intensive care, cardiac revascularization, or joint replacement surgery.

Tensions between patients' needs and coverage limits primarily involve routine non-acute care and services and technologies for maintaining, restoring, or maximizing function. Changes in four areas—medical necessity determinations, homebound requirements, coverage waiting periods, and office visit reimbursement—could considerably improve the lives of Medicare beneficiaries with disabilities. Related issues emerged repeatedly during 119 interviews I conducted with persons with mobility problems and their family members, physicians, physical and occupational therapists, and medical directors of health plans, as the following stories reveal (all proper names are pseudonyms, Iezzoni 2003).

Revising the Definitions of Medical Necessity

"I can't keep up with this walker," said Erna Dodd, moving slowly and laboriously, breathing oxygen from a canister dangling from her walker's handlebars. She had many medical problems: emphysema, diabetes requiring insulin, congestive heart failure, seizures, obesity, and debilitating arthritis. Nonetheless, she refused our proffered wheelchair. Ms. Dodd said, "[I don't] want people pushing me in a wheelchair. So Max [her nurse] put in to get me a [motorized] scooter. He had my doctor fill out some paper for it. This was a letter they send, telling me they wouldn't give it to me." Reaching into her handbag, she retrieved a legal-size envelope containing a single sheet of paper.

"Medicare sent this to you?" I asked, looking at the letterhead, then read aloud, "'We have received a prior authorization request for the above named beneficiary for a power operated vehicle. This request has been denied because the information did not support the medical necessity of the equipment. If you do not agree with this decision, you may request a review in writing within six months of the date indicated in this letter. Submit any additional documentation to the review department.' Did Max appeal this for you?"

"I don't know. I was going to call my doctor and talk to him about it. It would help me a lot." Dr. Baker, her primary care physician, did contest Medicare's denial, but Erna Dodd died during the appeals process (Iezzoni 1999, 2003).

Decisions on health insurance reimbursement typically involve two stages: organization-wide decisions about what services will be covered and case-by-case decisions about the medical necessity of covered services for individual persons

(Singer and Bergthold 2001). (As noted below, a third-order decision, critical for some individuals with disabilities, concerns whether persons can receive services at home.) Congress makes Medicare's broad benefit decisions, which are then codified in federal regulations. Local Medicare carriers determine whether individual beneficiaries receive the items or services they request, such as assistive technologies and physical and occupational therapy.

In its pamphlet *Your Medicare Benefits,* CMS informs beneficiaries that original Medicare covers services or supplies that are medically necessary or that:

- Are proper and needed for the diagnosis or treatment of your medical condition;
- Are provided for the diagnosis, direct care, and treatment of your medical condition;
- Meet the standards of good medical practice in the local area; and
- Are not mainly for the convenience of you or your doctor. (CMS 2003d)

Two major questions generally drive decisions regarding requests from individual Medicare beneficiaries: (1) How long will the person need the service? Chronic needs raise more questions than short-term demands; and (2) Will the service result in measurable improvement of physical deficits caused by medical illness or injury? Neither question is especially propitious for persons with disabilities. By definition, these individuals generally need services long-term, and their impairments are unlikely to improve. Medicare also explicitly denies items judged only for personal comfort or not primarily medical in nature, such as hearing aids, grab bars, and routine foot or dental care (42 C.F.R. Sec. 411.15). This prohibition against convenience items likely doomed Erna Dodd's request for a motorized scooter. Long-term physical, occupational, or speech-language therapy to maintain function or prevent further declines would likely also fail these tests as the term treatment assumes recovery or improvement. In addition, decisions regarding individual medical necessity often appear idiosyncratic and subjective and deficient communication compounds the problem (Rosenbaum et al. 1999). "Denial letters rarely explain who made the decision, the reason for the decision, what sources of evidence were considered, what coverage policies were applied" (Singer and Bergthold 2001, 204).

These problems are well recognized. The IOM's Committee on a National Agenda for the Prevention of Disabilities lauded the potential for rehabilitation services, assistive technologies, and even modest items like grab bars to improve safety and quality of life for persons with disabilities. The committee noted that coverage and payment policies impede people from getting these devices, which could potentially save health care dollars downstream: "Denial of reimbursement for technology that assists in the performance of daily activities and reduces risk of secondary conditions is likely to result in long-term costs that exceed initial savings. For example, Medicare regards grab bars for bathrooms as convenience items, even though falls in the bathroom are a leading cause of hip fractures and other injuries among the elderly. The health care costs associated with hip fractures alone are large and growing. This shortsightedness is also reflected in the inadequate coverage that most insurers provide for long-term maintenance and replacement of the few assistive technologies they do fund" (Pope and Tarlov 1991, 227).

Like this committee, a panel of the National Academy of Social Insurance put this topic among its short- to mid-range recommendations for making Medicare more responsive to chronic care.

> Strive to include services related to function and health-related quality of life:
> - Cover durable medical equipment with the specific intent of maintaining or restoring function.
> - Provide for assistive devices that compensate for sensory or neurological deficits.
> - Support rehabilitation as a tool to improve, maintain, or slow the decline of function. (Eichner and Blumenthal 2003, v)

Medical necessity judgments, while ostensibly ensuring that Medicare covers only "health-related needs," also serve as a form of rationing available resources. Yet Medicare's current provisions deny the realities of a large fraction if not the majority of its beneficiaries—people with chronic debilitating conditions that will not improve. With appropriate technological or rehabilitative support, many of these individuals could continue living independently in the community, postponing the overwhelming expense of long-term institutionalization. Revisiting Medicare's medical necessity limits on items and services that help people with disabilities function is long overdue.

Enabling People with Disabilities to Go Outside Their Homes

A colleague who lives in a small mountain town described his neighbor. "Mary Jo is her name. She lives three blocks from us. She's thirty-nine or forty, and she has diabetes. She's had one leg amputated, and the other leg is constantly in danger. She lives in a low-income apartment, one of those little places like a motel room. Some friends raised the money and gave her an electric wheelchair— a real cheap one, but it allowed her to get out the door and up to a small park. On a nice spring day, she can go out and sit under a tree and come back in. That's all she ever did with it."

A home health nurse treats Mary Jo's ulcerated leg, among other medical problems. "One day, the home health nurse saw the electric wheelchair sitting in the apartment, and she said, 'You know what? I can't come anymore.' Mary Jo is disabled under Medicare, and Medicare won't pay for home health unless the person is homebound. So the wheelchair has now been folded up and is gathering dust in the corner. It's been retired from use, and every time a home health aide comes, she tries not to see it."

Mary Jo's friends rightly assumed that Medicare would refuse to purchase her power wheelchair since she does not need it within her tiny apartment—as for Erna Dodd, it would not have been deemed medically necessary. So they bought it themselves. The independence conveyed by the power wheelchair, however, could risk Mary Jo's eligibility for home-based nursing care for her remaining leg ulcerated by diabetes: If Mary Jo sits under a tree in her power wheelchair, she risks losing home health care, so she stashed away her power wheelchair. Staying indoors when she could venture out not only diminishes Mary Jo's quality of life but also could compromise her overall health.

Two paradoxical Medicare policies entrap Mary Jo. The first policy relates to eligibility for Medicare home care. To qualify for home-based services, Medicare regulations stipulate that individuals be homebound, defined as "a normal inability to leave home, that leaving the home requires a considerable and taxing effort by the individual." While absences for medical care, adult day-care, and attending religious services are allowed, other absences must be "infrequent or of relatively short duration" (42 C.F.R. Sec. 1814[a] and Sec. 1835[a]).

Clearly, this policy makes little sense for Mary Jo. To qualify for nursing care in her home, Mary Jo first needed to demonstrate that skilled services were medically necessary. With diabetic ulcerations on her remaining leg needing constant clinical attention, Mary Jo easily met the medical necessity criterion. Traveling daily to a clinic or hospital for this care would pose an enormous, perhaps impossible, burden. Since Mary Jo obviously had compelling medical needs, as well as substantial physical impairments, why couldn't she take short jaunts out in her power wheelchair without risking home care coverage?

For years, concerns about increasing home care costs have stalled efforts to broaden the homebound definition. From 1989 to 1996, Medicare Part A home health spending soared from $2.8 to $11.3 billion (U.S. General Accounting Office 1997). To reverse this trend, the Balanced Budget Act of 1997 significantly changed Medicare home health care payment policies. Total home care expenditures plummeted by 50 percent between 1996 and 2001, and the average number of days on home care fell 28 percent, from sixty to forty-three days (Medicare Payment Advisory Commission [MedPAC] 2003b). Some worry that these cuts have gone too far, especially for home care recipients who are frail, disabled, or medically vulnerable. MedPAC (2003b) found evidence "that for beneficiaries with certain clinical conditions, SNF [skilled nursing facility] use may be partly replacing home health use." Furthermore, "A number of home health agencies reported changing the way they operated, being more careful about accepting long-term, chronic, or higher-cost beneficiaries" (MedPAC 2003b, 77). Someone like Mary Jo might now find it difficult to get Medicare home care.

One highly public case underscores the consequences of Medicare's homebound definition. Georgia resident David Jayne had developed amyotrophic lateral sclerosis (ALS) in 1988 at age twenty-seven, and over the years he had become totally physically incapacitated. In 1997 Medicare started paying for skilled nursing care in his home. In 2000, Mr. Jayne traveled out of town with a college friend to watch a Georgia Bulldog football game. The trip and Mr. Jayne's story appeared in an Atlanta newspaper, and shortly thereafter his home health agency discharged him for violating the homebound definition. His congressman arranged for Medicare to reinstate the services, and Mr. Jayne began campaigning to reform the homebound definition. He founded the National Coalition to Amend the

Medicare Homebound Restriction and proved an exceptional lobbyist, although now he speaks only with aid of a computer.

Prompted by Mr. Jayne's story and to commemorate the twelfth anniversary of his father's signing of the Americans with Disabilities Act, on July 26, 2002, President George W. Bush addressed concerns about Medicare's homebound requirement. Urging people with disabilities to meet friends, join family reunions, and even attend baseball games, President Bush announced, "We're clarifying Medicare policy, so people who are considered homebound can occasionally take part in their communities, without fear of losing their benefits" (White House 2002). However, Bush did not alter the language requiring considerable and taxing effort to leave home. Anecdotal reports suggest that little has changed since Bush's pronouncement and that Medicare carriers still interpret the homebound definition strictly.

The second paradoxical home-related Medicare policy entangling Mary Jo involves the purchase of her wheelchair. Since most mobility aids will not improve baseline physical function, medical necessity judgments cannot in this case rely on the usual standard of restoring function. Instead Medicare seeks to determine whether the equipment allows someone to perform minimal activity—moving around within one's home. Medicare "pays for the rental or purchase of durable medical equipment . . . [only] if the equipment is used in the patient's home or in an institution that is used as a home" (42 C.F.R. Sec. 410.38[a]). Getting around outside the home is a convenience and not medically necessary, as Erna Dodd found.

According to this stringent standard, many people with progressive chronic conditions who still get around inside their homes, such as by furniture surfing, cannot qualify for mobility aids through Medicare. Requirements are even stricter for power wheelchairs. To obtain a power-operated vehicle (POV) for their patients, physicians must complete the "certificate of medical necessity" (form DMERC 07.02B and OMB No. 0938-0679). Section B of the form asks:

- Does the patient require a POV to move around in their residence?
- Have all types of manual wheelchairs (including lightweights) been considered and ruled out?
- Does the patient require a POV *only* for movement outside their residence?

Medicare's intent is clear: It will pay for the more expensive POV only if cheaper options are ruled out. But standards for ruling out manual chairs remain unspecified, leaving considerable leeway for subjective judgments and denials. A social worker told me about a man paralyzed by a stroke whose POV request was refused. Medicare asserted that his elderly wife could push him in a manual wheelchair within their home although she is also frail and weak. In the past, compared with other types of durable medical equipment, POVs were relatively rarely requested, and no evidence suggested that they were over-prescribed (Wickizer 1995). However, since 1999, power wheelchair purchases through Medicare have soared, and fraudulent practices by unscrupulous vendors cost Medicare $84 million in 2002 (Janofsky 2004). Medicare has recently cracked down on abusive practices, causing consternation among advocates for persons with disabilities. POVs are now even harder to obtain than before. As one woman whose husband is severely debilitated by multiple sclerosis said, "I don't believe there's massive abuse, that people are buying things that they don't need. There's a 20 percent copay. My husband's wheelchair is $20,000. That's a $4,000 copay. Do you think I'm going to spend $4,000 just for the fun of it?"

Policymakers must recognize that requiring persons to remain in their homes and denying them mobility aids ignores a critical reality. Today's assistive technologies allow people with substantial physical impairments, such as Mary Jo and David Jayne, to leave their homes and participate within their communities. People with disabilities no longer accept being shut away in their homes.

Medicare Coverage from Day One of Disability

Jimmy Howard is in his late forties with arthritis and diabetes. He has a high school education and lifted heavy boxes in ManuCo's warehouse for years before being fired because he had difficulty walking. Mr. Howard moves firmly with an aluminum cane, although sometimes he falls unexpectedly. After ManuCo fired him, he applied to SSA for disability benefits. He has incapacitating stiffness each morning and other "objective medical evidence" of "arthritis of a major weight-bearing joint," as specified in *Disability Evaluation under Social Security* (SSA 1998).

Five months following his disability determination, Jimmy Howard started receiving cash SSDI benefits. According to federal regulations, he must wait another two years to obtain Medicare coverage—a total of twenty-nine months beyond the date of SSA's disability determination. Mr. Howard, however, can't wait for health insurance to keep his diabetes under control, as well as treat his arthritis. So he pays $400 per month for private health insurance under COBRA provisions. Sometimes he and his wife, who also doesn't work, can barely make this payment.

P.L. 92-603, signed by President Richard Nixon on July 1, 1972, granted Medicare coverage to individuals who have received SSDI cash benefits for twenty-four months (42 U.S.C. Sec. 226[b][2][A]). The law also reduced to five months the waiting period between qualifying for SSDI and actually receiving cash payments. On July 1, 2001, Congress passed a special waiver rescinding the twenty-four-month wait for Medicare coverage, but only for persons who qualify for SSDI because of ALS. This exemption, won through active lobbying by ALS advocates, reflects the reality of rapid debilitation that generally accompanies that disease. But what about other SSDI beneficiaries who also need care, including Jimmy Howard with his diabetes and arthritis?

Separating Medicare coverage from disability determination makes little sense. The 1972 law aimed both to limit Medicare costs and avoid dislodging private employer-sponsored health insurance that SSDI applicants presumably had. To receive SSDI, applicants must prove disability by meeting explicit medical criteria determined by the SSA: "The inability to engage in any substantial gainful activity by reason of any medically determinable physical or mental impairment(s) which can be expected to result in death or which has lasted or can be expected to last for a continuous period of not less than 12 months" (SSA 1998, 2). Surely applicants who might face imminent death and can't work ought to receive health insurance coverage immediately! Persons who qualify for Supplemental Security Income, another financial support program that uses identical application procedures as SSDI, obtain immediate Medicaid coverage.

The reasons for this baffling incongruity remain murky. Vladeck and colleagues explain the roots and tenacity of the Medicare gap as reflecting "ambivalence about the meaning of disability itself: The truly disabled—those who have a clear right to protection—cannot be easily identified in the modern social context in which disability is a matter of degree. . . . Disability consists of a hard physical core with an expanding penumbra of mental and psychological nuance not generally as visible (or acceptable) to society. As a result, gaps in services betray a deeply rooted ambivalence toward certain classes of the disabled. Most especially, a fundamental skepticism of those who are disabled because of a mental illness, alcoholism, or drug addiction seems ingrained in the culture" (1997, 87).

In earlier years, most new SSDI recipients qualified because of conditions that obviously warranted close medical attention. In 1981, circulatory conditions accounted for 25 percent of disability determinations, followed by other systemic diseases at 19 percent; musculoskeletal conditions contributed 17 percent, and mental disorders 11 percent (IOM 2002b). Two decades later, the situation has changed considerably. In 2001, mental disorders contributed the largest percentage (26.8 percent) of new SSDI beneficiaries (1.5 million persons), with musculoskeletal conditions in second place (21.7 percent, 1.2 million persons) (SSA 2002). Circulatory disorders fell to 9.6 percent.

No publicly available data describe SSDI beneficiaries during the waiting period. Dale and Verdier pieced together information from various sources to sketch this population, which they estimated at 1.26 million individuals in 2002. Approximately one-third, or 400,000 persons, lack health insurance during their waiting period, while roughly 40 percent, or 504,000 adults, enroll in Medicaid programs, costing the federal and state governments $7.6 billion in 2002. Eliminating the waiting period would add about $8.7 billion (3.4 percent) to Medicare costs at 2002 spending levels. However, lower state and federal Medicaid expenses would offset roughly 30 percent of the Medicare rise (Dale and Verdier 2003).

Questions remain about what health care services SSDI recipients obtain during the wait. Being uninsured, even for one to four years, may worsen general health status (IOM 2002a). Having financial access to health care services is essential to "fostering early interventions to prevent diseases or impairments from becoming permanent work disabilities" (Mashaw and Reno 1996, 135). While awaiting Medicare coverage, uninsured SSDI beneficiaries might skimp on care that could prevent or slow progression of their diseases, thus decreasing longevity, hastening functional declines, and increasing health care costs. One study of persons who had been continuously uninsured from ages sixty through sixty-four years found that, upon joining Medicare, they considerably increased their use of basic covered services. For instance, upon getting Medicare, "continuously uninsured adults with arthritis reported greater increases in arthritis-related medical visits and limitations of activity than continuously insured adults with arthritis" (McWilliams et al. 2003, 762).

Adding new SSDI beneficiaries to the Medicare rolls would undoubtedly fractionally increase costs, at least in the short term. However, longer-term savings could outweigh these costs. Jimmy Howard's primary care doctor told me a year or two later that his diabetes had been poorly controlled and he risked losing toes to gangrene. Might Medicare coverage have prevented or slowed that progression?

Paying the Right Amount for Office Visits

Joe Alto, a former backhoe operator in his late thirties, has had multiple sclerosis for twelve years and has used a wheelchair for three. Mr. Alto's primary care physician does not have an adjustable examining table—a table that automatically lowers to wheelchair height with the touch of a pedal. Instead, the physician uses a fixed-height table, conveniently positioned for standing physicians. "There's no way for me to get onto their examining tables—they're too high," Mr. Alto reported. He worries that his primary care physician gives him short shrift. "Most of the time, he wants to do my physical exam in my wheelchair. I'm not even undressed. All he does is listen to my heart and ask what's wrong. He can't diagnose me in my wheelchair. I want to get on the table. Get me undressed like the rest of the people—treat me like the others!"

Joe Alto believes that the problem is money and time. Examining tables with pedal-operated lifts cost at least twice as much as standard, fixed-height tables. He also worries that some physicians want to avoid patients who use wheelchairs. "When they see you coming in the wheelchair, they say, 'That's going to be a lot of work,'" said Mr. Alto. "Insurers don't pay extra for someone like me, so the doctor isn't going to want me there." Minute by minute, "The doctor's not getting as much money for a disabled person as he's getting for someone else."

Roughly 85 percent of Medicare beneficiaries belong to the traditional fee-for-service program, up several percentage points from 1998, the peak of managed care enrollments (MedPAC 2003a). In 2004, Medicare expects to pay about $48.7 billion to nine hundred thousand fee-for-service physicians and other providers, rising from an estimated $47.9 billion in 2003 (CMS 2003c). To be paid for the office visit, Joe Alto's primary care physician must submit a claim to Medicare listing an evaluation and management (E&M) code indicating the level (from one to five) of the visit. His physician will choose the E&M code that matches the extent of the clinical history, the physical examination, review of body systems, clinical issues discussed with Mr. Alto, and the time spent. Medicare's resource-based relative value scale, the basis for physician payment for the last decade, sets payments for each code physicians list on their claims. This scale attempts to narrow the reimbursement gap between primary care and specialist physicians. However, "reimbursement for routine primary care visits is insufficient for the care of many with chronic conditions, as care for this population usually takes a considerable amount of time, particularly when self-management and multiple conditions are addressed. . . . [Furthermore, the E&M classification] is a barrier to chronic care. E&M codes account for almost half of Medicare-paid physician services. These codes fail to adequately reflect the additional complexity and time requirements associated with care for many beneficiaries with chronic conditions" (Eichner and Blumenthal 2003, 30).

Other aspects of Medicare's physician reimbursement policies are also problematic. The Medicare statute requires adjusting up or down the physician fee schedule based on how actual expenditures compare to a target rate, the sustainable growth rate or SGR. CMS (2003c) calculates the SGR "based on medical inflation, the projected growth in the domestic economy, projected growth in the number of beneficiaries in fee-for-service Medicare, and changes in law or regulation." Substantial growth in Medicare physician outlays, combined with the slow economy, led to cuts in Medicare physician payments in the early 2000s. In fiscal year 2003, Medicare cut physician payments by 5.4 percent, and CMS proposed a 4.2 percent cut for 2004 (CMS 2003c).

Continued cuts in physician payments could make it harder for people like Joe Alto to find routine care. In 2002, 70.1 percent of physicians accepted new Medicare fee-for-service beneficiaries, down from 76.4 percent in 1999 (MedPAC 2003a). Even some generalist physicians avoid new Medicare beneficiaries. A spokesperson for the American Academy of Family Physicians reported that more than one-fifth of family physicians no longer accept new Medicare patients (Pear 2003b). In March 2003, MedPAC warned, "If the Congress does not change current laws, . . . then payments may not be adequate in 2003 and a compensating adjustment in payments would be necessary in 2004" (2003a, 72).

Physicians clearly need more time to fully examine persons using wheelchairs and persons with other disabling and complex conditions and to discuss their medical concerns. Paying more per visit for persons with disabling conditions than for healthier, able-bodied persons (i.e., "risk adjusting" office visit fees for patients' health-related risks) therefore makes sense. Risk-adjusting E&M codes could substantially improve quality of care (Eichner and Blumenthal 2003).

Ensuring Health Care Quality

Current Medicare coverage policies do not match basic needs of persons with disabilities for interventions to maintain, restore, or maximize their functioning. These policies pose barriers to "patient-centered" care—care that is "respectful of and responsive to individual patient preferences, needs, and values" (IOM 2001, 42). Many strategies now exist to allow persons even with significant disabilities to live independently in the community, minimizing their risks of developing debilitating and costly secondary conditions. But coverage gaps prevent people from obtaining this care.

Addressing the four targets described in the previous section could substantially ameliorate this situation. However, skyrocketing costs pose formidable obstacles. Total Medicare expenditures are expected to reach $450.1 billion by 2011, compared with $245.6 billion one decade earlier (Heffler et al. 2002). Expanding coverage to include more function-related services has always proved politically unpalatable: "The cost implications of disability-related services . . . frighten policymakers away from contemplating all but the narrowest of expansions. What looks like a half-empty glass when benefits are being designed may be a bottomless pit once the payments begin to flow" (Vladeck et al. 1997, 88).

Although I concentrate here on Medicare, deep cuts in state budgets are fraying Medicaid's safety net. In designing Medicaid, Congress recognized that low-income persons have little to spend on care, so it adopted broader benefits than for Medicare. All states must cover core services (e.g., inpatient hospitalizations, skilled nursing facility stays, home health care), but they can also offer various optional services including prescription drugs, physical and occupational therapy, prosthetic devices, eyeglasses, and durable medical equipment. In 2002, Medicaid insured about 42.8 million persons, including 7.7 million low-income individuals, eligible because of disability or blindness, who consumed 37.8 percent of Medicaid's resources (CMS 2002).

When facing substantial budgetary shortfalls, states frequently cut benefits, eliminating or reducing payments for optional items and services. In 2003, forty-five states implemented cost controls on prescription drugs, and twenty-five reduced Medicaid coverage for vision care; dental services; physical, occupational, and speech therapy; and home oxygen (Smith et al. 2003). With continuing budget deficits, state legislatures will likely continue chipping away at Medicaid benefits.

With these cuts, failures to expand Medicare coverage, and other related policy decisions, our nation consciously chooses to limit the quality of life, independence, and even health of many persons with disabilities. Politicians could credibly argue that coverage costs are too high, competing with other pressing societal needs. To counter such arguments, we need better evidence about potential cost trade-offs. For example, does providing a power wheelchair to improve independent mobility save money in the long run by reducing secondary disabilities, such as falls and depression, and lowering costs of home-based and institutional care?

As countless others have said, how we care for our most vulnerable citizens speaks volumes about our values as a nation. With mounting federal and state budget deficits, little will likely change in the next few years. But rethinking fundamental Medicare coverage policies may gain political momentum as millions of baby boomers care for aging parents and then retire themselves. Sally Ann Jones, a wheelchair user and SSDI recipient, feels that politicians have missed the obvious. "It amazes me that nobody's gotten this notion yet: the baby boomers are coming. Despite MS and other diseases, they're going to live longer. We're not going to warehouse them in nursing homes. These boomers simply won't do that. They're not going to go quietly into the night."

References

Arias, E. 2002. United States Life Tables, 2000. *National Vital Statistics Reports* 51, no. 3: 1–39. Available at *www.cdc.gov/nchs/products/pubs/pubd/nvsr/51/51_03.htm.*

Boult, C., M. Altmann, D. Gilbertson, et al. 1996. Decreasing Disability in the 21st Century: The Future Effect of Controlling Six Fatal and Nonfatal Conditions. *American Journal of Public Health* 86, no. 10: 1388–1393.

Centers for Disease Control and Prevention. 2003. Public Health and Aging: Projected Prevalence of Self-Reported Arthritis or Chronic Joint Symptoms among Persons Aged > 65 Years: United States, 2005–2030. *Morbidity and Mortality Weekly Report* 52, no. 21: 489–491.

Centers for Medicare and Medicaid Services (CMS). 2002. *2002 CMS Statistics.* Office of Research, Development, and Information. CMS publication no. 03437, April. Baltimore: CMS.

———. 2003a. Medicare and Medicaid Statistical Supplement, 2001. *Health Care Financing Review.* Publication no. 03441, April. Baltimore: U.S. Department of Health and Human Services.

———. 2003b. Medicare Data for Calendar Year 2002, Office of Research, Development, and Information. Table I.C1. Available at *www.cms.hhs.gov/publications/trusteesreport/2003/table1.asp* (accessed September 12, 2003).

———. 2003c. Medicare Proposes 2004 Physician Fee Schedule Changes. Available at *www.cms.hhs.gov/media/press/release.asp?Counter=825* (accessed August 14, 2003).

———. 2003d. *Your Medicare Benefits.* Publication no. CMS–10116, April. Baltimore: U.S. Department of Health and Human Services.

Dale, S. B., and J. M. Verdier. 2003. *Elimination of Medicare's Waiting Period for Seriously Disabled Adults: Impact on Coverage and Care.* New York: Commonwealth Fund, July.

Day, J. C. 1996. *Population Projections of the United States by Age, Sex, Race, and Hispanic Origin: 1995–2050.* Washington, DC: U.S. Bureau of the Census, Current Population Reports, P25–1130.

Eichner, J., and D. Blumenthal, eds. 2003. *Medicare in the 21st Century: Building a Better Chronic Care System.* Final Report of the Study Panel on Medicare and Chronic Care in the 21st Century. Washington, DC: National Academy of Social Insurance, January.

Foote, S. M., and C. Hogan. 2001. Disability Profile and Health Care Costs of Medicare Beneficiaries under Age Sixty-Five. *Health Affairs* 20, no. 6: 242–253.

Fox, D. M. 1993. *Power and Illness: The Failure and Future of American Health Policy.* Berkeley: University of California Press.

Freedman, V. A., L. G. Martin, and R. F. Schoeni. 2002. Recent Trends in Disability and Functioning among Older Adults in the United States: A Systematic Review. *Journal of the American Medical Association* 288: 3137–3146.

Heffler, S., S. Smith, G. Won, et al. 2002. Health Spending Projections for 2001–2011: The Latest Outlook. *Health Affairs* 21, no. 2: 207–218.

Iezzoni, L. I. 1999. Boundaries. *Health Affairs* 18: 171–176.

———. 2003. *When Walking Fails: Mobility Problems of Adults with Chronic Conditions.* Berkeley: University of California Press.

Institute of Medicine (IOM). 2001. *Crossing the Quality Chasm: A New Health System for the 21st Century.* Committee on Quality of Health Care in America. Washington, DC: National Academies Press.

———. 2002a. *Care without Coverage: Too Little, Too Late.* Committee on the Consequences of Uninsurance. Washington, DC: National Academies Press.

———. 2002b. *The Dynamics of Disability: Measuring and Monitoring Disability for Social Security Programs*, ed. G. S. Wunderlich, D. P. Rice, and N. L. Amado. Committee to Review the Social Security Administration's Disability Decision Process

Research, National Research Council, Committee on National Statistics. Washington, DC: National Academies Press.

Janofsky, M. 2004. Costs and Savings in Medicare Change on Wheelchairs. *New York Times*, January 30, NE A10.

Marmor, T. R. 2000. *The Politics of Medicare*. 2nd ed. New York: Aldine de Gruyter.

Mashaw, J. L., and V. P. Reno, eds. 1996. *Balancing Security and Opportunity: The Challenge of Disability Income Policy.* Report of the Disability Policy Panel. Washington, DC: National Academy of Social Insurance.

McWilliams, J. M., A. M. Zaslavsky, E. Meara, et al. 2003. Impact of Medicare Coverage on Basic Clinical Services for Previously Uninsured Adults. *Journal of the American Medical Association* 290: 757–764.

Medicare Payment Advisory Commission (MedPAC). 2003a. *Report to the Congress: Medicare Payment Policy*. Washington, DC: March.

———. 2003b. *Report to the Congress: Variation and Innovation in Medicare*. Washington, DC: June.

Mokdad, A. H., E. S. Ford, B. A. Bowman, et al. 2003. Prevalence of Obesity, Diabetes, and Obesity-Related Health Risk Factors, 2001. *Journal of the American Medical Association* 289, no. 1: 76–79.

National Spinal Cord Injury Statistical Center. 2001. *Spinal Cord Injury: Facts and Figures at a Glance.* Birmingham: University of Alabama. Available at *www.spinalcord.uab.edu* (accessed July 17, 2003).

Pear, R. 2003a. Adding Confidence, along with Drug Benefits, to Medicare. *New York Times*, June 11, NE A21.

———. 2003b. Medicare Fees for Physicians in Line for Cuts. *New York Times*, August 12, NE A1.

Pope, A. M., and A.R. Tarlov, eds. 1991. *Disability in America: Toward a National Agenda for Prevention*. Institute of Medicine, Committee on a National Agenda for the Prevention of Disabilities. Washington, DC: National Academies Press.

Rosenbaum, S., D. M. Frankford, B. Moore, et al. 1999. Who Should Determine When Health Care Is Medically Necessary? *New England Journal of Medicine* 340, no. 3: 229–232.

Singer, S. J., and L. A. Bergthold. 2001. Prospects for Improved Decision Making about Medical Necessity. *Health Affairs* 20, no. 1: 200–206.

Smith, V., K. Gilford, R. Ramesh, et al. 2003. *Medicaid Spending Growth: A Fifty-State Update for Fiscal Year 2003*. Menlo Park, CA: Henry J. Kaiser Family Foundation, January.

Social Security Administration (SSA). 1998. *Disability Evaluation under Social Security*. Office of Disability. Washington, DC: SSA, Pub. no. 64-039, January.

———. 2002. Table 4: Distribution, by Diagnostic Group and Sex, 2001. *Annual Statistical Report on the Social Security Disability Insurance Program*: 31.

———. 2003. *Fast Facts and Figures about Social Security*. Washington, DC: Office of Policy, Office of Research, Evaluation, and Statistics, Pub. no. 13-11785, June.

U.S. Census Bureau. 2003a. Definition of Disability Items in Census 2000. Available at *www.census.gov/hhes/www/disable/disdef00.html* (accessed June 14, 2003).

———. 2003b. Table 1: Characteristics of the Civilian Noninstitutionalized Population by Age, Disability Status, and Type of Disability, 2000. Available at *www.census.gov/hhes/www/disable/disabstat2k/table1.html* (accessed June 14, 2003).

———. 2003c. Table 2: Percentage of the Civilian Noninstitutionalized Population with Any Disability by Age and Selected Race and Hispanic or Latino Origin Groups, 2000.

Available at *www.census.gov/hhes/www/disable/disabstat2k/table2.html* (accessed June 14, 2003).

U.S. General Accounting Office. 1997. *Medicare Post-acute Care: Cost Growth and Proposals to Manage It through Prospective Payment and Other Controls.* Washington, DC: GAO/T-HEHS-97-106, April 9.

Üstün, T. B., S. Chatterji, N. Kostansjek, et al. 2003. WHO's ICF and Functional Status Information in Health Records. *Health Care Financing Review* 24, no. 3: 77–88.

Vladeck, B. C., E. O'Brien, T. Hoyer, and S. Clauser. 1997. Confronting the Ambivalence of Disability Policy: Has Push Come to Shove? In *Disability: Challenges for Social Insurance, Health Care Financing, and Labor Market Policy*, ed. V. P. Reno, J. L. Mashaw, and B. Gradison. Washington, D.C.: National Academy of Social Insurance.

White House. 2002. President George W. Bush. President Commemorates Twelfth Anniversary of Americans with Disabilities Act, July 26. Available at *www.whitehouse.gov/news/releases/2002/07/20020726-8.html* (accessed July 27, 2002).

Wickizer, T. M. 1995. Controlling Outpatient Medical Equipment Costs through Utilization Management. *Medical Care* 33, no. 4: 383–391.

CHAPTER 14

Specialization, Specialty Organizations, and the Quality of Health Care

—⸎⸎⸎—

ROSEMARY A. STEVENS

Specialization is a defining word for American medicine in our time. If it were still possible for a generalist to understand medicine as a body of knowledge and skills, we would not now have mighty health care corporations, millions of workers in hundreds of health care occupations, sprawling academic medical centers with their associated networks, or even managed care. However, while technological innovation and improvements in the quality of health care available to earlier generations testify to the manifold benefits of medical specialization, its downside has also long been evident.

For more than a century specialization has been portrayed as a force for disorganization in medical care, challenges in medical education, opportunities for profit seeking, and power plays among rival claimants (Rosen 1944; Somers and Somers 1961; Stevens 1971; Starr 1982; Ludmerer 1985, 1999). Today competition for market share in lucrative fields such as cardiology characterizes our health services, jurisdictional disputes mark professional organizations, and massive government programs, including Medicare, Medicaid, and the National Institutes of Health, subsidize and underpin the whole.

For the past two decades medical specialists have moved efficiently into market niches. Health policy has been largely silent about regulating and organizing such services, but signs of change are promising. Here I focus on four essentials: the need for a workable information infrastructure, strategic planning at the community level, encouragement of primary care, and public support of lifelong learning for physicians through "maintenance-of-certification" programs. Achieving these would enhance quality of care by better aligning the advantages of medical specialization with the needs of consumers searching for physicians with top-notch skills and expertise, the latest technology has to offer, and the most effective treatments.

Specialization in U.S. Medicine

Why do we have such a complex and confusing array of specialists? Partly because patients have long been complicit in the rush toward specialized medical practice. "Between us we have 10 or 12" specialists, reported an eighty-three-year-old Medicare beneficiary in Florida in 2003. His list included a pain specialist, neurologist, cardiologist, pulmonologist, rheumatologist, and urologist. His wife's experts were likewise defined by body parts, conditions, and diseases (Kolata 2003).

Historically, three social forces have combined to encourage specialization in the United States: the definition of medicine as a science that advances through the subdivision of effort; belief in the superior skills of experts; and competitive (rather than collaborative or bureaucratic) medical practice, supported by private and public health insurance. The managed care movement of the 1980s and 1990s promised to limit direct patient access to specialists by imposing a generalist or "gatekeeper" but roundly failed, attacked by both providers and consumers.

Specialization is an intrinsic, formalized aspect of American medicine. The medical profession is much more formally stratified than the legal profession; for example, and unlike law, which is largely state regulated, medicine is intensely subject to private regulation. Specialties do not just happen. The system that produces and credentials medical specialists is owned and operated by professional organizations, in the time-honored process of public deferment of responsibility. As I will show, specialties are based on demarcations negotiated among major associations. Those groups, working together, are now attempting a major expansion of specialty certification into a system of lifelong learning for all physicians.

For the individual U.S. physician, successful specialist practice requires favorable market conditions, including an available and willing patient base and supportive insurance programs. However, in our legalistic society, successful practice also requires some formal validation of experience that stands up to marketplace challenges such as denial of hospital privileges and malpractice insurance, that is accepted by third-party payers, and that is convincing in the case of costly lawsuits. For the U.S. medical profession and the public, the persona of a "specialist" may suggest success, expertise, and enhanced fees, but for practical purposes this persona must be accompanied by years of education, usually capped with examinations and the resulting certificates on the doctor's office wall. The credentials embedded in those certificates—ranging, alphabetically, from adolescent medicine to vascular surgery—are almost always those the medical profession has validated through its formidable specialty network: medical school departments and divisions in designated fields, professionally accredited residency programs, and specialty certification.

Specialty Credentials as Essential Standards in a Privately Organized System

In contrast to the constantly shifting organization and financing of U.S. health care, the production system for doctors runs like a finely tuned machine. Specialty identification and credentials provide a necessary standard for consumers (at least in theory, though often ignored) in America's competitive health care enterprise.

On a practical level, specialty credentials are important for at least four reasons. First, the MD degree is an intermediate, not a final, credential in a market where physicians are specialists, and thus the specialty (and increasingly subspecialty) diploma has taken over the role once marked by the MD alone. Second, common standards are essential in a context of decentralized, fragmented services without strong, local institutional controls, and where a physician may have relationships with multiple insurers, hospitals, and other providers. Third, credentials serve as markers for patients shopping for specialty services in a market-oriented system and help define a market niche. And fourth, credentials serve health care providers, auditors, accrediting agencies, bond raters, and insurers, all anxious to maintain standards, acquire prestige, protect patients from harm, and avoid legal difficulties.

In the absence of national, state-based, regional, or even large-scale corporate health services, there is no countervailing authority overseeing the quality and use of health personnel. Government has intervened from time to time to stimulate the overall supply of doctors and subsidize training programs, chiefly research fellowships in subspecialty fields and areas deemed undersupplied, such as (in the past) mental health. Federal "health manpower" legislation of the 1970s made a large impact on the number of doctors, but relatively little on their roles or the distribution of their services demographically and geographically (Weissert and Weissert 1996). Meanwhile specialists have made their career choices based on the training available and their perceptions of the changing health care market (Robinson 1999; Scott et al. 2000). Credentials that attest to residency, specialty, and often subspecialty training provide a gold standard in an otherwise uncertain health care environment.

Organized Medicine: One Voice or a Multitude of Agendas?

Through decades of debate over how to provide efficient specialty services, national organizations have represented U.S. physicians, but the pattern of representation has shifted significantly. From the early years of the twentieth century through Medicare legislation (1965) and beyond, the American Medical Association (AMA) offered a united front in political debates, successfully claiming to represent the entire profession. The growth of organized specialties, evident well before 1965 but increasingly powerful and activist, shifted physician allegiances away from the AMA. The specialty rather than the general medical society has become the primary allegiance for American doctors. Today the average internist, pediatrician, cardiac surgeon, and interventional radiologist identifies with his or her specialty organization, meetings, newsletters, and journals for both scientific information and policy representation.

Between 1950 and 1990, as organized specialties consolidated their institutional authority, AMA membership fell away. In 1950 almost 73 percent of all MDs were AMA members; in 1970, 64 percent were, and by 1989 little more than 40 percent of MDs were AMA members (AMA 2002). By the late 1990s the AMA was recognizably weak, representing less than half of all doctors, including those in training. Powerful specialty groups have focused on agendas such as child health policy (American Academy of Pediatrics) and a forty-eight-hour minimum hospital stay after childbirth (American College of Obstetricians and Gynecologists).

Specialty groups have also sought congressional support for a national trauma system, claiming that only eight states have well-organized trauma systems (American College of Surgeons) (Hawryluk 2003).

In the political arena, such focusing may make organized medicine more powerful and effective, at least on targeted policy issues. In the professional arena, though, too much fragmentation may ultimately be self-defeating, as medical leaders are well aware. As specialty credentialing has become ever more important, questions regarding common standards have acquired new significance.

For example, what does the array of specialty and subspecialty training programs say about the production of U.S. doctors? Does certification imply quality of services for patients? Are the certifying boards doing a good job? Should government support them more fully in the Herculean tasks they have set for themselves, which include greater coordination? Or can other groups do credentialing better or more economically? These are important questions with major implications for the quality of care, medical standards, professional responsibility and accountability, and the role of regulation. Though they cannot yet be answered fully, debates about health care quality and outcomes, cost controls, and state licensing require a better appreciation of where credentialing arrangements have come from and how they work.

The Production of Specialists in the United States

Twenty-four independent, "approved" boards divide the U.S. medical profession into specialties and subspecialties. An approved board is one formally affiliated with the American Board of Medical Specialties (ABMS), based in Evanston, Illinois. (Since 1999 I have served as one of three public members representing public policy perspectives on the ABMS). Subspecialty status requires that the individual physician first become certified in a primary specialty field. For example, internal medicine, pediatrics, and radiology are designated specialties, each with its own board: the American boards of Internal Medicine (headquartered in Philadelphia), Pediatrics (Chapel Hill), and Radiology (Tucson). Cardiology, pediatric allergy, and interventional radiology are among the formal subspecialties, respectively, of these boards, each responsible for granting subspecialty certificates.

Each board specifies training pathways, via approved residency or fellowship programs, and administers examinations. Approved training requires completion of residency programs accredited by a group parallel and related to the ABMS, the Accreditation Council for Graduate Medical Education (ACGME). An individual doctor leaves medical school with the MD degree, enters an approved residency program in a specialty for three to six years, and eventually becomes certified in that field. Those who are certified are called "diplomates."

Together the boards granted thirty-seven basic specialty certificates and ninety-two types of subspecialty certificates in 2003, with more subspecialty categories on the way (ABMS 2003a). In 2000 alone, almost twenty-four thousand physicians became diplomates. The "biggies" were internal medicine, which granted 29 percent of all primary certificates; family practice (15 percent); and pediatrics (11 percent). These three specialties—together with psychiatry and neurology (which for historical reasons joined together in one board), obstetrics/gynecology, radiology, emergency medicine, and surgery—granted 80 percent of all specialty diplomas in 2000, with the remaining 20 percent scattered across the other sixteen boards. Half of all subspecialties reside in three boards: internal medicine (with sixteen subspecialties), pediatrics (seventeen), and pathology (eleven).

ABMS-affiliated boards now certify 90 percent of U.S. practicing physicians, on a rising trend (ABMS 2003a). Thus these ABMS-approved twenty-four boards and their subspecialty committees define the formal structure of American medicine.

As might be expected, other credentialing groups also exist, perhaps as many as two hundred—there is no formal list. Osteopathic physicians have their own boards that maintain substantial affiliation with ACGME-approved residency programs. Other groups advance the cause of newer specialties not yet covered, in their view, by ABMS-approved boards. (The ABMS, in liaison with the AMA, has a formal process for approving applications from new boards.) Vascular surgeons, for example, though recognized as a subspecialty of the American Board of Surgery, have been pressing—so far unsuccessfully—for acceptance of the American Board of Vascular Surgery as an independent, ABMS-affiliated board (Burton 2003). Leaders of the American Board of Hospice and Palliative Medicine are similarly seeking recognition of end-of-life care as distinct from pain medicine, which is an ABMS-approved subspecialty. This group, too, may eventually seek ABMS approval (Beresford 2004).

Courts have generally upheld the authority of ABMS-approved boards. The American Academy of Pain Management brought an unsuccessful suit against the Medical Board of California for prohibiting physicians from advertising that they are "board certified" unless they meet certain requirements. These include certification by an ABMS-approved board or the "equivalent," as determined by the Medical Board or by completion of approved postgraduate training. Physicians certified in other ways, such as by attaining the academy's credentials for multidisciplinary pain practitioners, may not advertise in California that they are board certified. In upholding the Medical Board, the U.S. Ninth Circuit Court of Appeals noted that "'Board Certification' is a term of art that the ABMS popularized among physicians and has come to designate a certain level of qualification." The court also noted that the state has given the term "board certified" a "special and particular meaning," and that the plaintiffs' use of "board certified" was "inherently misleading" and thus not protected speech, as the plaintiffs had claimed (U.S. Court of Appeals 2004).

Such challenges push approved boards to recognize their public role, to ask what this means regarding quality of care, and to make major attempts to coordinate their efforts. The legal system thus provides a useful goad to responsible self-regulation.

The Origins of Specialties

The specialty board structure arose out of a long, negotiated history. Multiple professional associations typically organize a specialty board once they have become motivated to seek credentialing. Not surprisingly, these groups found boards at different times for different reasons. The first medical specialty board—for ophthalmology—incorporated in 1917 amid turf battles with well-organized optometrists, who were also seeking professional credentials (Stevens 1971). The newest specialty board is Medical Genetics, approved in 1991, affirming medical jurisdiction when many investigators in the field held the PhD as their primary credential.

The basic pattern was set in the 1920s when otolaryngologists followed the ophthalmologists with their own board (1924), thus making an effective claim for that field, too, as requiring expertise beyond that of the general practitioner. However, specialty boards blossomed into a movement with the economic pressures of the 1930s. By 1944, when sociologist George Rosen published a classic study of medical specialization, self-styled specialists outnumbered general practitioners, making specialization an "essential feature of modern medical practice" (Rosen 1944, 1). Specialism seemed tailor-made for the American public, with its faith in experts and the cachet accruing to those who charged high fees and offered esoteric treatments. As Rosen also observed, specialization intensified the U.S. view of medicine as an economic transaction, becoming a natural partner to and developing alongside market-oriented health care (Rosen 1944, 77).

The specialization movement proved a double-edged sword for the medical profession. As long as general practice remained its actual—or even symbolic—core, the training and recognition of specialists could remain at the margin of organized medicine. Specialization reinforced the profession's commitment to innovation based on an elite cadre working in science, technology, and clinical advancement in medical schools, while specialists could work as consultants to average practitioners without considering their demographic distribution. However, as the balance shifted toward an entirely specialized profession, the opportunistic and public policy aspects of specialties came more firmly into view.

The formation of the American Board of Family Practice in 1969—amid vocal concern about the decline of general practice and rousing calls for new roles for "personal physicians" and "primary care"—made generalism a "specialty" (Lee et al. 1976; Stevens 2001a). Somewhat similarly, emergency medicine achieved its own certifying board in 1979 following intense public interest in reforming emergency medical services. But by encompassing family and emergency medicine, the certifying boards acquired de facto responsibility, however unwillingly, for the design, specialty training, and evaluation of the entire medical profession. Equally, all physicians were now specialists.

At least in theory, the collective influence of the certifying boards, their associated specialty groups, medical school departments and sections, and the residency system on the structure and standards of medicine is now as great as that of universities. However, collective influence implies some cross-specialty collaboration so the profession has a unified voice, and this process is still in its infancy.

For the certifying boards and their associated specialty societies, the key question is whether, now that they have acquired the opportunity for power and influence, they can overcome their history of professional separatism.

Problems with Specialties

Rivalries across fields, encouraged by competitive practice, make it difficult to determine how well the specialty structure helps patients find the right expert for a specific condition. Surprisingly little research has been done on this question. Preliminary studies for the ABMS suggest lack of public awareness of the specialty boards, their standards, and their formal specialty and subspecialty delineations (ABMS 2003b). Left to her own decision, a patient with annoying back pain might decide to take it easy and self-medicate with over-the-counter preparations, consult her primary physician, or seek out a general orthopedic surgeon or one with additional spinal expertise. Or she might ask friends for advice and receive an enthusiastic recommendation for a specific neurologist—or rheumatologist, sports medicine specialist, or pain subspecialist with a background in anesthesiology, neurology, or physical medicine, each offering a different professional perspective. The patient might also try herbal remedies, acupuncture, and massage.

These consultations might produce recommendations ranging from exercise through behavior modification, prescribed medications, laminectomy, and spinal fusion. Becoming a wise consumer is difficult in such circumstances. Nevertheless, the U.S. system, based on free-standing groups of specialists, assumes that the consumer is competent to do so. Indeed, direct access to specialists requires that patients act not only as sophisticated and sensible first-line diagnosticians but also as general contractors for their care. In seeking (or avoiding the need for) specialists, many patients clearly need an intermediary, a role that may be performed by doctors, nurse practitioners, physician assistants, the Internet, or someone or something else.

The Internet may play a powerful role for some patients in initially diagnosing symptoms and matching them with appropriate specialists. But that process may be risky. "Primary care" has long recognized the beneficial role of a knowledgeable generalist who has the patient's interest at heart. Nevertheless, despite efforts from the 1960s through the managed care movement to designate a specific service role for primary care, no one "specialty" plays that role. Primary physicians may be family physicians, general internists, or general pediatricians, each with their own specialty board and associated subspecialties. Many subspecialists also act as primary care practitioners for their patients.

The field of sports medicine, for example, a formal subspecialty of family practice, internal medicine, pediatrics, and emergency medicine, will naturally appeal to patients primarily for sports injuries. Similarly, practitioners of endocrinology, oncology, and nephrology—among the subspecialties of internal medicine and pediatrics—are likely to draw patients with specialized rather than general needs. Yet these and other specialists may take on primary care roles for at least some of their patients. For example, an obstetrician/gynecologist may serve that role for a woman, while a child psychiatrist may do so for a child with behavioral problems. The U.S. health system makes no direct connection between the training and credentialing of physicians and the clinical roles they play.

Turf Wars

Market and policy conditions ranging from managed care and Medicare reimbursement through varying competition among specialties and the relative burden of malpractice rates (heaviest for surgeons and obstetricians) affect clinical roles. The AMA designated seventeen states as in "tort crisis" over medical liability insurance rates in 2003 (Albert 2003). Meanwhile, physicians have looked for income opportunities outside their own specialties. To "limit economic shortfalls and to expand boundaries," primary care physicians have reportedly been offering fee-for-service cosmetic procedures and dermatology, adding their own laboratories and imaging and bone density equipment, and setting up physical therapy programs (Reece 2003). Investment in imaging centers serving privately insured patients by physicians who are not radiologists has evoked public concern, "pitting radiologists against other doctors, and hospitals against free-standing centers, in a fight for health care dollars" (AP/*Dallas Morning News* 2003). Cosmetic surgery may endanger patients when performed by inadequately trained practitioners in unregulated facilities, yet it has been a steadily growing field for men as well as women (Haiken 1997).

Two movements are occurring simultaneously: the encouragement of health care as a market commodity allows patients relatively unfettered access to specialists while muddying specialty roles. Since the 1990s, market forces have stimulated competition between physicians practicing in the same specialty (such as rival groups of orthopedic surgeons), fanned turf wars between specialties, and fostered a decline in multi-specialty practice in favor of single-specialty groups and centers. "As HMOs and hospitals have seen their profit margins narrowed," wrote one analyst in 1999, "entrepreneurs have turned to niche industries" such as ambulatory surgery centers, eye care companies, oncology, and cosmetic services (Kuttner 1999).

Medicare has also encouraged single-specialty practice by abolishing separate payment codes for the same procedure performed by radiology and internal medicine, for example. Medicare fees for family and general practitioners also rose much faster than for specialties such as ophthalmology, cardiology, gastroenterology, and urology in the 1990s, while fees for some specialized procedures such as cataract removal and insertion of a lens dropped significantly (Iglehart 1999). The Medicare Payment Advisory Commission and its predecessor effectively encouraged interests to lobby for (or against) specialty fields and procedures. A large multispecialty group had thus become "too unwieldy," claimed members of such a group in Charlotte, North Carolina, as it disbanded. In contrast, a single-specialty group cited an "alignment of incentives" regarding reimbursement and few interspecialty tensions (Page 2000).

In a competitive, single-specialty system, the patient cannot rely on doctors in different fields to provide comprehensive, coordinated care. Many Americans do have primary physicians in one specialty field or another whom they trust to manage their care. Many patients, though, make their own choices from a list of specialists who are part of their insurance network or who participate in Medicare. No one is directing the patient to the physician who can best meet the patient's needs.

Better information on clinical results among specialty practices in different communities would greatly help consumers. In a consumer-oriented system, patients should have access to standard information. The simplest way of providing such information is to work toward standardized, computerized patient records with firewalls to ensure confidentiality. If the relatively impoverished National Health Service in England is able and willing to establish a universal health care database over the next two years, entertaining bids for contracts from global corporations such as IBM, why can't the United States (Naik 2003)?

Cooperation across Specialties

Paralleling these market trends are two promising signs of cooperation. The first is joint planning among subspecialties, and the second is a move toward lifelong learning and evaluation of physicians, known as maintenance of certification.

Cooperation is important in designing innovative cross-specialty training and evaluation to advance the quality of care, standardizing credentialing, providing consumer-friendly information to help patients choose specialists, and assuring lifelong commitment to learning and quality improvement. Cross-specialty alliances are also essential in enabling the medical profession to play a significant role in health care policy (Stevens 2001b).

The human urge to protect and extend one's property applies to organizations as well as individuals. As with primary boards, the creation of subspecialties tends to have a domino effect. One board's creation of a new subspecialty sparks similar moves by other specialties interested in the same field. Oncology is an early case in point. The ABMS approved oncology as a subspecialty of internal medicine in 1972, of pediatrics in 1973, and of gynecology in 1974, following applications from each of these boards. The growing importance of critical care has similarly led to subspecialties in six different boards (anesthesiology, pediatrics, internal medicine, obstetrics/gynecology, neurosurgery, and surgery). Newly visible fields such as geriatrics, sports medicine, toxicology, pain management, adolescent medicine, head and neck surgery, and neurodevelopmental disabilities have sparked the interest of more than one board. Five boards offer immunology as a subspecialty, while four boards offer sports medicine. Part of this movement reflects the fact that clinical medicine and market opportunities continue to shift.

The subspecialty movement has made the specialties less rigid than in, say, the 1960s. Sometimes painful negotiations precede a move toward integrated standards. Recent fights between otolaryngologists and plastic surgeons over the subspecialty of head and neck surgery resolved only after years of negotiation involving the ABMS and two ABMS boards, the American Board of Plastic Surgery and the American Board of Otolaryngology. The latter two were undoubtedly energized by the American Board of Facial and Reconstructive Surgery (ABFRS) and the

American Board of Cosmetic Surgery, neither of which the ABMS recognizes. The potential of state licensing boards to preempt professional standard setting was also clearly an ingredient. Licensing boards in Florida, Colorado, and California recognized the ABFRS as "substantially equivalent" to the ABMS boards in the 1990s. State boards usually work with ABMS-approved boards to set standards for licensing and advertising, but that could change, particularly in areas with "non-approved" specialties, such as physicians without board certification who perform cosmetic surgery in Florida.

Negotiations between otolaryngologists and plastic surgeons within the ABMS were difficult. An editorialist for a major plastic surgery journal wrote in 1996 that "it appears that the old embers of suspicion and distrust still glow too hot to permit closure of this issue" (Neale 1996, 223). Nevertheless, the groups did reach consensus: the ABMS approved a subspecialty program for each board, administered jointly. The otolaryngologists received their approval first, in 1999.

All twenty-four ABMS-approved specialty boards also recently agreed to develop requirements for all physicians to maintain their certificates throughout their careers, thereby spurring "continuous quality improvement" (ABMS 2003a). This move, if successful, will represent a giant step toward integrated education and evaluation of physicians from medical school through their entire careers. The boards are also working with the ABMS and related specialty societies to develop tools for teaching and evaluating physicians in patient communication, professionalism, and systems improvement as well as knowledge and skills. How this commitment plays out will determine the influence of specialty organizations in U.S. health care and health policy. It will also determine whether those groups can meet challenges from state licensing boards, thus maintaining a national credentialing process rather than fifty or more separate ones, and whether public or private entities such as a national quality board, health insurers, or hospitals supercede self-regulation.

Avenues for Change

One could argue that the physician production system is exquisitely attuned to the diffused American health care marketplace, meeting the demands of both doctors and patients. While some evidence shows that physician incomes are declining as managed care, Medicare, and Medicaid fees tighten, few physicians are unemployed. Physicians have become adept at responding to perceived signals in the market. This is not surprising in a climate that encourages consumer choice and specialty proliferation, and where the average doctor is an owner or participant in a clinical corporation.

Proponents of market approaches in the 1980s and 1990s suggested that shaking up the health care system would spur innovation, and, indeed, entrepreneurial medical specialists and many patients enthusiastically embraced innovations (Robinson 1999). These included the rise of single-specialty medical groups and the buying and selling of lucrative specialty corporations, such as orthopedic groups and organ transplantation teams by hospitals and health care systems. Other innovations included the development of specialty hospitals (such as heart hospitals) and the rise of decentralized specialty office procedures (sometimes unlicensed, such as cosmetic surgery). With or without ABMS approval, newly defined subspecialty fields such as back surgery, sleep medicine, and Alzheimer's disease were part and parcel of the larger redefining movement.

However, assuming a totally free market in heath care would be naïve—and blatantly ahistorical. We have long lived with the benefits and distortions of major public insurance programs (notably Medicare), tax subsidies (to employers providing workers with health insurance), federal grants (to states for Medicaid and other programs), federal assistance (for research and university-based postdoctoral training in new fields), and national policies that encourage organizations deemed socially important, such as cancer centers. States have also been a vital resource, funding training programs for family physicians. The policy question is not whether subsidy and regulation of the complex, specialized U.S. system will continue, but how, for what purposes, and by whom.

How best can we improve the overall quality, effectiveness, and efficiency of patient care? Does it make most sense—politically and operationally—to try to regulate the behavior of consumers so they seek services more prudently? Are there practical ways to improve information for consumers in a direct-access system, or to provide incentives for collaborative practice in corporate systems? Or to reform Medicare via compelling incentives for private corporations to establish new systems and for Medicare beneficiaries to participate? Or to change the behavior of specialists as providers? And at what point does it make sense for government to preserve valued social institutions such as hospitals serving the poor, medical teaching institutions, and professional organizations?

These questions have no simple answers. However, some avenues for change appear promising. First, the quality movement is off and running. The U.S. population, steeped in direct access to specialists, is unlikely to flock to HMOs that restrict access, however good their care may be. Quality data may eventually show real advantages to patients in organized health systems or through primary care. Databanks of comparable evidence from competing systems can make a compelling case for consumers attuned to making their own, often intuitive decisions in the marketplace for specialty care. Here is a strong argument for establishing a compatible, national clinical information infrastructure based on automated patient records, and for providing trustworthy analyses that can advance medicine for the public, professions, and health care organizations. The automated medical record—as a basis for public accountability—may even be a necessary precondition for effective Medicare reform.

A second positive sign of change is the apparent willingness of Congress to consider planning and regulating health care, as expressed in the eighteen-month moratorium on new starts of physician-owned specialty hospitals in the 2003 Medicare law (Section 507). This legislation specifically mentions hospitals devoted primarily to cardiac or orthopedic surgery, but the secretary of health and human services may also designate other specialties under the moratorium. The law also restricts such hospitals from adding physician investors, expanding beyond the main hospital campus, extending services into a new specialty, and increasing the number of beds. Meanwhile, the Medicare Payment Advisory Commission (MedPAC) will study the financial impact of physician-owned hospitals on local full-service hospitals. MedPAC is already studying free-standing centers for plastic and other forms of outpatient surgery to establish Medicare payment rates. The relative value of different forms of medical service is likely to become more prominent in public debates.

The reasons are obvious. "Specialty niche" has become a common health care term, but it is a potential bombshell in its policy implications. Heart and orthopedic hospitals have shown that these specialty centers can be lucrative, but they threaten to strip services and reduce quality in neighboring general hospitals, with potentially serious implications for their bottom line. Not surprisingly, hospital associations lobbied vigorously for Section 507. However, communities also face splintering services and rising costs of care without added value (and perhaps with negative value). Common sense alone suggests that quality will decline when a community sees its general hospital lose its leading cardiologists or orthopedic surgeons.

Hospitals facing competition from new specialty hospitals, particularly those started by their own medical staff, face difficult choices. These range from launching an aggressive campaign of their own—perhaps involving expensive recruitment of another specialist team—to pressing the state legislature and regulatory agencies to limit specialist services to high-volume facilities. The first scenario involves added expenses and duplicated services; the second, expanded state and federal regulation (Devers, Brewster, and Ginsburg 2003). Community benefit and protection of well-established general hospitals may become more powerful considerations in health policy debates as efforts to curb "cream skimming" of patients yield public payoffs.

The need to coordinate and improve access to medical care can also spur strategic planning across traditional specialties. A cancer center offering multiple services, for example, may include subspecialists in radiology, surgery, gynecology, colon and rectal surgery, internal medicine, psychiatry, and pediatrics. The cancer center coordinates the efforts of professionals who come to oncology with diverse training. The concept of bringing multispecialty skills within a larger hospital or health system to patients with identifiable conditions may extend to areas such as Alzheimer's disease, healthy aging, and stroke.

A third promising movement stems from calls by family physicians and others for renewed attention to the advantages for patients of a "medical home." To be successful, such a movement may require substantial investment in consumer education regarding the value of primary care and (again) coordinated patient records, so both the primary doctor and the patient can discuss their options and make good decisions. A renewed market for primary care would prompt more medical students to become residents in family medicine, internal medicine, and pediatrics. The move away from such general fields is a rational economic response to present conditions, but these are not immutable. Here again public policy may seek to intervene.

Finally, the move toward maintenance-of-certification programs should attract broader policy attention. The most intense policy focus on physicians now stems from the Medicare payment system. However, except for the studies of specialty hospitals and ambulatory surgery, this focus is narrow, and it encourages specialties to compete to maximize their fees rather than set standards for the entire profession. In this instance public policy is divisive. At the very least, policy analysts need to know how U.S. physicians are being educated and in what fields, how they are evaluated by their professional organizations, what changes are under way, and how that process can advance the broader quality movement. A possible physician shortage, shortages in specific fields, quality of care, patient safety, and computerized patient records and ordering systems are best addressed in conjunction with—rather than in opposition to—specialty organizations, whose members may otherwise be reluctant to move ahead.

Overall, for the past twenty-five or thirty years, coinciding with the shift toward market-oriented health care, hospitals and physicians alike have been seen as self-interested competitors rather than guardians of the public interest or worthy of the public's trust. This dominant perspective views specialty organizations as fighting for turf, new revenue sources, and status. Fight they do. Yet they also pursue more altruistic activities. As noted, ABMS-approved specialty boards are trying to improve standards for communication with patients and peers, professionalism, and effectiveness under the maintenance-of-certification program, which all boards have endorsed. Representatives of the ABMS and the Council of Medical Specialty Societies have been meeting to expedite the program. I speak from experience as a public member representing ABMS in that group.

The broader policy question is whether health professions as well as medical schools and hospitals will be regarded as merely self-serving or as invaluable, irreplaceable social institutions. The former assumes a hostile, confrontational political and regulatory context; the latter, self-regulation to serve the public good. I hope the policy tide will turn from the former to the latter. Government and the medical profession should work together. Absent organized health care on a major scale, it is difficult to see an effective alternative.

Acknowledgments

For background data I am indebted to the American Board of Medical Specialties. Special thanks to Stephen H. Miller for helpful comments on the text.

References

Albert, T. 2003. Tort Crisis Spreads, Few Signs of Abating. *American Medical News* 8 (December): 1.

American Board of Medical Specialties (ABMS). 2003a. *Annual Report and Reference Handbook*. Evanston, IL: ABMS Research and Educational Foundation.

———. 2003b. Unpublished reports to the Executive Committee.

American Medical Association (AMA). 2002. Personal communication.

AP/*Dallas Morning News*. 2003. Imaging Centers: Physician Investment in Facilities Examined, December 1. As reported by *American Healthline*, December 3.

Beresford, L. 2004. Doctors to the Dying: The Growing Specialty of Palliative Care Attracts Physicians Who See It as a Noble Calling. *American Medical News,* January 26.

Burton, T. M. 2003. The Surgery Your Doctor Shouldn't Perform: Vascular Surgery Carries Greater Risks When Done by General Surgeons. *Wall Street Journal,* December 30.

Devers, K. J., L. R. Brewster, and P. B. Ginsburg. 2003. Specialty Hospitals: Focused Factories or Cream Skimmers? Issue brief. *Center for Health Systems Change* 62 (April): 1–4.

Fye, W. B. 1996. *American Cardiology: The History of a Specialty and Its College.* Baltimore: Johns Hopkins University Press.

Haiken, E. 1997. *Venus Envy: A History of Cosmetic Surgery.* Baltimore: Johns Hopkins University Press.

Hawryluk, M. 2003. Surgeons Push for Federal Funding for Trauma Care. *American Medical News* 23 (June): 8.

Iglehart, J. K. 1999. The American Health System: Medicare. *New England Journal of Medicine* 340: 327–332.

Kolata, G. 2003. Patients in Florida Lining Up for All That Medicare Covers. *Wall Street Journal*, September 13, A1.

Kuttner, R. 1999. The American Health Care System: Wall Street and Health Care. *New England Journal of Medicine* 340: 664–668.

Lee, P. R., et al. 1976. *Primary Care in a Specialized World.* Cambridge, MA: Ballinger.

Ludmerer, K. M. 1985. *Learning to Heal: The Development of American Medical Education.* New York: Basic Books.

———. 1999. *Time to Heal: American Medical Education from the Turn of the Century to the Era of Managed Care.* New York: Oxford University Press.

Naik, G. 2003. England Plans Major Revamp of Health Care. *Wall Street Journal*, December 3, B1.

Neale, H. W. 1996. ABMS-ABPS-ABO to Negotiations: Where We've Been and Where We Are Now. *Annals of Plastic Surgery* 36: 221–223.

Page, L. 2000. N.C. Clinic Abandons Multispecialty Trend. *American Medical News* 24 (April): 15–16.

Pisacano, N. J. 1964. General Practice: A Eulogy. *GP* 19: 173–181.

Reece, R. L. 2003. Observing Health Care: Realities and Boundaries in Revitalizing Primary Care, Part I. *HealthLeaders News*, December 3. Available at *www.healthleaders.com/news* (accessed December 3, 2003).

Robinson, J. C. 1999. *The Corporate Practice of Medicine: Competition and Innovation in Health Care.* Berkeley: University of California Press.

Rosen, G. 1944. *The Specialization of Medicine with Particular Reference to Ophthalmology.* New York: Froben Press.

Scott, W. R., et al. 2000. *Institutional Change and Healthcare Organization: From Professional Dominance to Managed Care.* Chicago: University of Chicago Press.

Somers, H. M., and A. R. Somers. 1961. *Doctors, Patients, and Health Insurance: The Organization and Financing of Medical Care.* Washington, DC: Brookings.

Starr, P. 1982. *The Social Transformation of American Medicine: The Rise of a Sovereign Profession and the Making of a Vast Industry.* New York: Basic Books.

Stephens, G. G. 1979. Family Medicine as Counter-Culture. *Family Medicine Teacher* 11, no. 5: 14–18.

Stevens, R. 1971. *American Medicine and the Public Interest*. New Haven, CT: Yale University Press. Reissued 1998, with new introduction. Berkeley: University of California Press.

————. 2001a. The Americanization of Family Medicine: Contradictions, Challenges, and Change, 1969–2000. *Family Medicine* 33, no. 4: 232–243.

————. 2001b. Public Roles for the Medical Profession in the United States: Beyond Theories of Decline and Fall. *Milbank Quarterly* 79, no. 3: 327–353.

U.S. Court of Appeals for the Ninth Circuit. 2004. *American Academy of Pain Management v. Joseph*. No. 01-15764. DC No. CV-96-02108-LKK. Filed January 2.

Weissert, C. S., and W. G. Weissert. 1996. *Governing Health: The Politics of Health Policy*. Baltimore: Johns Hopkins University Press.

PART IV

Frameworks for Fairness in Health Care

CHAPTER 15

Integrating People with Mental Illness into Health Insurance and Social Services

———— ∽∾∾ ————

RICHARD G. FRANK AND THOMAS G. MCGUIRE

Mental disorders are prevalent, impair functioning, and impose a large economic burden on American society and the global community. Careers are cut short, investments in education and training are erased, and families are torn apart. Affected individuals are routinely victimized, and jails and prisons are increasingly filled with people whose conduct is a direct result of their mental illnesses (Harwood et al. 1999).

Medical science has advanced the understanding of mental illnesses and led to improved treatments. *Mental Health: A Report of the Surgeon General*—which summarized much of what is known about mental illness and its treatment—emphasized that mental disorders are a complex mix of biological and psychosocial features, blurring distinctions between mental and physical illness (U.S. DHHS 1999).

Running parallel to the science that, according to the report, "mends the destructive split between 'mental' and 'physical' health" is an evolving health care delivery system (U.S. DHHS 1999). Public provision, directed by state mental health agencies, dominated mental health care in the 1950s and 1960s. In 1956, for example, the budgets of state and local psychiatric hospitals and specialty mental health clinics accounted for 84 percent of spending on mental health care (Fein 1958). Individual households accounted for the remaining 16 percent, which largely paid for psychotherapy and care in private psychiatric hospitals. Aside from a small sector serving a high-income clientele, governments planned and paid for mental health delivery, markets played a small role in allocating resources, and a small set of specialized providers supplied the care.

Recent analyses of spending on mental health care show how things have changed. Coffey et al. (2000) report that in 1997 government played a significant role in financing mental health care, accounting for about 59 percent of spending, but most of that spending occurred through public insurance programs such as Medicare and Medicaid. Less than 15 percent of total spending went directly from government to state and local public mental hospitals. Now a diverse set of private providers and professionals deliver mental health care, including general hospitals, nursing homes, primary care physicians, psychologists, and social workers, among others. Private insurance now accounts for over a quarter of all spending.

The advent of insurance as the central form of financing for mental health care has decentralized decision making and given markets a prominent role. Thus, at the start of the twenty-first century, mental health care delivery looks more like general health care delivery than at any time in the last 150 years (Grob 1994). This is largely because the United States has integrated mental health care into the organization, financing, and delivery of medical care.

These broad trends notwithstanding, integrating mentally ill individuals into health insurance and other social programs continues to be a central challenge with a number of dimensions. The first is how clinical care for mental disorders fits into the health care delivery system. Patients with mental illness often initially present their problem to a primary care physician (Morlock 1989). Recent improvements in diagnostic screening and treatment technologies allow primary care providers to identify and treat a high percentage of cases of depression (Wells et al. 1996). However, many primary care physicians and general medical clinics are still reluctant to do so, and depression and other disorders often go unrecognized and untreated (Wells et al. 1996). One set of integration issues thus involves how to manage mental disorders in the context of general medical care.

A second aspect of integration concerns the organization and financing of mental health care. As Medicare, Medicaid, and private insurance have come to dominate financing, coverage and payment have become matters of public policy. The long-standing debate about parity—equality in insurance coverage for mental health care and other treatments—can be cast as an issue of integration. Full parity would make no distinction between mental and physical conditions and treatments (Frank, Goldman, and McGuire 2001). But parity in coverage is only one side of the story: integration also relates to the design of the payment system. For example, when Medicare implemented its prospective payment system in 1983—which was based on diagnosis-related groups, or DRGs—it exempted psychiatric hospitals and specialized psychiatric units of general hospitals. Advocates asked policymakers not to integrate mental health into the new hospital payment system because of evidence that DRGs failed to account for case-mix differences among providers (Lave 2003).

As treatment of people with severe mental disorders has moved from the public mental hospital to community-based settings, care has intersected with social programs aimed at poor and disabled people—a third dimension of integration. (Concerns about equal treatment for people with mental illness also apply to social insurance, job training, housing, education, and criminal justice, although equal treatment may be hard to define in many of these areas.) Integrating people with mental disorders into mainstream social insurance programs such as Temporary Assistance for Needy Families (TANF), Social Security Disability Insurance (SSDI), and Supplemental Security Income (SSI) raises questions regarding whether applying program rules equally to people with mental disorders is fair and efficient. A common theme in these debates is how to design policies that recognize the special (and disabling) features of mental disorders and would result in fair and efficient treatment of people with mental illness.

Integrated payment systems can create incentives to underserve or otherwise discriminate against persons with mental illness, leading to efficiency problems. Since people with mental disorders are most costly to insure, and payments to plans do not generally recognize such differences, health plans have an incentive to avoid enrolling persons with mental illness. Recent tabulations from the Medical Expenditure Panel Survey show that the per capita health spending of people with mood disorders is more than four times that of individuals without any chronic diseases (Anderson and Knickman 2001; Druss et al. 2001). As we argue, adverse incentives associated with integration pose a serious threat to fair and cost-effective treatment of people with mental illness.

We first encounter this argument in the context of integrated health insurance, but incentives to avoid serving people with mental disorders extend beyond insurance coverage. Social insurance programs generally apply uniform rules to all beneficiaries. Since the early years of the Reagan administration, courts have supported the principle of equal treatment of people with mental illnesses in social insurance programs. Policymakers often make these decisions on simple fairness grounds. In the case of social insurance, however, as with health care financing, fully integrating persons with mental illnesses into social programs can create incentives that will disadvantage those individuals.

Integration in Health Insurance: Parity for Mental Health Services

Parity in insurance coverage for mental health means literal equality in demand-side cost sharing—deductibles, co-payments, and limits—between general health and mental health services. Data on private health insurance from the 1990s show that mental health care is commonly subject to higher demand-side cost sharing, sustaining a discrepancy in benefit coverage that has lasted more than forty years (Buck and Umland 1997).

Governments are passing and implementing parity—or at least partial parity—laws. For example, the federal Mental Health Parity Act required, beginning in 1998, that group health plans provide the same annual and lifetime spending caps for mental and physical illness. Although this legislation delivered a symbolic victory for mental health advocates, it eliminated only differences in annual and lifetime caps, and not the deductible and co-payment features that matter more, thus exerting little impact on equality of coverage. By mid-2000, Gitterman et al. counted thirty-one states with parity laws of their own, ranging from laws that simply matched the federal regulation to those that defined mental illness broadly and applied to virtually all aspects of coverage (2000). In 1999, an executive order established full parity for plans serving federal employees and their families through the Federal Employees Health Benefits Program. Meanwhile, some private employers voluntarily expanded coverage to create parity for mental health while introducing managed care (Goldman, McCulloch, and Sturm 1998; Ma and McGuire

1998a). In fact, the generally favorable experience of the private sector with managed care and parity-like benefits stimulated federal and state regulations (National Advisory Mental Health Council 1998).

Parity, Fairness, and Efficiency

Parity has been the stated objective of mental health advocates since differences in coverage first arose in the early days of private health insurance (Reed, Myers, and Scheidemandel 1972). These advocates have based their case primarily on the fairness argument: insurance should not discriminate against persons with mental illness. This argument usually focuses on equality of benefit design— that is, on cost sharing and coverage limits. Such parity may or may not result in equity of *use* for persons with mental illness compared with those with physical illness (in relation to measured need).

However, advocates for parity in coverage had to contend with a central question: If parity is such an attractive idea, why were buyers in private health insurance markets not demanding it? Stigma was one answer, but economic analysis supplied another, based on adverse selection. That is, competing health plans may under-provide coverage for some health conditions because of fears that they will attract costly enrollees, even if enrollees value the coverage more than the costs of providing it (McGuire 1981). Thus, competition focuses on avoiding "bad risks": plans reduce coverage that attracts costly enrollees, such as mental health coverage. Low-cost individuals are drawn to plans offering more limited coverage at a lower premium, leaving the "sickest" enrollees in plans with relatively generous coverage. If premiums do not reflect differences among enrollees, health plans offering more generous coverage will lose money. This distorted competitive dynamic in health insurance is referred to as a death spiral.

Some of the most compelling evidence for adverse selection in mental health comes from the Federal Employees Health Benefits Program, where the dynamics of coverage approached death spiral proportions in the 1980s and 1990s. The proportion of total dollars accounted for by behavioral health claims fell from 7.8 percent in 1980 to 1.9 percent in 1997 (Foote and Jones 1999; Padgett et al. 1993). What was once model coverage for mental health care deteriorated to very limited benefits, as plans cut back on coverage to drive away users of mental health care. Short-circuiting such market failures is the economic rationale for benefit mandates passed by states during the 1970s and 1980s (Frank 1989). While these mandates were popular and effective, they succeeded only in establishing a low floor for coverage, and only for plans within reach of state regulation. Mandates were also often denominated in dollar terms and eroded in purchasing power with medical price inflation.

The equity-in-access argument and adverse selection argument for parity have been articulated for many years, but they have not, until recently, been on the winning side. Against parity policies stood both equity and efficiency objections. Fairness involves issues of vertical equity (fair relative treatment of those better or worse off) as well as horizontal equity (people with mental disorders should be covered the same as those with physical conditions). The most common vertical equity standard is fairness across income groups. Simply put, vertical equity implies that redistribution favoring higher-income groups is bad, while actions that favor lower-income groups are good. Although the days of insurance-paid long-term psychotherapy are gone, use of outpatient mental health care remains highly correlated with income (Alegria et al. 2000). Thus, adding full coverage for outpatient mental health care to private health insurance serves to redistribute income from lower-income to higher-income groups.

The efficiency argument against parity is well-known in mental health services research (Frank and McGuire 2000). The concern is that offering the same level of insurance coverage for mental health as for general medical care will produce a disproportionate rise in health care spending. And, in fact, studies show that the demand response to changes in coverage is greater for mental than for physical health care (Frank and McGuire 1986, 2000). This is seen as overuse and implies that an insurance-related drop in the price of care would create more inefficiency in mental than in general health care (Frank and McGuire 2000; Newhouse and Insurance Experiment Group 1993). This finding sets up the main efficiency argument against parity: in the interest of consumers, coverage should not be equal for physical and mental conditions.

Parity in the Age of Managed Care

Managed care changes all the arguments—pro and con—bearing on parity. Virtually all private insurance plans include some elements of managed care, including some for behavioral health (Kaiser Family Foundation 1998). Managed care has altered methods of rationing both general health care and mental health care (Glied 2000).

Managed care weakens or even reverses arguments against parity. For example, under managed care, benefit designs help determine people's use of mental health care. No study since the advent of managed care has considered the aspects of parity concerned with regressive income distribution. However, given that managed care has controlled the use of psychotherapy, and that these treatments are highly correlated with socioeconomic status, it seems likely that managed care would attenuate the regressive effects of parity.

Managed care also undercuts the cost containment argument against parity. Since managed care introduces a number of tools to curtail overuse and control spending, plans no longer have to rely on high levels of cost sharing and service limits. If other mechanisms can better contain costs, benefit design can focus on risk protection. Supply-side payment mechanisms—such as capitation and other forms of prospective payment—enlist providers' financial self-interest in efforts to restrain use and cost. This line of argument implies not only parity in coverage but—with effective managed care—parity at full coverage for all services (Frank, Glazer, and McGuire 2000; Ellis and McGuire 1993; Ma and McGuire 1998b).

However, a key issue is whether health plans will use their cost-containment tools to ration mental health services according to the same standards as for other services. Parity in managing health care implies that health plans would apply the same cost-per-unit-of-quality criteria across all clinical service areas, such as heart disease, mental health, and cancer care (Frank and McGuire 1998; Burnam and Escarce 1999). Economic analysis implies that full parity in this sense is also efficient. Parity in benefit coverage is thus a necessary but not a sufficient condition for an efficient health plan.

Unfortunately, the very mechanisms that have weakened the traditional cost-control argument against parity imply that competitive insurance markets may continue to supply inefficiently low levels of mental health coverage in the presence of parity laws in the era of managed care. As noted, managed care tactics substitute for demand-side cost sharing. Thus, parity laws regulate just one dimension of cost and access control (benefit design) and leave others (utilization review, network design, physician incentives) open for use by plans to discourage enrollment by persons with mental illness. As Mechanic and McAlpine put it, "Parity in benefit structures means little if ADM [alcohol, drug, and mental illness] care is managed more stringently than other types of health care" (1999, 10).

One could take comfort in observing that parity fixes one problem (benefit design) related to equitable treatment of mental health care. However, this fallback position has problems. If regulators force a plan to make demand-side cost-sharing provisions more generous, the plan will presumably react by managing utilization more tightly. Do we know that the net result is more access, or better access in any sense? Overall, the traditional incentives to avoid enrolling people with high expected costs remain at least as strong as in the past, while the mechanisms available to health plans for affecting selection have expanded with managed care.

Why Integration Fails to Ensure Equal Treatment: Selection Incentives

Adverse selection is an issue for all of health insurance, but may be especially serious in the mental health arena. Deb et al. found that individuals with a family member with mental illness were more likely than similar U.S. residents to choose coverage with more generous mental health provisions (1996). Sturm and colleagues analyzed the treatment of depression across health plans as part of the Medical Outcomes Study, finding that depressed individuals receiving care from specialists were more likely to migrate from prepaid to fee-for-service plans (1994).

Ellis examined the persistence of spending over time and its implications for health plan choice (1985). Individuals with a history of using mental health care had persistently higher levels of spending than otherwise similarly insured individuals. He also found that a history of mental health care utilization had a significant impact on an individual's choice of health plan. Higher levels of prior-year mental health spending increased the likelihood that an enrollee would choose a low-deductible plan. These studies imply that health insurance plans will anticipate this demand behavior and take steps to prevent it—including offering poor coverage for mental illness to discourage these "risks" from enrolling.

As mentioned, during the 1970s and 1980s, insurers channeled competition in avoiding bad risks into limiting coverage for treating mental and addictive disorders. As health insurance moved away from traditional fee-for-service toward managed care, plans shifted from using co-insurance, deductibles, limits, and exclusions to relying on internal management processes (which are more difficult to regulate) to ration treatment. The question these changes raise about efficiency is whether incentives to cut back on mental health care in an integrated plan are greater than for other services. Is the threat of underservice for mental health care any worse than for cancer or diabetes care or other medical services?

Empirical research has shown that certain characteristics of services under- lie market-driven incentives to ration tightly (Frank, Glazer, and McGuire 2000). If a service is *predictable,* consumers will base decisions on whether to join a plan on their expected future use. If a service is *predictive* of total health care use, a person using this service will tend to use more of all services. Predictable-predictive services are the ones that integrated health plans have the greatest incentive to ra- tion tightly.

The empirical question then becomes, how does mental health compare with other services in incentives to ration tightly under integrated managed care plans, and is there any evidence that integrated plans are acting on this incentive? Frank, Glazer, and McGuire examined these questions in the context of a Medicaid popu- lation (2000). They found that plans applied more stringent cost-effectiveness stan- dards to mental health and substance abuse care than to any other service studied, including cancer care, gastrointestinal care, and heart care. This outcome occurred because plans assumed that individuals could predict their service use based on past use, and was primarily driven by the fact that mental health care was much more predictable than the other services.

Some evidence shows that plans act on these incentives. If Medicare rations mental health care more strictly than other services, people using such care may be less likely than other beneficiaries to leave traditional Medicare and join HMOs. Cao compared the health care costs of Medicare enrollees during the year before they switched into HMOs with those who did not switch and found that people who used mental health care were more likely to stay in traditional Medicare than people who used other services (2003). The implication is that people who use mental health services are less willing to subject themselves to health plans that tightly ration services. And the inference is that the plans in the study subjected mental health services to special control.

Cao and McGuire examined another implication of tighter mental health ra- tioning (2003). If mental health users tend to stay in traditional Medicare as HMO market share rises in an area, the average cost of mental health care in regular Medicare should rise with HMO share, compared with other services. Using na- tional data from 1996, the researchers found that average mental health care costs (both Part A and Part B) rise for people who remain in traditional Medicare as HMO market share rises. This contrasts with some other services such as primary care, where the average cost falls in traditional Medicare. These findings are also consistent with tight rationing of mental health compared with loose rationing of primary care.

In sum, empirical evidence shows that health plans' incentives to avoid people likely to use mental health services are stronger than for most other types of ser- vices. The evidence is also consistent with the notion that health plans ration mental health services more stringently than other services. This evidence implies that the main efficiency concern that led to the impulse to use parity laws and benefit mandates to regulate mental health coverage persists in the era of managed care. Unfortunately, parity in benefit coverage fails to solve the problem.

Fixing the System: Separation and Risk Adjustment

Two market-based approaches can counter selection-related incentives to distort the allocation of treatment resources away from mental health care: managed behavioral carve-outs and risk adjustment. Although managed behavioral carve-outs are usually regarded as cost-control devices, they may also moderate selection-related incentives. A carve-out refers to the use of a separate contract—usually with a company specializing in behavioral health care—to provide and manage mental health and substance abuse care.

The economic role of a carve-out program can differ significantly depending on its form. Carve-outs that simply enlist health plan subcontractors may have little impact on adverse selection because consumers continue to choose among integrated health plans where the use of rationing rules across services can affect enrollment patterns. The incentives for an organization to give mental health care special attention in rationing are present with or without a carve-out subcontract.

However, carve-outs that take the form of separate risk contracts from payers (such as employers) remove the risk of mental health service from overall health care, and thus eliminate its management from competition among health plans. Separating mental health care and coverage means that the contract between the payer and the specialty behavioral health company will determine rationing. Of course, carve-out programs have disadvantages that must be considered along with the potential gains in minimizing adverse selection. These disadvantages include high administrative costs (estimated at 8–15 percent), difficulties in coordinating (integrating) care between general medical and mental health providers, and incentives to shift responsibility for care across insurance segments (such as to pharmacy benefits).

Risk adjustment—the other methodology for stemming selection-related incentives in managed care—retains integration in health insurance. The basic idea is that if plans are paid more for care of enrollees likely to be costly, plans will not actively avoid such enrollees. Most risk-adjustment systems rely on demographic factors and clinical information for individuals from past time periods. The clinical information usually consists of diagnoses and procedures arranged in clusters based on judgments about the complexity and intensity of past treatment (Weiner et al. 1996). If individuals choose among plans based partly on predictable medical expenses, then a risk-adjustment scheme capturing this predicted spending variation may be able to address some potential distortions.

Research on risk adjustment shows that careful choice of weights for risk-adjuster variables can improve the incentives to supply care for chronic illness (Glazer and McGuire 2002). However, risk-adjustment methodologies are still evolving and currently explain only 7 percent of general health care spending, and researchers have paid little attention to mental health care (Newhouse 1998). In

1992 and 1993 Ettner et al. examined several commonly used risk adjusters among some 450,000 privately insured employees and their dependents (1998). The investigators showed that no classification system displayed strong predictive ability, and analysis of naturally occurring selection across plans for two large employer groups illuminated the weaknesses of all the classification systems.

So far, risk adjustment in general has failed to make significant progress in stemming the incentives to avoid enrollees who are likely to be costly. Risk adjustment in the mental health and substance abuse area is especially challenging. An important reason is the heterogeneity of conditions that are represented within a diagnostic group. For example, some people with major depression respond quickly to simple pharmacological treatment while others do not, and might require a complex mix of services. Indeed, diagnosis even in the absence of heterogeneity is not tightly tied to a particular course of treatment. One of the characteristics of modern psychiatry is that several evidence-based treatments are available for many mental disorders (U.S. DHHS 1999). The implication is that personal circumstances, patient preferences, and location explain variation in treatment in addition to diagnosis. The result is weak explanatory power of traditional diagnosis-based risk adjusters.

Fully integrating mental health into health insurance, in our view, means applying the same principles to rationing mental health care as to other medical care. Adverse selection incentives stand in the way of this type of integration. Public policy has responded by attempting to regulate benefit design to ensure that it is the same for mental health and general medical care. While we believe this to be a step in the right direction in the context of managed care, it does not meet our standards for full integration. For example, highly effective mental health treatments such as assertive community treatment have no clear parallels in medical care. As a result, health insurance will typically not pay for certain elements of that treatment technology. In that case, simply paying the same amount does not accomplish full integration because the approach fails to apply the same rationing principles to all types of treatment.

Integration in Social Insurance: The Case of Employment Policy

The previous section points to special features of mental illness and mental health care and the resulting selection incentives as key barriers to integrating health insurance. In this section we discuss how selection incentives can compromise the aims of social insurance programs and disadvantage people with mental illness.

Since the 1970s the majority of people with severe mental disorders have spent an increasingly large portion of their time living in communities rather than in institutions. A majority of adults with severe mental disorders receive financial support from Supplemental Security Income (SSI) and Social Security Disability Insurance (SSDI). The Temporary Assistance for Needy Families (TANF) program—established under welfare reform—also provides financial support for low-income women and children with mental disorders, among other recipients. Glied and Frank show that these social insurance programs support, at least to some degree, well over 70 percent of the population estimated to have severe mental disorders (2003).

People diagnosed with mental disorders account for a substantial share of SSI and SSDI enrollees: some 27 percent and 35 percent, respectively, suffer from a mental disorder. People with mental illnesses as their primary cause of disability are the fastest-growing group of beneficiaries in both programs, along with people suffering from musculoskeletal disorders. In the National Survey of American Families, 28 percent of adult TANF recipients had significant mental health problems, as measured by diagnostic questionnaires and symptom counts (Loprest and Zedlewski 1999). Moreover, research has linked improvements in mental health with income support and employment (Alegria, Perez, and Williams 2003).

Social insurance programs have made new efforts to move beneficiaries to employment. Welfare reform is well-known, but the newer Ticket to Work (TTW) program also exerts potential effects on work for persons with a range of disabilities. The TTW program equips SSI and SSDI recipients with vouchers they can use for work-related training from private and some public agencies. Welfare and TTW program rules generally apply to people with mental disorders just as to all other program participants—a form of program integration. The question is, does this form of simple integration, or parity, serve people with mental illness fairly and efficiently?

The Economics of Disability Programs
and Challenges to Simple Integration

Social insurance, including disability insurance, spreads risk among members of society, just as health insurance does. The financial support offered by a disability program alters the behavior of individuals and can create moral hazard. Disability insurance provides workers with an income-support payment if they are deemed disabled by a physical or mental condition. If income-support payments were available if—and only if—workers did not recover from disabling conditions, they could receive some protection against the risk of disability at no efficiency cost. Transfer payments cannot be made with such precision, however, and workers typically know more about their own condition than does the social insurance program (e.g., the Social Security Administration). Some workers for whom it would be socially efficient to reenter the workforce will not do so. Low-wage workers and workers less likely to become attached to jobs will be least likely to reenter the labor force.

A range of policy initiatives has tried to address this problem since the creation of social insurance programs. Both welfare reform and TTW rely on employment services to help match workers with jobs. But again moral hazard will prompt too few workers to accept these services. In particular, low-wage workers and workers with lower probabilities of obtaining a match will not seek out employment services. What's more, employment agencies that are paid and evaluated according to their ability to place and maintain beneficiaries in jobs will have incentives not to work with people who have a lower likelihood of success (Frank and McGuire 2003). These incentives are similar to the health insurance selection incentives discussed earlier. Employment agencies that are paid for performance will potentially lose money if they take on clients that are costly to support and have a low probability of reentering the labor market. Such agencies are more likely to profit from serving clients who have a greater likelihood of obtaining employment.

People with mental illness are among those who may be least likely to either reenter the labor force or seek employment services. People disabled by mental illness are less likely to work than people with most other disabilities. Ettner, Frank, and Kessler used the National Comorbidity Survey to study labor market outcomes and estimated that employment rates are 10–15 percent lower among males and females with diagnosable mental disorders (1997). Mechanic, Bilder, and McAlpine report that about 50 percent of people with a mental disorder work, while just 20 percent of people with serious mental illness hold any type of job (2002). Only 12 percent of people with schizophrenia work full time. Similarly Yellin and Cisternas analyzed the National Health Interview Survey and found that people with mental disabilities have the lowest rates of employment among people reporting disabilities (1996).

Workers with mental disorders earn less than otherwise similar workers, and those with severe mental illnesses are more likely to hold low-wage jobs than similar people without such diseases (Mechanic, Bilder, and McAlpine 2002). Ettner, Frank, and Kessler report that earnings were somewhat lower among workers with mental disorders than among people without such illnesses (1997).

People with mental illnesses are also less likely to keep jobs when they find employment. After examining the Survey of Income and Program Participation, Salkever estimated significantly lower rates of continuing employment for people with mental illnesses (2003). In analyzing the follow-up to the Epidemiologic Catchment Area Survey—the most comprehensive survey of mental disorders ever conducted in the United States—Slade and Albers found that people with recurring symptoms of depression are more likely to exit the labor market than are other similar individuals (2000).

The empirical evidence bolsters the notion that without special accommodation, people with mental disorders enrolled in TANF, SSDI, and SSI will be less likely to participate in voluntary employment services such as those of the TTW program, owing to the disincentives for both workers and employment agencies. People with mental illness will also reenter the labor force less often than people with other disabilities. Welfare-to-work programs that fail to recognize the special difficulties that people with mental illnesses confront in gaining employment will mean that those enrollees will experience sanctions and benefit expirations (Polit, London, and Martinez 2001). This would be an unintended and possibly undesirable program outcome. Thus, the incentives associated with welfare reform and the TTW program will tend to reinforce incentives for people with mental disorders not to return to work, even part time.

Conclusion

To stem the adverse consequences of market failures, some state legislators and policy analysts have proposed to directly regulate managed care contracts and to measure and pay for care based on quality (Gopelrud and Rosenbaum 1998). However, rationing within managed care is a complex, heterogeneous, and poorly understood business. It involves hundreds of decision points within managed care organizations, making direct regulation of these practices costly, complex, and difficult to monitor. Furthermore, given analysts' meager understanding of rationing in managed care, it is unclear whether incomplete regulation will improve or hinder the fair and efficient provision of mental health and substance abuse care.

The science and practice of quality measurement is still developing. Direct measurement of health plan performance is a subject of active research, but efforts to measure the quality of specific services such as mental health care lag behind the overall effort (IOM 1997). Developing quality indicators to regulate rationing thus remains a distant goal. Given the state of these measures, carveouts and risk adjustments remain ways to address the effects of moral hazard and adverse selection in mental health services.

The integration of people with mental illness into social insurance and social services is widespread and a sign of progress toward full integration of mental and physical illness. At the same time, policies that promote social goals such as employment but do not account for unique features of mental illness appear likely to disadvantage people with mental disorders and compromise progress. The search for ways to improve on the application of all program policies to all populations is a pressing challenge for researchers and policymakers alike.

Acknowledgments

Support from The Robert Wood Johnson Foundation Investigator Awards in Health Policy Research program, the National Institute of Mental Health, and the John D. and Catherine T. MacArthur Foundation for research underlying this chapter is gratefully acknowledged.

References

Alegria, M., D. Perez, and S. Williams. 2003. Mental Health Disparities among People of Color. *Health Affairs* 22, no. 5: 51–64.

Alegria, M., R. V. Bijl, E. Lin, E. E. Walters, and R. C. Kessler. 2000. Income Differences in Persons Seeking Outpatient Treatment of Mental Disorders: A Comparison of the U.S. with Ontario and the Netherlands. *Archives of General Psychiatry* 57, no. 4: 383–391.

Anderson, G., and J. R. Knickman. 2001. Changing the Chronic Care System to Meet People's Needs. *Health Affairs* 20, no. 6: 146–160.

Buck, J., and B. Umland. 1997. Covering Mental Health and Substance Abuse Services. *Health Affairs* 16, no. 4: 121–126.

Burnham, M. A., and J. J. Escarce. 1999. Equity in Managed Care for Mental Disorders. *Health Affairs* 18, no. 5: 22–31.

Cao, Z. 2003. Comparing the Pre-HMO Enrollment Costs between Switchers and Stayers: Evidence from Medicare. Manuscript. Center for Multicultural Mental Health Studies, Cambridge Health Alliance, Cambridge, MA.

Cao, Z., and T. G. McGuire. 2003. Service-Level Selection by HMOs in Medicare. *Journal of Health Economics* 22, no. 6: 915–931.

Coffey, R. M., T. Mark, E. King, et al. 2000. *National Estimates of Expenditures for Mental Health and Substance Abuse Treatment, 1997.* Rockville, MD: U.S. Department of Health and Human Services.

Deb, P., J. Rubin, V. Wilcox-Gok, and A. Holmes. 1996. Choice of Health Insurance by Families of the Mentally Ill. *Health Economics* 5, no. 1: 61–76.

Druss, B. G., S. C. Marcus, M. Olfson, T. Taniellan, C. Elinson, and H. A. Pincus. 2001. Comparing the National Economic Burden of Five Chronic Conditions. *Health Affairs* 20, no. 6: 233–241.

Ellis, R. P. 1985. The Effect of Prior-Year Health Expenditures on Health Coverage Plan Choice. In *Advances in Health Economics and Health Services Research*, ed. R. Scheffler and L. Rossiter. Greenwich, CT: JAI Press.

Ellis, R. P., and T. G. McGuire. 1993. Supply-Side and Demand-Side Cost Sharing in Health Care. *Journal of Economic Perspectives* 74, no. 4: 135–151.

———. 2003. Predictability in Health Spending. Manuscript. Department of Health Care Policy, Harvard Medical School.

Ettner, S. L., R. G. Frank, and R. C. Kessler. 1997. The Impact of Psychiatric Disorder on Labor Market Outcomes. *Industrial and Labor Relations Review* 51, no. 1: 64–81.

Ettner, S. L., R. G. Frank, T. G. McGuire, J. P. Newhouse, and E. H. Notman. 1998. Risk Adjustment of Mental Health and Substance Abuse Payments. *Inquiry* 35, no. 2: 223–229.

Fein, R. 1958. *Economics of Mental Illness.* Joint Commission on Mental Illness and Health, no. 2. New York: Basic Books.

Foote, S. M., and S. B. Jones. 1999. Consumer-Choice Markets: Lessons from FEHBP Mental Health Coverage. *Health Affairs* 18, no. 5: 125–130.

Frank, R. G. 1989. Regulatory Policy and Information Deficiencies in the Market for Mental Health Services. *Journal of Health Politics, Policy, and Law* 14, no. 3: 477–503.

Frank, R. G., and T. G. McGuire. 1986. A Review of Studies of the Impact of Insurance on the Demand and Utilization of Specialty Mental Health Services. *Health Services Research* 21, no. 2: 241–266.

———. 1998. Parity for Mental Health and Substance Abuse Care under Managed Care. *Journal of Mental Health Policy and Economics* 1: 153–159.

———. 2000. Economics and Mental Health. In *Handbook of Health Economics*, ed. A. J. Culyer and J. P. Newhouse. Amsterdam: North Holland.

———. 2003. Setting Payments in the Ticket to Work Program: Applying Experience from Capitation Payments in Health Insurance. In *Paying for Results in Vocational Rehabilitation,* ed. K. Rupp and S. H. Bell. Washington, DC: Urban Institute Press.

Frank, R. G., H. H. Goldman, and T. G. McGuire. 2001. Will Parity in Coverage Result in Better Mental Health Care? *New England Journal of Medicine* 345, no. 23: 1701–1704.

Frank, R. G., J. Glazer, and T. G. McGuire. 2000. Measuring Adverse Selection in Managed Health Care. *Journal of Health Economics* 19, no. 6: 829–854.

Gitterman, D. P., D. Schwalm, M. C. Peck, and E. Ciemens. 2000. The Political Economy of State Mental Health Parity. Paper presented at the tenth NIMH Biennial Research Conference on the Economics of Mental Health: Economics of Parity for Mental Health. Bethesda, MD, September 18–19.

Glazer, J., and T. G. McGuire. 2002. Setting Health Plan Premiums to Ensure Efficient Quality in Health Care: Minimum Variance Optimal Risk Adjustment. *Journal of Public Economics* 84: 153–173.

Glied, S. 2000. Managed Care. In *Handbook of Health Economics,* ed. J. P. Newhouse and A. Cuyler. Amsterdam: North Holland.

Glied, S., and R. G. Frank. 2003. Better but Not Well. Monograph.

Goldman, W., J. McCulloch, and R. Sturm. 1998. Costs and Use of Mental Health Services before and after Managed Care. *Health Affairs* 17, no. 2: 40–52.

Gopelrud, E., and S. Rosenbaum. 1998. State Medicaid and MCO-CBO Contracting. *Behavioral Healthcare Tomorrow* 7, no. 1: 21–27.

Grob, G. N. 1991. *From Asylum to Community: Mental Health Policy in Modern America.* Princeton, NJ: Princeton University Press.

———. 1994. *The Mad among Us: A History of the Care of America's Mentally Ill.* New York: Free Press.

Harwood, H., A. Ameen, G. Denmead, E. Englert, D. Fountain, and G. Livermore. 1999. *The Economic Costs of Mental Illness, 1992.* Fairfax, VA: Lewin Group.

Institute of Medicine (IOM). 1997. *Managing Managed Care.* Washington, DC: National Academies Press.

Kaiser Family Foundation. 1998. *Trends and Indicators in the Changing Health Care Market Place.* Menlo Park, CA: Kaiser Family Foundation.

Lave, J. 2003. Developing a Medicare Prospective Payment System for Inpatient Psychiatric Care. *Health Affairs* 22, no. 5: 97–109.

Loprest, P. J., and S. R. Zedlewski. 1999. *Current and Former Welfare Recipients: How Do They Differ?* Assessing the New Federalism, paper no. 99-117. Washington, DC: Urban Institute.

Ma, C. A., and T. G. McGuire. 1998a. Cost and Incentives in a Behavioral Health Carve-Out. *Health Affairs* 17: 53–67.

———. 1998b. Optimal Health Insurance and Provider Payment. *American Economic Review* 87, no. 4: 685–704.

Manning, W. G., and S. Marquis. 1992. The Effect of Mental Health Insurance: Evidence from the HIE. Working paper. Ann Arbor: University of Michigan.

McGuire, T. G. 1981. *Financing Psychotherapy: Costs, Effects, and Public Policy.* Cambridge, MA: Ballinger Publishing.

Mechanic, D., and D. D. McAlpine. 1999. Mission Unfulfilled: Potholes on the Road to Mental Health Parity. *Health Affairs* 18, no. 5: 7–21.

Mechanic D., S. Bilder, and D. D. McAlpine. 2002. Employing Persons with Mental Illness. *Health Affairs* 21, no. 5: 242–253.

Miller, R. H., and H. S. Luft. 1997. Does Managed Care Lead to Better or Worse Quality of Care? *Health Affairs* 16, no. 5: 7–25.

Morlock, L. L. 1989. Recognition and Treatment of Mental Health Problems in the General Sector. In *The Future of Mental Health Services Research*, ed. C. Taube, D. Mechanic, and H. Hohmann. Washington, DC: Government Printing Office.

National Advisory Mental Health Council. 1998. *Parity in Financing Mental Health Services: Managed Care Effects on Cost, Access, and Quality.* Interim report to Congress. NIH Publication no. 98-4322, May.

Newhouse, J. P. 1998. Risk Adjustment: Where Are We Now? *Inquiry* 35, no. 2: 122–131.

Newhouse, J. P., and the Insurance Experiment Group. 1993. *Free for All? Lessons from the RAND Health Insurance Experiment.* Cambridge, MA: Harvard University Press.

Padgett, D. K., C. Patrick, B. J. Burns, et al. 1993. The Effect of Insurance Benefit Changes on Use of Child and Adolescent Outpatient Mental Health Services. *Medical Care* 31, no. 2: 96–110.

Polit, D., A. London, and J. Martinez. 2001. *The Health of Poor Urban Women: Findings from the Project on Devolution and Urban Change.* New York: Manpower Demonstration Research Corp.

Reed, L. S., E. S. Myers, and P. L. Scheidemandel. 1972. *Health Insurance and Psychiatric Care: Utilization and Cost.* Washington, DC: American Psychiatric Association.

Salkever, D. S. 2003. Tickets without Takers? Potential Economic Barriers to the Supply of Rehabilitation Services to Beneficiaries with Mental Disorders. In *Paying for Results in Vocational Rehabilitation,* ed. K. Rupp and S. H. Bell. Washington, DC: Urban Institute Press.

Slade, E., and L. A. Albers. 2000. Syndromal Effects of Psychiatric Disorders and Labor Force Exits. In *The Economics of Disability,* ed. D. Salkever and A. Sorkin. Greenwich, CT: JAI Press.

Sturm, R. 1997. How Expensive Is Unlimited Mental Health Care Coverage under Managed Care? *Journal of the American Medical Association* 278, no. 18: 1533–1537.

Sturm, R., et al. 1994. Provider Choice and Continuity for the Treatment of Depression. RAND Paper DRU-692-AHCPR. Santa Monica, CA.

U.S. Department of Health and Human Services (DHHS). 1999. *Mental Health: A Report of the Surgeon General.* Executive summary. Rockville, MD: Substance Abuse and Mental Health Services Administration, Center for Mental Health Services, National Institute of Mental Health. *Available at www.surgeongeneral.gov/library/mentalhealth/home.html.*

Weiner, J. P., A. Dobson, S. L. Maxwell, K. Coleman, B. H. Starfield, and G. F. Anderson. 1996. Risk-Adjusted Capitation Rates Using Ambulatory and Inpatient Diagnoses. *Health Care Financing Review* 17, no. 3: 77–99.

Wells, K. B., C. Sherbourne, M. Schoenbaum, et al. 2000. Impact of Disseminating Quality Improvement Programs for Depression in Managed Primary Care: A Randomized Controlled Trial. *Journal of the American Medical Association* 283, no. 2: 212–220.

Wells, K. B., R. Sturm, K. D. Sherbourne, and L. S. Meredith. 1996. *Caring for Depression.* Cambridge, MA: Harvard University Press.

Yellin, E. H., and M. G. Cisternas. 1996. Employment Patterns among Persons with and without Mental Conditions. In *Mental Disorder, Work Disability, and the Law,* ed. R. J. Bonnie and J. Monahan. Chicago: University of Chicago Press.

CHAPTER 16

Accountability for Reasonable Limits to Care

CAN WE MEET THE CHALLENGES?

———— ✀ ————

NORMAN DANIELS

*A*ll health systems, whether public or private or rich or poor, limit access to medical care. Occasionally, this limit setting takes the form of a public melodrama focused on the "heartless" denial by an "evil" insurer or bureaucrat of a "last-chance" treatment for a dying patient. Such drama leaves little room for the limit setter to claim moral authority. For example, when Medicaid denied coverage for a bone marrow transplant to young Coby Howard in Oregon, the script of the public drama barely mentioned the fact that he was not in remission from his leukemia and therefore was not even eligible for a transplant.

The backlash against this case propelled the state to evaluate its Medicaid coverage through a process that attracted international attention. Yet most lightning-rod cases yield no such positive, if unintended, side effects. In *Fox v. Health Net* (Sup. Ct. 219692 [1993]), for example, a California jury decided that a private insurer's initial denial of an unproven bone marrow transplant contributed to the patient's death. The resulting $89 million judgment, combined with lobbying by interest groups, helped make bone marrow transplant the standard of care for advanced breast cancer—delaying discovery that such treatment was ineffective.

Public melodramas generally mislead people about efforts to set limits on health care, for most such efforts do not involve last-chance rescues. Avoiding these dramas—and viewing extreme situations more critically and dispassionately—requires that we learn how to set limits fairly and well in more typical settings.

Consider a case that entailed more established treatments and no life-saving rescue. When Massachusetts Medicaid recently faced cuts owing to steep declines in state revenue, the high cost of psychiatric drugs became a target (Sabin and Daniels 2003a). The agency established a process through which key stakeholders would develop a cost-reducing coverage policy acceptable to psychiatrists and patient advocates. Despite opposition by the American Psychiatric Association (APA) to limits on drug coverage, including requirements that providers obtain prior approval, the decision-making process secured acceptance of the plan among local psychiatrists and patient advocates.

Kaiser Permanente, the giant nonprofit, California-based HMO, also won general acceptance for a generics-first policy for prescribing antidepressants, this time after a careful internal review process (Sabin and Daniels 2003b). In contrast, when the Michigan legislature targeted Medicaid drug coverage for cost savings in 2001, a panel developed a preferred-drug list replete with forty-four categories requiring prior approval. The panel did not consult important stakeholders or conduct follow-up outreach efforts (Bernasek et al. 2003). This limit-setting process provoked considerable resistance and even litigation from patients and providers.

In another case in the mid-1990s, the Centers for Medicare and Medicaid Services (CMS) faced extreme pressure to approve coverage for lung volume reduction surgery for advanced cases of emphysema, even while private providers were making contradictory decisions on whether to cover the procedure. Medicare successfully delayed a decision until the National Emphysema Treatment Trial—a randomized clinical trial—produced clearer evidence on the procedure's effectiveness. CMS recently decided to cover the procedure only for limited groups of patients in controlled settings.

Why do some attempts to set limits on health care coverage win legitimacy and moral authority, while others convince patients and clinicians that their interests are taking a back seat to cost-cutting efforts? As I recount below, these cases support a model for ensuring accountability and fair decision making in health care coverage while also revealing unresolved policy challenges.

Legitimacy and Fairness Problems

Limit setting creates winners and losers, and thus conflict. These outcomes reflect not only competing interests but also the fact that reasonable people often disagree on how to weigh competing values. Should we refrain from giving a dying child or a woman with cancer a last chance with an unproven therapy because of concern about scarce resources? How much weight should limit setters give to reducing drug costs versus allowing individual patients to escape policies that might force them to accept less-than-optimal drugs? In the Medicare decision regarding lung volume reduction surgery, should decision makers approve only carefully selected patients and providers for an unproven therapy?

Fundamental issues regarding human well-being force decision makers to wear a mantel of moral authority. Under what conditions do those affected by the decisions appropriately grant that moral authority? I refer to this as the legitimacy problem (Daniels and Sabin 1997, 2002).

Legitimacy might be less important if the fairness problem had a straightforward, principled solution that was clear to all. Unfortunately, no such consensus exists. Instead, as the examples suggest, controversy over unproven technologies reflects the competing values of human compassion versus stewardship of scarce resources. There is similar controversy about the fair distribution of burdens and benefits in the drug management cases. Society also lacks consensus on how much priority to give the sickest patients, and on whether modest benefits for large numbers of people should outweigh significant benefits for a few.

In the absence of consensus on such principles, we must develop a decision-making process whose outcomes all who participate in the process and are affected by it will accept as just. The process must eliminate obvious sources of bias and conflict of interest and recognize the values and interests of different stakeholders. This is a classic appeal to procedural justice, wherein a fair process yields a just outcome in the absence of prior agreement on criteria and principles (Rawls 1971).

Some market advocates would claim that my appeal for procedural justice is unnecessary, as consumers can set limits by choosing different health plans. What could better legitimize limits than people's choices? Choice brings consent, and consent brings legitimacy.

Both theoretical and practical problems undercut this appeal to market accountability, however, even if we were to rely entirely on private insurance. Uncertainty about people's needs, the performance of health care plans, and the effectiveness of treatments make the purchase of medical services very different from the purchase of computers or cars. What's more, half of all workers with insurance have no choice of plans, and those who do have choices usually do not understand the limits that affect them until they have medical problems, at which point switching plans is difficult or impossible. Thus, I propose a process—accountability for reasonableness—for resolving disputes over scarce health care resources.

Accountability for Reasonableness

Four general conditions can ensure accountability for reasonableness. If met, they should lead health plan enrollees, patients, and the public to respect the fairness and legitimacy of decisions by managed care organizations and public officials regarding coverage of new technologies and treatments:

Publicity: Decisions and their underlying rationales must be publicly accessible.

Relevance: These rationales must rest on evidence, reasons, and principles that plan managers, clinicians, patients, and consumers agree are pertinent to deciding how to meet diverse needs under resource restraints.

Revisability and appeals: A mechanism must allow challenges to limit-setting decisions, help resolve those challenges, and allow revisions in light of further evidence and arguments.

Enforcement: A voluntary or public regulatory process must ensure that decision makers fulfill the first three conditions.

These four conditions can convert behind-the-scenes deliberations by public agencies and private health plans into a public—and ultimately democratic—deliberation concerning how limited resources might best be used to maintain the health of populations with diverse service needs. A culture of openness would also facilitate learning among clinicians and enrollees about the need for limits on health care coverage. Many people claim that the litigious public will accept no limits;

changing that culture requires a concerted educational effort both outside and inside the institutions that deliver and finance care. Education begins with openness about the reasons for decisions by public and private health providers and insurers. Over time, this process can spur broader deliberation by a public better educated to think about how to share medical resources fairly and its elected officials.

Though some, and perhaps many, health plans proceed carefully and thoughtfully when deciding which procedures to cover, private plans generally fail to make their rationales public. Rationales would make it crystal clear to patients and clinicians alike why the plan's cost and quality controls lead to its criteria for coverage. A public record of a plan's decisions, like case law in legal judgments, provides a basis for judging their coherence and consistency. Such a record enables those affected by those decisions, who often have no real ability to seek alternatives, to understand why they face the restrictions they do. The publicity condition thus satisfies a fundamental requirement of justice.

Participants in a health plan—patients, their clinicians, and plan managers—pursue a common goal: they aim to meet their diverse needs under resource constraints on terms they can justify to each other. Since hard decisions must be made about how to meet those needs fairly, the grounds that decisions are based on must be ones that fair-minded people can agree are relevant. (Being fair-minded means being willing to play by rules of the game they accept and can justify to each other.) The relevance condition imposes constraints on the rationales supporting coverage decisions, thus narrowing the range of disagreement. Involving diverse stakeholders is one way to secure greater agreement.

The relevance condition does not mean that all parties will agree with specific decisions; parties may agree on which reasons are relevant but still weight them differently. As long as fair-minded parties who make the decision and are affected by it can accept that the grounds are relevant, however, even those who do not agree cannot complain that it is unreasonable. Desperate parents and spouses who demand last-chance treatments for loved ones may not behave as fair-minded people interested in mutually justifiable rationales, but a public with experience in limit setting may resist unreasonable demands (Edgar 2000).

Fair-minded people will accept many kinds of evidence and reasons as relevant to decisions regarding health care coverage. These can include scientific evidence on a treatment's effectiveness and safety and even information on its cost-effectiveness, especially when a less-costly approach delivers equal or superior benefits. Controversy occurs when decision makers must sacrifice achievable benefits for some people in favor of greater overall cost-effectiveness. The situation becomes even more controversial when the cost-effectiveness comparison weighs treatments for patients with different conditions. Decision makers must carefully explicate their choices in these cases.

Except for some decisions concerning drug coverage, health plans do not seem to evaluate treatments as competitors within an overall budget for new technologies. If such comparative budget-driven judgments do become common, decision makers will have to pay even more attention to distributive fairness.

Because accountability for reasonableness is intended to apply in various public and private settings, consumer participation itself is not essential to fairness. Yet such participation, when properly supported, enhances legitimacy. Because such a process does not select consumer participants democratically, they do not make it more democratic, nor do they act as proxy consenters on behalf of other consumers. Rather, consumer participation reassures stakeholders that decision makers are addressing their arguments, broadens stakeholders' perspectives on which rationales are relevant, and ensures transparency.

Coverage decisions often rest on specific evidence about efficacy and cost. Because such evidence can change over time, and because decisions that apply to most patients with a condition may not apply to all, plans must make provision for revising decisions when new evidence emerges or when patients or doctors feel they should be exceptions to coverage rules. Enforcement of the publicity, relevance, and revisability conditions might be achieved by building them into accreditation requirements for health plans, or this may require some legislative mandates, as in the case of state laws regarding independent review of coverage decisions.

Accountability for Reasonableness in Practice

An ideal test of the effectiveness of accountability for reasonableness in solving the legitimacy problem would compare situations that implemented its central tenets and those that did not. Such an evaluation would measure outcomes such as stakeholder perceptions of legitimacy (represented by fewer appeals and complaints), consistency and coherence of decisions, and equitable access to services. This ideal test is not yet feasible, however, as no significant part of the U.S. health care system has explicitly adopted such an approach, and serious obstacles often prevent decision makers from pursuing it. Still, if we examine the narratives cited above in closer detail, we can find explicit use of such principles as well as situations where skilled managers implement those ideas on their own.

Weighing Pharmacy Benefits

In the late 1990s, James Sabin and I worked with executives at Merck-Medco (now Medco Health Solutions), one of the nation's two largest for-profit companies managing pharmacy benefits, to analyze limit setting in a broad range of designs for pharmacy benefits. These executives wanted to make the ethical rationales underlying their decisions available to practitioners, pharmacists, and patients. Consulting with Medco's clients, including large purchasers of pharmacy benefits, clinical managers, pharmacists, and marketing personnel, we developed an "ethical template" for many different pharmacy benefits (Daniels, Teagarden, and Sabin 2003).

This template maps the decisions entailed in designing such benefits onto types of ethical rationales appropriate for each. These decisions include which drug categories a plan will cover, which drugs each category will include, which symptoms each drug can address, and what limitations the plan will impose on the use of a drug. We found that officials based the first two decisions largely on need, while cost considerations drove decisions on the latter two criteria. The ethical rationale for covering certain drugs, for example, weighs the overall cost advantage of using a cheaper drug against the need to protect patients for whom the cheaper drug does not work.

Our work with one major Medco client, a private health plan, aims to translate the template into a Web site tool that explains the reasons for coverage limits to clinicians, pharmacists, and patients. Many decision makers remain skeptical of using such a template. Health plans often fear that transparency will open them to accusations that they are "the first rationer in town" or to litigation if they are explicit about their decision-making process. Other decision makers are simply not persuaded that such an approach adds value, even if it seems ethically justified ("business is business").

Two policy challenges are clear. Though strong support for ethically defensible decision making sometimes emerges even in for-profit firms, overcoming skepticism requires showing that transparency yields payoffs, such as fewer patient complaints and lower turnover, or a better market image. And producing such evidence requires research on natural experiments in accountability for reasonableness as they arise. (The Canadian Priority Setting Research Network recently sponsored a workshop to develop a research agenda to measure the value of such an approach.) Overcoming these fears may require regulatory rules that put all players on the same playing field, removing the risks of early experiments. One model for such rules is the independent review processes that forty-two states now mandate.

Return now to the examples of Medicaid drug limits in Michigan and Massachusetts. To avoid the problems encountered in Michigan, Massachusetts decision makers explicitly involved all key stakeholders in the limit-setting process and aimed at transparency. Stakeholders included organized psychiatry (through the Massachusetts Psychiatric Society, MPS) as well as consumer and family groups. These groups nominated psychiatrists to participate in a Psychopharmacology Work Group; consumers chose James Sabin, my collaborator and a psychiatrist, as their representative. He provided information on the accountability-for-reasonableness approach to work group members.

To fulfill two criteria of that approach—transparency and flexibility—the state agency responsible for Medicaid mental health circulated the work group's proposals for wider review and revised them to address stakeholder criticisms. The result was a set of policies—reinforced through an educational campaign by the MPS—designed to prevent providers from prescribing more than one selective serotonin reuptake inhibitor (SSRI), and five or more psychiatric medications, at a time. This policy curbed expensive and risky co-prescriptions.

Then, as the budget crisis in Massachusetts intensified, the Division of Medical Assistance, which administers the state's Medicaid program, decided to develop a list of preferred drugs. This approach directly conflicted with the APA's policy of exempting psychiatric medications from such lists and from requirements that providers obtain prior approval for prescriptions. The Psychopharmacology Work Group carefully evaluated the rationale for the national APA policy and weighed it against the reality of state budget cuts. Local psychiatrists, many of whom wanted to ensure the widest-possible access to psychiatric drugs given budgetary limits, supported this approach.

In the end, the work group recommended generic fluoxetine as the SSRI for an initial prescription. This decision required careful education of providers throughout the state as to its underlying evidence and rationale. The policy also required reassuring consumer and family groups that people already successfully treated with other antidepressants could easily win exemptions from the policy. Decision makers further added a drug to the list whose slow release diminished the risk of seizures for some patients. Stakeholders initiated some of these consumer protections, while the template spurred the Psychopharmacology Work Group to consider others. Key elements of accountability for reasonableness—transparency, careful deliberation with stakeholder involvement, and revision in light of appeals—may well explain why the Massachusetts approach worked without conflict while Michigan's did not.

This evidence concerning the effectiveness of accountability for reasonableness suggests its potential as best practice. Solidifying and refining this approach requires meeting two policy challenges. The first is to carefully study such natural experiments to determine differences in the value they add. The second is to establish incentives and rewards for individuals and organizations that grab the limit-setting bull by its horns. For example, the state Department of Mental Health's Executive Office of Health and Human Services gave the MPS a Clinical Excellence Distinguished Service Award for its leadership in enlisting local psychiatrists to participate in the Massachusetts decision-making process.

Kaiser Permanente, which serves over 8 million members nationally, including 6 million in California, also instituted a generic fluoxetine–first policy. Its pharmacy policy board based its decision on a controlled study comparing the effectiveness of various SSRIs and on an internal survey of physicians' prescribing patterns that showed that patients switch equally among all SSRIs. Whereas Massachusetts had to secure clinician buy-in to a new policy by soliciting stakeholder involvement, Kaiser had already established such a mechanism: the organization monitors clinicians' prescribing patterns, and clinicians meet to debate the merits of different approaches.

The ethical template requires an easy exception for patients whose conditions do not justify use of a cheaper drug first. In Kaiser's case, all physicians retain the authority—without prior authorization (a sticking point for the APA)—to override drug restrictions whenever they feel that is medically necessary for individual patients. Because of the organization's careful education regarding its rationales for recommended practice, variations in prescribing patterns are not widespread. This kind of peer management embodies central elements of accountability for reasonableness: transparency, deliberation of rationales, and openness to revision. This approach also allows a health plan to emphasize cost-effectiveness while protecting individual patients. These two examples show how a large insurer and a state Medicaid program relied on key elements of accountability for reasonableness to arrive at similar outcomes.

Kaiser's best practice also serves as a policy challenge. Although organizations like Kaiser have a long-standing culture that encourages cost-effective practice, loosely structured physician practice organizations (PPOs) and independent practice organizations (IPOs) lack this culture. Nevertheless, such provider groups can benefit from accountability for reasonableness, at least if they operate on a level playing field.

Moving such highly decentralized health organizations in the right direction will require quantified evidence of success. States that rely on key aspects of accountability for reasonableness to produce cost-effective pharmacy benefits can provide such evidence, especially if they win broad public support for fair limits on coverage. Alternatively, such evidence may encourage regulators to compel the private sector to move toward a more cost-effective approach based on accountability for reasonableness. To propel thinking in that direction, the federal Agency for Healthcare Research and Quality sponsored a conference for senior state policymakers on how to structure cost-effective state pharmacy benefit programs. The conference featured discussions of the ethical template, limit setting for psychiatric drugs, and a case study of the activities of the Massachusetts Medicaid program.

Independent Review: The Underdeveloped Potential of Regulation

Amid growing consumer distrust of managed care organizations, in 1998 California passed the Friedman-Knowles Experimental Therapy Act, which established the first mandatory independent review of decisions by HMOs to deny coverage for care. Some forty-two states have since established such review processes. These reviews overcome the deep conflict of interest entailed when health plans rely on experts who work for them to analyze denial of coverage. The movement toward independent reviews—clearly an idea whose time had come—codifies the appeals-and-revisions condition that underpins accountability for reasonableness.

Michigan has taken the bold step of posting the denial decisions it reverses on a Web site, providing one model of transparency. Advocates overcame resistance to such public posting by arguing that it would provide a body of unofficial case law, even if it lacked legal authority. California also posts brief summaries of its case reviews online.

State-level review of health plan decisions does put all players on a common playing field and reduces barriers to transparency and revisability. Existing legislation falls short, however, of providing incentives for converting the rich body of case evidence into an effective tool for improving health care quality. For example, although Michigan posts its redacted cases, it has no mechanism for encouraging the challenged organizations to change their decision-making policies. Nor does any research mechanism examine the cases and patterns underlying overturned denials and propose the steps insurers might take to modify their practices. Existing regulation of independent review activities could be refined to require health care organizations to systematically analyze the reasons the state reverses their coverage decisions. The resulting information could become the basis for improving quality, offsetting some of the costs of such review and evaluation.

Medicare Coverage Decisions

I noted earlier that the Centers for Medicare and Medicaid Services delayed—courageously, I believe—a decision on whether to cover lung volume reduction surgery until the National Emphysema Treatment Trial (NETT) could provide better evidence on the procedure's safety and effectiveness. To see why that delay took courage, we must look beyond the intense pressure on Medicare to the private sector, where insurers were also considering whether to cover the procedure. In a case study completed just as NETT began, James Sabin and I found that Northern California Kaiser Permanente decided to cover the procedure at "centers of excellence," while Health Partners in Minnesota, also a nonprofit plan, decided not to provide coverage. PacifiCare and Aetna, two for-profit plans, also reached opposing decisions on coverage (Daniels and Sabin 2002).

These contrasting conclusions did not reflect differing assessments of the technology or understanding of evidence-based practice. Rather, the decisions reflected member demand for the procedure, the presence of strong internal champions, and local practice patterns and beliefs. The decisions also reflected the degree to which the organizations felt confident of their ability to implement eligibility criteria and coverage limits for the procedure, and the weight they gave to values such as stewardship of scarce resources and rescue of desperate patients.

Such conflicting pressures affect both the private and public sector, so understanding how CMS persuaded stakeholders to wait for better evidence is important. With input from the Agency for Healthcare Research and Quality, CMS established a broad partnership backing NETT, including the National Heart, Lung, and Blood Institute. The authority and prestige of these institutions, and the resulting buy-in from many clinicians, enabled the organization to withstand pressure to provide immediate coverage of the procedure.

Also crucial to managing the social tension was creating public awareness that the decision hinged not only on rising costs but also on the need for better evidence concerning which patients would benefit. In the absence of better evidence, clinicians would be unable to secure proper consent for the procedure's benefits and risks. Thus, CMS took important steps to create transparency around reasons stakeholders can see as relevant—two key conditions entailed in accountability for reasonableness. Meeting these conditions helped avoid the rush to coverage that occurred with bone marrow transplants for advanced breast cancer.

Moving from the results of a trial like NETT to a coverage decision by both public and private plans still requires accountability for reasonableness. Unfortunately, CMS's actual coverage decision lacks some elements of that accountability, though the failing may reflect the organization's legislative charge more than its process.

After public input from its Medicare Coverage Advisory Commission, CMS decided to cover the procedure for several subgroups of patients despite strong warnings that evidence of benefits for those subgroups lacked statistical significance (Ware 2003). By itself, the decision may have been a case where reasonable people disagreed about how much caution to impose in the face of results showing measurable benefit for some subgroups.

Study results also showed that the procedure was not terribly cost-effective, however (NETT Research Group 2003). Unfortunately, the legislative charge to CMS gave decision makers little room to consider the opportunity costs of covering a potentially very expensive treatment with very modest benefits. No one explicitly asked, if Medicare funds this technology, what other new procedures or services can it not afford, and which are more important? The agency would have to make such tradeoffs explicit if it had to consider novel treatments within a budget for new coverage. And given budget neutrality pressures, still larger questions would loom if adding new benefits meant that services already covered by Medicare would have to be limited further.

The possibility that further delay was not politically feasible, and that attempts to meet urgent needs took precedence over caution concerning treatments not fully proven, suggests that Medicare may find it difficult to hold the line on coverage limits. Pressure from enthusiastic clinicians and desperate patients may lead to coverage "creep." Such an outcome not only would be costly but might bring harms whose magnitude society is not in a good position to measure. Accountability for reasonableness would require more careful deliberation premised on the convictions that health care resources are limited and that fair and legitimate decisions must evaluate a range of social effects.

Meeting the Accountability-for-Reasonableness Challenge

Efforts to secure accountability for reasonableness in setting limits on health care coverage face three main policy challenges. First, as the discussion of pharmacy benefits shows, resistance to transparency among both public and private health providers and insurers reflects a lack of clear evidence that acting virtuously will yield clear payoffs. Winning support for more transparent decisions will require research on the positive benefits of doing so.

Second, even where regulation has helped improve accountability in decision making, as in the state-level independent review processes, such accountability has not fulfilled its potential for improving quality. Meeting this challenge will require research on reviewed cases and on how incentives and sanctions can encourage health plans to put to good use the information produced by the reviews.

Third, cultural resistance to making hard choices about opportunity costs remains. I see no quick solution to this problem, but public education and broader deliberation can produce change over time. This is a bit of a chicken-and-egg problem: implementing accountability for reasonableness is one mechanism for producing that education, but boosting implementation is difficult without initial education. Perhaps, to switch metaphors, the solution requires "bootstrapping" our way from modest changes in process to modest changes in culture and so on to broader cultural and institutional change.

Acknowledgments

This paper draws primarily on material that I have coauthored with James Sabin. I also wish to thank Russell Teagarden for his crucial help on the work on pharmacy benefits. Both provided helpful comments on earlier drafts.

References

Bernasek, C., J. Farkas, H. Felman, et al. 2003. *Case Study: Michigan Medicaid Prescription Drug Benefit.* Washington, DC: Kaiser Family Foundation. Available at *www.kff.org/content/2003/4083/4083.pdf.*

Daniels, N. 1985. *Just Health Care.* New York: Cambridge University Press.

———. 1992. Growth Hormone Therapy for Short Stature: Can We Support the Treatment/ Enhancement Distinction? *Growth: Genetics and Hormones* 8, no. 2: 46–48.

———. 1993. Rationing Fairly: Programmatic Considerations. *Bioethics* 7, no. 2–3: 224–233.

Daniels, N., and J. Sabin. 1997. Limits to Health Care: Fair Procedures, Democratic Deliberation, and the Legitimacy Problem for Insurers. *Philosophy and Public Affairs* 26, no. 4: 303–350.

———. 2002. *Setting Limits Fairly: Can We Learn to Share Medical Resources?* New York: Oxford University Press.

Daniels, N., R. Teagarden, and J. Sabin. 2003. An Ethical Template for Pharmacy Benefits. *Health Affairs* 22, no. 1: 125–137.

Edgar, W. 2000. Rationing Health Care in New Zealand: How the Public Has a Say. In *The Global Challenge of Health Care,* ed. A. Coulter and C. Ham. Philadelphia: Open University Press.

Kamm, F. 1993. *Morality, Mortality: Death and Whom to Save from It.* Vol.1. Oxford: Oxford University Press.

National Emphysema Treatment Trial (NETT) Research Group. 2003. *New England Journal of Medicine* 348: 2059–2073.

Nord, E. 1999. *Cost-Value Analysis in Health Care: Making Sense of QALYs.* Cambridge: Cambridge University Press.

Rawls, J. 1971. *A Theory of Justice.* Cambridge, MA: Harvard University Press.

Sabin, J., and N. Daniels. 2003a. Improving Psychiatric Drug Benefit Management. I: Lessons from Massachusetts. *Psychiatric Services* 54, no. 7: 949–951.

———. 2003b. Improving Psychiatric Drug Benefit Management. II: Kaiser Permanente's Approach to Selective Serotonin Reuptake Inhibitors. *Psychiatric Services* 54, no. 10: 1343–1344, 1349.

Ware, J. H. 2003. The National Emphysema Treatment Trial: How Strong Is the Evidence? *New England Journal of Medicine* 348: 2055–2056.

CONTRIBUTORS

LINDA H. AIKEN, PhD, RN, is director of the Center for Health Outcomes and Policy Research, the Claire M. Fagin Leadership Professor of Nursing, professor of sociology, and senior fellow at the Leonard Davis Institute of Health Economics at the University of Pennsylvania. She is a member of the Institute of Medicine of the National Academy of Sciences, the American Academy of Arts and Sciences, and the National Academy of Social Insurance; a fellow and former president of the American Academy of Nursing; and an honorary fellow of the United Kingdom's Royal College of Nursing. Dr. Aiken is the winner of the 2003 Individual Earnest A. Codman Award from the Joint Commission on Accreditation of Healthcare Organizations.

DAVID C. COLBY, PhD, is interim vice president for Research and Evaluation at The Robert Wood Johnson Foundation. He came to the foundation in 1998 after nine years of service with the Medicare Payment Advisory Commission and the Physician Payment Review Commission, most recently as deputy director. Dr. Colby was a Robert Wood Johnson Faculty Fellow in Health Care Finance, serving in the Congressional Budget Office. His published research has focused on Medicaid and Medicare, media coverage of AIDS, and various topics in political science.

NORMAN DANIELS, PhD, is professor of ethics and population health at Harvard School of Public Health. His most recent books include *From Chance to Choice: Genetics and Justice* (with Allen Buchanan, Dan Brock, and Dan Wikler, Cambridge University Press, 2000); *Is Inequality Bad for Our Health?* (with Bruce Kennedy and Ichiro Kawachi, Beacon Press, 2000); and *Setting Limits Fairly: Can We Learn to Share Medical Resources?* (with James Sabin, Oxford University Press, 2002). Dr. Daniels is a fellow of the Hastings Center, a member of the Institute of Medicine, and a founding member of the National Academy of Social Insurance and the International Society for Equity in Health.

Richard G. Frank, PhD, is the Margaret T. Morris Professor of Health Economics in the Department of Health Care Policy at Harvard Medical School and a research associate with the National Bureau of Economic Research. Dr. Frank serves on the Biobehavioral Sciences Board of the Institute of Medicine and is the co-editor of the *Journal of Health Economics*. He was awarded the Georgescu-Roegen Prize from the Southern Economic Association for his collaborative work on drug pricing, the Carl A. Taube Award from the American Public Health Association for outstanding contributions to mental health services and economics research, and the Emily Mumford Medal from Columbia University's Department of Psychiatry.

Sherry A. Glied, PhD, is professor and chair of the Department of Health Policy and Management of Columbia University's Mailman School of Public Health. In 1992–1993, she served as a senior economist for health care and labor market policy on the president's Council of Economic Advisers under Presidents Bush and Clinton and participated in the Clinton Health Care Task Force. Professor Glied's principal areas of research are in health policy reform and mental health care policy. Her book on health care reform, *Chronic Condition*, was published by Harvard University Press in January 1998.

David Hemenway, PhD, is professor of health policy at Harvard School of Public Health, where he has won more teaching awards than any other faculty member. Dr. Hemenway is director of the Harvard Injury Control Research Center and the Harvard Youth Violence Prevention Center. He is the author of *Private Guns, Public Health* (University of Michigan Press, 2004).

Lisa I. Iezzoni, MD, MSc, is professor of medicine at Harvard Medical School and codirector of research in the Division of General Medicine and Primary Care, Department of Medicine, at Beth Israel Deaconess Medical Center in Boston. She has conducted numerous studies on risk adjustment and quality measurement methods and has edited *Risk Adjustment for Measuring Health Care Outcomes* (Health Administration Press, 2003), now in its third edition. Dr. Iezzoni recently published *When Walking Fails: Mobility Problems of Adults with Chronic Conditions* (Milbank Memorial Fund and University of California Press, 2003). She is a member of the Institute of Medicine of the National Academy of Sciences.

Patricia Seliger Keenan is a PhD candidate in health policy at Harvard University. Her dissertation focuses on the implications of the growth in spending on medical care. She previously held positions at the Henry J. Kaiser Family Foundation and the Health Care Financing Administration.

James R. Knickman, PhD, is the president and chief executive officer of the New York Charitable Asset Foundation which focuses on improving access to health care and public health in New York State. Previously, Dr. Knickman was vice president for Research and Evaluation at The Robert Wood Johnson Foundation, where he was responsible for external evaluation of national initiatives. Before joining the RWJF staff in 1992, Dr. Knickman was on the faculty at New York University and its Health Research Program, where he conducted research on a range of issues related to health care delivery.

LUCIAN L. LEAPE, MD, is adjunct professor of health policy in the Department of Health Policy and Management at the Harvard School of Public Health. Before joining the Harvard faculty in 1988, he was professor of surgery and chief of pediatric surgery at Tufts University School of Medicine. Dr. Leape was a founder of the National Patient Safety Foundation, the Massachusetts Coalition for the Prevention of Medical Error, and the Harvard Kennedy School Executive Session on Medical Error. He was a member of the Institute of Medicine's Quality of Care in America Committee, which published *To Err Is Human* (National Academies Press, 1999) and *Crossing the Quality Chasm* (National Academies Press, 2001). He has published over one hundred papers on quality of care and patient safety.

BRUCE G. LINK, PhD, is professor of epidemiology and sociomedical sciences at Columbia University's Mailman School of Public Health and a research scientist at New York State Psychiatric Institute. He is director of the Psychiatric Epidemiology Training Program and the Center for Violence Research and Prevention at Columbia, and codirector of The Robert Wood Johnson Foundation's Health and Society Scholars Program. His interests include the nature and consequences of stigma for people with mental illnesses, the social epidemiology of homelessness, the connection between mental illnesses and violent behaviors, and explanations for associations between social conditions and morbidity and mortality.

THOMAS G. McGUIRE, PhD, is professor of health economics at Harvard Medical School. His research focuses on the design and impact of health care payment systems, the economics of health care disparities, and the economics of mental health policy. Dr. McGuire is a member of the Institute of Medicine of the National Academy of Sciences and coeditor of the *Journal of Health Economics.* He received the 1998 Arrow Award (jointly with Albert Ma) from the International Health Economics Association and the 1991 Carl A. Taube Award from the American Public Health Association.

DAVID MECHANIC, PhD, is the René Dubos University Professor of Behavioral Sciences and director of the Institute for Health, Health Care Policy, and Aging Research at Rutgers, the State University of New Jersey. He also directs The Robert Wood Johnson Foundation's Investigator Awards in Health Policy Research and the National Institute of Mental Health's Center for Research on the Organization and Financing of Care for the Severely Mentally Ill at Rutgers. Dr. Mechanic is a member of the National Academy of Sciences, the American Academy of Arts and Sciences, and the Institute of Medicine. He has written or edited twenty-four books and some four hundred research articles, chapters, and other publications in medical sociology, health policy, health services research, and the social and behavioral sciences.

MICHAEL L. MILLENSON is the Mervin Shalowitz, MD Visiting Scholar at Northwestern University's Kellogg School of Management and a nationally recognized consultant on the quality of health care, on patient empowerment, and on e-health. He is the author of *Demanding Medical Excellence: Doctors and Accountability in the Information Age* (University of Chicago Press, 1997). A former Pulitzer Prize–nominated journalist, he has written for a range of peer-reviewed and general interest publications including *Health Affairs* and the *Washington Monthly*.

JAMES A. MORONE, PhD, is professor of political science at Brown University. His most recent book is *Hellfire Nation: The Politics of Sin in American History*, published by Yale University Press, 2003. Dr. Morone's *Democratic Wish: Popular Participation and the Limits of American Government* (Basic Books, 1990, Yale University Press, 1998) won the American Political Science Association's Gladys Kammerer Award for the best book on the United States and was named a "notable book of 1991" by the *New York Times*. He has written more than one hundred articles on American politics, history, and health care policy. The Brown University classes of 1993, 1999, and 2001 voted Dr. Morone the Barret Hazeltine Citation as teacher of the year.

JO C. PHELAN, PhD, is associate professor of sociomedical sciences at Columbia University's Mailman School of Public Health. Her research focuses on social inequalities, including objective conditions of inequality and social psychological factors that contribute to and result from those conditions. Her current research interests include socioeconomic disparities in health and mortality, and public attitudes and beliefs about mental illness, especially the potential impact of the genetics revolution on those attitudes.

JAMES C. ROBINSON, PhD, is professor of health economics and chair of the Division of Health Policy and Management at the University of California, Berkeley. His research focuses on medical groups, hospital systems, health insurance, health care consumerism, and capital finance. Dr. Robinson has published over seventy-five papers in peer-reviewed journals and two books through the University of California Press, *The Corporate Practice of Medicine* (1999) and *Toil and Toxics* (1991). He is a contributing editor to *Health Affairs* and a member of the board of directors of the Integrated HealthCare Association.

LYNN B. ROGUT, MCRP, is deputy director of The Robert Wood Johnson Foundation Investigator Awards in Health Policy Research. Before joining the Investigator Awards program, she served as executive director of the New York Center for Liver Transplantation, a consortium of liver transplant programs in New York State. She previously held positions at the United Hospital Fund, the SUNY Health Science Center at Brooklyn, and M. Bostin Associates, Inc. Her interests include quality of care and organ transplantation policies.

SARA ROSENBAUM, JD, is the Harold and Jane Hirsh Professor of Health Law and

Policy and chair of the Department of Health Policy at the School of Public Health and Health Services, George Washington University Medical Center. She also directs the Hirsh Health Law and Policy Program and the Center for Health Services Research and Policy. Professor Rosenbaum is coauthor of *Law and the American Health Care System* (Foundation Press, 1999). From 1993 to 1994, Professor Rosenbaum worked for the White House Domestic Policy Council, where she directed the drafting of the Health Security Act. She has been named one of America's five hundred most influential health policymakers and has been recognized by the U.S. Department of Health and Human Services for distinguished national service on behalf of Medicaid beneficiaries.

THEDA SKOCPOL, PhD, is the Victor S. Thomas Professor of Government and Sociology and director of the Center for American Political Studies at Harvard University. Her research focuses on the politics of U.S. social policies and on changing patterns of civic engagement in American democracy. Her most recent books include *Boomerang: Health Reform and the Turn against Politics* (W. W. Norton, 1996); *The Missing Middle: Working Families and the Future of American Social Policy* (W. W. Norton, 2000); and *Diminished Democracy: From Membership to Management in American Civic Life* (University of Oklahoma Press, 2003).

ROSEMARY A. STEVENS, PhD, MPH, is Stanley I. Sheerr Professor in Arts and Sciences, Emeritus, in the Department of History and Sociology of Science at the University of Pennsylvania. She has also served as a senior fellow at the Leonard Davis Institute of Health Economics and as dean of the School of Arts and Sciences at the University of Pennsylvania. Dr. Stevens's current research is on the impact and implications of specialization in American medicine. She is a public member of the American Board of Medical Specialties and a long-time member of the Institute of Medicine. She has published six books and numerous articles on the history of medicine and health policy research.

ALVIN R. TARLOV, MD, is a professor of medicine at the University of Chicago. Previously, he was professor in the School of Public Health at the University of Texas, and the Sid Richardson and Taylor and Robert H. Ray Senior Fellow in Health Policy at the James A. Baker III Institute for Public Policy at Rice University. He has also served as a professor at Tufts University and at the Harvard School of Public Health, and was president of the Henry J. Kaiser Family Foundation. Dr. Tarlov is a former Markle Foundation scholar and NIH Research Career Development awardee. He was elected to the Association of American Physicians and the Institute of Medicine and is a master of the American College of Physicians. From 1997 to 2000 he served as the national program director of The Robert Wood Johnson Foundation's Investigator Awards in Health Policy Research.

JOEL TEITELBAUM, JD, LLM, is associate professor and vice chair of the Department of Health Policy and managing director of the Hirsh Health Law and Policy Program at the School of Public Health and Health Services, George Washington

University Medical Center. His research interests include civil rights issues in health care, health care financing and delivery systems, and quality-of-care issues. Professor Teitelbaum serves on the Board of Directors of the Center for the Study of Race and Bioethics at DePaul University College of Law, and as a faculty mentor to Project HEALTH, a national student organization addressing socioeconomic, medical, and environmental causes of poor health in children who are disadvantaged.

KENNETH E. WARNER, PhD, is the Avedis Donabedian Distinguished University Professor of Public Health at the University of Michigan and director of the university's Tobacco Research Network. His research focuses on the economic and policy aspects of disease prevention and health promotion, with an emphasis on tobacco and health. Dr. Warner was a founding member of the Board of Directors of the American Legacy Foundation. In 1989 Dr. C. Everett Koop awarded him the Surgeon General's Medallion. In 2003, he received the inaugural award for Outstanding Research Contribution of the Luther L. Terry Awards for Exemplary Leadership in Tobacco Control. Dr. Warner is a member of the Institute of Medicine of the National Academy of Sciences.

DAVID R. WILLIAMS, PhD, is on the faculty at the University of Michigan, where he serves as the Harold W. Cruse Collegiate Professor of Sociology, senior research scientist at the Institute for Social Research, professor of epidemiology in the School of Public Health, and faculty associate in the Center for Afro-American and African Studies and the Program for Research on Black Americans. His previous academic appointment was at Yale University. He is interested in the trends and determinants of socioeconomic and racial differences in mental and physical health and has authored more than one hundred scholarly papers in scientific journals and edited collections. He is a member of the Institute of Medicine of the National Academy of Sciences.

Name Index

255

SUBJECT INDEX

academics, vs. clinicians, 157

access to health care: differential, 117–118; limiting, 238; and racial disparities, 138; and resources, 80; and variations in spending, 157

accountability: lack of, 170; public, 142

accountability for reasonableness, 240–243; challenge of, 247; effectiveness of, 244; in practice, 242–247

Accreditation Council for Graduate Medical Education (ACGME), 166, 173, 209

accreditation surveys, 165

Acheson report, 125

Addams, Jane, 19

adolescents: and firearm policy, 91; health problems of, 20–21; illegal firearms obtained by, 93; suicide of, 94

adverse selection, 40, 41, 226

advertising: bans on food, 110; cigarette, 101; public-service, 111; tobacco, 106

Aetna, 246

African Americans: and health disparities, 118–119; and segregation, 118–119; and socioeconomic status disadvantages, 125; substance abuse of, 117. *See also* blacks

Agency for Healthcare Research and Quality (AHRQ), 155, 164, 166, 167, 168, 172, 245, 246

aging, 191–192. *See also* elderly

AIDS, 17; deaths from, 154; and health disparities, 80; private coverage for, 45; response to, 21

air bags, 79

Alaska, tobacco-control program of, 104

alcohol abuse: disability because of, 199; and public health, 107–108; and socioeconomic status, 117

Alexander v. Sandoval, 137, 142, 143, 144–145

Allina, 166

"all products" clauses, 140

alternative medicine, 42–43

Alzheimer's disease, 217

ambulatory surgery, 218; centers for, 56–57, 213; and Stark regulations, 64

American Academy of Family Physicians, 201

American Academy of Pediatrics, 91, 208

American Association for the Advancement of Science, 163

American Board of Family Practice, 211

American Board of Medical Specialties (ABMS), 166, 173, 209, 214, 215, 216, 218; "maintenance-of-certification" programs of, 206, 218

American Cancer Society (ACS), 104

American Civil Liberties Union (ACLU), 94

American College of Obstetricians and Gynecologists, 208

American College of Physicians, 166

American Hospital Association (AHA), 155, 166